iTunes™, iPhoto, iMovie™, and iDVD Bible

Includes Mac OS X Bible bonus chapter!

iTunes™, iPhoto, iMovie™, and iDVD Bible

Bob LeVitus
Dennis R. Cohen

Wiley Publishing, Inc.

iTunes™, iPhoto, iMovie™, and iDVD Bible
Published by
Wiley Publishing, Inc.
909 Third Avenue
New York, NY 10022
www.wiley.com

Copyright © 2003 by Wiley Publishing, Inc., Indianapolis, Indiana

Library of Congress Control Number: 2002110313

ISBN: 0-7645-3702-4

Manufactured in the United States of America

10 9 8 7 6 5 4 3 2 1

1B/SS/QR/QT/IN

Published by Wiley Publishing, Inc., Indianapolis, Indiana
Published simultaneously in Canada

No part of this publication may be reproduced, stored in a retrieval system or transmitted in any form or by any means, electronic, mechanical, photocopying, recording, scanning or otherwise, except as permitted under Sections 107 or 108 of the 1976 United States Copyright Act, without either the prior written permission of the Publisher, or authorization through payment of the appropriate per-copy fee to the Copyright Clearance Center, 222 Rosewood Drive, Danvers, MA 01923; 978-750-8400, fax 978-750-4470. Requests to the Publisher for permission should be addressed to the Legal Department, Wiley Publishing, Inc., 10475 Crosspoint Blvd., Indianapolis, IN 46256; 317-572-3447, fax 317-572-4447, e-mail permcoordinator@wiley.com.

> LIMIT OF LIABILITY/DISCLAIMER OF WARRANTY: WHILE THE PUBLISHER AND AUTHOR HAVE USED THEIR BEST EFFORTS IN PREPARING THIS BOOK, THEY MAKE NO REPRESENTATIONS OR WARRANTIES WITH RESPECT TO THE ACCURACY OR COMPLETENESS OF THE CONTENTS OF THIS BOOK AND SPECIFICALLY DISCLAIM ANY IMPLIED WARRANTIES OF MERCHANTABILITY OR FITNESS FOR A PARTICULAR PURPOSE. NO WARRANTY MAY BE CREATED OR EXTENDED BY SALES REPRESENTATIVES OR WRITTEN SALES MATERIALS. THE ADVICE AND STRATEGIES CONTAINED HEREIN MAY NOT BE SUITABLE FOR YOUR SITUATION. YOU SHOULD CONSULT WITH A PROFESSIONAL WHERE APPROPRIATE. NEITHER THE PUBLISHER NOR AUTHOR SHALL BE LIABLE FOR ANY LOSS OF PROFIT OR ANY OTHER COMMERCIAL DAMAGES, INCLUDING BUT NOT LIMITED TO SPECIAL, INCIDENTAL, CONSEQUENTIAL, OR OTHER DAMAGES.

For general information on our other products and services or to obtain technical support, please contact our Customer Care Department within the U.S. at 800-762-2974, outside the U.S. at 317-572-3993 or fax 317-572-4002.

Wiley also publishes its books in a variety of electronic formats. Some content that appears in print may not be available in electronic books.

Trademarks: Trademarks: Wiley, the Wiley Publishing logo and related trade dress are trademarks or registered trademarks of Wiley Publishing, Inc., in the United States and other countries, and may not be used without written permission. iTunes and iMovie are trademarks or registered trademarks of Apple Computer, Inc. All other trademarks are the property of their respective owners. Wiley Publishing, Inc., is not associated with any product or vendor mentioned in this book.

Wiley Publishing, Inc. is a trademark of Wiley Publishing, Inc.

About the Authors

Dennis R. Cohen has written or contributed to many books, including *Macworld Mac OS X Bible*, *Macworld Microsoft Office 2001 Bible*, *Macworld AppleWorks 6 Bible*, *AppleWorks 6 for Dummies*, and *Mac Secrets*, 6th Edition, as well as being the technical editor for over 70 titles in just the past few years. A software developer for over 20 years and a Mac developer since 1984, he brings a history not only with the Mac, but also with other platforms (including Unix). Dennis lives in Sunnyvale, California, with his Boston Terrier, Spenser.

Bob "Dr. Mac" LeVitus is the author of over 40 books, including *Dr. Mac: The OS X Files, or, "How to Become a Mac OS X Power User,"* and *Mac OS X For Dummies* for Wiley, and *The Little iTunes Book* and *The Little iDVD Book* for Peachpit Press. He's been a newspaper columnist for the *Houston Chronicle* for five years penning the popular "Dr. Mac" column every Friday for their award-winning Business section, and has been published in most magazines with the word "Mac" in their title. He's known for his expertise, trademark humorous style, and ability to translate "techie" jargon into usable and fun advice for regular folks.

Credits

Acquisitions Editor
Tom Heine

Project Editor
Andy Marinkovich

Technical Editor
Lisa Spangenberg

Copy Editor
Maarten Reilingh

Editorial Manager
Rev Mengle

Vice President and Executive Group Publisher
Richard Swadley

Vice President and Executive Publisher
Bob Ipsen

Executive Editorial Director
Mary Bednarek

Project Coordinator
Regina Snyder

Graphics and Production Specialists
Beth Brooks
Heather Pope
Kathie Schutte
Jeremey Unger

Quality Control Technicians
John Bitter
John Tyler Connoley
Andy Hollandbeck
Carl Pierce

Proofreading and Indexing
TECHBOOKS Production Services

Thanks to all my friends and family, especially Spenser (who gets me out from in front of the computer for regular walks). — drc

Thanks to my family, once again, for putting up with me. — BL

Acknowledgments

Dennis would like to thank Bob LeVitus for agreeing to work on this project with him; Apple Computer for providing software that is not only useful, but fun to use; Wiley Acquisitions Editor Tom Heine for believing in this book, Andy Marinkovich for coordinating all the logistics, Lisa Spangenberg for her careful and insightful technical review, and Maarty Reilingh for catching our typos and style goofs. Finally, he'd like to thank various folks at Apple, in particular Ken Bereskin (Mac OS X Product Manager) and Sal Soghoian (AppleScript Product Manager and iDVD guru) for their help, intentional or not, in providing some very cool tips and ideas. He would also like to join Bob in thanking Carole McClendon, their agent, for her help in making this project a reality.

All Bob has to say is: "Ditto."

Introduction

Popular folklore suggests that Macs are so easy to use that manuals and books aren't necessary. Apple has bought into that philosophy by not providing a user manual for any of the applications in this book. In fact, Apple doesn't provide a user manual for Mac OS X or AppleWorks, either. We disagree; and most of the user base seems to agree with us as the demand for books and other documentation grows.

Apple's online help is pretty good as online help systems go, but it leaves a lot out, is slow, and requires that you know what questions to ask in the first place.

Who Should Read This Book

Anyone who uses or wants to use Apple's wonderful "digital hub iApps" — iTunes, iPhoto, iMovie, and iDVD — will benefit from this book.

We do make a few assumptions, though. The primary ones are that you're using Mac OS X (three of the four applications work only in Mac OS X) and that you already know Mac and OS X fundamentals — point and click, dragging items, opening windows, choosing commands from menus, selecting items in a window or list, editing text, and what a Home directory is. If you don't have this knowledge, we'd recommend either *Mac OS X for Dummies* (by one of the authors of this book) or *Macworld Mac OS X Bible* (co-authored by the other author of this book).

Apple frequently updates the subject applications, so we had to draw the line somewhere as to what versions if the iApps programs to cover — iTunes 3, iPhoto 1.1.1, iMovie 2.1.2, and iDVD 2.1 are current as we went to print and the ones on which this book is based. Other than iMovie, these applications require Mac OS X (usually 10.1 or later), and OS X is strongly recommended for iMovie as well.

Normally, a Bible title is a little dry, but normally the subject matter is, too — word processors, spreadsheets, databases, operating systems, and so forth. We're blessed with software that, while productive, is primarily fun to use. Because of this, we're going to present the material in a lighter style than is usual, with a little repartee, some personal anecdotes, and occasional opinions.

iTunes, iPhoto, and iMovie come with all currently shipping Macs and with boxed copies of Mac OS X. iDVD comes with all current Macs that include a SuperDrive. You might (but probably won't) find it on some other Macs, but it won't run unless a SuperDrive is present. You have the software; now you can read this book and learn how to use the software Apple provided.

What's Inside

The *iTunes, iPhoto, iMovie, and iDVD Bible* covers each of the title applications in detail. Not only does it tell you what the applications do and how to use them, but it also points out the limitations and suggests software or hardware to augment the applications or function as alternatives. The book is divided into six parts:

✦ **Part I** provides a very basic overview of the four applications and lays some groundwork for what is to follow.

✦ **Parts II through** V cover iTunes, iPhoto, iMovie, and iDVD, respectively. Each part consists of five chapters, as follows:
  - Introduction
  - Getting Started
  - Getting Advanced
  - Tips, Tricks, and Techniques
  - Hardware and Software Enhancements

✦ **Part VI** covers ways to share your work between the different applications and what software to consider if one of the applications no longer satisfies your needs.

Conventions Used in This Book

We use the following conventions in this book in an effort to assist you through the material:

Version References

Apple regularly updates Mac OS X and the applications described in this book, each update bringing with it a new version number. When we don't list a version number, you can assume that we are talking either about the book's subject versions: iTunes 3, iPhoto 1.1.1, iMovie 2.1.2, and iDVD 2.1. If we list a version without a decimal point (such as iDVD 2 rather than iDVD 2.0), we're talking about all versions whose version numbers start with that digit.

Mac OS X (10.2, aka "Jaguar") was released while we were writing this book. Some interface elements (such as the Info window) changed. In general, our screen shots and discussions were taken with Mac OS X (10.1.5), but where there is a difference in 10.2, we note it parenthetically.

Sidebars

Certain discussions are expanded with sidebars. These are shaded boxes containing background information, advanced technical details and references, and other helpful ancillary information.

Icon Paragraphs

We augment the basic discussion of our topics with special information, set apart from the regular text and marked with one of the following distinctive icons:

 A note icon is an "aside," calling attention to an interesting or unexpected aspect of the current topic. This includes our personal opinions and experiences where we feel them germane to the discussion.

 A tip icon indicates an advisory discussion. When you see one of these, you can expect to learn a shortcut or other useful information concerning the current topic.

 A caution icon warns you of possible pitfalls and will include workarounds (even if that workaround is "don't do that.")

We hope you enjoy using this book at least as much as we enjoyed writing it. If you have feedback or suggestions for future editions, please let us know about them.

Contents at a Glance

Acknowledgments ix
Introduction xi

Part I: Getting Started with Digital Media 1
Chapter 1: The Big Picture: What's the Digital Hub all About? 3
Chapter 2: Tools and Terms 11

Part II: iTunes 19
Chapter 3: Introducing iTunes 21
Chapter 4: Getting Started with iTunes 45
Chapter 5: Getting Advanced with iTunes 71
Chapter 6: More iTunes Tips, Tricks, and Techniques 95
Chapter 7: Enhancing Your iTunes Experience 103

Part III: iPhoto 115
Chapter 8: Introducing iPhoto 117
Chapter 9: Getting Started with iPhoto 135
Chapter 10: Getting Advanced with iPhoto 193
Chapter 11: More iPhoto Tips, Tricks, and Techniques 211
Chapter 12: Enhancing Your iPhoto Experience 219

Part IV: iMovie 235
Chapter 13: Introducing iMovie 237
Chapter 14: Getting Started with iMovie 259
Chapter 15: Getting Advanced with iMovie 309
Chapter 16: More iMovie Tips, Tricks, and Techniques 351
Chapter 17: Enhancing Your iMovie Experience 363

Part V: iDVD 373
Chapter 18: Introducing iDVD 375
Chapter 19: Getting Started with iDVD 387
Chapter 20: Getting Advanced with iDVD 409
Chapter 21: iDVD Tips, Tricks, and Techniques 421
Chapter 22: Enhancing Your iDVD Experience 433

Part VI: Putting it All Together 437
Chapter 23: Using the Four "i"s Together 439
Chapter 24: Movie- and DVD-Making Like the Pros 447
Chapter 25: Taking Slideshows Beyond iPhoto 457
Chapter 26: When You Outgrow the "iStuff" 469

Appendix: System Requirements 477

Index 481

Bonus Chapter from *Mac OS X Bible* B-1

Contents

Acknowledgments ix

Introduction xi

Part I: Getting Started with Digital Media   1

Chapter 1: The Big Picture: What's the Digital Hub All About? 3

    Bringing the Studio into Your Home 4
    Sharing Your Work with Others 5
        On the Web 6
        Via e-mail 7
        On CD/DVD 9
    Summary 9

Chapter 2: Tools and Terms 11

    Meeting the iApplications 11
        Rolling out iMovie 12
        Hitting the high notes with iTunes 13
        Be your own producer with iDVD 13
        Smile for iPhoto 14
    Learning a Little Jargon 15
    Summary 18

Part II: iTunes   19

Chapter 3: Introducing iTunes 21

    Discovering iTunes (and What It Does) 22
    What You Need to Use iTunes 24
        CD burner 25
        Media 25
        Speakers or headphones 26
        An iPod or other MP3 player 26
        Internet access 26
    Getting Started with iTunes 27
    Exploring the iTunes Window 30
    Getting Help 37

Setting iTunes Preferences 38
    General 38
    Effects 40
    Importing 41
    CD Burning 43
    Advanced 43
Summary 44

Chapter 4: Getting Started with iTunes 45

Checking Out the Library 45
    Adding songs to your Library 46
    Removing songs from the Library 48
    Searching the Library 51
    Browsing the Library 52
    Creating and Managing Playlists 53
    Creating and deleting playlists 54
    Modifying playlists 55
Importing Songs 56
    Preparing to rip 58
    It's time to rip 58
Making Your Own CDs 61
    Burning the CD 62
    If something goes wrong 63
Listening to Internet Radio 64
    What's available on Internet radio 64
    Listening to the built-ins 65
    Adding your own stations 66
Introducing Smart Playlists 68
Summary 70

Chapter 5: Getting Advanced with iTunes 71

Exploring the Song Information Dialog Box 71
    Viewing the Info tab 72
    Using the Tags tab 73
    Adjusting on the Options tab 74
Working with MP3 Players 75
    Interfacing the iPod to iTunes 76
    Using MP3 players other than the iPod 80
Adjusting Sound with the Equalizer 83
    What is an equalizer? 83
    Roll your own or use presets 84
Exploring the Visualizer 85
    Adjusting Visual Effects 85
    Installing additional Visual Effects 87
Burning MP3 CDs 88

Choosing the Right Bit-rate 89
Advanced Importing and Converting 89
Advanced Smart Playlists 90
Accessing Audible.com 92
Summary 93

Chapter 6: More iTunes Tips, Tricks, and Techniques 95

Smarten Up Smart Playlists 95
Relocating Your iTunes Library 96
Backing Up Your Music 98
Adding Visual Effects 99
AppleScript and iTunes 99
Summary 102

Chapter 7: Enhancing Your iTunes Experience 103

Hardware Accessories 103
   The Apple iPod 104
   Speakers and headphones 104
   MP3 players 107
   External storage 107
   CD burners 108
Software Add-ons 108
   Roxio Toast with Jam 108
   AppleWorks and Apple's iTunes AppleScripts 109
   MP3 Rage 110
   Amadeus II 111
   Visualizer plug-ins 113
Summary 114

Part III: iPhoto   115

Chapter 8: Introducing iPhoto 117

Introducing Digital Photography and iPhoto 118
   Choosing a digital camera 118
   Focusing on iPhoto 123
Exploring the iPhoto Window 125
   Import mode tools 127
   Organize mode tools 128
   Edit mode tools 128
   Book mode tools 129
   Share mode tools 130
Setting iPhoto Preferences 131
Summary 133

Chapter 9: Getting Started with iPhoto 135

Importing Pictures 135
    Importing from a supported digital camera or equivalent 136
    Importing other digital images 138
Organizing Your Photos 139
    Using iPhoto's organizational tools 140
    Creating your own albums 146
    Searching your Photo Library 148
    Removing photos from albums and the Library 149
Making Adjustments to a Photo 153
    Rotating an image 154
    Cropping an image 154
    Adjusting brightness and contrast 156
    Removing red-eye from an image 157
    Converting to black-and-white 157
Laying Out Books 158
    Putting together your album 158
    Choosing a theme 160
    Designing your pages 163
    Previewing your book 170
Printing Photos 171
    Preparing to print 171
    Printing from iPhoto 172
Ordering Photos 175
    Prints 175
    Coffee table books 178
E-mailing Your Photos 180
Publishing Your Pictures on Your .Mac HomePage 181
Creating a Slide Show 185
    Playing a slide show 186
    Controlling your slide show 187
Using Your Photos on the Desktop 187
    Desktop pictures 188
    Screen savers 188
Summary 191

Chapter 10: Getting Advanced with iPhoto 193

Exporting Your Photos 194
Sharing a Slide Show 195
Creating Custom Web Pages 199
Using an External Program for Photo Editing 204
Plugging in to iPhoto 205
Summary 209

Chapter 11: More iPhoto Tips, Tricks, and Techniques 211

Inside an iPhoto Library 211
Managing Your iPhoto Library 213
Taking Better Pictures 214
    Photo composition 214
    Make use of your camera's capabilities 217
Summary 218

Chapter 12: Enhancing Your iPhoto Experience 219

Hardware to Consider 219
    Digital camera 220
    Scanner 221
    Burning drive 222
    Tripods 223
    Lenses and filters 223
    Color printer 224
Software Acquisitions to Consider 225
    Toast 5 Titanium 226
    iView Media/iView MediaPro 226
    Adobe Photoshop 7/Photoshop Elements 228
    GraphicConverter 229
    iPhoto Library Manager 230
    iPhoto Librarian 230
    SmartSound MovieMaestro 231
    Educational Web sites 234
Summary 234

Part IV: iMovie   235

Chapter 13: Introducing iMovie 237

Discovering Digital Video 237
    Proliferating formats 238
    Video compression 239
Gathering the Bare Essentials 240
    What your Mac needs 240
    What you need to connect to your Mac 240
    Jargon break 243
Exploring the iMovie Window 243
    Viewing the monitor 245
    Seeing what's on the shelf 247
    The clip viewer 250
    The timeline viewer 251
    Status indicators 252

Setting iMovie Preferences 253
    Managing your Import preferences 254
    Selecting your Playback Preference 254
    Moving up to Advanced preferences 256
Summary 257

Chapter 14: Getting Started with iMovie 259

Acquiring Video from a Digital Camcorder 259
    Connecting your camcorder 259
    Starting iMovie 261
    Importing the video 264
Working with Clips 267
    Renaming clips 267
    Editing clips 268
    Working with the clip viewer 273
    Working with the timeline viewer 287
    Unleashing iMovie Audio effects 292
Importing Images 298
    Getting the image into iMovie 299
Exporting Your Video 302
    Exporting back to a camera 302
    Exporting to QuickTime 304
    Exporting for iDVD 307
Summary 307

Chapter 15: Getting Advanced with iMovie 309

The Cutting Room Floor 309
    The art of the intercut 310
    The coolest cuts of all 313
Working with Non-DV Video 316
    Converting compatible formats 318
    Knowing what to import 319
    Translating to DV Stream in QuickTime Pro 322
    Importing DV Streams into iMovie 323
Plugging into iMovie 324
    Installing plug-ins 325
    Exploring iMovie Plug-in Pack 2.1.1 for Mac OS X 326
    Adding other stuff to iMovie 327
Becoming Expert with QuickTime Export 329
Postproduction Tricks with QuickTime Pro 334
    Masking out part of the screen 336
    Making better subtitles with Text Tracks 339
Putting Your Movie on the Web 341
    Creating the HTML for a downloadable movie 342
    Embedding a movie in your Web page 343
    Streaming your movie 346
    Putting your iMovies on your iDisk 347
Summary 349

Chapter 16: More iMovie Tips, Tricks, and Techniques 351

Sharing Clips between Projects 351
Making Menu-driven VideoCDs 353
    Planning for chapters 354
    Building a menu-driven VideoCD 354
    Burning a VideoCD 356
Plan Your Shoot and Shoot Your Plan 357
Taping Tips for Better Footage 358
    Bouncing is bad 358
    Getting good lighting 359
    Huh? What'd they say? 360
Summary 362

Chapter 17: Enhancing Your iMovie Experience 363

Hardware Enhancements 363
    Adding RAM 363
    Boosting mass storage 364
    Burning drives 365
    Getting out of the shadows 365
    Keeping a steady hand 366
    Filtering and focusing 366
Software Enhancements 367
    Going Pro with QuickTime 367
    Have a little toast with your iMovie 368
    Adding effects, transitions, and scoring 369
    Putting a dent in your plastic 371
    Free software 371
Summary 372

Part V: iDVD   373

Chapter 18: Introducing iDVD 375

Understanding DVDs 376
    Authoring a DVD 377
    DVD-R burning application 378
Exploring the iDVD Window 379
    The Main Window 379
    The Themes drawer 381
    The Slideshow pane 384
Setting iDVD Preferences 384
Summary 386

Chapter 19: Getting Started with iDVD 387

Creating DVD Menus 388
    What's your theme? 388
    Adding movie content 390

Customizing your theme 392
Saving your favorite themes 398
Creating a Slideshow 399
Previewing Your DVD 404
Burning Your DVD 405
Summary 407

Chapter 20: Getting Advanced with iDVD 409

Storing Data on Your DVD 409
Monitoring Your DVD's Status 412
Using iDVD Companion 412
Employing the iDVD Companion palette 414
Using the iDVD Companion menu bar 415
AppleScripting iDVD 418
Summary 420

Chapter 21: iDVD Tips, Tricks, and Techniques 421

Inside Projects 421
Inside Themes 424
Borrowing a background 424
Resurrecting an iDVD 1 theme 426
Planning Your iDVD Project 428
Inside Encoding and Compression 429
Summary 432

Chapter 22: Enhancing Your iDVD Experience 433

Hardware Enhancements 433
Pioneer A104 (SuperDrive) 433
DVD players 434
Media 435
Software Enhancements 435
QuickTime Pro 435
Photoshop or Photoshop Elements 436
iDVD Companion 436
Summary 436

Part VI: Putting it All Together 437

Chapter 23: Using the Four "i"s Together 439

What's the Score? 439
Slip, Slideshowing Away 443
Basic slideshows 444
Complex slideshows 445
Feeding iDVD 446
Summary 446

Chapter 24: Movie- and DVD-Making Like the Pros 447

Storyboarding the Movie. 447
    Collecting your notes 448
    Outlining or charting your project 448
    Scripts 450
    Shot lists 451
    Storyboards 451
    Budgets 451
    Schedules 452
Shooting Extra Footage. 453
Setting the Stage in iMovie 453
    Plan for iDVD's limitations 454
    Preparing more than just the movie 454
Choosing Transitions 454
Planning the DVD 455
Summary 456

Chapter 25: Taking Slideshows Beyond iPhoto 457

Getting More Control over iPhoto Slideshows 457
Taking Slideshows to VideoCD 462
    Converting QuickTime to VideoCD 462
    Creating menus 465
    Building the VideoCD 466
Summary 468

Chapter 26: When You Outgrow the "iStuff" 469

When iTunes Isn't Enough 469
    Sound Studio 470
    Roxio's Jam 471
Moving Beyond iPhoto 471
Moving Beyond iMovie 473
Authoring Beyond iDVD 474
Summary 476

Appendix: System Requirements 477

Index 481

Bonus Chapter from *Mac OS X Bible*. B-1

Getting Started with Digital Media

PART

I

In This Part

Chapter 1
The Big Picture: What's the Digital Hub All About?

Chapter 2
Tools and Terms

The Big Picture: What's the Digital Hub All About?

CHAPTER 1

✦ ✦ ✦ ✦

In This Chapter

Bringing the studio into your home

Sharing your work with others

✦ ✦ ✦ ✦

On October 5, 1999, Apple rolled out the iMac DV, the first iMac ready for digital filmmaking that did not require any additional hardware or software. Every iMac DV came with iMovie, Apple's revolutionary new digital video editing software. For the first time ever you could edit high-quality digital video at home for well under $2,000.

Fourteen months later, Steve Jobs premiered iTunes and iDVD, and ballyhooed Apple's new digital hub strategy: To make the Mac "the Hub of your digital lifestyle."

Amid great speculation and phenomenal hype, Apple announced the iPod on October 23, 2001. It was a huge hit, selling far more units than Apple had forecasted.

Then, on January 7, 2002, Jobs introduced iPhoto, "the missing link," according to Apple, in digital photography and the missing spoke on Apple's digital hub.

Note As you've probably noticed, none of the digital hub products has a printed User's Manual or any documentation beyond a ReadMe file or short Getting Started pamphlet. You're expected to rely upon the often terse, and occasionally helpful Help files. That's where we come in. In this single volume, you get what amounts to a manual for each of the four applications (iPhoto, iTunes, iMovie, and iDVD), packed with easy-to-follow, step-by-step instructions for just about anything you'll ever need to do, topped off with plenty of tips, tricks, and techniques. (And some puns, jokes, and old song references at no additional charge.) Think of the book you hold in your hand as our version of the four missing iManuals.

Bringing the Studio into Your Home

Apple's iPhoto Web page starts with the caption, "Shoot like Ansel. Organize like Martha." While the first sentence may be a bit of an exaggeration, iPhoto certainly provides tools making such a result less improbable. Similar claims, with different names, could be made about the other hub applications.

That's the whole point of Apple's digital hub: You now have the tools in hand to be all that you can be as a multimedia producer. All you have to provide is the vision and talent.

For years, we've all been reading and hearing about "the computer revolution" and the "digital revolution" and, being in the industry, your savvy authors knew that "revolution" was generally an overstatement. Since the iMovie debut, "revolution" stopped being an exaggeration, and each new hub application adds momentum to this ongoing revolution from Apple.

In just the past three years, we've watched iMovie take film-making out of the hands of professionals and dedicated hobbyists and put it squarely in the grasp of the average consumer. iDVD now lets that typical consumer create DVDs — a process, which not too long ago was the exclusive province of studios with hundreds of thousands of dollars worth of equipment. iTunes can enable anybody to become a DJ or album maker. iPhoto and a digital camera (an increasingly affordable tool) provide an escape from film and photo developers.

You're now the master of your own digital destiny. Here's just a sample of what you can do:

- ✦ iPhoto lets you use your photographs as more than just prints to frame, paste in albums, or store in a drawer. If you want prints, you've got them, but you also have slide shows, bound and printed albums, screen savers, Web pages, desktop backgrounds, and on and on.

  And you get all of this without any fancy professional equipment, smelly chemicals, or darkroom. (Save the closet for your clothes.)

- ✦ iTunes lets you create your own recording mixes and burn your own CDs without splicing tapes.

- ✦ iMovie eliminates all the nastiness of splicing scenes together as well as the fancy (and expensive) equipment required to add special effects and transitions. And, through the wonders of FireWire and QuickTime, you can easily save the finished product to videotape or to disk.

- ✦ Using iDVD you can take your iMovies and burn your own DVDs, complete with static and live-motion menus just like the ones on commercial DVDs.

Only a few short years ago, the software and hardware required to perform these tasks cost astronomical amounts. Now you find the software included in your

OS X Dock when you first start up your $1900 flat panel iMac (or a number of other Mac configurations), as shown in Figure 1-1. Additionally, these hub applications have rendered a lot of the hardware unnecessary. Of course, you'll still need to own digital still and video cameras to make full use of iPhoto and iMovie, but even without cameras the programs can be useful, as you'll see in Parts III ("iPhoto") and IV ("iMovie") of this book.

Figure 1-1: The standard OS X Dock, with iPhoto, iTunes, iMovie, and iDVD all ready to use.

With some additional software, most notably Roxio's Toast 5 Titanium, you can also create VideoCDs from your iMovies and your iPhoto Slide Shows or create photo collections on CD directly from iPhoto.

Note

VideoCDs, also referred to as VCDs, are a popular distribution format for video almost everywhere in the world except the United States, with quality equivalent to that found on prerecorded videotapes. Since most (but not all) DVD players also play VCDs, the format is starting to gain momentum in the US, as well. And why not? Eighty minutes of VHS-quality video on a 19 cent CD-R disc that you can view on your set-top DVD player, or almost any Mac is a very good thing.

We usually cringe when we encounter phrases using words like *empower,* but it's hard to think of a better word to use when describing what the digital hub applications do. They empower you, turning your Mac into a combination Hollywood studio and Fotomat.

Sharing Your Work with Others

Although there are exceptions, most people enjoy sharing music, movies, and their photographic memories. Of course, we enjoy being reminded of our trip to London, our tour of the Smithsonian, or the way Junior looked as a baby, but more than that, we like to show the photos and home movies to our friends and family.

Similarly, no matter how much we enjoy just sitting back and listening to music, most of the time we enjoy it even more at a party or with friends.

Because of this normal human desire to share our pleasures and memories, Apple has included lots of sharing capabilities in both the Mac OS and in the hub applications.

On the Web

The Web is a little over ten years old now and, for the past few years, ISPs (Internet Service Providers) have touted personal Web page space as one of their selling points. Unfortunately, except for some truly awful automated tools (usually Windows-only), creating and publishing your own Web pages required a Web page editor or knowledge of HTML (HyperText Markup Language) to create your pages and using an FTP (File Transfer Protocol) program to transfer them to your ISP-provided space.

Apple decided this whole process should be easier for their customers and created iTools, a collection of Internet-related tools for Mac users (OS 9 and later). The two iTools of particular interest to us here are the iDisk, a mountable 20MB disk volume, and HomePage, Apple's Mac-only Web page builder that uses your iDisk as your personal Web space. At the July, 2002 Macworld Convention, Apple morphed iTools into a for-pay service named .Mac.

The first hub application to exploit Apple's HomePage iTool was iMovie, which isn't surprising as it's also the oldest of the four hub programs. In fact, Apple has promoted the Web presence of home iMovies with the iMovie Gallery (`http://homepage.mac.com/imovie/`), not only putting a few iMovies on iMovie's own iTools page to amuse and entertain, but also demonstrating how easy it is to provide a Web browser interface to your finished movie.

> **Note** Using your own products both for everyday operations and to show what they can do is often referred to as, "eating our own dog food." If you want to see a can of Bob's, it's on his Apple HomePage:
>
> `http://homepage.mac.com/boblevitus/iMovieTheater1.html`
>
> If you have a dial-up modem connection, it may not stream but you can control-click and download it since it's only about 5MB.

With iPhoto, Apple went even further, automating the page-creation process even more by having iPhoto interact directly with both iDisk (loading the photos into the iDisk's Pictures folder for you) and HomePage (linking directly into HomePage's PhotoAlbum page themes without using your Web browser). An example Web page created in this way (photos of Dennis's canine companion) is shown in Figure 1-2.

So far, we haven't seen a Music page, linking iTunes with iDisk and HomePage, but there is a Music folder on your iDisk. Who knows what the future holds in this area? Apple's probably wise not to provide tools for sharing music at this time — the RIAA (Recording Industry Association of America) doesn't have much tolerance for companies that facilitate sharing music. (Remember what happened to Napster.)

> **Note** We don't *know* that the RIAA has anything to do with Apple's ommision of MP3 distribution in its HomePage and e-mail tools. That's just a guess on our part, owing partly to our skeptical natures and partly to the fact that we read the newspapers and follow the battles between the recording industry and consumers with great interest and mixed emotions.

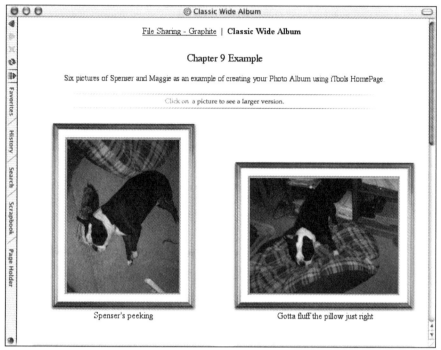

Figure 1-2: iPhoto's HomePage connection makes creating and posting a Web page easy.

Suffice it to say, though, that if you're willing to design your own Web pages, it isn't difficult to make a few MP3s available. We'll even show you how in Chapter 6, "More iTunes Tips, Tricks, and Techniques."

Caution

We'll warn you again in Chapter 6, but be very careful about what songs you post. Make sure that you have the right to post them. The DMCA (Digital Millennium Copyright Act) was used to go after Napster and others for just this sort of thing. "Sharing" copyrighted music is a no-no without specific, written permission from the copyright holder.

Via e-mail

Once again, Apple has concentrated on iPhoto and iMovie when dealing with e-mail. Of course, sending a DVD by e-mail doesn't make much sense, even with a very fast connection. Transferring an MP3, though, does make sense, but Apple hasn't automated that process — again, probably something to do with the RIAA.

One of iMovie's default formats for exporting (Save As in most Mac programs) is designed specifically for e-mail attachment. Just fire up your e-mail program, create a new message, address it, drag the movie file(s) into it, and click Send.

The Care and Labeling of Optical Media

We're going to focus on CD-R media here, but what we write applies also to CD-RW and DVD-R discs.

In the olden days of computing, before Apple introduced the Macintosh with its Sony 3.5" floppy disk, floppies really were, well, floppy. The thin Mylar disk was enclosed in an insubstantial, flexible case and writing on that case with anything other than a soft felt-tip pen was likely to damage the disk inside. Adhesive labels came with floppies. You wrote on the label, telling what the disk held, then affixed the label to the case. This was fine, so long as you didn't have to change what was on the label by adding to the disk's contents or replacing them. If so, you were back to square one.

With CDs, you have much the same problem. Writing on the (nondata) surface can, if you don't use a soft writing implement, apply sufficient pressure to deform the substrate layer behind it, where the laser burns your data.

On the other hand, applying a label can unbalance the disc, resulting in problems when the drive has the disc spinning and tries to read from it. This is less of a problem with full-coverage labels, properly applied using the tool that comes with your labels and/or labeling software, but it's still a consideration.

Just writing on a CD or DVD that you want to give as a gift looks tacky, so what are you to do?

For backups and the like, we just scribble something with a soft pen designed for this purpose, such as the TDK CD Mark (www.tdk.com). On some discs, though, presentation is important and we create our labels using various software. Dennis has templates for both Photoshop and Illustrator that match his label stock, Bob collects Avery products and has templates in Word and Photoshop, and a script that exports a playlist from iTunes and lays it out in a jewel box insert template in AppleWorks. Then, very carefully, making sure that the label is applied evenly, we use an applicator. (The one that comes with CD Stomper [www.cdstomper.com] is our favorite.)

One tip, though: The instructions that come with the label applicators suggest using fingertip pressure in the center ring to press the CD onto the label. We've found something better, eliminating the risk that our fingers will slip and damage the recorded surface. If you purchase your CDs in bulk on spindles, there are usually clear plastic CD-sized protective "discs" at the top and bottom of the stack. These protective discs can serve the same purpose when you're applying a label. Just put the non-label side down on the plastic, flip the pair of discs over and press the discs down onto the label. Since you're only touching the protective disc, you can actually spread your fingers more, ensuring a more even application.

Oh, and don't try to peel labels off the discs. You're guaranteed to flex the media and that will separate the disc's layers, resulting in an unusable disc.

Just as with Web pages, iPhoto automates sending photos via e-mail. iPhoto will do everything for you except address the message and click Send.

On CD/DVD

Don't get us wrong, sharing via Web pages and e-mail is great when the files are few and small. But, even with all the compression performed to create MP3s, QuickTime movies, and JPEG photo files, you sacrifice a lot of quality getting them small enough to transfer quickly over an Internet connection, especially for folks dialing in via modem.

In today's world of large multimedia files and massive hard disks, portable media like floppy disks are all but useless (which might be why they aren't built into Macs any more); and Zip disks are often inadequate and are very expensive. Apple was one of the pioneers in delivering software on CD and including CD drives as a standard feature in some models as far back as 1990. CDs and DVDs become even more attractive when you consider that you can create music CDs playable in your CD players and DVDs that you can play on the DVD player hooked to your TV set. With 650MB to 700MB capacities and a very low per-MB cost, optical media (CD-R, CD-RW) seems like the next evolutionary step in backup and transport media. DVD-R, with its 4.7GB capacity, is a little more expensive than CD-R per unit, but costs about the same per megabyte.

Apple also recognized the importance of integrating disc-burning capabilities into the Finder (data CDs and DVDs), iTunes (Audio CDs and MP3 CDs), and iDVD (DVDs), and at about the same time (early 2001) they started including burners for CDs and/or DVDs in most Mac models. The integrated disc burning is simple, straightforward, and for most people, adequate to meet their disc burning needs. We're going to mention Roxio's Toast 5 Titanium frequently in this book. In our opinion, it is an invaluable tool for anyone who burns more than an occasional CD. Roxio (www.roxio.com) includes an iMovie and QuickTime plug-in for creating VideoCDs and El Gato Software (www.elgato.com) created a free iPhoto plug-in so that you can burn photo collections directly to CD using Toast.

Summary

In this chapter, you've seen the evolution of Apple's digital hub. You've also seen how the digital hub applications integrate with Apple's Internet strategy and take advantage of Mac OS's built-in disc-burning software, which makes sharing your digital creations much easier.

✦ ✦ ✦

Tools and Terms

In This Chapter

Meeting the iApplications

Learning a little jargon

Apple continues expanding the scope of their digital hub concept and frequently updates the applications and services comprising the hub.

Anything we write will, eventually, become outdated. Dealing with an evolving technology base (like the digital hub) just means that "eventually" isn't a very long time.

Our snapshot in time is iTunes 3, iPhoto 1.1.1, iMovie 2.1.4, and iDVD 2.1. It's possible, even likely, that one or more of these applications will be out in a newer version by the time you read this, but that's the nature of software.

Fortunately, when new versions of these applications appear, the things you learned about the previous version still apply, you just have some new tools to use. Thus, even with a newer version the information in this book will still be useful — it will just be a little less complete with respect to the new version.

Having said that, here's an introduction to the four applications and some of the jargon (including acronyms) that we'll be using throughout the book.

We will occasionally refer to the collection of these four applications as the *iApps*.

Meeting the iApplications

Although this isn't the order in which we'll cover them in Parts II through V of the book, Apple introduced iMovie first, followed by iTunes and iDVD, and then iPhoto. The order we're following is the order of most users to fewest users, which has nothing to do with the applications' relative complexity and everything to do with the dollar (or equipment) cost of entry. Here, though, we'll introduce them in the order Apple presented them.

Rolling out iMovie

With the release of the iMac DV models in autumn 1999, Apple shook up the digital video world by bundling iMovie, the industry's first easy-to-use and affordable digital video editing program. Taking advantage of the iMac DV's high-speed FireWire connectors, common on most digital camcorders (though usually referred to as i.Link or IEEE-1394), iMovie made the iMac the least expensive platform for editing high-quality video.

Now at version 2.1.4, iMovie is the only one of the four applications whose current version can still run under OS 9. With Apple's pronouncements that development for OS 9 is dead and that Macs produced in 2003 won't even boot OS 9, we are pretty certain that the next version of iMovie (whatever number they give it) will be OS X-only.

Figure 2-1 shows you the iMovie 2 screen you'll see the first time you launch iMovie. In Chapter 13, "Introducing iMovie," we'll cover what all the parts are for.

iMovie comes with a very nice tutorial to give you practice using the application. We believe in hands-on use, so if you want some ready-made footage to use when you're reading this book, the tutorial is a good place to look.

Figure 2-1: iMovie welcomes you with just a hint of its capability.

Hitting the high notes with iTunes

In January 2001's Macworld Expo keynote, Apple introduced both iTunes and iDVD. In that keynote, Steve Jobs commented that Apple was late to the game in including CD burners with their hardware, but they were making up for it in a big way. And, to make the CD burners even more useful, he showed iTunes burning audio CDs directly from user-created playlists.

As the second half of this one-two punch, Jobs also demonstrated burning a CD directly from the Finder, eliminating the requirement for third-party applications for basic CD burning.

Eighteen months later, iTunes had two major revisions and now stands at version 3. Figure 2-2 shows what you see the first time you run iTunes (after you first answer a number of configuration questions).

Figure 2-2: iTunes is ready to shake, rattle, and roll.

Be your own producer with iDVD

At the same time Jobs announced CD-R availability in Macs, he announced an industry breakthrough with the first consumer-priced DVD burner, the Apple SuperDrive (based on the Pioneer A103 mechanism). Using a simple drag-and-drop metaphor, iDVD enables anyone with a suitably configured Mac to create DVDs with navigation menus virtually indistinguishable from those on commercial DVDs that would play in most set-top DVD players.

Now in version 2.1, iDVD has added some bells and whistles, such as motion menus (animated menus and buttons), without sacrificing any of its simplicity of use. Figure 2-3 shows the initial iDVD screen, which starts you off ready to work with the iDVD tutorial.

Figure 2-3: iDVD starts out ready to create a menu-driven DVD.

Smile for iPhoto

January 2002's Macworld Expo saw Apple introduce iPhoto, hailing it as the "missing link" in digital photography. Sporting a simple, yet elegant, user interface, iPhoto leverages OS X's Image Capture technology to recognize a wide variety of USB-connected digital cameras without any user configuration, as well as Picture CDs and various Smart Media readers. With iPhoto's organizational tools, a typical user can manage photo collections containing hundreds or even thousands of images. Basic built-in editing tools let you crop, rotate, adjust hue and saturation, and remove red-eye and, if those tools prove insufficient, you can specify an external editing program to use when a photo is double-clicked. Finally, iPhoto includes a number of ways to share your photos, including printing, commercial print processing, coffee table books, slideshows, screensavers, Web pages, and many others.

The initial iPhoto window is shown in Figure 2-4, although it seems a bit barren with no pictures yet imported. The current iPhoto version is 1.1.1.

Figure 2-4: iPhoto starts you out with an empty photo library, just waiting to be filled.

Learning a Little Jargon

Every vocation and avocation has its own lingo. Photography, cinematography, and music are great examples of this, and the addition of computers to the mix has spawned additional dialects.

There's no way we can give you an exhaustive list (an unabridged dictionary, as it were), but we can get you started with those words, phrases, and acronyms you're most likely to encounter — in fact, you'll run across a number of them while reading this book, such as:

AIFF (Audio Interchange File Format): The Apple-standard specification for audio such as that used on CDs.

aspect ratio: The horizontal to vertical ratio. For example, 320 x 240 and 640 x 480 are both 4:3 aspect ratios.

authoring: The act of assembling the various elements of a video production and creating a consumer-ready end product including navigational aids. One example would be creating the menus and background music that present the video and slideshows on a DVD and then encoding and burning the result.

bit depth: Describes how many bits are used to determine the color space of each pixel in an image. A bit depth of 8 gives 256 possible colors, 16-bit depth allows for 65,536 possible colors.

burner: A CD or DVD drive that has the capability of writing CDs and DVDs in addition to reading them.

cap: Digital video captured from other media. For example, when you transfer video footage from a VHS or Super-8 tape, you are said to have capped it.

CBR (constant bit rate): Used in reference to digital video streams that transfer data with the same number of bits-per-second, regardless of the content.

CD-DA (compact disc-digital audio): The format specification for audio compact discs such as those played in standalone CD players.

CD-R (CD-recordable): An inexpensive write-once, read-many disc format that has become popular for use in CD burners.

CD-RW (CD-rewritable): Similar to CD-R, but it can be erased and written over.

decoding: The conversion process that reads compressed audio or video and reconstructs the sounds and images you hear and see

dpi (sometimes ppi): Dots (or pixels) per inch is used to describe the density of an image and is used primarily as a measurement for how well (or poorly) an image will print.

DVD: Either digital versatile disc or digital video disc depending on context and whom you ask.

DVD-R (DVD-recordable): A user-writable disc medium that can be played in most modern DVD players.

encoding: Changing the format of the data to comply with a transmission standard. The term is used most often when referring to the process of creating the MPEG files from DV stream source material for video or the MP3 file from AIFF or WAV files for audio.

FireWire: Apple's name for the IEEE-1394 data transmission standard, a high-bandwidth technology. Also known, primarily on Sony products, as i.Link, it is the standard high speed data transfer technology used on current Macs and almost all digital camcorders.

fps (frames per second): Tells how many digital images per second are being decoded for display.

JPEG: Joint Photographic Experts Group, also the image-compression algorithms that organization developed and which are in common use by digital cameras and for use on Web sites.

lossy: The word used to describe data compression techniques which involve removing detail as part of the compression process. When lossy compression is employed, the decompressed image will differ from the original. *Lossless* compression, on the other hand, completely reconstructs the original from the compressed data. JPEG and the various MPEG formats are lossy, GIF and PNG are lossless.

MP3 (MPEG-1, Audio Layer 3): Audio compression technology specified by MPEG and in common use for digital audio to produce near-CD quality encodings in substantially less disk space.

MPEG: Motion Picture Experts Group, an industry organization which has developed the algorithms and formats used for DVD, VideoCD, SuperVideoCD, and streaming video.

NTSC (National Television System Committee): Group who specifies the U.S. television standard and for whom the standard is named.

PAL (phase alternating line): The European TV standard.

resolution: The number of pixels in an image's horizontal and vertical dimension.

rip: Extracting audio from CD, tape, or record.

SCSI (small computer systems interface): A medium-to-high bandwidth data transfer technology that, until recently, was the standard on Macintoshes. SCSI has been supplanted by FireWire as the Mac standard, although it is still available as an extra-cost option.

SuperDrive: Apple's name for the DVD-R/CD-RW drive available on many Mac models. It was originally based upon the Pioneer A103 mechanism, but now uses the Pioneer A104, which allows 2x writing.

SVCD (Super VideoCD): A format based on MPEG-2 and developed by Philips for use in China on enhanced VCD players. It has achieved significant popularity due to its near-DVD quality while still allowing the use of inexpensive CD media.

USB (universal serial bus): A standard for the transmission of serial data between electronic devices. It is the current standard for low-bandwidth transfers on the Mac, such as between the keyboard and the computer.

VBR (variable bit rate): Used in reference to digital video streams that vary the amount of data transferred per second depending upon the content.

VCD (VideoCD): A format based on MPEG-1 for digital video to be played on both computers and standalone VideoCD players. The format is playable on most commercial DVD players as well, with quality approximately equal to VHS tape.

WAV: The Windows standard format for phase-encoded audio such as that used on CDs.

Summary

In this chapter you've learned the history and purpose of our four title applications and how Apple has positioned the iApps. You've also picked up some of the jargon common to these applications and their venues. Every vocation and avocation has terminology (jargon) specific to it, and computers, audio, and video sometimes carry that to an extreme — knowing these terms in context will help you follow not only our discussion, but what you read on the Web and in magazines as well.

✦ ✦ ✦

iTunes

P A R T

II

In This Part

Chapter 3
Introducing iTunes

Chapter 4
Getting Started with iTunes

Chapter 5
Getting Advanced with iTunes

Chapter 6
More iTunes Tips, Tricks, and Techniques

Chapter 7
Enhancing your iTunes Experience

iTunes

Introducing iTunes

In This Chapter

Discovering iTunes

What you need to use iTunes

Getting started with iTunes

Exploring the iTunes window

Using iTunes Help

Setting iTunes preferences

Since time immemorial (or at least a decade ago), Mac users have listened to music on their Macs, with programs such as (not necessarily in this order) QuickTime Player, HyperCard, AppleCDAudio Player, SoundJam, and a plethora of other players by third-party developers (i.e., not Apple). These all-Mac solutions were popular in their day, but none came close to the universal and ubiquitous popularity MP3 has today.

Today, regardless of what kind of computer you have, what operating system it runs, or even what portable device you choose for your listening enjoyment, chances are it understands MP3 files.

MP3 is a file format that uses compression to create smaller audio files that sound almost as good as the original. Most computers, regardless of make, model, or operating system, can read and write MP3 files using either included software (such as iTunes) or third-party software (such as Toast). MP3 is also the file format used by many portable music-playing devices. These devices come in all sizes and shapes — from software players for the Mac or PC to teeny-tiny wearable players that weigh less than an ounce, including the ear-buds!

Note The very coolest (in our opinion) is Apple's revolutionary 10GB, 2000-song, FireWire-fast, iTunes-savvy iPod.

Note Many portable CD players and DVD players sold today will play MP3-formatted disks, as well as regular Audio CDs. MP3 discs, which you can burn with iTunes (as you'll see shortly), let you pack up to ten times more music on each CD you burn (vs. the Audio CD format).

Bob once burned his whole Beatles boxed set — around 250 songs — onto one 700MB CD and listened to it on his pre-iPod music player, a RioVolt.

Photo courtesy of Apple Computer

Now consider the phenomenal popularity of peer-to-peer file sharing services such as Napster and Gnutella and you'll realize that the MP3 file format has become the proverbial 900-pound gorilla. And, as such, we've seen a profusion of cool Mac programs to play, organize, manage, burn, and transfer MP3 files.

iTunes can do all that and more. When Steve Jobs showed iTunes to the Mac faithful during his January 9, 2001 Macworld Expo keynote, jaws were dropping all over the room.

Note

Of course, there were those few jaded individuals who gleefully noted that iTunes was actually the spawn of best-selling MP3 player SoundJam (written by Jeffrey Robbin and published by Casady & Greene), and that Apple must have made Casady & Greene and Robbin an offer they couldn't refuse to get it.

In this chapter, we'll discuss what iTunes can do for you and explore the iTunes interface. In the next few chapters we'll show you how to perform specific tasks using iTunes.

Discovering iTunes (and What It Does)

Ask a half-dozen Mac users what iTunes is and you're likely to get at least a dozen different descriptions. We've been told that iTunes is our Mac's CD player, and it is. We've also been told that it is the way we burn audio CDs, and it is that, too. In addition, we've been told (also accurately) that it is the conduit to our MP3 players, such as the iPod or Rio; our radio connection to Internet radio station broadcasts; and the database managing our Mac's collection of MP3s, AIFFs, and WAVs.

WARNING: Some so-called "CDs" may damage your Macintosh!

One thing you should be really careful of are so-called audio CDs that are "copy-protected." Check new CDs you purchase—according to Apple KnowledgeBase article #106882, the industry is starting to produce CDs that not only won't play in your computer's optical drive, but may actually cause damage to your computer.

These renegade disks shouldn't even be called CDs—they don't conform to the Red Book, the standards document that describes a properly created audio CD. And, in fact, the aforementioned article says as much:

The (copy protected) audio discs are technically and legally not Compact Discs (CD format), and the CD logo has been removed from the disc. In the logo's former place is the printed message:

"Will not play on PC/Mac"

This appears both on the cover and on the disc. Inserting this disc in a computer may cause the system to stop responding. It might not be possible to eject the disc on computers without a manual eject hole.

Unfortunately, not all Mac users notice the fine print in time to prevent damage to their Macs. Some Macs reportedly require hardware repairs not covered by Apple's warranty, which only covers "real" CDs, and states:

If a disc with copyright protection technology remains inside the drive after following the procedures above, or if the computer does not start up normally, it is recommended that you contact an Apple Authorized Service Provider (AASP) or Apple Technical Support. Audio discs that incorporate copyright protection technologies do not adhere to published Compact Disc standards. Apple designs its optical disc drives to support media that conform to such standards.

The first such disk that came to our attention was Sony's *A New Day Has Come* by Celine Dion. Released in Europe, this disk reportedly causes some Macs to crash. Apple rightfully places the blame squarely on the record label. If a copy-protected disk (note that we avoided calling it a "CD") messes up your Mac, blame it on labels like Sony, not on Apple.

The bottom line is to be very careful about what you stick into your Mac's mouth. Shiny disks that look like CDs (but are not really CDs) may be hazardous to your Mac's health.

 We use the words *song* and *track* interchangeably and generically throughout the book. And we do it even though we know that not every track on a CD is a song (for example, the CD might be a "book on disc"); and that not every item in your library will be a song even though that is what iTunes calls them.

iTunes is all these things and more. We use it to play the MP3 files on our hard disks and the Red Book CD-audio files on our CDs. We use it to display soothing, stimulating, or otherwise satisfying visual effects. And we use it to send information to AppleWorks, which can automatically generate jewel-box covers and CD labels, complete with artist names, song titles, and track lengths.

Most would agree, though, that iTunes' ability to rip songs — encode Red Book audio files from a music CD and magically turn them into great sounding yet much smaller MP3 files on your hard disk — is its most valuable capability.

Now, even though the music industry tries to equate this ripping with the idea that you're ripping them off, it's not true unless you start giving away or, worse, selling copies of copyrighted material. If you're just enjoying copies of songs you've purchased on another device, such as your computer, iPod, cassette player, or car stereo, you're probably okay under what is called the courts decided in what's called the *BetaMax decision*. You're even okay if you're playing the copy you made on your regular CD player to prevent risking damage to the original.

Posting these files on your Web site, though, would almost certainly be an infringement unless you have the copyright holder's express written consent. (Good luck getting that, by the way, in most cases.)

As the MP3 craze has gathered momentum, manufacturers of CD and DVD players have found a niche to fill. Creating players that play not only standard audio CDs, but also properly formatted data CDs containing MP3 files seemed like a natural evolution. While they are not yet in the majority, the number of CD and DVD players that boast MP3 CD support is rapidly growing. In Chapter 5, "iTunes Advanced Operations," where we discuss how to create an MP3 CD, we also describe the differences in formatting between an audio CD (called a CD-DA, for Compact Disc-Digital Audio) and a data CD (sometimes called an MP3-CD). iTunes has a Preferences setting to create an MP3 CD instead of a CD-DA. And iTunes converts AIFF, WAV, and MP3 files to Red Book audio files automatically when it creates an audio CD (a.k.a. CD-DA).

Caution   Don't convert between formats more than once, especially between MP3 and either AIFF or WAV. MP3 is a *lossy* compression format. This means that some (hopefully unnecessary) data is thrown away (lost) when the compression is applied, to reduce the file's size. The bad news is that once that data has been lost, it is lost forever. So if you later convert that MP3 file to either AIFF or WAV, it won't sound as good as the original. Further, if you were to re-encode the resulting AIFF or WAV file back into an MP3, even more data would be discarded and the sound quality would deteriorate further.

As you can imagine, looping through this cycle a few times could seriously degrade the quality of the recording.

What You Need to Use iTunes

iTunes requires a Mac with at least one USB port running Mac OS X. Technically, that's all iTunes requires. But unless you have some of the things in this section, you won't be able to do much with it. For starters, you're also going to need some free disk space (probably a lot of it) if you're going to rip tracks to disk and build a library of songs.

Note Bob's music collection uses more than 6GB of disk space and contains over 1500 songs. All of the songs fit easily on his 10GB iPod, with room to spare for things such as a cleanly-installed bootable System Folder (Mac OS 9.2.2), DiskWarrior, Disk First Aid, Norton Disk Doctor, and some folders he backed up from his PowerBook the other day in a hotel room somewhere.

Dennis's music collection, not including the stuff he has yet to put on the computer, uses more than 8 gigabytes of disk space and doesn't come close to fitting on his 5GB iPod. But that's okay, because he mostly sits at home writing and finds listening to a CD in his computer or listening to audio files with iTunes more convenient than listening to music straight from his iPod.

CD burner

A CD-R, CD-RW, or SuperDrive isn't required to use iTunes, but you won't be able to create (burn) your own CDs without one.

Fortunately, most current Mac models come with such a drive as a standard component or offer it as an optional configuration. If your Mac doesn't have such a drive, you can always hook one up through USB or FireWire. We'd say SCSI, too, except that SCSI support, particularly in OS X, is limited.

Note Be sure to verify that any external CD burner you acquire is compatible with iTunes and your Mac's built-in burner software. A list of compatible drives is maintained on the iTunes Web page at www.apple.com/iTunes.

We also encourage you to seriously consider FireWire drives over USB. USB is much slower and, due to other activity on the USB bus, rarely burns successfully at speeds beyond 2x. Failed burns result in what we long-time burners call *coasters* (worthless CDs useful as a drink coaster and nothing more).

Media

No, you don't need a newspaper, magazine, TV station, or radio station to enjoy iTunes. In this instance, when we say *media* we mean blank discs. They're only necessary if you're planning to burn CD-DAs or MP3 discs, but since that's half the fun, you'll want to try it if your hardware supports it.

Note We strongly recommend that you stick to CD-R media rather than CD-RW since CD-R discs are much more compatible with audio CD players. Also, most drives burn CD-R discs two or three times faster than CD-RWs. Finally, although CD-RW discs can be erased and reused, they cost more than even high-quality blank CD-R discs. Many users don't use CD-RW discs at all since they find them not worth the additional cost, burn-time, and bother. Finally, Apple includes a cautionary note concerning CD-RW media in Knowledge Base article 58585: "Apple CD-RW Drive: Cannot Write to High Speed CD-RW Discs."

Caution Even CD-R media might not be recognized by some audio CD players. This is mostly true for older models.

Please note that some Audio CD and DVD players can be sensitive to the color or brand of the CD-R. We have encountered players that have only liked silver, only liked blue, only liked gold, or liked just two of the three. There's no hard rule of thumb to follow here—trial and error is your best method.

For all these reasons, it is best to buy small quantities of media at first until you find a brand/color of CD-R that works well on the player(s) you're going to use. As to the brand, CD-burning folklore says that Verbatim, Fuji, TDK, and other so-called name brands are usually your best bet. Bob has had good luck lately with spindles of 50 top-of-the-line discs from Memorex (Black; 700MB; 16X) and iMation (Silver; 700MB; 16X).

One thing you can be sure of is that the cheapest no-name CD-R discs, often sold under the store's own brand name, are usually no bargain unless you have a thing for coasters.

Oh, and be very careful if you stumble across CD-Rs that advertise greater than 80 min/700MB capacity. Some burners won't recognize them and there are stories floating around about damage to burners when they were used. We haven't experienced this, but we haven't ever used such questionable media.

Speakers or headphones

Even though your Mac does have built-in speakers, you can probably use external speakers or headphones. If you work in an office or not everyone in your household appreciates your excellent musical taste, you certainly will need a set of headphones. And, unless you have more of a tin ear than Dennis does, you'll really enjoy the extra sound quality from a set of good external speakers. We'll discuss specific speakers and headphones in Chapter 8, "Enhancing Your iTunes Experience."

An iPod or other MP3 player

While not a necessity, once you've started using an MP3 player (particularly the iPod), you'll be hooked. Being able to download your favorite playlists to a pocket-sized portable device that you can take with you to the park, the pool, or on a trip is habit-forming. We'll also discuss these in Chapters 6 and 8.

Internet access

If you never intend to make use of iTunes' Internet radio capabilities, don't want to download MP3s from newsgroups and Web sites, and don't want iTunes to automatically look up the track names and lengths when you insert an audio CD, then Internet access isn't necessary.

Otherwise, it is, and having it makes iTunes that much more fun (and useful).

Note In the interest of full disclosure, both authors believe Internet access is as necessary as things like water, shelter, and even food. We also believe that the faster the Internet connection, the better.

Getting Started with iTunes

It isn't really necessary, but you might find it convenient to be in front of your Mac with iTunes running for this section. We're going to include pictures as we go along, but keep in mind they're in black-and-white whereas your Mac screen is in living color.

We think you'll remember better if you explore these things as you read. Experimentation is a great way to learn things and you'll rarely hurt anything experimenting with software as forgiving and friendly as iTunes.

So let's get going. Start by launching iTunes. It's usually found in the Applications directory. (*Directory* is OS X/UNIX-speak for that thing we longtime Mac OS 9 users called a *folder.*) When you find it, double-click the iTunes icon to launch it.

Or, since Apple assumes that you'll be using iTunes often, they pre-install it in your Dock for you, as shown in Figure 3-1.

iTunes

Figure 3-1: Apple is so thoughtful that they've put iTunes in your Dock for easy access.

If this is the first time you've launched iTunes, the first screen you'll see is brought to you courtesy of the Apple legal eagles. Fortunately, no trees were killed to bring you the iTunes Software License Agreement screen (Figure 3-2).

Figure 3-2: Count on the lawyers to get into the act nice and early.

You have four options, from left to right:

1. Click the Save As button to save a copy of the license agreement to disk.
2. Click the Copy button to copy the license agreement to the Clipboard (so you can paste it into another application, such as TextEdit).
3. Click the Decline button to exit the license agreement and the iTunes installer.

   If you want to read the agreement, you'll have to scroll down quite a few times. Or, do what everyone does:
4. Click the Accept button to proceed.

The iTunes Setup Assistant's Welcome screen (Figure 3-3) should now appear. Read it, then click Next.

Figure 3-3: Welcome to the iTunes Setup Assistant.

The polite iTunes assistant will help you get iTunes configured quickly. It will ask if you want your Web browser to play audio MP3 streams from the Internet and whether you want iTunes to automatically connect to the Internet (when you choose a streaming radio broadcast or to obtain a track list when you insert an audio CD). As you can see in Figure 3-4, iTunes defaults to turning them both on.

Set these radio buttons as you desire. If you have a broadband Internet connection (cable or DSL), we suggest you answer Yes to both. If you have dial-up (telephone/modem) access to the Internet, you might wish to change the settings to No and No.

When you're done, click Next.

iTunes generously offers to search your hard disk (really just the areas accessible to you as a user under Mac OS X), locate any MP3 files, and add copies to your music library for easy access, as shown in Figure 3-5.

Figure 3-4: Set your iTunes Internet access preferences here.

Figure 3-5: iTunes asks if you want it to find all your MP3 files.

If you change the setting to "No, I'll add them myself later," you'll be on your own when it comes to populating your iTunes library and will be forced to either drag the MP3 files into the iTunes window or utilize the File⇨Add to Library command. Which you choose will depend primarily upon whether you want to duplicate the disk space and whether you want everything or just certain items in your Library.

Caution

Note that if you answer "Yes," iTunes will populate your music library with every single MP3 file on your hard disk. If you have games or applications that include MP3 files, you may end up with a library full of so-called "songs" with names like "DwarfHeadExplosion" and "MortalWoundScreamLong."

After making your choice, click Done.

Assuming you answered affirmatively in the previous step, iTunes searches all available files looking for MP3s and copies them to the iTunes library (Figure 3-6).

Figure 3-6: iTunes searches your hard disk for MP3 files.

When the search is complete, you'll see a populated iTunes Library window similar to the one in Figure 3-7, the difference being that it shows your music collection rather than Dennis's.

Figure 3-7: The iTunes window with all the |MP3 files iTunes could find.

Note   As mentioned previously, iTunes finds *all* files that contain MP3 tracks, even games, applications, and MPEG video files, as shown in Figure 3-7. We'll discuss MPEG video in the iMovie and iDVD sections of this book.

Exploring the iTunes Window

The iTunes window, shown in Figure 3-8, sports the brushed-metal look made (in)famous by QuickTime when Apple released QuickTime 4. There are some advantages to this window type over that used in most OS X windows. For one thing, you can drag it by clicking in any part of the frame, not just in the window's title bar.

If that's not enough, the brushed-metal look is evocative of high-end audio and video equipment's finish, letting folks know right away that this is a multimedia application.

Figure 3-8: Welcome to iTunes. Here's a brand spanking new iTunes Library.

As you can see, there are many (many) parts to the iTunes window. In fact, if you have an iPod plugged in, there will be an iPod button to the left of the equalizer button on the bottom of the window. You'll see that in Chapter 5 when we discuss the iPod and MP3 players.

Here are the features of the iTunes window:

✦ **Close, Minimize, and Zoom:** These are those three buttons you find in the upper left corner of virtually every window you find in OS X. As usual, Close (red) is self-explanatory; Minimize (amber) reduces the window to an icon in your Dock; and Zoom (green) switches you back and forth between the window shown in Figure 3-8 and a much reduced window, as shown in Figure 3-9.

Figure 3-9: Clicking the zoom box shrinks the iTunes window down to this basic status display.

✦ **Status Display:** This little area tells you a lot when a song is playing, as shown in Figure 3-10a. There are three rows in the Status Display that enable you to do the following:

- On the top row you can view the song name, artist name, and album name, which appear in rotation. Or, you can force it to switch at your whim just by clicking on it.
- On the second row you can view how much of the song has played, how much is remaining to play, and the full length of the song.
- The bottom row is a graphic bar indicating the current position of the virtual playhead within the song. You can drag the little diamond (which is called, not coincidentally, the *playhead*) or just click on the bar where you want the playhead to be.

The status display also has another mini-icon that looks like an arrowhead inside a circle. Clicking this icon toggles the display from showing the information as described above and displaying the animated graphic equalizer shown in Figure 3-10b.

When you're connected to a streaming radio broadcast, the Status Display shows the station you're playing and how long you've been connected, as shown in Figure 3-10c.

When you're ripping a CD, the Status Display also shows the name of the track (if known) and the speed at which the song is being ripped in the form of how many minutes is being imported per minute of real time. For example, if the display says 6.6x, as shown in Figure 3-10d, then 6.6 minutes of content is being imported each minute.

✦ **Source List:** The Source List specifies all the various sources iTunes accesses to play songs (or whatever) for you. At the top of the list is your iTunes Library, the master database of all the songs iTunes tracks for you. This is followed by any external sources, such as inserted audio CDs, iPods, and supported MP3 players that are currently connected to your computer. Next is your portal to Internet radio, called the *Radio Tuner*. Finally, you'll have a list of *playlists*. Playlists are subsets of your library that you've created. *Smart playlists* are dynamic playlists whose contents change according to criteria you specify, and they'll appear first among your playlists and bear the distinctive icon shown next to, for example, My Top Rated, in Figure 3-8. We'll discuss all of these source types in Chapter 4, "Getting Started with iTunes," and Chapter 6.

Tip Double-clicking an item in the source list will open that item in its own window.

✦ **Song/Detail List:** Once you've selected an item in the Source List (the Library is the default), its contents will be enumerated in this large list area. (There is one exception to this, covered under the Search option later in this section.) When you select the Radio Tuner, you'll see categories of stations with disclosure triangles to their left, as shown in Figure 3-11. Clicking one of the disclosure triangles will present an indented list of stations within that category (you must have an active Internet connection for this to work). In all other cases, you see a list of the songs available in that Library, device, or playlist.

Following guidelines almost as old as the Mac itself (dating back to the introduction of the List Manager in 1985) you can select multiple items in a list by holding down the Command button (⌘) as you click on the items you want. Or, you can select a contiguous range by clicking the first item you want and then holding down the Shift button when you select the last item.

You also have control over which columns are displayed for a particular source item by choosing Edit⇨View Options (or ⌘-J), which opens the View Options dialog box (Figure 3-12).

Figure 3-10: The status display when a song is playing (a); with the equalizer shown (b); when listening to Internet radio (c); and when ripping songs from a CD (d).

Figure 3-11: Internet radio stations are grouped just like folders in a Finder list view.

✦ **Back:** This is your rewind button. Hold it down to move back through the song being played or click it to move back to the beginning of the current song. When no song is playing, but a song is selected in the song list, this button will move you to the previous song in the list. If no song is selected in the song list, the button will be disabled.

✦ **Forward:** This is the opposite of the Back button, providing a Fast Forward feature when held down or moving to the next song when clicked.

Figure 3-12: In the View Options dialog box you can specify which columns are displayed for a source item.

For both Back and Forward, if you've enabled Shuffle (described later in this chapter), the previous or next item will be based upon the shuffle order and not the one displayed.

✦ **Play/Pause:** When nothing is playing, this button is the right-pointing triangle shown in Figure 3-13a. When a song is playing this button becomes the two vertical line Pause button shown in Figure 3-13b.

(a)   (b)

Figure 3-13: To start a song playing, click the Play button (a), which will then change to the Pause button (b), which you can click to pause play.

✦ **Volume slider:** You can adjust iTunes' volume to anything from Mute (far left) to maximum (far right) by sliding the little knob.

These volume settings are relative to the current system volume setting, so if you have your system volume (Sound Preferences panel) set low, a maximum setting will still be quite low.

✦ **Browse/Burn:** This button takes on many appearances and functions, depending upon what is displayed in the center of the window. When the Library is selected, this button is a colorful eyeball named Browse. Selecting a playlist changes it to the camera shutter Burn button. With Radio Tuner selected, it changes to Refresh, and so forth. We'll cover its many faces in Chapters 5 and 6 where we discuss iTunes capabilities in greater detail. One major point is that when you click Browse for the Library, an additional pane with three columns is displayed above the detail list. You will see this in Chapter 5 when we cover browsing the Library.

✦ **Search:** Typing in this field allows you to search for a string of characters in the detail list. iTunes will display only those entries containing the string. This is called *filtering* the list.

✦ **Add playlist:** Click this button to create a new, untitled playlist in the source list. When you create the list, iTunes will turn *untitled playlist* into an editable text field so that you can begin typing immediately to (re)name it. Chapter 5 contains an extensive discussion of playlists.

✦ **Shuffle:** Click this button to have iTunes play the songs in the current list in (pseudo) random order.

✦ **Repeat:** You get two different repeat functions for the price of one with this little button. Clicking it once loops the current list, repeating it over and over until you intervene. A second click of the button changes the repeat from focusing on the list to just repeating the current song. When just the current song is being looped, the button changes appearance slightly, as shown in Figure 3-14a–c. If you can't tell the difference between the buttons shown in Figure 3-14a and Figure 3-14b, it's because they're in black-and-white. On your computer screen, you'll see the looped arrows change from gray to blue when Repeat List is on.

Figure 3-14: The three faces of Repeat: (a) Repeat off; (b) Repeat list; (c) Repeat song.

(a)   (b)   (c)

✦ **Eject CD:** This is a quick way to eject an inserted CD-DA or CD-ROM. Don't press this while burning a CD unless you want that CD ruined.

✦ **Equalizer:** Clicking this button displays the dialog box shown in Figure 3-15. Using this dialog and all its various controls and menu selections allows you to adjust specific sound frequencies, working much like the treble and bass controls on stereo equipment. We discuss the Equalizer in Chapter 6.

✦ **Visual Effects:** We don't think this button has a practical application, but it sure is fun to play with. When you click it, iTunes will replace the source and detail lists with a colorful animated display, as shown in Figure 3-16. Okay, so you can't see the color or the animation in this black-and-white still shot — that's one of the reasons we recommended that you read this material in front of your Mac!

Figure 3-15: The Equalizer dialog lets you fine-tune the sound.

 Note When you have Visual Effects turned on, the Browse/Burn button turns into an Options button (see Figure 3-16). We'll cover iTunes Visual Effects in Chapter 5.

+ **Resize box:** Both the shrunken and full-sized iTunes windows can be resized by clicking and dragging the resize box at the lower right corner of the window. The shrunken window resizes only horizontally with a minimum size showing just the control buttons and hiding the status box, and a maximum size just large enough to show the buttons and the status field. Resizing the regular iTunes window resizes the status box, resizes the search field, and hides/reveals columns in the detail list, leaving everything else intact.

+ **Info text:** iTunes displays text here that tells you how many items are in the detail list and, if the selected item in the Source List is either the Library or a playlist, how long it will take to play them all, as well as how much disk space they consume.

Figure 3-16: Visual Effects can relax or entertain.

As you can see, iTunes packs a lot of buttons and other items into its window and there's going to be a lot to learn if you want to learn it all.

Getting Help

Apple actually does a pretty decent job with its iTunes Help files. That's a good thing, because iTunes doesn't come with a manual (hence the reason for this book). Unfortunately, as with most help systems, you must have some clue about what you want to ask before you can get the help you need. If you don't know if a feature is available then you can't ask about it and, thus, probably won't ever discover that feature or how to use it.

Since this is the first of the four applications, we'll just say it here. Apple doesn't include manuals for any of its digital hub applications (or other consumer software, such as AppleWorks). This creates a larger market for books such as this, simply because these products pack so much power and capability that just can't be adequately expressed and demonstrated with the Help systems available.

Obtaining Help with iTunes is the same as other OS X applications — choose *application-name* Help from the Help menu. In this case it is iTunes Help (⌘-?). After a short wait, Help Viewer will start up and display the window shown in Figure 3-17 or something very similar if you have a different version of iTunes (which is a possibility, considering how often Apple revises the software).

Figure 3-17: The initial iTunes Help window.

The text field above the Ask a Question label is your friend. Type a word or phrase and click the Ask button to get some help. The Help Viewer searches the entire iTunes Help database for anything that might answer your question or provide information about the words you entered. In Figure 3-18, you can also see the result of a query about MP3s. Help Viewer tells you that it is displaying the first page (nine entries, max, per page) of three containing topics that might be pertinent. The bullets to the right of a listed topic (from 1 to 5) are relevancy rankings. In other words, that's an approximation of how appropriate the topic might be. When you see five bullets, you can bet that the topic is completely germane to the discussion, unless you weren't very specific in the words you entered. When you see one bullet, that topic probably won't be too helpful, but there is some wording in it that is related to your query.

Note   The Help Viewer displayed here is the one for Mac OS X 10.1 – 10.1.5. The Help Viewer that comes with Jaguar (Mac OS X 10.2 and later) has a different appearance and uses a scrolling list rather than multiple pages.

Note   Those left and right arrows at the bottom right of the window aren't next page, previous page as you might hope or expect. They're similar to the Back/Forward buttons in a Web browser (which is really what Help Viewer is, a mini-HTML browser). You'll need to find the Previous and Next text hyperlinks to navigate sequentially. The question mark button at the bottom left takes you to the main Help Center where you can choose other applications about which to ask questions.

Setting iTunes Preferences

iTunes allows you to customize a number of settings through the iTunes Preferences dialog box. To access Preferences, choose iTunes⇨Preferences (or ⌘-Y). You'll be presented with a dialog box with five buttons in its toolbar: General, Effects, Importing, Burning, and Advanced.

General

As shown in Figure 3-19, the General display has three sections. The top section has two pop-up menus and a check box that control how things will look in the main iTunes window. If you have trouble making out the text in either the Source List or the Song List, you can choose to make them larger. Apple doesn't let you set the actual size, just Small (which is about 10 pt) and Large (which is about 14 pt). The Show genre when browsing check box determines whether the Genre column joins the Artist and Album columns when you browse. (See Chapter 5 for a full discussion of browsing the Library.)

Clicking the On CD Insert pop-up menu presents you with four choices as shown in Figure 3-20.

- ✦ **Show Songs:** The default option, tells iTunes to check with its database and, if necessary, to check the Internet database for the CD's track list.
- ✦ **Begin Playing:** Tells iTunes to automatically start playing with the first track.
- ✦ **Import Songs:** Tells iTunes to start ripping the tracks from the CD into MP3 files stored in your Library.
- ✦ **Import Songs and Eject:** A variation on Import Songs where iTunes will eject the CD when the import is done.

Figure 3-18: iTunes Help answering a query about MP3s.

Figure 3-19: General Preferences control basic iTunes appearance and behavior. The On CD Insert pop-up menu is to the right of the label.

The bottom section of General Preferences tab should be familiar to you, since it is very similar to the iTunes Setup Assistant discussed earlier in this chapter in the "Getting Started with iTunes" section.

Note Remember that if you enable Connect to Internet when needed, iTunes will attempt to dial your modem whenever you insert an audio CD or do anything else that might need Internet access. If you're using just one phone line for both your modem and your (real) life, you might want to leave this unchecked and manually make the connections either beforehand or when iTunes complains about not being able to communicate with the cyber world.

Figure 3-20: The On CD Insert pop-up menu.

Effects

The Effects display, shown in Figure 3-21, lets you specify whether and how much each of two sound effects are used. You can also tell iTunes to do the math and equalize sound playback volume for all songs, regardless of how you manually adjust the volume slider.

Crossfade playback controls whether iTunes will have silent gaps between songs or whether finishing songs will fade out while new songs fade in. You can specify how many seconds (from 0 to 12) of fade are employed.

Figure 3-21: The Effects display lets you specify whether and how the Sound Enhancer is employed, as well as whether and how much crossfade is used between songs.

Bob thinks this may be iTunes' most annoying "feature." Songs, for the most part, should start and end the way the performer recorded them. "Crossfade is the music industry equivalent of colorization. In both cases the end product is not what the artist intended. It also attenuates the beginning and ending of songs, possibly losing notes and words. We both suggest that this feature be set to 0 if you want to hear the music as it was recorded."

The Sound Enhancer lets you control the *depth* and *liveliness* (Apple's terms) of your music. Barring really good speakers you're probably not going to notice much difference, but you can see a difference in the Equalizer status display. A high Sound Enhancer setting will raise the level near the display's center.

The Sound Check checkbox provides an override to the volume slider. If you have this box checked, all songs will play at the same volume. iTunes will go through your entire Library to determine the various volume levels and evening them out.

Importing

The Importing display (Figure 3-22) enables you to specify whether tracks imported from CDs should be encoded as MP3, AIFF, or WAV. When you choose either AIFF or WAV, the Configuration pop-up menu offers two choices: Automatic and Custom. Specifying Custom displays the dialog box shown in Figure 3-23, where you can specify whether your rip will be mono or stereo, 8-bit or 16-bit, and what the Sample Rate will be (from 8kHz to 48kHz). Unless you really have a specific need and know what you're doing, it is advisable to leave this set to Automatic.

Figure 3-22: The Importing tab is where you can specify how songs are ripped from disc and in what format they're to be stored.

Most of the time, you'll probably be importing your songs as MP3s where iTunes offers three choices for CBR (constant bit rate) importing (Figure 3-24a) and a Custom choice, which displays the MP3 Encoder dialog box (Figure 3-24b). If you turn on the Use Variable Bit Rate Encoding (VBR) check box, the bit rate pop-up menus specify the minimum rates to be used and the Quality pop-up menu becomes enabled, where you can choose from seven quality levels, which iTunes will attempt to maintain by varying the compression bit rate. If the music is relatively complex, like an orchestral offering, using VBR can help reduce the file size.

Tip If you're importing voice recordings, such as speeches or narratives, you should consider lower bit rates. Unless your ears are even worse than Dennis's, you should probably keep music at 128 Kbps or greater, disk space permitting, since higher bit rates mean larger files and, usually, better fidelity. Bob, who claims he used to hear like an audiophile, rips his MP3s at 160 Kbps and can tell the difference.

Figure 3-23: A true audiophile can control AIFF and WAV imports using the Custom dialog box.

(a)   (b)

Figure 3-24: The MP3 Encoder's Configuration pop-up menu (a) and the Custom choice's MP3 Encoder dialog box (b).

The Smart Encoding Adjustments check box tells iTunes to compare your encoding settings to the source music and, when beneficial to the quality, modify your settings. The Filter Frequencies Below 10Hz check box tells iTunes to eliminate these (essentially) inaudible frequencies from your encoding, which results in smaller files.

The Channels settings let you specify whether iTunes should create one (Mono) or two channels (Stereo) of sound. Mono files are about half the size of stereo files. Auto tells iTunes to use the same setting as the incoming data: Mono input is saved as mono and stereo input as stereo.

In the Stereo Mode settings, selecting Normal Stereo means your MP3 files will contain one track for the left stereo channel and one track for the right stereo channel. Frequently, this means that information is duplicated on the two channels. The Joint Stereo option allocates one channel to the duplicated information and the other channel to be unique information. At lower bit rates (128 Kbps and below), this will often improve the quality of your encoding.

Choosing Auto for the Sample Rate tells iTunes to use the same rate as the music being imported. This will give you the highest possible quality for the space consumed, but you won't be in control of how much space is consumed.

The Play Songs While Importing check box is self-explanatory.

CD Burning

The CD Burning display, shown in Figure 3-25, tells you what CD burner is going to be used. You can specify the speed at which the disk should be burned and whether to burn an Audio CD or MP3 CD. When you choose Audio CD, you can also specify how large a gap to place between song tracks.

 Even though the pop-up menu will allow you to specify up to 24x as a burn speed, settings greater than the maximum speed your burner supports will be ignored and reset to the maximum for your burner.

Advanced

Figure 3-26 shows the Advanced display. One of iTunes' best-kept secrets is the Change button, which allows you to change the location of your iTunes music folder. The iTunes Music folder's default location is in your Home directory's Music folder. Click the Change button to specify a different folder or to create a new folder in another location in the standard Choose a Folder dialog box if, for example, you wish to keep your iTunes music in the Shared folder (so that other users of your Mac can access it) or on another hard disk if you wish to offload it to a portable FireWire disk that you can move from computer to computer.

Figure 3-25: The CD Burning preferences tab is where you specify the type of CD you want to burn and how fast you'll burn it.

Choose among a Small, Medium, and Large buffer when listening to Internet radio stations in the Streaming Buffer Size pop-up menu. By allocating a larger buffer size, you are less susceptible to breaks in the sound resulting from short Internet connection interruptions.

You can use the Shuffle by radio buttons to specify that iTunes shuffle the songs when playing or shuffle the album order (but maintain the song order within the albums).

The Keep iTunes Music folder organized tells iTunes to organize your library into folders for each artist, with folders for albums under each artist's name, and then for discs within the album (for those multi-disc sets). Whenever you change song information (which we discuss both in Chapters 4 and 5), iTunes will (if necessary) move the song from one folder to another when this box is checked.

Copy file to iTunes Music folder when adding to library can be a boon or a curse, depending upon your individual style. The major upside is that the Library is always intact, even if you accidentally delete a folder containing a song from elsewhere on your disk or if one of your disks is not connected. The major complaint is that making the copy consumes more disk space, which isn't too bad if you're religious about deleting the original MP3s after you've added them to iTunes.

Figure 3-26: In the Advanced tab you can set your Music Folder Location, how much memory to provide the Radio's streaming buffer, how Shuffle operates, and two organizational preferences.

Summary

This chapter gave you a very brief overview of iTunes and its multifaceted interface. Now that we've gotten that overview, let's go on to Chapter 4 and learn how to really start using it!

✦ ✦ ✦

Getting Started with iTunes

In This Chapter

Checking out the Library

Creating and managing playlists

Importing songs

Making your own CDs

Listening to Internet radio

Introducing Smart Playlists

In Chapter 3, we gave you a thorough overview of iTunes and showed just how many capabilities are crammed into the deceptively simple iTunes interface. Now, we're going to get right down to the real nitty-gritty and examine the iTunes features you're likely to use most.

Checking Out the Library

The very first item in the iTunes Source List is Library, with its own distinctive icon. You can't remove the Library from the Source List, nor can you create another one. Sure, you can create a playlist (see "Creating and Managing Playlists" later in this chapter) and name it Library, but it won't have the same capabilities as the real thing. For example, the button in the upper-right of the window will be Burn rather than Browse — the wonderful browser capability we'll discuss shortly will be missing.

Okay, so what is the Library? The Library is the database of all the songs on all the volumes connected to your Mac that iTunes knows about. iTunes will keep track of all the songs you show it, regardless of where you have them stored on whatever disk or disc — as long as the disk is online and accessible. But iTunes reserves a favorite place, in the iTunes Music folder (which iTunes Help calls the Music Library), for the songs it manages. In Chapter 3, we discussed the (Advanced) Preferences setting that tells iTunes where to look for this folder. We like it in our Music folder, but that's just us being a bit compulsive. Wherever you choose to keep it, be aware that when you let iTunes manage songs for you, this is where they'll be, neatly organized by artist and album.

Note As we've just mentioned, the Library is a database. Entries in a database are called records (one for each song, in this case). Records are divided into fields and, in the case of iTunes, these fields are named "Song," "Track," "Artist," "Album," "Rating," and so forth. We'll be using these terms when talking about the Library.

Adding songs to your Library

There are four ways to add songs to your Library:

+ **Choose File➪Add to Library** to display a standard Choose Object dialog box, named Add to Library as shown in Figure 4-1. You can select either a file or a folder and click the Choose button. iTunes will add any song (MP3, WAV, or AIFF) files to your Library.

 Note If the file isn't a song file and the folder doesn't contain any song files, then nothing will get added to your Library, although iTunes won't tell you that. You just won't see any change to your Library.

Based upon your Advanced Preferences settings (Chapter 3: "Introducing iTunes"), iTunes will either add the file references or copy the songs into your iTunes Music folder. Figure 4-2 shows the copying process in operation— note the slightly dimmed items that have not yet been copied as well as the progress information in the Status Display area.

 Tip In previous versions (before iTunes 3), iTunes didn't copy the files to your Library, leaving you to do so manually and displayed a warning alert that the files wouldn't really be in your Library for iTunes to manage, just references to them elsewhere on your disk. Bob says it took him a day to avail himself of this checkbox. Dennis wasn't quite as patient and checked it the second time the alert appeared. We both avail ourselves of, and applaud, the new default. We strongly recommend that you leave the Copy files to the iTunes Music folder when adding to library box checked. It's just too easy to end up with unresolved references if you don't.

Figure 4-1: Select a file or folder in the Choose Object dialog box to add songs to your Library.

Chapter 4 ✦ Getting Started with iTunes

Figure 4-2: iTunes copies the songs into your Music Library by default.

Now, your Library will be populated with some songs, as shown in Figure 4-3. By the way, this figure and the others in this section reflect Dennis's taste in music, not Bob's (which tends more to Heavy Metal and Hard Rock).

Figure 4-3: Your Library now has some songs on the shelf.

✦ **Drag** a song file or folder full of (folders of) song files to either the Library item in the Source List or to the detail list area when Library is selected in the Source List. Figure 4-4 shows a folder being dragged onto the Source List's Library icon.

Tip iTunes will automatically create Playlists for folders (or disks) dragged directly into the Source List. This is a handy feature. If you don't want the Playlists created, drag the folders onto the Library icon.

Figure 4-4: You can also drag files and folders from the Finder into the Library.

- **Choose Advanced⇨Convert Selection to MP3** to convert any file from which QuickTime can extract the audio to an MP3 file. This is a very powerful feature and makes full use of QuickTime's broad support for multiple formats. Not only can you convert (as expected) sound files like AIFF and WAV to MP3, but you can even extract the sound tracks from QuickTime-readable movie files, as shown in Figure 4-5. Just add the file to your iTunes Music Library and choose Convert Selection to MP3 from the Advanced menu. iTunes will start the extraction and then the conversion process, put a small Converting Songs entry in the Source List if a playlist is being converted, and tell you how things are progressing in the Status Display while the extraction and conversion takes place. When the conversion is done, the converted file(s) will play.

Tip

This is a handy way to extract and convert the sound track from movies you create with iMovie, which we discuss in Part IV of this book.

- **Import** songs from a CD. We'll cover ripping (importing) from a CD later in this chapter in the "Importing Songs" section.

Removing songs from the Library

In true Macintosh fashion, deleting one or more files from your Library is simplicity itself. You just select them in the Library's detail list and press the Backspace (Delete) key on your keyboard or the Clear key on the numeric keypad or, if you like to work with the mouse, choose Edit⇨Clear. In each of these cases, iTunes produces one of its cautionary "Are you sure?" alerts (Figure 4-6a), but you can check a box in the alert telling iTunes not to bother you with it again. If any file you're deleting is in your Music Library folder, iTunes will ask with yet another alert whether you would like it removed from the disk as well (Figure 4-6b). iTunes doesn't provide this service unless the songs are in your iTunes Music folder.

Figure 4-5: iTunes will convert anything with a sound track it can read into an MP3 file for you.

(a)   (b)

Figure 4-6: iTunes asks whether you really want to delete files (a); iTunes offers to trash files you remove if they're in your Music Library (b).

If you want the file removed from the folder, click Yes. If you want the song deleted from the Library, but the file left on the disk, click No. One would expect Cancel to tell iTunes to ignore the request and leave the song in the Library and the file on disk. However, you already confirmed in the previous alert that you wanted the file removed from the list, so clicking Cancel is the same as clicking No.

Dealing with the Detail List

The iTunes detail list has a lot in common with a Finder list view. Click on a field title (like Artist or Rating) and iTunes sorts the list based upon that field's contents. Click the triangle on the right end of that title and reverse the sort order from low-to-high to high-to-low, or vice versa. An up-pointing triangle indicates an ascending (A–Z, 0–9) sort and a down-pointing triangle indicates a descending sort. Reorder the fields (other than the Song field) dragging a field title into a new position.

The question is, how does all this data get into the fields? As we see in Importing Songs, when iTunes can get the information from the Internet database, it fills the fields automatically. Sometimes, though, the information isn't there or is inaccurate or you may not have an Internet connection available while you're ripping a CD.

You can enter data into these fields in two ways. You can always type directly into the detail list, but you'll probably find it easier to click on the song in the detail list and choose File⇔Get Info (or type ⌘-I) and click on the Tags tab to display the dialog box shown in Figure #1. We cover the Song Information dialog box and ID3 tags in Chapter 5, "Getting Advanced with iTunes."

Figure #1: Change the song's detail information in the Tags tab.

This technique is especially handy when you select multiple songs and choose File⇔Get Info. iTunes will now (after presenting another nagging "Do you really wanna..." alert) present the Multiple Song Information dialog box with all the common fields filled in, as shown in the Figure #2. You should be very careful before clicking OK in this dialog box because every selected song will have the check marked fields replaced with the values displayed in this dialog box. Therefore, be sure that you have checkmarks next to only those fields that you want changed. iTunes automatically checks the box on any field in which you type and, if you remove the change but don't uncheck the checkmark, you could inadvertently wipe out the contents of that field in every song you selected.

Figure #2: Make bulk changes to multiple songs using the Multiple Song Information dialog box.

By the way, the little checkbox to the left of the song title (we're back in the detail list now) tells iTunes whether to play or skip the song when playing songs sequentially. It also can be used to designate which songs to download to your iPod. (There's an iPod preference for this; if you have an iPod you can choose to ignore checkmarks or not.)

Tip

Other than the leftmost column, which does nothing in the Library (it shows the sequence order in a playlist), and the song column (which always appears in both the Library and your playlists), you control which columns are displayed in the Detail List and playlists, by choosing Edit➪View Options (⌘-J).

Searching the Library

We told you that the Library is a database. No database interface is complete without a search capability. After all, databases are often large collections of information and it is easy to overlook an entry you're trying to find if you scan manually.

iTunes provides a very basic search facility with the Search text box. Type a string into that Search box and your detail list will shrink down to just those records that contain the string in one of the text fields, as shown in Figure 4-7.

In addition to displaying only those songs that match your search string, iTunes tells you how many songs were found out of however many were displayed in the window originally. It does this by displaying the information directly below the Search field at the top of the iTunes window (16 of 420 in Figure 4-7b).

Note

iTunes only searches the text fields displayed in the detail list. If the string appears in a hidden field (one turned off in View Options), it won't be displayed. Similarly, if you enter digits, iTunes still won't search the Time, Size, Date, or similar fields because they are numeric and not text.

Figure 4-7: Before you search (a); After you search (b).

The advantages of Search are that it is blindingly fast and incredibly easy to use. The disadvantage is that it isn't very discriminating. You can't, for example, tell it to search only one or more specific fields.

Browsing the Library

It is now time to discuss the "button of many faces" in the iTunes window's upper-right corner. When the Library is selected in the Source List, this button is an eyeball called "Browse." Clicking the Browse button changes the detail list appearance, as shown in Figure 4-8, adding three (or two, depending upon your Preferences settings as discussed in Chapter 3—turned off Genre display) columns at the top. These columns list all the genres, all the artists, and all the albums included in your database.

Figure 4-8: Browse lets you filter your detail list display on three criteria.

Note Figure 4-8 also gives an example of the possible inconsistencies and misspellings that occur in Internet-downloaded Song Information. The album, "The King and I" is spelled three different ways, and the artist, Al Jolson, is spelled two different ways. This is why you should check the information obtained from the Internet and, when necessary, edit it.

Select an item from any of the three columns and the other two columns rearrange themselves to include only items shown after the filter is applied. Click on an entry in one of the two remaining columns and the third will get even smaller, as shown in Figure 4-9. Simultaneously, the detail list will be filtered, displaying only those songs that match the criteria specified. Figure 4-9 shows the result of filtering a database to display only songs on Soundtracks (Genre) where F. Sinatra is the Artist. Another difference you'll note is that, where a search looks for an occurrence of the search string within any field, Browse only finds exact matches. Thus, in the example shown in Figure 4-9, those songs where the artist field contains "G. Kelly, F. Sinatra" are not displayed.

Caution It is very important to be consistent in entering the data if you want to take advantage of browsing. For example, using both "Platters" and "The Platters" as the artist on different songs by that group will result in two different Artist entries and a filter on one won't catch songs with the other entry in the Artist field.

Browsing and searching are not mutually exclusive activities. Trimming a list down by browsing and then doing a search lets you search subsets of your Library.

Figure 4-9: Multiple Browse criteria further narrow the search.

Creating and Managing Playlists

Playlists are groupings of songs in your Library constructed according to your whims. They might be an album, all the songs by a specific group, or just some random collection of songs that you think complement each other. It doesn't matter or have to make sense to anyone but you. They do have one very important function, though, since iTunes uses playlists as its interface to burning CDs, as you'll see later in this chapter in the "Making Your Own CDs" section.

Playlists work almost exactly like the Library, which is not surprising since playlists are subsets of the Library. You select, sort, search, and edit items in the Library and playlists the exact same way. The biggest difference is that you can't use the three-column browse mode in a playlist — that feature is only available in the Library.

Creating and deleting playlists

iTunes provides three methods for creating playlists. You can click the Create a playlist button at the bottom-left of the iTunes window or you can choose File⇨New Playlist (⌘-N) to create a new, empty playlist. Alternatively, and the method we employ most often, you can select a group of songs by Shift- or ⌘-clicking them in the Library and choosing File⇨New Playlist From Selection (Shift-⌘-N) to create an already populated playlist that shows up untitled in the Source List, ready for you to type in a real name for it (Figure 4-10).

Figure 4-10: It's easy as 1-2-3. . . . Select the songs, then choose New Playlist From Selection (rear); a new untitled playlist with those songs is created for you (middle); rename the playlist (front) and you're done.

Tip

To rename a playlist, click once to select it in the Source List, pause briefly, and then click again (not a double-click) to make the name editable. This is just like renaming a file in the Finder.

Note

Unlike the rest of the pictures in this chapter, Figure 4-10 was created by Bob, not Dennis. Could you tell from the song list?

Deleting a playlist is simplicity itself. Select it in the Source List and choose Edit➪Clear or press Backspace (Delete) or Clear. iTunes will ask you, unless you turn the alert off by clicking the Do not ask me again check box, whether you really want to delete the playlist.

Note

In general, iTunes provides these cautionary alerts for any activities that are not undoable. So, if you see one of these "do you really wanna?" alerts, you can be pretty sure that Undo won't be available if you change your mind.

You can even open a playlist in its own window by double-clicking the playlist in the Source List. There is no menu equivalent for this operation.

Tip

This feature is useful when you're copying a song or songs from one playlist to another. Open both in their own windows, arrange them on screen just the way you like, and drag songs from one list to the other to your heart's content.

Modifying playlists

You can add songs in your Library (or another playlist) to a playlist by dragging the song to the target playlist's entry in the Source List. You can also drag songs from the Finder onto the playlist's Source List entry or, if the playlist is selected, to its detail list area. Figure 4-11 illustrates the process of dragging a couple of files from the Finder onto a playlist entry.

Figure 4-11: Dragging songs from the Finder to a playlist.

Dragging from the Finder is a "kill two birds with one stone" approach. You not only add the song(s) to the Library (remember, the playlist can only display songs that are in the Library), but you get them in the playlist in one fell swoop.

If you have a playlist opened in its own window, you can drag Library entries or songs from other playlists directly to the playlist window's detail list.

Removing playlist entries is Mac-easy. Select the entry or entries and choose Edit⇨Clear or press Backspace (Delete) or Clear on your keyboard. The entry is gone, again with the warning since you can't use Undo. Fortunately, removing a playlist entry does nothing to the underlying Library entry. The song is still in your Library.

You might have noticed that a playlist has a number in the leftmost column, a column that is empty in the Library. If you select this column as the sort column, iTunes will let you drag songs into a different order as shown in Figure 4-12. iTunes automatically renumbers the play order.

Note When Shuffle is turned on, you don't control the sequence of play, so iTunes doesn't let you reorder the playlist. You can turn Shuffle off by either clicking the Shuffle button (turning it back to black crossed arrows) or by choosing Controls⇨Shuffle.

Importing Songs

Commonly called ripping, importing tracks from an audio CD and converting them to smaller MP3 files is one of iTunes great strengths. In Chapter 3, "Introducing iTunes," you learned that you can import MP3, AIFF, or WAV format into iTunes (see Chapter 2, "Tools and Terms," for definitions of these formats). The default behavior is to import as MP3 files, because they are the smallest (typically about 10 percent the size of an AIFF or WAV) and they are the format recognized by the iPod, portable players like the Rio, and the growing number of CD and DVD players that also recognize MP3 CDs.

Since iTunes can play the tracks directly from your audio CD, why should you import them? Good question, and here are just a few of the answers:

- ✦ **Convenience:** If they're on an accessible hard disk, iTunes need only look them up in your Library and play them with a double-click. You don't have to go to the shelf, find the CD, take it out of the case, Insert it in your CD drive (thus rendering it unavailable for other uses), and start it playing.

- ✦ **Customization:** You can easily build playlists that play only the songs you want, in the order you want. While many CD players are programmable, it is always considerably more complicated than using a playlist to create that program, and the program isn't as easily modified.

- ✦ **Searchability:** As we saw, finding the song(s) you want in iTunes is really fast and easy. If you know a manual system for doing this with CDs that is anywhere near as fast, we'd love to hear about it.

✦ **Burnability:** You can create your own CDs (either audio CDs or MP3 CDs) with the songs you want in the order you want them. We don't know about you, but with rare exceptions we usually are only interested in a small number of songs from the CDs we purchase.

✦ **Flexibility:** You can download the songs into your iPod or other MP3 player for convenient, portable use.

(a)

(b)

Figure 4-12: You can drag songs into a different play order in a playlist: (a); after you let go (b).

Again, the best reason to import songs as MP3s rather than using AIFF or WAV is the size difference. On the other hand, if your goal in ripping songs from a group of CDs is solely to construct a tailored composite of your favorite tracks on those CDs and burn that composite to a new CD, you should probably import them as AIFF and avoid any of the data loss that comes with MP3 compression (however minor).

Preparing to rip

Unless you're a masochist, if you have an Internet connection available, have it up and running when you insert a CD for ripping. If you don't, you'll get no help with names or titles, as you can see on the left side of Figure 4-13. But if your connection is up and active, you will almost always get a filled-in display, as you see on the right side of Figure 4-13.

We say that you can "almost always" get the CD information online because sometimes you will run across a CD that isn't in the Internet database as yet. If you're ambitious and want to help out others who might have the same CD, you can enter the information manually and choose Advanced⇨Submit CD Track Names, as we'll discuss in Chapter 5.

Deciding whether to have iTunes connect to the Internet automatically whenever you insert a CD will depend on your connection type and, possibly, your patience level. Frankly, if you have an "always-on" connection such as a cable-modem, DSL, or T1 line, we can't think of any good reason to disable the automatic connection. On the other hand, if you use a dial-up connection, you might want automatic connection disabled because your Mac will attempt to dial in on every CD insertion if it isn't already connected and this can try your patience as you wait for the connection to be established.

With such a dial-up connection and automatic checking disabled, you can still get the information. When you're ready, with the CD already inserted and showing in your Source List, initiate your Internet connection and choose Advanced⇨Get CD Track Names. iTunes will fill in the information just as if you had automatic checking enabled.

It's time to rip

Assuming that you have all the track information displayed, click the Import button (refer to Figure 4-13) at the top-right of the iTunes window — yes, it's another face for the "button of many names." iTunes will proceed to import the CD's tracks and store them in your Music Library.

You don't have to import every song on the CD. Those little checkmarks to the left of the song names tell iTunes which tracks to rip. Uncheck any songs you don't want ripped. If you have either Import Songs or Import Songs and Eject chosen in your iTunes General Preferences for On CD Insert (see Chapter 3 for more on Preferences), iTunes will be ripping the first track before you can uncheck its box.

While iTunes is importing the songs, the Status display reports which song is being ripped, how much time it estimates the remainder of that song will require, and how fast the import is progressing, as shown in Figure 4-14. Songs display a green-circled checkmark when they're completed; the song currently ripping has an orange-circled, animated squiggle (that's supposed to look like a sine-wave, for those of you who know about such things). Though not in color, you can see both marks — the green checkmark for tracks one and two; the orange squiggle for track three — in Figure 4-14. Unless you unchecked the default preference (on Preferences' Importing tab), iTunes will play the songs while importing. The import will finish well before the CD is done playing unless your Mac is really, really slow.

When iTunes finishes ripping everything you want imported from the CD, it will notify you with a chime sound. All of these songs will be located in your Music Library (Figure 4-15), neatly organized by Artist and then by Album for that artist, or as compilations (such as our "The Wizard of Oz" soundtrack).

(a)

(b)

Figure 4-13: iTunes can't get the information when you aren't connected to the Internet (a); iTunes gets the CD information when you are connected (b).

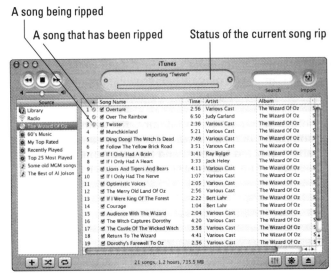

Figure 4-14: iTunes shows you which songs have been ripped, which one is being ripped, and the status of the song being ripped.

Figure 4-15: iTunes keeps your Music Library organized when it imports a CD.

iTunes organization is fine, as far as it goes. Additional soundtrack CDs will be stored alongside "The Wizard of Oz" (to use the pictured example). Assume however, that you're importing Ella Fitzgerald albums — if the Internet database has an album marked as just "Ella" for the artist, they'll be stored separately, as will the albums she made with Louis Armstrong.

If you're concerned about the size versus quality trade-off when importing as MP3 files, check out the "Choosing the Right Bit-rate for Import" section in Chapter 5.

Making Your Own CDs

Now that you know how to create a playlist, how to add songs to your Library, and how to import songs from CDs, you pretty much know all you need to know in order to burn your own CDs.

In addition to what you know, there are just a few things you need to burn a CD: the desired songs in your Library organized into a playlist, a supported CD-R or CD-RW drive, and a blank CD-R.

- **Songs:** Since CD-Rs are "burn once" media, you only get one chance to write to them, so whatever you burn will be all you get on that CD. Thus, you should have everything you want, up to the 74 or 80 minutes (depending upon your media) capacity of your blank CD-R. If you only burn 26 minutes, that's all you're ever going to have on that CD.

- **CD Burner:** Many (most?) Macs these days come with built-in CD burners — some of them even burn DVDs as well. If you have such a Mac, this requirement is solved. If not, make sure that whatever CD-R(W) drive you attach is compatible with iTunes and your version of MacOS. You can find a compatibility list at www.apple.com/itunes/notes.html.

- **Blank CDs:** Originally, Apple recommended only using 74-minute (650MB) CD-R media; however, they've relented and are now selling Verbatim 80-minute (700MB) media as their preferred media. We'll repeat the advice we gave in Chapter 3: Check out whether a particular brand and style works in your CD player before buying in bulk.

- **Soft-tipped Pen:** Never use anything sharp to write on your CDs. We tend to use Fine or Extra-Fine Sharpies, which aren't sharp, or pens like the TDK CD Mark, made specifically for writing on CD-Rs, to keep track of what we put where.

But There's More than 700MB on That CD!

If you rip to AIFF files, avoiding any audio degradation, you will find considerably more data in 80 minutes of audio than the 700MB listed as the CD's capacity. We're going to explain how that happens.

Primarily, the two capacities — 80 minutes and 700MB — have (almost) nothing to do with each other. Every sector of a CD is 2352 bytes in size. The 80 minutes describes how much audio data will fit on the CD if it is formatted according to CD-DA specification. One thing about the CD-DA specification is that it mandates a packet size of 2324 bytes. The 700MB lists how much data will fit when the CD is formatted as a data disk, and a data disk's packet size is 2048 bytes (so is DVD data, by the way). What this means is that audio CDs get 276 more bytes of data into each sector of the disk, about 23 percent more data. If you want us to do the math, that means that a CD-DA can contain over 850MB of data to the data disk's 700MB.

Burning the CD

iTunes places a gap (default is 2 seconds) between tracks on CDs it burns. You can alter this (as mentioned in Chapter 3) in your CD Burning Preferences. Figure these gaps in when you're figuring out how many songs will fit on the CD you're going to burn. Thirty songs will add a full minute to the time. iTunes helps you out by showing the playtime of your playlist at the bottom of its window.

Okay, it's time to burn a CD. Here's how:

1. Create your playlist
2. Put the songs you want on your CD in the playlist, in the order you want them, as shown in Figure 4-16.

Figure 4-16: Fill your playlist and order the songs the way you want them to occur.

3. Click the Burn CD button (it looks like a closed camera shutter)
4. The Burn CD button changes to look like a radiation warning symbol (Figure 4-17) and you're prompted to insert a blank CD. Do so and click the button again and, after checking the media, the status display tells you to click Burn CD to start. When you're sure that you're ready, click Burn CD.
5. The iTunes Status display keeps you informed as to what's happening as it prepares the data.

Figure 4-17: Click Burn CD again when you're ready to start the burn.

Caution Make certain that your Mac doesn't go to sleep. As per Apple's Knowledge Base document 60841, you'll end up with ruined CDs and your Mac may stop responding, requiring a restart. So, set Sleep to Never in your System Preferences' Energy Saver panel before burning CDs.

The first thing iTunes does is prepare the CD tracks. A major part of this preparation is converting the MP3 files back to CD-DA format. iTunes will compute whether it needs to convert the files before starting to burn or whether your Mac is fast enough for it to do the conversion while burning. How long this takes will be a function of how fast your Mac is, how much data has to be prepared, how much memory is available to iTunes, how fast your hard disk is (temporary files are created), and how many other things your Mac is doing at the same time. After iTunes is done preparing the data, the Status display will tell you that it is now writing tracks, at what speed, and which track is currently being burned, as shown in Figure 4-18. In another typical Apple touch, the Burn CD button is animated, pulsing slowly while the disk is burned.

Again, the burn time will depend on multiple factors, especially how much data has to be burned and how fast your burner is. How long the burning takes is roughly the length of the CD divided by the burn speed of your burner, plus a little extra for closing out the CD burn. For example, Dennis's 8x drive takes about 9 minutes plus just short of a minute of preparation and closing to burn the 71minute CD used in the example illustrated in Figure 4-18. On completion, iTunes will notify you by playing a chime.

Figure 4-18: iTunes tells you when it starts actually burning tracks to the CD

Note A nice feature of the CDs you burn is that, if you insert them back into your Mac's CD drive, iTunes will find the track list in its internal database without going out to the Internet (where it probably won't find the disk listed).

If something goes wrong

Being true paranoids, we verify our newly burned discs immediately. You can stick it back in your Mac's CD drive, although even if your Mac recognizes it that doesn't mean other CD players will. We generally use audio CD players for that purpose. Bob, being a true audiophile, has some top-flight equipment, whereas Dennis slips it into a small CD boombox to try it out.

Here are some of the things that can go wrong with a burned CD:

- ✦ The burn fails partway through. This can be caused by various problems, but the most common are
  - You were burning data at a higher speed than the Mac could deliver. This is particularly common with USB burners, but can also occur when your Mac is doing so much that iTunes doesn't get enough time to deliver the data. If you're using USB, burn at 2x or even 1x instead of 4x (you can set the speed on the CD Burning tab of iTunes Preferences). If you're connected via FireWire or using an internal burner, you could try slowing the burn or you could quit some of the other activity on your Mac. (Heavy network activity with a lot of disk access sometimes causes this problem for Dennis.)
  - You were using media with defects. Remember what we've said about using quality CD-R blanks.
- ✦ The burn completes, but the CD has odd noise (pops, hisses, and clicks) when played back. The first thing to do when you encounter this problem is to check the MP3s from which you burned. If the MP3s have the same problem, you will probably want to rip the song again (maybe to AIFF this time), but check the source CD first — the problem may have been on the original.
- ✦ The burn completes and the CD plays fine in your Mac, but fails in some audio CD players. First, not all audio CD players can handle CD-R media, particularly older models. Check it in a player known to support CD-Rs. Second, some audio players are sensitive to the brand/color of CD-Rs. If you've burned other CDs that were recognized in this player, try to use the same brand and color media.

Listening to Internet Radio

The iTunes Radio tuner lets you listen in to a growing number of Internet radio stations transmitting music and conversation. (Yes, even the Internet has talk radio.) So long as the stations *netcast* (transmit over the Internet) in streaming MP3 format, iTunes can connect and play their netcasts. Unfortunately, some Internet radio stations lock themselves into proprietary formats such as WMA (Windows Media Audio) or RealAudio (requires RealPlayer).

What's available on Internet radio

iTunes comes with access information for hundreds of Internet radio stations organized in 22 (at the time we wrote this) categories, as shown in Figure 4-19.

In addition to the hundreds of stations Apple packs into these categories for you, you can add more from the thousands of other stations available. We'll show you how to do that later in the "Adding your own stations" section.

Figure 4-19: Twenty-two categories of radio come prepackaged with iTunes.

Listening to the built-ins

There are few things easier than listening to one of the built-in stations. Just follow these steps:

1. Make sure you have an active Internet connection.
2. Select Radio Tuner in iTunes' Source List.
3. Find a category that interests you in the detail list and click its disclosure triangle.
4. In the list of stations that gets revealed (Figure 4-20), double-click a station that interests you (or select it and either click the Play button or press Return).

Very shortly (it's just about immediate with Dennis's cable modem connection), the station will start playing. While you're listening, iTunes will tell you about the current station in the Status display, as shown in Figure 4-21.

As you can also see in Figure 4-20, some stations (such as Puregold ROCK'N'ROLL) offer multiple bit-rates from which to choose. The higher the bit-rate, the higher the quality; however, the higher the bit-rate, the faster the connection needed to support it. You should choose a bit-rate no faster than your Internet connection. For example, with a 56K dial-in connection, choose 56kbps or less.

Tip Use the Refresh button periodically to update iTunes database of available stations.

Figure 4-20: Find a station that interests you in whatever category you chose.

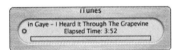

Figure 4-21: Internet radio does live radio one better — it tells you what's playing while you listen.

Adding your own stations

We previously told you that you can add your own stations and that's true. Unfortunately, this process isn't as easy as most things you can do with iTunes. First, you have to know the URL of the netcast. Unfortunately, that is almost never anything but a string of four numbers separated by periods (an IP address), so they aren't the easiest things to remember for most people.

Fortunately, there is a wonderful Web site called Live365.com that maintains a database of thousands of Internet radio stations, which are organized (like iTunes) by genre. Just launch your Web browser and go to www.live365.com. You can search its genres using keywords (like Redneck in the Comedy genre, for example, if you're looking for Jeff Foxworthy–style comedy). Live365 presents a list of matches. Click on one of them and, when the popup window tells you that you need an MP3 player, tell it you have one. (They even give iTunes top-billing in their list of compatible players.) The next thing you know, iTunes will be back in front with a new entry in your Library's detail list, as shown in Figure 4-22.

Figure 4-22: iTunes adds new stations to your Library's detail list.

If you select the entry and choose File➪Get Info (⌘-I), you will see the Song Information dialog box shown in Figure 4-23. Check out the "Where" field — aren't you glad you didn't have to type in that URL?

Figure 4-23: The Info dialog shows that the URL isn't easy to remember.

If this doesn't satisfy your craving for Internet radio, you can also do searches using various search engines such as Google (`www.google.com`) or Bob's favorite Big Mamma (`www.mamma.com`). Good keywords are Internet, radio, and MP3.

Additionally, you can check Internet newsgroups such as `alt.radio.internet` to find station announcements and references.

The biggest problem we have with adding your own stations is that they go in your Library and don't appear in the Radio Tuner, so if you want to change stations, you might have to change lists as well. On the other hand, you can easily make a playlist with all of your favorite Internet radio stations if you like.

Introducing Smart Playlists

We could have buried this topic under "Creating and Managing Playlists"(earlier in this chapter), but we feel it is a really cool feature and deserves its own heading. Introduced with iTunes 3, Smart Playlists are dynamic — you set criteria and iTunes fills the list for you. Even better, iTunes updates the list automatically, keeping the list in compliance with your specifications as you continue to use iTunes.

iTunes 3 comes with four predefined Smart Playlists, just to give you a headstart:

- **'60s Music:** Songs (and other MP3s) whose tags indicate that they were recorded between 1960 and 1969, inclusive.
- **My Top Rated:** Songs that you've rated as better than 3-star
- **Recently Played:** Songs you've played in the past two weeks
- **Top 25 Most Played:** The 25 songs you've played most often

If all you could do is make use of the provided Smart Playlists, this feature wouldn't be very interesting, but iTunes lets you create your own Smart Playlists and modify them (and the provided ones) when and as you like.

You start the creation process by choosing File⇨New Smart Playlist (Option-⌘-N), at which point iTunes displays the Smart Playlist dialog box (Figure 4-24).

We're only going to deal with the Simple tab at this point, and discuss the Advanced tab, along with other advanced iTunes topics, in Chapter 5.

Although they're not outlined or otherwise separated, each of the three rows is a group of related controls, as follows:

Figure 4-24: The Smart Playlist dialog box.

- ✦ The checkbox, popup menu (which defaults to Artist), and the large text field are where you specify the criteria by which you want selections made. The popup menu limits you to Artist, Composer, or Genre and you can enter any text by which you wish to filter the specified field. As a nice touch, if you start to type in the text field, iTunes will check the box for you, so you don't have to take your hands off the keyboard.

- ✦ The second row's checkbox, limit to text item, units popup, and selected by criterion let you control the size of the playlist. Using the text field and the units popup, you control either the number of songs, the duration of the playlist, or the amount of disk space the playlist consumes. The selected by popup lets you tell iTunes to select the playlist's constituents at random or by sorting on a criterion and then taking as many as it takes to meet your limit from the start of that list. You can choose artist, last played, most played, or song name as your criterion.

- ✦ The final row contains just a single checkbox, Live updating. When checked, iTunes will continually adjust the playlist as you continue to use iTunes. For example, if you limited your Smart Playlist to your 15 most played Beatles tunes and then you started playing a newly-added Beatles song over and over, that song would automatically appear in the Smart Playlist when its play count surpassed whatever song was previously fifteenth on your list.

As an example, creating the simple playlist shown in Figure 4-25a creates the Smart Playlist shown in Figure 4-25b. Notice that the Smart Playlist will take its name from the criterion specified in the Contains text field, if it is non-blank (otherwise it gets a numbered name of the form *untitled playlist n*, where "n" is whatever number is next in iTunes' automated numbering sequence).

In order to edit or view an existing Smart Playlist's criteria, select the Smart Playlist in the Source List and choose File⇨Get Info (⌘-I).

Figure 4-25: The criteria specified in (a) result in the Smart Playlist shown in (b).

Summary

In this chapter you've learned about building, organizing, and searching your Library; creating playlists; burning CDs; listening to Internet Radio; and how to create simple Smart Playlists. In Chapter 5, you'll learn even more about these and other (more advanced) iTunes features.

✦ ✦ ✦

Getting Advanced with iTunes

CHAPTER 5

In This Chapter

Exploring the Song Information dialog box

Working with MP3 players

Adjusting sound with the Equalizer

Exploring the Visualizer

Burning MP3 CDs

Choosing the right bit rate

Advanced importing and converting

Advanced Smart Playlists

Accessing Audible.com

Now that we've covered the basics of using iTunes to manage our collections of MP3s, burn audio CDs, listen to CDs, rip songs from CDs, and listen to Internet Radio, we're going to explore other things you can do.

Exploring the Song Information Dialog Box

As we mentioned in Chapter 4, the Song Information dialog box lets you enter and modify information displayed in your Library: title, artist, year, album track number, genre, and comments. It also displays information about the song that can't be modified (at least not by changing something in this dialog box): time, size, date, location on your hard disk, kind, bit rate, sample rate, channels, ID3 tag, and encoder.

This dialog box, accessed by selecting a song and choosing File⇨Get Info (⌘-I), is subdivided into three parts (each in its own tab), each of which you'll explore in detail. But before you even get to those tabs, look at the top of the dialog box at the icon with a text field to its right. The icon echoes the file's Finder icon and the text field lets you change the title of the song displayed in the Library and playlists, but it does not rename the actual song file on your hard disk.

Note If you're like Bob, you'll use this text field often, if only to correct spelling and punctuation errors you didn't make. The database iTunes uses to automatically fetch song titles via the Internet is notorious for mistakes; they drive Bob nuts.

What Are ID3 Tags?

When MP3 was a very young standard there was no way to include such textual information about songs as title, artist, album, year, genre, and other user-specific information. After all, MP3s were originally "computer only" files. At that time, no players existed for them other than computer programs, and many operating systems (such as MacOS pre-X) didn't allow for much information to be encoded into the name. Someone (reputedly Eric Kemp) came up with a 128-byte text block to be added at the end of the music data and named it ID3, supposedly because it was ID information for MP3s.

As with any software implementation that acquires a following, enhancements were made. The first was an "upgrade" to ID3 version 1.1, for which a Windows developer created an extension to Windows Explorer that allowed the user to edit the ID3 information and to add the track number as a field in the ID3 block.

Various folks, in particular Martin Nilsson, decided that this 128-block, located at the end of the stream/file was inadequate to the descriptive task set for ID3. Thus was born ID3 version 2 (popularly known as ID3v2). At the time we're writing this (May, 2002), the current version is ID3v2.3.0 and the tags can now specify a lot more than just the fields listed above. The tags are now divided into frames and can store a wealth of data in addition to the textual information for which the tags were initially intended. A draft for ID3v2.4.0 is now circulating. For more detail, check out `www.id3.org/easy.html`.

You can only have one text frame of a given type within a tag and there are now a slew of text frame types in addition to the initial ones. In fact, iTunes doesn't display much more than what was possible with ID3v1.1.

If you want to know virtually everything there is to know about ID3, check out the Web site, `www.id3.org`, the home of the ID3 standards group.

And now, back to our regularly scheduled programming....

Viewing the Info tab

The first tab, Info (Figure 5-1), has no user-modifiable fields. It just tells you about the song selected.

iTunes separates the information into two categories: General Information and Detail Information. You might want to think of General Information as the "What, Where, and When" data and the Detail Information as the "How" data. The "Why and Who" is left to you — after all, you're the one who acquired it and put it in your Library.

The first three General Information items (Kind, Time, and Size) tell you what the file is. In the example shown in Figure 5-1, we see that we have a 2 minute 16 second MPEG audio file that consumes 2.7MB of disk space. Next we get to see when the file was created, how often it has been played, when it was last played, and finally we get to see where it is stored.

Figure 5-1: The Info tab tells you a lot about the selected song.

Under Detail Information, we see how the file is formatted and how it will play back. In the same example, we see that the MP3 was created at 160kbps (kilobits per second) with 44,100 samples taken per second, two-channel joint stereo, version 2.2 ID3 tags, and with no information stored as to who/what did the encoding.

Using the Tags tab

The Tags tab (Figure 5-2) should be somewhat familiar from Chapter 4. This is where you can change most of the text fields associated with the song. There is no checking for accuracy or even that the information placed in a field makes sense. For example, you could enter that it was track 31 of 14 and recorded in the year 2131 and iTunes wouldn't object in the least. Think of these tags as your own personal, embedded notes about the file.

Figure 5-2: The Tags tab is where you can record and edit information about the song.

As you can see in Figure 5-3, the Genre pop-up comes preset with a number (26) of provided genres, to which you can add. Bob likes to add British Invasion and Dennis likes to add Rock & Roll and Broadway to the list (as seen in Figure 5-3). You can add a genre by selecting the text in the Genre field and typing in a new value, which is the same as clicking the pop-up menu button and choosing Custom, which highlights the text for editing. Similarly, if the genre information downloaded from the Internet is not in iTunes list, it gets added.

Figure 5-3: The Genre pop-up helps you classify the song type.

Other tags, such as time, size, and date added, are calculated and not user-editable and appear on the Info tab.

It's a good thing that the fields on this tab are user-editable, because, as we mentioned before, you'll find that many song, album, and artist entries are misspelled in the Internet database. Additionally, not all the fields will be populated with data (such as genre or number of tracks on an album) and you'll often want to supply that data.

Adjusting on the Options tab

The Options tab is one of the more powerful tools in iTunes (Figure 5-4). By modifying the default settings you can significantly alter the way a song sounds when you play it in iTunes (or on an iPod). You can increase or decrease the volume, set the beginning or end point, and specify an Equalizer preset (see the "Adjusting Sound with the Equalizer" section later in this chapter) for the selected song (Figure 5-5).

Figure 5-4: The Options tab lets you specify how a song plays.

Figure 5-5: The Equalizer preset pop-up lists all the Equalizer adjustments of which iTunes is aware.

Working with MP3 Players

MP3 CD players aren't the only inexpensive and compact way to take your music on the road with you. There's a broad range of small, dedicated MP3 player devices. Some of the most popular are from SonicBlue and Creative Technologies.

Note   Until Apple released the iPod, a compatibility list of MP3 players was prominently displayed on the iTunes Web pages. The page is still there at `www.apple.com/itunes/notes.html`, but you probably won't find a link to it from the main iTunes pages and it hasn't been updated in a while. Be forewarned that even though some of these devices are linked to the Apple Online Store, the only one Apple sells is the iPod.

For the purposes of this discussion, we're going to divide MP3 players into two categories: the iPod and everything else. We do this partly because the iPod is cooler than any of the other MP3 players we've seen or used and partly because iTunes treats it differently than other MP3 players.

Interfacing the iPod to iTunes

Although we have lots of gadgets hooked to our Macs either permanently or intermittently (scanners, digital cameras, digital camcorders, external hard disks, printers, Zip drives, and so forth), the single coolest item is the little iPod that Apple introduced in late 2001. You can see a photo of one in Figure 5-6. Fitting easily in a shirt pocket, it contains a 5GB, 10GB, or 20GB FireWire hard disk and, without recharging, the battery has stood up to over 10 hours of steady use for us. It comes with earbuds, a FireWire cable, and a recharger that plugs into a standard electrical outlet and, get this, uses the FireWire cable and connection to do the recharging. The 10GB and 20GB models also come with a carrying case and a remote control. In addition to being an MP3 player, your iPod can also serve as a portable hard disk, allowing you to copy files between it and your Mac's hard drives.

Tip   You cannot see or access the iPod's Library from the Finder. Similarly, the iPod's MP3-playing feature will not recognize songs that are placed on the iPod's hard disk any way other than via iTunes. At least, that's the way Apple intended things to work. Enterprising hackers (in the best sense of the word) have gotten around these limitations with utilities like Podestal, PodMaster 1000, XPod, and iPod2iTunes — all of which can be obtained through Version Tracker (www.versiontracker.com).

When you connect your iPod to your Mac with iTunes running, the iPod appears in your Source list as shown in Figure 5-7a. Select the iPod in the Source, and iTunes sprouts an iPod button just to the left of the Equalizer button along the window's bottom and shows you how much of the iPod is filled and how much free space remains below the detail list (Figure 5-7b).

Figure 5-6: The iPod: compact, light, and just plain cool in looks and functionality.

(a)

(b)

iPod status   iPod button

Figure 5-7: The iPod shows up in your Source list (a). Select the iPod and iTunes displays a new button and status area (b).

iPod preferences

That little button opens the iPod Preferences dialog box (Figure 5-8). Your choices include allowing iTunes to copy all your songs and playlists to the iPod, copying only the playlists you specify, or copying manually, as shown in Figure 5-8.

When you choose to manually manage the iPod, the "Enable FireWire disk use" checkbox is automatically selected and the item disabled — in other words, you can't turn off FireWire disk use if you manually manage your iPod. Similarly, the

"Only update checked songs" option is off and disabled since you're going to be in complete control. If, however, you select either of the Automatic options, you can update only those songs with a checkmark next to their names in your various playlists.

Figure 5-8: The iPod Preferences dialog box is where you tell iTunes just how much control it should exert over the iPod's contents.

 Your iPod is also a Contact Manager, if you wish. You can obtain AppleScripts to export your contact database to your iPod from a wide variety of e-mail clients and contact managers, including the OS X Address Book, Microsoft Entourage, FileMaker Pro, and Now Contact.

Applications, written in AppleScript Studio, for the first two are available as free downloads at `www.apple.com/iPod/contacts.html`. For other scripts, you should check at `www.versiontracker.com` (a good place to check for just about any Macintosh software) or ask the developer of the contact database program. The contacts interface expects *Virtual business Card Files* (.vcf), a standard (if not completely universal) format for text transmission of contact information.

Enterprising folks have also "adapted" the contacts interface, allowing you to store notes and various other types of data, rather than just the .vcf files that were originally intended. Check for iPod at Version Tracker to see what is current—new items appear almost daily.

Apple has also made it a clock and calendar application, interfacing with the iCal application in Mac OS X 10.2 (more commonly known as "Jaguar"), so you can take your iCal calendars with you.

Between the Contacts, Calendar, and Clock, the iPod is looking more and more like a PIM (Personal Information Manager) every day.

Automatic updating

Your iPod will synchronize with only one iTunes Library. Choosing Automatically update all songs and playlists tells iTunes to check whether the iPod "belongs" to it. If not, you get the alert shown in Figure 5-9. Assuming you answer affirmatively, iTunes will erase the current iPod library and copy your iTunes Library and all your playlists to the iPod.

Figure 5-9: You get the option of starting with a clean slate when you connect your iPod to a different Mac.

You also get the same alert if you choose Automatically update selected playlists only. The difference is that now, only the playlists you checked in the iPod Preferences dialog box will be copied, replacing the previous iPod Library contents.

Caution

In either Automatic case, songs deleted from the iTunes Library will also be removed from the iPod on the next synchronization. The same holds true for playlists. If you don't want these songs removed, choose Manually manage songs and playlists, as described in the next section.

If you want your iPod to be a reflection of your iTunes Library, without any conscious involvement on your part, choose one of the Automatic settings. All you have to do is plug the iPod in and let iTunes do all the work for you. Well, at least up until the point where the iPod is full, at which point iTunes informs you that there is no more space and stops copying files to the iPod.

Manually updating

This selection, Manually manage songs and playlists, appeals to those people (like your authors) who have libraries larger than the iPod can hold or who might want to keep songs and playlists on the iPod which they've already removed from their iTunes Library. For example, on a recent trip Dennis wanted an audiobook on his iPod in addition to his tunes, but saw no reason to keep the book around on his PowerBook's hard disk, chewing up hard disk space that he needed for work. If he had chosen to update automatically, the audiobook would have disappeared when he hooked up the iPod.

Additionally, using manual updating allows you create a new iPod playlist and drag files from your hard disk, MP3 CD, Zip, or other storage device, which are not in your iTunes Library, directly to the iPod playlist item in the Source list, as shown in Figure 5-10.

Figure 5-10: You can add tunes and playlists to your iPod that aren't in your iTunes Library when you use manual updating.

After you release the mouse, iTunes starts adding the selected items to your iPod as indicated by the Status display shown in Figure 5-11.

Figure 5-11: iTunes lets you know what it is adding to your iPod.

Using MP3 players other than the iPod

Before Apple announced and shipped the iPod, they touted compatibility with a wide range of portable MP3 players, to the point of selling devices like the Rio (Figure 5-12) through the Apple Store and advertising them on the iTunes Web pages.

These devices connect to your Mac via USB, so the transfer of songs to such a device is significantly slower than to an iPod with its FireWire connection. More importantly, you can't play from these MP3 players in iTunes; you can only copy files to the device or erase the player's contents. They also have substantially smaller capacities (generally between 32 and128MB), much shorter battery life, and a much higher cost of storage per song. Their primary advantages are that they tend to cost less than an iPod (between $100 and $300 for the Rio and similar devices compared to $300 for a 5GB, $400 for a 10GB, and $500 for a 20GB iPod), and they can be used with computers other than a Mac, or with other Macintoshes.

Note We both have Diamond Rio MP3 players, made before SonicBlue took over the product from Diamond. Since we got our iPods, about the only time the Rios get any use is when we're writing about them. They're okay, but they're really slow, have limited battery life, and are severely restricted compared to the iPod.

As you can see in Figure 5-13, iTunes sports two new buttons to the left of the Equalizer button when a Rio (or other MP3 player) is selected in addition to the status line below the detail list. The Preferences button (cog wheel) invokes the player's Preferences dialog box and the Erase button (lightning bolt) erases the player's memory. For the Rio 600, the only things you can do in Preferences is rename the device and apply firmware upgrades. Other players might (probably will) offer other options.

Figure 5-12: The Rio 600 from SonicBlue, one of the many iTunes-compatible MP3 players.

Tip If you want to delete individual tracks rather than all the songs in the player's memory, select them and press Backspace (Delete) or Clear (or choose Clear from either the Edit menu or the contextual menu).

To add songs to your MP3 player's memory, either drag them from the Library or another playlist within iTunes or, if it's an MP3 file, drag it from the Finder. iTunes will display transfer progress in the Status display, as shown in Figure 5-14. Many of these devices also play WMA files (Windows Media Audio) and dragging from the Finder is the only way to add them to the player's memory since iTunes can't play them.

Figure 5-13: Connecting the Rio adds it to the Source list and sprouts two new buttons at the bottom of the iTunes window, to the left of the Equalizer button.

Figure 5-14: iTunes displays the transfer status. USB transfers can take a long time.

Note Microsoft's Windows Media format files (both audio and video) are proprietary formats. Few tools (other than those from Microsoft) exist to create or edit Windows Media files, and those tools are not available for MacOS.

We don't go into more specifics here because you absolutely must read the manual that comes with your particular MP3 player. Every one of them is a little (some are a lot) different. For example, the Rio 600s we have don't support multiple playlists, but your player might. So check the user manual or the company's Web site.

Note It is possible that there is a plug-in for your MP3 player, even if it isn't one of the ones iTunes already knows about. Check the Web site for the company which made your player to see whether they have such a plug-in for your version (9 or X) of MacOS. If so, download it and install it in Library:iTunes:iTunes Plug-ins (creating the subdirectories of Library if necessary). If you're going to be the only one using this plug-in, you can instead place it in your Home directory's Library:iTunes:iTunes Plug-ins folder (again, creating the directory path if necessary). Also, be aware that the underlying software is Unix and the names are case-sensitive, so capitalize as we did.

Adjusting Sound with the Equalizer

In version 1, iTunes had no equalizer, and audiophiles who wanted to tweak their sound based upon the type of music being played were screaming bloody murder. Adding an equalizer was among the most-requested features for iTunes 2. Luckily, Apple responded with a quality tool.

Clicking the Equalizer button at the bottom of iTunes' window displays the Equalizer window shown in Figure 5-15. Flat is the default setting and, as you can see, all sliders are at their midpoints.

Figure 5-15: The Equalizer lets you change the sound level at a number of different frequencies.

What is an equalizer?

Okay, we hear you screaming, "But what does it all mean?"

This is going to get a bit technical, but we'll try to make it as clear as possible. The human ear can hear across a range of frequencies, but not across the entire sound spectrum. For example, you've probably all seen those whistles that produce a sound so high that dogs can hear it but we can't. Typically, the frequency range for human hearing is from about 32Hz (a deep bass) to about 16kHz (a high treble). This is not a linear scale. What we consider *mid-tones* (normal frequencies) tend to lie in the 250–500Hz range. Each of these frequencies has a volume, expressed in decibels (abbreviated dB) and these are also nonlinear. (They're logarithmic.) The sliders (called *faders*) on the different frequency bars in Figure 5-15 allow you to adjust the volume of sounds only in that frequency range without affecting any others. Dropping below the midpoint mutes the sound while raising the fader above the midpoint enhances the volume in that range.

The preamp is a secondary adjustment and applies equally to all the frequency ranges. You might want to employ preamp if the original recording was particularly quiet or particularly loud.

Roll your own or use presets

As we saw earlier, in Figure 5-5, iTunes comes with a wide range of presets (predetermined equalizer settings provided by Apple). The names are descriptive and cover a broad range of likely settings to enhance your audio experience.

Note

If you've never used an audio equalizer, here's how to get up to speed quickly. Choose a song you're familiar with and select each of the built-in presets for a few seconds. Watch the *faders* (the technical term for those blue dohickies you slide up and down) and notice how they affect the way the music sounds. The leftmost fader controls the lowest (bass) frequency; the rightmost fader controls the highest (treble) frequency; the faders in the middle control the rest. Move a fader up to make that frequency louder; move it down to make that frequency softer. That's how it works. Play around with it for a few minutes and you'll have it mastered.

Once you have everything just so, you'll want to save these equalizer settings. Click on the pop-up menu and choose Make Preset (it's at the top of the menu). In the dialog that appears, give your preset a name and click OK. From now until you delete it, that preset will be available to you in the Equalizer window and on the Song Information dialog box's Options tab.

Tip

Tweak the faders until it sounds the best to you. Now save the preset and forget about the equalizer. Bob says his older ears don't hear high or low sounds as well as they once did. So, as you can see in Figure 5-16, he's boosted the lowest and highest frequencies more than the others. He uses this preset for all the songs he listens to and swears that it sounds much richer, fuller, and better this way. Your mileage, of course, may vary.

Figure 5-16: Bob's Rock4OldDudes setting.

Choose Edit List from the pop-up menu to use the dialog box shown in Figure 5-17 to delete or rename a preset. Just select the preset in the list and click the appropriate button. If you click Delete, iTunes will ask if you really want to do so. Clicking Rename just brings up a naming dialog where you can enter a different name.

Figure 5-17: You can remove or rename presets on the list.

Exploring the Visualizer

Visual Effects is probably the iTunes feature Bob enjoys most. Clicking the Visual Effects button (between Equalizer and Eject) at the bottom right of iTunes' window lets you play with this electronic lava lamp and light show. If you're more menu- or keyboard-oriented, you can choose Visuals⇨Turn Visual On (⌘-T). iTunes comes with some Visual Effects built-in, but you can add more as we'll describe in a bit.

Note   The Visualizer is the software component in iTunes that plays the Visual Effects. The built-in Visual Effects are what we're referring to as the lava lamp and light show.

Adjusting Visual Effects

Just to be agreeable, iTunes will let you choose any size for your Visual Effects, providing that you choose one of Small, Medium, Large, or Full Screen. The first three sizes are shown in Figure 5-18 and we're going to let you guess (we're sure you can do it) what Full Screen looks like.

Just choose your size from iTunes' Visuals menu.

Visual Effects even has some built-in help. With the Visualizer at play, press the Help key (?) on the keyboard and you'll see some information appear, as shown in Figure 5-19. The listed keystrokes are modifiers for the visual effect being shown.

Figure 5-18: Small (a), Medium (b), and Large (c) Visual Effects displays.

Figure 5-19: Press the Help key on the keyboard to display a list of which keys will modify the Visual Effect's behavior.

Clicking the Options button, which is what the multipurpose button becomes when Visual Effects are active (Figure 5-18), displays the Visual Options dialog box (Figure 5-20) for the built-in Visual Effects. Different Visual Effects (see the following section, "Installing additional Visual Effects") will have their own Options dialog boxes. In this dialog box, you set bounds on the speed at which the Visualizer plays and determine whether the frame rate and song information (assuming a song is playing) is always displayed.

Figure 5-20: The Visual Options dialog box lets you control Visual Effects' speed and information display.

Here are the choices in the Visual Effects dialog box for the built-in Visual Effects:

- **Display frame rate:** When you check this box, the frame rate being employed will display in the visual.

- **Cap frame rate at 30fps:** This box is checked by default and limits the number of visual frames calculated and displayed per second to 30 (about the same as a TV picture in the US).

- **Always display song info:** Checking this box tells the visual to display the song title, artist, and album information in the corner of the display.

- **Use OpenGL:** This tells iTunes to use OpenGL (a library of 2-dimensional graphics functions) to generate its displays. Using OpenGL accelerates graphics performance.

- **Faster but rougher display:** Checking this box tells the Visualizer to display the effect as fast as it can, and not worry about keeping the flow smooth.

Installing additional Visual Effects

Like the Equalizer, the ability to add Visual Effects was very high on the list of most-requested features for iTunes 2, and Apple responded again. Additional Visual Effect plug ins are available on the Internet through such sites as Version Tracker. (At the time we wrote this there were 15 listed and all were freeware.) Make sure that the plug-ins you download are appropriate for your version of MacOS. (Some are for OS 9, some for OS X.)

Here's how to make the Visual Effect available to all users of your Mac:

1. Check to make sure that there is a folder named iTunes Plug-ins inside a folder named iTunes inside the Library folder at the top level of your startup disk.

2. If the folders aren't present, create them (you'll need to be running from an Administrator account to do this).

3. Drag the plug-in or plug-ins to this iTunes Plug-ins folder.

Now, wasn't that easy? If, on the other hand, you want the plug-ins to be available only to your account, drag them to the Library:iTunes:iTunes Plug-ins folder in your Home directory (creating the folder[s] if necessary). You will need to quit from iTunes if it is running and relaunch to have the new Visual Effect show up at the bottom of the Visuals menu. Choose the Visual Effect you want from the Visuals menu and you're good to go. Figure 5-21 shows the DHG-FlowerPowerX plug-in in action. Since it has no Options dialog box, the Options button is disabled.

Figure 5-21: Flowers, flowers, everywhere: the DHG-FlowerPowerX Plug-in.

Note If you're into programming, check out developer.apple.com/sdk for the software development kit allowing you to create your own visual effects plug-ins.

Burning MP3 CDs

As we've said over and over, MP3s take up a lot less space than the equivalents on an Audio CD. Further, more and more CD Players and DVD Players are appearing that will play properly formatted discs containing MP3s. Not surprisingly, these are called MP3 CDs.

Note Calling them MP3 CDs is a bit of a misnomer. They're really just PC-standard ISO9660 CDs, but your burning software generally makes sure that the names of all the MP3 files end in the .mp3 extension.

iTunes makes burning MP3 CDs a breeze. All you have to do is choose iTunes⇨ Preferences (⌘-Y) and, on the CD Burning tab, click the MP3 CD radio button instead of the Audio CD radio button and then click OK. Chapter 3 covers iTunes Preferences.

Now, you just burn the CD as described for Audio CD burning in Chapter 4. Doesn't iTunes make this simple?

Choosing the Right Bit rate

There is very little about bit-rate selection that is cut-and-dried. What can generally be stated is that the higher the bit rate, the larger the file and the more faithfully the original will be reproduced.

After we get past that point, things get a little murkier. Usually, any bit rate below 128kbps should be reserved for such things as recordings of the spoken word (books on disc, comedy monologues, lectures, etc.). While 128kbps is pretty much the default used for most MP3 music, the folks who are serious about their MP3s trade some disk space and insist on 192kbps at a minimum and some opt for 320kbps. All of this is, of course, for stereo. Mono material is captured at half the bit rate of stereo for equivalent reproductive fidelity.

The only way you can tell which bit rate to use for a particular album or genre is to run some tests on the music you're going to rip. First, rip a representative track at one bit rate and then do it at least one more time at a different bit rate. Play them both on the device and through the speakers you intend to use and, if you can hear the difference, choose the bit rate that sounds better to you. If you can't hear a difference, you might as well use the smaller one.

Typically, we encode anything where there is significant audio range (such as an orchestra recording) at no less than 192kbps and usually at 320kbps. In fact, Dennis keeps his default set at 192kbps as a reasonable balance between fidelity and size.

Advanced Importing and Converting

Since iTunes can recognize and play MP3, AIFF, and WAV files, it isn't surprising that iTunes can also convert between the formats. This is one of the few places where iTunes doesn't make an operation straightforward. You would think that converting a song from one format to another would be a simple matter of selecting the song and choosing a conversion format. Unfortunately, in an effort to make the conversion as general-purpose as possible, you need to take several steps:

1. Choose iTunes⇨Preferences (⌘-Y).
2. On the Importing tab, select your desired format (from the Import Using pop-up menu) and configuration. Click OK when done.
3. Select the song(s) in your Library
4. You'll see that the Advanced⇨Convert to <format> item now specifies your destination format rather than, necessarily, MP3.

   For example, if you set AIFF as the Import Using selection in your Importing Preferences, you would see the Advanced menu shown in Figure 5-22.

Figure 5-22: The Advanced menu reflects your destination format in the Convert to item.

When we described this process as "general-purpose" we really meant it. You can convert a 320kbps MP3 to 192kbps using this same method. We think that Apple could have simplified this process while retaining its flexibility by making the menu selection bring up a dialog box similar to the Importing Preferences tab. For now, you'll have to make the trip back to Importing Preferences when you're done with the conversion to reset your Importing Preferences.

Caution Be aware that you cannot improve the quality of an MP3 by converting it to a higher bit rate. Any data that was lost in the original encoding is still lost. All reencoding to a higher bit rate will do is make the file larger. Similarly, reencoding as AIFF will not improve the quality, but it will allow you to use the song in programs that require AIFF files.

Advanced Smart Playlists

We promised (in Chapter 4, "Getting Started with iTunes") to cover the Smart Playlist Advanced tab, and that's where we are now. At a cursory glance (Figure 5-23a and 5-23b), the Simple and Advanced tabs look very similar, but that small visual difference conceals significant functionality differences.

All of those differences reside in the condition-matching area — first row of the Simple tab and the "Match the following condition" checkbox and area in the Advanced tab. The most significant of these differences are:

+ You're no longer limited to Artist, Composer, and Genre for your conditions. You can now use any field that might be shown in the Detail List except for Disc # and Equalizer — that's 18 fields at your disposal instead of 3.

+ You can create multiple criteria, used simultaneously. For example, you could search for all Elvis Presley songs recorded in 1961–1963 that you've played at least 4 times and rated 4 stars or better.

Note When you specify multiple criteria, you can tell iTunes to match all conditions or any condition.

✦ You're no longer limited to "contains" as the match condition, but also have exact matches (is) and a variety of comparison matches: "is not" is greater than, is less than, and is in the range for numeric and time fields; "does not contain" is not, starts with, and ends with for text fields.

The plus and minus buttons shown here allow you to add and remove conditions as you develop your Smart Playlist. Click a + button and a new condition line is added immediately after the line whose + button you clicked. Click a – button and that button's line disappears.

iTunes' four presupplied Smart Playlists all use the Advanced tab, but are a single condition. They use the Advanced tab because they're based on criteria other than Artist, Composer, and Genre.

Figure 5-24 shows one of Dennis's Smart Playlists. Growing up an Elvis Presley fan, he has dozens of Elvis CDs and he's imported them into iTunes. Some songs, though, he likes far more than others, so he has this playlist to select all his 5-star, Rock & Roll, Elvis songs and then randomly choose up to 78 minutes worth (in case he wants to burn a CD of the selected songs).

To view or edit a Smart Playlist, select it in the Source List and choose File⇨ Get Info (⌘-I).

(a)

(b)

Figure 5-23: The Smart Playlist's Simple tab (a) doesn't look that different from the Advanced tab (b).

Figure 5-24: Create a playlist of 5-star, Rock & Roll, Elvis songs that will fit on a CD.

Accessing Audible.com

Books on disk, books on tape, and all the variations arising from these technologies have grown by leaps and bounds in the past few years. Audible.com is a Web-based service providing these audiobooks, audiomagazines, and even radio programs as downloadable items you can listen to in iTunes, transfer to your iPod, or even burn to CD. Something like a book-of-the-month club, you can choose one audiobook and one periodical per month for $14.95 or two audiobooks per month (no periodicals) for $19.95 per month. If you're into books on disk or tape, these prices are generally lower than purchasing the books through traditional channels.

When you purchase a book from audible.com, you don't have to worry about losing it — you can store it in your personal space at audible.com and redownload it if and when necessary.

The files you download aren't MP3 files, though. They're audible.com files and have the filename extension .aa. All you have to do in iTunes is open General Preferences (iTunes⇨Preferences and click General in the toolbar), click the Set button next to "Use iTunes for Internet Music Playback" and click OK in the dialog box that appears, and in the Preferences dialog box. From then on, you can download audiobooks from audible.com and work with them in iTunes almost as though they were MP3 files (the big difference is that you can't convert between aa and other formats).

Neither of us is a fan of audiobooks, but we know many people who are. The ones whose opinions we value all think that audible.com is a great thing, and a big improvement over purchasing the books on CD or tape. If you're into audiobooks, check out www.audible.com. We think you'll be pleased.

If you ever want to remove audible.com access, choose Advanced⇨Remove Audible Account.

Summary

In this chapter you've learned how to work with the song information dialog box, in particular how to enter and edit song information. You've learned about using MP3 players with iTunes, with an emphasis on the iPod. Additionally, you saw how to adjust sound levels with the Equalizer and provide yourself with some visual entertainment using iTunes Visual Effects. You also learned how to burn your own CDs in iTunes, convert between file formats (WAV, AIFF, and MP3), and select bit rates for encoding. Finally, you learned how to use the Smart Playlist's Advanced tab and obtain audiobooks from audible.com.

✦ ✦ ✦

More iTunes Tips, Tricks, and Techniques

In This Chapter

Smarten up Smart Playlists

Relocating your iTunes Library

Backing up your music

Adding Visual Effects

AppleScript and iTunes

At its core, iTunes is a database. The player, the Smart Playlists, the Visualizer, and the disc-burning interface are all just ways of presenting the (audio) data stored in the database. The ID3 tags are text data and the songs are audio data.

If you treat iTunes as a database and approach it as a database, you'll be more productive and iTunes will be more responsive.

In this chapter, we're going to point out a few ways that you can work with your iTunes data that might not be immediately obvious.

Smarten Up Smart Playlists

Smart Playlists got a big play (pun intended) when Steve Jobs showed them off at Macworld Expo, New York in January 2002. By adding a few fields to the database record, such as times played, user rating, and last played date/time, Apple enables us to apply some numerically-based selection and sorting criteria to the data in our iTunes database. That's really all Smart Playlists are: sorted selections of songs based upon the text and numeric fields in the database.

Looking at a Smart Playlist's Advanced tab (Figure 6-1) makes this very clear. You can select based on one or more fields, either as an AND condition (select "all" in the Match pop-up menu) or an OR condition (select "any") and then limit the selection based upon a sorting criteria such as "most played."

Note Since you can't mix AND and OR conditions, we expect (okay, hope) that the Smart Playlist feature will continue to evolve, allowing even more complex and useful criteria specifications. We know that we would like to be able to create a playlist of our 20 most frequently played Beatles and Elvis songs that have a 4- or 5-star rating. We'll show you a little later in this chapter how to use AppleScript to create a normal playlist that meets the criteria we specified, though.

The Internet lookup is a mixed blessing. While it gives you a lot of really good information, you will sometimes find misspellings, abbreviations, or different artist naming conventions. For example, songs by the King might be up there as Elvis Presley or just Elvis. If you want to build a Smart Playlist of your 25 favorite Elvis Presley numbers, you'll surely want to include the ones with just Elvis as the artist. However, if you make "Elvis" the "contains" criteria for Artist, you're also going to have songs by Elvis Costello. The Advanced tab lets you work around this by allowing you to specify multiple criteria (i.e., any), for example, choosing "is" Elvis or "contains" Presley as your criteria.

Note You can also use "contains" Elvis and "does not contain" Costello for this example. The NOT options are worth exploring to exclude specific items. For example, if you wanted all the songs that had Frank Sinatra in a duet or trio performance, you could choose "contains" Frank Sinatra and "is not" Frank Sinatra.

Remember, to get maximum use out of Smart Playlists, use the Advanced tab to construct useful filters. The Simple tab is a very small subset of it, and not nearly as useful.

Figure 6-1: Smart Playlists are dynamic database searches.

Relocating Your iTunes Library

MP3s are compressed, but that doesn't necessarily make them small. Just because they only take up about 1MB/minute instead of 10MB/minute, a 72-minute CD will still be over 70MB in size. To paraphrase Everett Dirksen: A megabyte here and a megabyte there, before you know it, you're talking about some real disk space.

Even in these days of multigigabyte hard disks, dedicating 10 or 20 gigabytes to MP3s is a bit extravagant. If you think those numbers are out-of-line, just remember that Apple is selling iPods in those capacities and some people are still asking for bigger disks. After all, even your small iMovie projects will chew up gigabytes of space and your steadily growing digital photo collection will rapidly consume additional gigabytes. Then, of course, there are your "real" documents — word processing, spreadsheets, and all the rest. Before you know it, your internal hard drive is going to be getting cramped for space. Thirty gigabytes (or whatever your internal disk size is) just doesn't go very far in a digital media world.

In Chapter 7, "Enhancing Your iTunes Experience," and Chapter 17, "Enhancing Your iMovie Experience," we recommend that you get an external hard drive for your songs and movies. In the case of iTunes, there are benefits beyond freeing internal hard drive space — you can carry your iTunes Library to other computers (say at the office) with a minimum of fuss.

The key here is to use the iTunes Preferences' Advanced pane (iTunes⇨Preferences or ⌘-Y and then click the Advanced icon in the toolbar) to change the iTunes Music Folder Location. Click the Change button shown in Figure 6-2 and select a location on your external hard disk.

Both Dennis and Bob use lightweight external 30GB FireWire drives (a FireLite and a FireWireDirect, respectively) and recommend them. They're reliable and compact in addition to being light.

Figure 6-2: Click the Change button to relocate your iTunes Library to another drive (or folder).

If all the Macs you're using have drives that will read DVDs and your main Mac has a SuperDrive, you might consider creating an archive library containing your favorite 4+ GB of songs, and burning it on a DVD-R disc. This is close to the capacity of the original iPod and will only cost you about $5 (or roughly $1.25/GB) for the storage. Then, moving your library from computer to computer becomes very inexpensive.

Backing Up Your Music

Dr. Mac's (that's Bob) most frequently (m)uttered advice is "Back up your data. There are only two types of users: those who have lost data and those who are going to lose data." And Dennis concurs in that admonition. We both back up our data, though Bob is more thorough in this respect than Dennis. Even so, we've both lost data, but we've lost a *lot* less than we would have without our backups.

Do your MP3s qualify as data worth backing up? We would respond with a resounding and unequivocal "maybe." The larger your collection, the more likely the answer is a "yes." A small collection can be reripped with a minimum of effort and all you'll have to do is recreate your playlists. Of course, if you have a .mac account, you can use the Backup utility almost effortlessly to back your collection up to CD-R or DVD-R — even a small collection will quickly overflow a 100MB iDisk Backup folder.

If you have an iPod and your collection will all fit on the iPod, you could (rightly) consider that a backup, assuming that you have one of the myriad utility programs we mention in Chapter 7, "Enhancing Your iTunes Experience," capable of copying your songs back off the iPod and onto your hard disk. Dennis currently uses Christian Vick's iPod2iTunes, available through Version Tracker (`www.versiontracker.com/macosx`), as it handles recreating the playlists as well. (Other programs will almost certainly come out after this book is published.)

Tip   Backing up a large iTunes Library can run into lots of CDs or DVDs. Be sure to label them and have a catalog (both on your computer and on paper) of what can be found where. While you might not be the packrats we are, when archiving music, video, book projects, and so forth to CDs, it is likely that you will get to the point where you start grumbling, "Where in the <expletive-deleted> is the disc with 'Yellow Submarine' on it?" (or whatever). We recommend iView Media as an excellent cataloging tool — it comes with Toast Titanium — or the even more powerful iView Media Pro. Dennis uses Unikeeps (`www.univenture.com`), which he buys in lots of 20 and each of which holds 10 CDs and their catalog sheets. They look great; Bob ordered his own 5-pack of them after reading the previous line.

Assuming that you want to back up to CD/DVD, you have essentially two choices. You can manually drag the files and folders to the CD and then burn, although that is a cumbersome and error-prone method since you have to remember what needs to be backed up and make sure that you have the latest copy of everything. This method is best suited to archiving material you're going to delete from your hard disk. Alternatively, you could use a backup program, which does the bookwork for you — tracking what has already been backed up and what still needs to be, thus minimizing your effort and the amount of backup disk space consumed. Until recently, our unequivocal recommendation would have been Retrospect (`www.dantz.com`). If you're going to back up to anything other than CD/DVD, it is still our recommendation. If you have a .Mac account, you have a decent CD/DVD backup tool called Backup (a very suggestive but not very innovative name) included with your membership.

Adding Visual Effects

As noted elsewhere (Chapters 3, 4, and 5), Bob loves the iTunes Visualizer. Dennis considered it just a cute and, occasionally, relaxing display until he started trying out some of the downloadable visual plug-ins so that he could write about them in this book. While still not the fan that Bob is, he is using the Visualizer occasionally, even when not showing it to a Mac-deprived friend. You'll find lots of possibilities to explore at Version Tracker, just search the Mac OS X section for "iTunes Visual" and you'll get page after page of potential additions to your software collection and, best of all, most of them are freeware.

Some of the visual effects plug-ins will come with installers, making installation a trivial matter. Luckily for all of us, Apple made it almost as easy to add plug-ins even if they don't have an installer.

In your Home folder's Library folder, you should find a folder named iTunes. Inside that folder should be two additional folders, iTunes Plug-ins and Scripts. We're interested in the iTunes Plug-ins folder. Deposit a downloaded plug-in in this directory and relaunch iTunes. You'll now have additional entries in iTunes' Visuals menu, as shown in Figure 6-3.

Figure 6-3: Place your visual plug-ins in your Home/Library/iTunes/ iTunes Plug-ins folder (a); they'll be available next time you launch iTunes (b).

AppleScript and iTunes

We both find it a little hard to believe that AppleScript hasn't generated a cottage industry abounding with freeware and shareware to dwarf the HyperCard revolution of the late 1980s. The only reason we can come up with is that the visual metaphor provided by the cards in a HyperCard stack made the difference. As a language, there is virtually no difference in complexity between AppleScript and HyperTalk and the fact that AppleScript can drive program operation of numerous commercial products (such as Entourage, BBEdit, StuffIt, and Photoshop) instead of self-contained stacks makes AppleScript enormously powerful.

We're not going to attempt to teach you AppleScript. That's not what this book is about and, frankly, to do the job properly would require at least a few hundred pages. Apple makes extensive AppleScript documentation and tutorials available via their Web site at `www.apple.com/applescript`.

Apple made iTunes scriptable starting with iTunes 2.0.3, and iTunes 3.0's scriptability is enhanced beyond that initial offering. Enhancing iTunes functionality, Apple has made a number of iTunes-related AppleScripts available at `www.apple.com/applescript/itunes`. You'll be able to find even more at such sites as AppleScript Central (`www.applescriptcentral.com`) or MacScripter (`www.macscripter.net`). Many (we're tempted to say "most") such scripts are available in source form, giving you the opportunity to learn how to script various functions and to modify scripts that do almost what you want so that they do precisely what you want.

When we talked about plug-ins in the previous section, we mentioned the Scripts folder within your Home Library's iTunes folder. If you place your iTunes AppleScripts in this folder, they will appear in your menu bar when running iTunes for quick and convenient access.

Note An application hosting a Scripts menu so that you may invoke AppleScripts from within the application as if they were built-in commands is called *being attachable*.

Using AppleScript won't let you match Smart Playlists' dynamic capabilities, but you can do some things that Smart Playlists won't do, in particular mix AND and OR conditions when constructing a playlist. For example, you can build a playlist that includes all your unrated songs featuring Elvis Presley or Janis Martin. The script for that is shown below:

```
property required_version : "2.0.3"
property artist1 : "Elvis Presley"
property artist2 : "Janis Martin"
property targetrating : "0"

tell application "iTunes"
    activate
    try
        -- VERSION CHECK
        set this_version to the version as string
        if this_version is not greater than or equal to the required_version then
            beep
```

```
            display dialog "This script requires iTunes version: " &
required_version & ¬
                return & return & ¬
                "Current version of iTunes: " & this_version buttons {"Update",
"Cancel"} default button 2 with icon 2
            if the button returned of the result is "Update" then
                my access_website("http://www.apple.com/itunes/download/")
                return "incorrect version"
            end if
        end if

        display dialog "Creating a playlist for "" & artist1 & " & " & artist2 &
" that have not been rated"." buttons {"•"} default button 1 giving up after 1
        set this_playlist to make new playlist
        set the name of this_playlist to artist1 & "-" & artist2

        display dialog "Adding tracks to the playlist." & return & return & ¬
            "One moment..." buttons {"•"} default button 1 giving up after 1
        tell source "Library"
            tell playlist "Library"
                duplicate (every track whose (rating is targetrating) and
(artist is artist1 or artist is artist2)) to this_playlist
            end tell
        end tell

        display dialog "Process completed." buttons {"•"} default button 1
giving up after 2
    on error error_message number error_number
        if the error_number is not -128 then
            beep
            display dialog error_message buttons {"Cancel"} default button 1
        end if
    end try
end tell

on access_website(this_URL)
    ignoring application responses
        tell application "Internet Explorer"
            GetURL this_URL
        end tell
    end ignoring
end access_website
```

> **Note**
>
> You'll notice that we used constants (properties) at the top of the script to handle the rating and artist names. By the way, for ratings, each star is worth 20 points, so if you're looking for songs with ratings greater than 3 stars, you should check for ratings greater than 60.

We'd like to thank Apple for their example scripts, from which we shamelessly cadged the version check code and the `access_web site` routine.

Using parentheses for grouping your conditions, you can quickly create complicated conditionals that are not remotely possible via Smart Playlists. AppleScript opens a wealth of possibilities when it comes to managing your iTunes database (for example, deleting all tracks that have a 1-star rating), building playlists (as discussed previously), and communicating between iTunes and other scriptable programs (such as the Apple-provided script that creates CD jewel box covers in AppleWorks corresponding to your selected iTunes playlist).

Summary

Treating iTunes as the (programmable) database that it is and its contents as the valuable data that it comprises can pay dividends. You've seen that following a backup strategy will save you from a great deal of unnecessary effort in the event of a disk crash or other related problem and that relocating your iTunes Library can pay dividends both in your enjoyment of iTunes and, to a lesser extent, in your use of OS X on your Mac. You've seen that using AppleScript with iTunes, or just employing the scripts Apple and others make available enhances iTunes functionality. You've also seen how to add visual effects plug-ins to iTunes. Additionally, you've learned that the Smart Playlist Advanced tab is the secret to getting truly useful Smart Playlists.

✦ ✦ ✦

Enhancing Your iTunes Experience

CHAPTER 7

✦ ✦ ✦ ✦

In This Chapter

Picking hardware accessories

Choosing software add-ons

✦ ✦ ✦ ✦

We haven't done a scientific survey or anything like that, but we'd guess from talking to people and watching the traffic in user group forums, on Usenet, and on the Web that more people use iTunes than any of the other iApps. This isn't surprising when you realize that you can enjoy iTunes with less investment than any of the other programs in this book. Every OS X-capable Mac comes with a CD drive. You don't need a CD burner (though it helps), you don't need a peripheral device like a digital camera, digital camcorder, or set top DVD player (much less the SuperDrive) to make the program useful. Stick in a CD or download some music from the Internet (paying the obligatory attention to not violating copyright) and you're good to go.

This doesn't mean that you can't add hardware and software to make your iTunes experience richer, just that you can get pretty decent use out of iTunes with your basic Mac.

Now, we're going to start tempting you with some of the things you can add to create an even better iTunes world for yourself.

Hardware Accessories

One thing that will become clear throughout this book is that each of the four iApps programs is useful in and of itself. Starting with iTunes, let's start seeing how you can make your use of them even more enjoyable with the addition of hardware and software accessories.

These accessories have a price range from free (for some software) to "Do I have enough credit before I max out this card?" When making the decision whether to shell out large chunks of money for something, try to decide whether the pleasure you'll derive henceforth is worth the short stabbing pain in the wallet you'll experience now.

The Apple iPod

You have to know that this wonderful combination MP3 Player, PIM, and portable FireWire hard drive is right at the top of the iTune user's hardware wish list. Coming in 5MB, 10MB, and 20MB sizes (as of September 2002) and priced at $300, $400, and $500 respectively, you're looking at a versatile tool that provides good value relative to its price. Check out the "Working with MP3 Players" section in Chapter 5 for a picture and some more detail.

One iPod accessory worth mentioning is an auto adapter so that you can listen to your iPod while driving since using headphones (or plugs) while driving is illegal in many jurisdictions. Dennis likes the iRock 300W (www.myirock.com). You just plug it into your iPod, choose one of four available FM frequencies, tune your car stereo to that station, and enjoy. For $25, it's a great buy, especially if you don't have a cassette player in your car that will utilize the Dr. Bott adapter Bob likes (see the next couple of paragraphs).

Bob bought an iRock also, but wasn't happy with it. With iRock, you must use one of four FM radio stations — 88.1, 88.3, 88.5, and 88.7. Unfortunately, in Austin, where Bob lives, there are FM stations on all four frequencies and they interfere with the iRock no matter which station you choose.

Bob recommends the cassette audio adapter he bought from Dr. Bott (www.drbott.com) for about the same price as the iRock. It does the same thing as the iRock (albeit, with a little cord instead of wirelessly) but doesn't suffer from FM bleed-through.

Speakers and headphones

iTunes is an auditory experience. Unless you can hear what's playing it really isn't very compelling. The better the sound, the greater the enjoyment (assuming it's music to which *you* want to listen). All Macs have built-in speakers, but there is a reason that they also have jacks to connect external speakers and/or headphones.

Bob's attitude on speakers is that Mac speakers are significantly better than those found on other PCs, but that isn't saying much because he thinks that even the Mac's are pretty bad. Dennis, who has a less discerning ear, thinks that the built-in speakers aren't acceptable for listening to music, but the external Apple Pro Speakers that came with his flat-panel iMac are more than adequate. We both agree, though, that good external speakers (or headphones) are a must if you want to really enjoy iTunes.

Some Macs include just a stereo audio-out jack, some include both a headphone jack and an audio-out jack, and at least one (the discontinued G4 Cube) had neither, requiring that USB speakers be used. But, we're not done yet — some audio-out jacks use a standard connector, but some newer models (like the flat-panel iMacs) take a shorter plug with a shield around its base for Apple Pro Speakers, and some (the Summer 2002 G4s) have both the stereo audio-out jack and the Apple Pro jack. Although adapters are available in some cases, you're best advised to make certain the speakers you choose have the appropriate connectors for your Mac model.

Note At least currently (September 2002), Apple Pro Speakers can only be used with the Apple Pro jack that comes with the flat-panel iMacs and the G4s.

If you're playing your tunes in an isolated environment, speakers are a great investment; however, if you're in a shared office environment (like a Dilbertian cubicle farm) or you're at home but not everyone there shares your discerning musical taste, you should consider getting a good set of headphones. One advantage to headphones is that, while they prevent (or protect) others from sharing your music, they also shield you from distracting noises such as other people talking while you're trying to relax.

What to look for in a speaker

Obviously, the first thing you should check out is that the speakers will plug into your Mac, either via USB or one of your Mac's available jacks. In some cases, it won't be possible without an adapter (and sometimes, such as for the Apple Pro Speakers and an iBook, no such adapter exists).

Note Adapters add an extra connection and, possibly, one more thing that can go wrong. We've (more than once) experienced signal loss or breakup when a stereo jack is plugged into an adapter. If you absolutely must have a certain speaker, by all means get the adapter and make sure the connection is solid and secure. But, if there is an option that doesn't involve an adapter, you should opt for it.

When it comes to USB-connected speakers, we're in complete agreement. The Harmon-Kardon Sound Sticks are the class act in the field. The only controversy is whether their appearance or their sound quality is their greatest strength. With a list price of $199, they aren't the least expensive offering available but they'll work with any USB-equipped Mac — including every iTunes 3-compatible Mac except for the Beige G3 — and they look and sound great.

Bob's favorite non-USB speakers are also his overall favorite — the Sonigistix Monsoon iM700s. These flat-panel speakers with a separate subwoofer can really be cranked up without any quality loss. Priced at $170, they're not exactly inexpensive, but their quality warrants the price. The iM700 can also be used via a USB connection if that is your desire.

Dennis prefers a Harman-Kardon (www.harmankardon.com) product as his non-USB choice, the JBL Sonnet Power Satellite Speakers ($100). This is the Harman-Kardon M310J model; it can be plugged into any Mac with a headphone jack, as well as into other audio devices like the iPod. Since anything "cranked up" gives Dennis a headache, he really doesn't know how they perform compared to the Monsoons at high levels. (Nothing cranked up sounds good to him.) Although he uses them with his G4 tower on occasion, he mostly has them hooked to the iPod, running off its power adapter while he's working. Another Harman-Kardon offering, at $150, is more visually appealing and is, in fact, prominently displayed and demonstrated in Apple's Retail Stores — the Creature series.

Tip

For flexibility, you might consider speakers that also have a headphone jack. We regret that Apple no longer makes such a speaker, but Dennis's old AppleDesign Powered Speakers still do a great job with current Macs and he can plug headphones into the left speaker when he wants to without having to unplug the speakers from the computer.

Another option, for those of you who have quality home stereo systems and a Mac with an Apple Pro Speaker jack, is the Griffin Technology ProSpeaker Breakout Cable. Using this cable you can connect your home stereo speakers (even high-end ones like Boston Acoustics or B&W) directly to your Mac's Apple Pro jack without requiring an amplifier. Priced at $25, it's a serious value.

Headphones, for a personal listening experience

Like the Harman-Kardon M310Js, headphones with a ministereo plug can serve double-duty. You can plug them into either your Mac or your iPod (or Sony Discman, an MP3 player, and so forth). Additionally, you don't have to worry about speaker placement relative to where you're sitting or standing since you're always perfectly centered between the speakers.

Dennis hasn't yet found a compelling reason to purchase new headphones and still uses the old lightweight Sonys he bought in the early '90s to use at work. If your taste runs more toward ear buds, like those that come with the iPod, they'll also work just fine plugged into your Mac's headphone jack.

Near the high end in terms of price, features, and quality is the BOSE QuietComfort Acoustic Noise Cancelling Headset. This is not a common, cheap set of headphones and, at $300, it's not inexpensive either, but it is lightweight, with cushioned earcups that are adjustable both in size and angle for a proper and comfortable fit. A nice touch is the inclusion of two adapters, one for standard home stereo systems and one dual-plug to fit those airline headphone jacks so that you don't need to rent their cheap headphones to listen to music or hear the movie's sound. (And the quality will be much higher.)

If, however, you have an aversion to cords and like to listen from the other side of the room or in an adjacent room, cordless headphones just might be your thing. Dennis is partial to the Sony MDR-IF630RK and considers it the most likely candidate to replace his old corded headphones when the time comes. With a 33-foot (10-meter) range he's tempted because he would still have "right there" sound, even if he had to go into another room. With a street price of $115, they're not exactly inexpensive, but they probably won't break the bank, either.

Bob's favorite headphones so far are the Grado SR-60s he bought on the Web for about $70. They're regular over-the-head style cup headphones but they sound so much better than any earbuds he's tried that he often stuffs them in his briefcase and uses them when he travels.

MP3 players

In addition to the iPod, there are a number of iTunes-supported MP3 players on the market. Check out "Working with MP3 Players" in Chapter 5 for more information on using them with iTunes and finding Apple's compatibility list.

With their slower USB interfaces, limited capacity and feature set, and (generally) shorter battery life when compared to the iPod, the primary redeeming feature of these players is price. Also, they are solid-state devices that can withstand more punishment than a hard disk-based device like the iPod.

Some MP3 players, like the Rio, provide all their storage on internal memory and upgrading the memory is both awkward and costly. Others, like the iRock 530, provide a compromise with a certain amount of internal storage (the iRock 530 has 128MB) and a SmartMedia card slot for additional memory. One advantage of the card system is that you can purchase multiple cards, load each of them up with a collection of tunes, and then swap them in and out as desired. Of course, by the time you purchase the iRock ($130) and a four 128MB cards for $50 each, you still only have 640MB on a slow USB connection and you've spent more than the 5GB iPod's cost.

Note: Of course, the SmartMedia cards can serve more than one purpose. You can also use them in a number of digital cameras, as described in our iPhoto chapters (Chapters 8–12).

If you aren't ready to spring for an iPod but want a way to carry your tunes with you, an MP3 player like the iRock 530, Rio, or Nomad provides a reasonable compromise.

External storage

If you're looking for a way to take your tunes with you from home to the office or vice-versa, portable FireWire drives should be on your list. Even though MP3 files are compressed, it doesn't take long to accumulate a huge library. Dennis doesn't even have a tenth of his CD collection in iTunes yet and it's already way too big to fit on his 5GB iPod, to say nothing of the space it consumes on his main hard disk. Bob's in the same predicament (though the exact numbers vary a bit).

An external hard disk can be designated as your iTunes Library location and that will free up space on your boot disk, eliminate some contention between iTunes and other applications for disk access, and provide you with more flexibility if you (like we do) have more than one Mac.

Bob is partial to VST products and uses an ultrathin 30GB VST FireWire drive. Dennis opted for the SmartDisk FireLite 30GB drive as his solution. At just a few ounces each, they're easily transported and don't require an external power supply. (They draw their power from the FireWire bus.)

> **Note** SmartDisk recently bought VST, so both of our drives actually come from the same company. Bob adds, "with prices so low, I've bought a variety of inexpensive FireWire drives from Other World Computing and FireWire Direct lately, and they've all performed flawlessly."

There are plenty of options in all price ranges — more than we can even start to cover here. Besides, whatever we write here will very likely be out-of-date by the time you read this.

CD burners

These days, most Macs come with a CD burner, but if yours didn't you should really consider acquiring one. They're great for backing up your Mac (you do back up, don't you?) and also provide a handy method for archiving your tunes to free up hard drive space. Those functions are in addition to a burner's main iTunes-related use — creating your own audio and MP3 CDs. Check out the "Making Your Own CDs" section in Chapter 4 and "Burning MP3 CDs" in Chapter 5 for more information on how to burn CDs.

When looking for an external CD burner, USB burners are usually a little less expensive than FireWire burners, but we can't seriously recommend them. USB is just too slow to reliably burn CDs at any reasonable speed. Though most USB burners list a maximum speed of 4x, we've never successfully burned at higher than 2x, and have had failures even at that speed.

One critical feature to look for, in addition to the burn speed, is Buffer Underrun Protection. Without this protection, your burn failure rate will go up, especially if you're trying to do other work while burning CDs. Most built-in Apple drives (since 2002) have this feature built-in, but even today, not all third-party drives offer it.

Software Add-ons

There are so many software enhancements available for iTunes and MP3 that we'll limit ourselves to a few of the high points in some different categories.

Roxio Toast with Jam

Roxio's Toast 5 Titanium ($90) is going to be a recurring recommendation throughout the book, but for iTunes we're going to recommend a variation: Toast with Jam, which is currently retailing for $190.

Toast goes far beyond Mac OS's built-in disc burning technology, supporting VideoCD, Multitrack CD-ROM XA, and other formats. Add in the QuickTime component to convert movies to VideoCD format and the iMovie plug-in to do so directly (covered in detail in Chapter 17, "Enhancing Your iMovie Experience"), and it becomes a very compelling addition to the digital hub enthusiast's arsenal. It also includes some useful-in-their-own-right utilities: Discus for creating and printing CD labels and covers; iView Media for managing libraries of sounds, images, movies, and other documents; and Panic's Audion to import music from analog sources such as cassettes or LPs, removing hisses, clicks, and pops along the way.

Jam is a professional quality audio editing package. In addition to supporting additional formats beyond MP3, AIFF, and WAV, Jam's editing tools let you tweak the actual waveforms. You can soften peaks, add reverb to vocals, and create a variety of audio special effects, all in real time. Additionally, you can create Red Book standard audio CD masters, suitable for mass duplication. Along the way, you can create crossfades between tracks, edit the gain on individual audio channels, and introduce index points to break a live recording session into individual tracks.

Check out Figure 7-1 to see Jam in action, editing the crossfade between two tracks.

Figure 7-1: Use Jam to control crossfades between tracks.

AppleWorks and Apple's iTunes AppleScripts

If you're going to burn your own CDs, it's quite likely that you're going to want to have some way to find out what's on which disc. Apple has provided some

AppleWorks jewel-case templates that are iTunes AppleScript targets. You can download the templates and AppleScript from www.apple.com/applescript/itunes. There are a number of other useful iTunes-related scripts available on that page.

Note   Frankly, we don't think that the artwork on Apple's supplied templates is very compelling, but one of the beauties of AppleWorks is that you can easily change the artwork or create your own templates based upon their model.

Figure 7-2 shows an example jewel case cover created using the Build CD Tray Insert AppleScript and the provided Party Mix template.

Figure 7-2: Create CD tray inserts easily with AppleWorks and the iTunes AppleScripts.

MP3 Rage

Bob refers to MP3 Rage (shareware, $25, from Chaotic Software, www.chaoticsoftware.com) as a Swiss Army knife when it comes to working with MP3 files, everything in one compact bundle. Dennis thinks of it more as a Sears Tool Center—everything is there, but the selection is overwhelming. The MP3 Rage menu screen is shown in Figure 7-3 and you can decide how easily you can find the MP3-related tool you're looking for.

Figure 7-3: MP3 Rage's menu screen provides an almost overwhelming option set.

iTunes' search capabilities are pretty good, assuming that you have the fields in which you want to search displayed and are willing to scroll around a bit (or a lot). MP3 Rage will search the ID3 tags in your iTunes database quickly and builds a list for you, as shown in Figure 7-4.

MP3 Rage is also helpful when you want a catalog of your MP3s. With iTunes, you can Export to text and end up with a lot of information you don't really want. MP3 Rage will produce a tab-delimited report formatted with just the fields you specify, in the order you specify them, as shown in Figure 7-5. We will admit that the specification syntax is a little geeky, but it isn't too difficult and you don't have to memorize anything with the cheat sheet displayed right below the text box.

Amadeus II

A useful shareware tool ($25) from Hairer Soft (www.hairersoft.com/Amadeus.html), Amadeus II lets you generate, analyze, and edit MP3 files. You can use it to trim and combine MP3 files and actually process the audio waveforms. You can speed the music up or slow it down, either in toto or in chunks.

Amadeus II doesn't have the most intuitive of interfaces, as its author, Martin Hairer, will concede. What it does, it does well, at least on our Macs. In Figure 7-6, you can see Amadeus playing an MP3, displaying the combined waveform as well as the waveforms for both stereo channels.

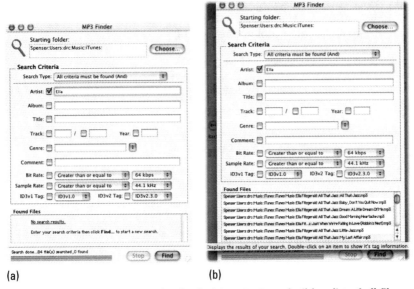

(a)   (b)

Figure 7-4: Setting your search criteria (a); MP3 Rage builds a list of all files with matching ID3 Tag information (b).

(a)   (b)

Figure 7-5: Specify the fields you want, in the order you want them (a); MP3 Rage will generate the catalog for you. This report was opened in Excel (b).

Figure 7-6: Amadeus II shows you both channels and the combined waveform.

Neither of us is audio geek enough to know what all of the functions do, but we each find a few of its functions very useful, particularly in cleaning up MP3s we bring in from older analog sources such as cassette or LP.

Visualizer plug-ins

Bob is a huge fan of the iTunes Visual Effects functionality and Dennis uses it primarily to entertain and amaze Windows-using friends. Wherever you fall on the continuum between these two positions, you should check out Version Tracker's collection of Visualizer plug-ins. The assortment grows steadily — far beyond the prosaic effects Apple includes with iTunes 3 — and you're almost sure to find something you'll like. Best of all, most of the visual effects plug-ins are *free*.

One of our favorites (and a big hit with guests) is the Zoomify plug-in, shown in Figure 7-7 transitioning from one photo to the next in a slide show.

Figure 7-7: The freeware Zoomify plug-in plays a slideshow in the iTunes Visualizer.

Summary

Depending upon your interests and budget, the material in this chapter should start you on the road to even greater iTunes enjoyment. Whether hardware or software, there are plenty of items with which you can deck out both your Mac and iTunes. Some work directly with iTunes and others work with the MP3 files that provide iTunes its fodder.

✦ ✦ ✦

iPhoto

In This Part

Chapter 8
Introducing iPhoto

Chapter 9
Getting Started with iPhoto

Chapter 10
Getting Advanced with iPhoto

Chapter 11
More iPhoto Tips, Tricks, and Techniques

Chapter 12
Enhancing your iPhoto Experience

Introducing iPhoto

In This Chapter

Introducing digital photography and iPhoto

Exploring the iPhoto window

Setting iPhoto preferences

The newest spoke in Apple's Digital Hub is iPhoto, introduced at Macworld San Francisco in January 2002 to a very appreciative audience. Paraphrasing Steve Jobs, iPhoto filled the gaping hole in the Macintosh digital hub strategy. Apple already had iTunes for digital music, iMovie for digital video editing, and iDVD for digital video production, but nothing for managing digital images.

This oversight is especially amusing and amazing to those of us who remember that Apple was among the first to seriously promote digital photography with their QuickTake 100 digital camera almost a decade ago. The first digital camera with a three-digit price tag at about $600 ($10,000-plus was the norm for even a 640×480 digital camera in those days), the QuickTake once again demonstrated that Apple recognizes technology trends early. Since then, almost every major camera and printer manufacturer (and a whole slew of others) have been producing and selling digital cameras, offering more and more features and resolution for the same or lower prices. You can now purchase a pocket-sized equivalent of the QuickTake 100 for $29, and cameras costing $600 will have ten to fifteen times the resolution and a raft of special features (such as panoramas and minimovies).

Apple's Mac OS X Public Preview (Spring 2000) again highlighted digital photography, when the standard Steve Jobs demo featured Image Capture recognizing USB-connected digital cameras and mounting them on the desktop like any (other) volume, downloading pictures, and even automatically creating Web page photo albums. But thereafter, for 18 months, through two versions of iTunes, a major upgrade to iMovie 2, and the introduction of iDVD, digital photography on the Mac languished.

In contrast, Apple released the critically acclaimed iPhoto software and then significantly upgraded it to iPhoto 1.1.1 in less than six months.

Introducing Digital Photography and iPhoto

If you're like most of the people we know, you have been exposed to albums, shoeboxes, envelopes, and drawers full of old photographs most of your life. Most of these photos are part of a totally disorganized mess, never looked at but never discarded. On the rare occasion that you think, "Aha, I have a photo of that event," you probably can't find it or, if you do, it is creased, smudged, or otherwise damaged.

Here comes digital photography, freeing you from the tyranny of purchasing film, the drudgery of hauling the exposed film rolls to wherever you choose to have your pictures developed, and the confusion of sorting through the results when you get the processed pictures back to see if any of them turned out the way you hoped. No film to deal with and no agonized wait to see how the pictures look — sounds like photographic nirvana, doesn't it?

In those respects, it is. When you take a picture with a digital camera, you can check it out immediately on the camera's LCD screen. If you don't like the result, just delete the picture from the camera's memory (or memory card) and take more pictures.

Choosing a digital camera

There is a price to be paid for going digital, though. While pictures of just about any size printed from a photographic negative can look sharp, digital photos don't print out well past a certain size, which is determined by the camera's *resolution*. For example, a camera that advertises 640×480 resolution will be limited to about wallet size printouts, unless you like blocky artifacts in your picture. To print an 8×10 that looks like it came from film, you'll need at least 2 megapixels (about 1600×1200) and probably 3.3 megapixels (about 2048×1536).

Resolution and Pixels

Since digital cameras don't use film, they require a different technology to acquire an image. Like a scanner, digital cameras use what is called a *CCD* (Charged Coupled Device). A CCD reacts to light, storing color information in the pixels (picture elements) that comprise it. Each of these pixels is one dot in your digital photo — the more dots you have, the more accurate the picture. A 640×480 image measures 640 dots in one (normally thought of as the horizontal) dimension and 480 dots in the other dimension. This is just over 39 percent of a typical 1024×768 monitor's display area. Since it is smaller than the screen, to scale it and fill the screen will introduce blur and jagged edges, which explains the constant race for higher and higher resolution cameras. Similarly, if you want to print an 8×10 inch photo on an inkjet printer that prints 360 dots per inch and not introduce any *interpolated* (estimated) pixels, you need 360×8 pixels in one dimension and 360×10 pixels in the other (2880×3600 resolution) — that's over 10 megapixels. Fortunately, those dots are so small and the interpolation is so good that you can get by with much less, about 2 to 3 megapixels, before your eye will start to notice a lack of fidelity.

Higher resolution cameras do have their upsides and downsides. The upsides:

✦ A printed image can be bigger without pixelization (blocky artifacts).

✦ The more you can enlarge a portion of a picture and still print without pixelization.

The downsides:

✦ The fewer images you can store in memory at a time.

✦ The more the camera will cost.

Cap'n, We need more power

You'll quickly learn that digital cameras go through batteries like food through a goose. Most digital cameras take two to four AA batteries and will exhaust that set of alkaline AAs in twenty to thirty minutes of use. Lithium ion (sometimes called photo lithium or just lithium) batteries last longer (maybe 60–90 minutes of use), but cost a lot more than alkaline. The best way to go, at least at present, is with rechargeable NiMH (nickel metal hydride) batteries. NiMH batteries are even more expensive than lithium ion, but they don't get exhausted as quickly, lasting two to three hours in our informal testing, and you can recharge and reuse them.

Those cameras that don't take AAs generally have their own, proprietary batteries that require recharging while the camera is plugged into an electrical outlet. While the life of these batteries is good, you can't get too far from a power source and you have to wait for the camera to recharge before you can continue shooting pictures.

Possibly the best of the lot are cameras that have their own power packs, but will also run off AAs. These aren't common and tend to be high-end (read "expensive") purchases.

Tip

Although it negates one of the major advantages of digital cameras, instant feedback, turning off the LCD display will greatly extend battery life. That little screen is a major power drain. So, you might want to turn it off while you're shooting and only turn it on to review groups of pictures during a lull.

Resolving resolution

If your only use (and don't get us wrong, it's a good use) of a digital camera is to take photos to use on Web pages and view on the computer, 640×480 resolution is all you'll ever need. For one thing, larger pictures take longer to download and for your Web browser to render. For another, anything much larger than 640×480 won't fit in a lot of users' browser windows without scrolling.

Note It has long struck us as curious that even though the image aspect ratio of digital photographs is generally 4:3, that pictures are usually printed at 4×6 and 8×10, which aren't true 4:3 ratios. (True 4:3 ratios are 7.5×10 or 4.5×6.) We're also unsure if the film photography world knows how to measure. When we put the ruler to the allegedly 4×6 prints, we almost never get 4×6 (more like 4×5.875) on a full-bleed (edge to edge) print, and we know (from looking at the negative), that the picture's edges were cropped. The fact is you're going to be trimming and cropping if you want to print your digital photos at standard picture sizes. Fortunately, iPhoto makes that an easy task, as you'll see in the "Adjusting a Photo" section in Chapter 10, "iPhoto Advanced Operations."

The next step up in resolution is the "megapixel" camera, generally with 1280×960 resolution. Since most computer screens are smaller than this, you'd have to scroll the picture or reduce it in size to view on-screen. The megapixel cameras (often listed as 1.1 megapixel) are good for printing pictures up to 4×6 inches.

The cameras in the 2-megapixel family (those designated as 2, 2.1, or 2.2 megapixels) are usually sufficient for images up to 8×10 inches. Three megapixel (usually marked as 3.3 megapixel) cameras generally suffice for pictures up to 11×14 and you can get good results at 12×16 inches with a 4-megapixel camera.

Trying to print a lower resolution picture than those listed results in a picture that appears pixilated or, to use a more common term, *jaggy*. For those of you who have been around a while, you might recall trying to print bitmap fonts on a laser printer, and the ugly jagged characters that would result. Those are the jaggies. Figure 8-1 shows an example of the jaggies in a photograph.

Lies, Damn Lies, and Specifications

If you want to do the math, you can discover that camera manufacturers lie (okay, exaggerate) when they list a camera's resolution. For example, Dennis's Kodak DX-3500 is listed as 2.2 megapixels. The image is 1800×1200 (yes, we know that isn't a 4:3 ratio), which multiplies out to 2,160,000 pixels. With computers, "mega" generally means 1,048,576 (that's 1,024 times 1,024) and we're way short of the 2,306,867 that 2.2 megapixels should mean ($1{,}024 \times 1{,}204 \times 2.2$). Now, even using the generous definition of "mega" to mean "million," we still aren't at 2,200,000 pixels. The cameras advertised as 3.3 megapixel (2048×1576) are *exactly* 3 megapixels in computer terms, which makes the exaggeration a nice round 10 percent. Be aware of this, but don't worry about it too much—everybody lies, but at least they're all telling pretty much the same lies.

Yes, they lie about expected battery life, too. Of course, we're used to that because everybody in the electronics business lies about battery life. Ask any PowerBook owner. We've yet to encounter a single instance of *anyone* who got the stated battery life on their laptop computer in anything resembling normal use, or in their Walkman, or in their portable TV, or . . . Well, you get the picture.

Our best advice is to take electronic product specifications with a grain of salt.

Figure 8-1: Attempting to print a low-resolution picture at too large a size introduces the jaggies.

The number of pixels is not, however, the only item affecting how good your printouts will look. You also need a good printer, appropriate paper, and a good clean shot from which to start. That last item is really not within our areas of expertise. We'll give you a few tips that will help in Chapter 11, "More iPhoto Tips, Tricks, and Techniques," but there are whole college-level courses and large books dedicated to teaching the photographic art.

Thanks for the memory

The bigger your picture (higher resolution), the more memory it is going to consume in your camera. Even with the JPEG compression used by most digital cameras, these pictures are going to fill your camera's built-in memory (usually 8MB or 16MB) pretty quickly. Using a 2-megapixel camera, you shouldn't expect to get more than about 7 to 15 pictures in 8MB of memory. That's why most digital cameras also accept memory cards, which come in a variety of flavors and sizes (both physical and capacity). The more common of these are:

- **Smart Media** are small (about 2 square inches), thin, reasonably priced, and commonly used cards that come in sizes ranging up to 128MB.
- **CompactFlash** is another relatively inexpensive and widely used format, boasting capacities up to 1GB. They have varying write speeds, so if you're going to be taking pictures rapidly, you might want to make sure that yours are up to the task.
- **Memory Sticks** are pretty much a Sony-only format that is used in Sony cameras, camcorders, and laptop computers. (Not that the latter should interest you — you have a Mac.) Memory sticks top out at 128MB and are not cheap.

- **Secure Digital** is a very small (postage stamp-sized) card that comes in capacities up to 128MB. They aren't common, but are starting to appear in some handheld devices (Palms, for example). They're a little more expensive than Smart Media or CompactFlash in the same capacity, but a little less expensive than Memory Sticks.

If you have other devices that use memory cards (Dennis has an old MP3 player that uses Smart Media and a Sony digital camcorder that uses Memory Sticks), you might consider that an incentive to favor one format over another.

Tip

Manufacturer hype notwithstanding, there is almost never a quality difference between brands. We say "almost" just to cover our posteriors—we've never encountered a difference, nor do we personally know anyone who has, except with Memory Sticks. Although they're more expensive, Sony's seem more reliable, but then, Sony is just about the only manufacturer that uses them. Bob has been buying whichever brand of CompactFlash card is least expensive and hasn't had a problem with any of the four or five different brands he's purchased.

Fathoming feature lists

Digital cameras have one more thing in common with film cameras: bells and whistles. These bells don't ring and the whistles don't blow, but if you want to take the best pictures you can under a variety of conditions, you're going to have to know about them. Then the real problem arises: deciding how much you're willing to pay for the features. Adjustable f-stops, aperture control, shutter mode control, color balance, auto-focus assist, variable film speeds, swivel LCDs, and so forth give you more flexibility, but they come with a price that is measured in both dollars and, often, size.

Without these additional features, your digital camera, available for $19.95 and up, is roughly the digital equivalent of simple Instamatic film cameras. It'll work fine in normal conditions: outdoors on a sunny day or at relatively close range indoors, where the flash will be effective or you have a lot of natural light. But they'll work poorly for action shots, night shots, pictures in mood lighting, or any of the other atypical conditions you're going to encounter when you really want to capture a memory.

Here are some of the more desirable options to look for in a digital camera:

- A **swivel or flip LCD** lets you see what is in your shot when you're holding the camera somewhere other than right in front of you. For example, you could be holding the camera down low to take an eye-level shot of your child's first steps or up high to get an elevated perspective without climbing a ladder or standing on a chair.

- **Color balance** means that you can adjust how the camera sees light. Our eyes automatically adjust to what's called the *color temperature* of light. Shots taken in the shade or indoors without a flash are "cool" and can display a bluish tint. Pictures taken under incandescent lighting are "warm" and display a yellow or reddish tint. Color balance is sometimes listed as white balance.

- **Aperture priority control** lets you specify how wide the shutter opens. This provides control over how much light gets in.

- **Shutter priority control** lets you set how quickly (or slowly) the shutter cycles. You can use this to great effect in taking action shots (quick) or nighttime shots (slow).

- **Manual mode** lets you control the aperture and shutter independently.

- **Variable film speeds** let you simulate the effects you achieve with different film speeds (ISO 100, 200, 400) in traditional cameras.

- **Optical zoom** gives you control over how close objects appear to be without sacrificing quality. Don't pay much attention to digital zoom numbers. Using digital zoom is just like taking the picture and cropping the edges — you end up with fewer pixels.

- **Attachment ready** cameras let you hook up real flashes (helps eliminate red-eye and other side effects of having the built-in flash right next to the lens) and different lenses and filters.

- **Burst mode operation** means that you can take pictures one after another, just like you see the fashion photographers do in the movies and on TV. A camera with burst mode operation is going to be expensive because it requires a large memory buffer to hold these images. Storing the image on a memory card is not the world's fastest operation.

Finally, some digital cameras can record short movies and/or record audio.

Almost all digital cameras are threaded to attach a tripod, but you might want to check whether the threading is metal or plastic. Metal is better since it is less likely to go out of shape or strip the threads when used.

Tip

To get a rundown on these features and others, check out a Web site like www.shortcourses.com.

Focusing on iPhoto

Okay, you have your digital camera and you want to use your Mac to view, edit, organize, and print your pictures. Those are just some of the tasks iPhoto performs. iPhoto will download your pictures from your camera when you connect it to your Mac and store them in your photo library. iPhoto will even erase the pictures from your camera after they're downloaded, if you wish.

Caution There are pluses and minuses to automatically erasing pictures after they're downloaded. The biggest plus, obviously, is that it frees up room in your camera's memory (or on the memory card) for new pictures. Erasing the pictures from the camera also means that you won't be downloading the same pictures the next time you attach your camera. Weighing against these pluses is the fact that "stuff happens" and, if you accidentally erase a picture from your Library before doing a backup, it will be irrevocably lost. Paranoid, (uh, make that cautious), people will eschew this option and make sure that everything got into the Library without a problem and that a backup has been made before manually erasing the camera's contents. Bob rarely follows this advice and hasn't lost a picture yet (though it's probably just a matter of time).

In addition to being a photo importer, iPhoto wears many other hats, as described in the sections that follow.

A photo organizer

When iPhoto downloads pictures from your camera, they are added to your Photo Library. At first glance, this Library resembles nothing so much as huge drawer full of apparently unrelated pictures. iPhoto keeps track of what's there by both roll number (groups of simultaneously imported photos) and by date. Additionally, iPhoto lets you create albums of related pictures, including sharing pictures between multiple albums (without having to pay for additional prints).

We'll cover this and a lot more in the "Creating Your Own Albums" section in Chapter 10.

A basic photo editor

No one is going to seriously suggest that iPhoto is competition for Photoshop as a photo editor. iPhoto does, however, provide you with a handful of the basics for cleaning up your digital photos: trimming them to print on different paper sizes and at different aspect ratios, converting to black and white for that retro look, and adjusting the brightness and contrast.

The "Adjusting a Photo" section in Chapter 10 will fill you in on iPhoto's editing tools, capabilities, and limitations.

A photo publisher

It matters not whether you're talking about publishing a book or a Web site containing your photos. iPhoto publishes both the traditional hardcover coffee table book and the Web photo gallery currently in vogue. Well, for the book it actually connects via the Internet to a printer/bindery, but what gets printed are your photos and text as you laid them out in one of the supplied iPhoto templates. When publishing your Web page, iPhoto can create a one-click page on your .Mac account or let you customize the layout and produce a page you can publish on either your .Mac homepage, or any other account.

We cover iTools Homepages in the "Creating a .Mac Homepage" section in Chapter 10, and custom Web pages in the "Creating Custom Web Pages" section in Chapter 11.

A photo printer

Whether you want to print your photos on your own printer or order prints from Kodak, iPhoto fills the bill. In addition to individual prints in various sizes, you can print *contact sheets* (collections of miniatures on a single page).

In the "Printing Photos" section in Chapter 10, you'll see how to print your own and how to send them off to be printed.

A photo delivery service

Using the Mail program that comes with OS X, iPhoto creates messages with your chosen photos attached just waiting for you to address and send.

Check it out in the "Sharing Your Photos" section in Chapter 10.

A photo jack-of-all-trades

iPhoto runs on a Mac and we all like to personalize our Macs. Apple realized this and made iPhoto capable of creating slideshows, desktop pictures, and screen savers using your photos.

The "Sharing Your Photos" section in Chapter 10 covers these features.

Exploring the iPhoto Window

What you see when you first open iPhoto depends upon whether you launched it by connecting a digital camera through the USB connection (Import mode) or clicked the iPhoto icon in the Dock (Organize mode). iPhoto has five modes, accessible via the buttons shown in Figure 8-2: Import, Organize, Edit, Book, and Share. Each mode displays its own set of tools in the iPhoto window's bottom panel.

Figure 8-2: These buttons set iPhoto's mode, determining which controls show up in the toolbox at the bottom of the window.

Except for this mode-specific tool panel, the rest of the iPhoto window is the same regardless of the current mode (Figure 8-3).

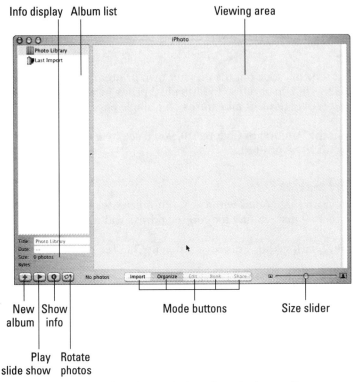

Figure 8-3: Most of the iPhoto window doesn't change if you change modes.

The parts and controls you see in Figure 8-2 are:

- ✦ The **Album list** is very reminiscent of the iTunes Source List (see the "Exploring the iTunes Window" section in Chapter 3). The first item is fixed and that's your Photo Library, the repository and database for all the photos iPhoto knows about. Working under the assumption that you're often going to want to work with your newest pictures, Last Import is a special album that contains whatever group of pictures you last imported into iPhoto. Beneath that will appear any albums you create.

- ✦ The **Viewing area** is where you view your photos. Depending upon your mode, you'll see one (Edit) or more pictures or thumbnails.

- ✦ The **Info display** might be hidden, normal-sized as shown in Figure 8-3, or expanded to include a Comments box. If no image or more than one image is selected, the name and date of the current album are displayed; otherwise, the current photo's name and date are shown. For a single image, the dimensions are shown next to Size; otherwise, the number of selected photos or photos in the album is displayed. Bytes shows the size on disk of the photo, photos, or album selected.

- ✦ The **Add button** creates a new entry in the Album List when clicked, presenting the New Album dialog box where you can name your new album.

- ✦ The **Play button** starts playing a slide show of the currently selected photo(s) or Album, using the settings established in Preferences (see the "Setting iPhoto Preferences" section later in this chapter).

- ✦ The **Information button** cycles the Info Display through its three states.

- ✦ The **Rotate button** will rotate the photos 90 degrees in the direction of the arrow, which you can set in Preferences (see the "Setting iPhoto Preferences" section later in this chapter). Pressing Option while clicking this button rotates the photo(s) 90 degrees in the opposite direction.

- ✦ iPhoto displays how many photos are in the current album and, if any are selected, just how many are selected in the **Info Display**.

- ✦ The five iPhoto **Mode buttons** are used to switch between iPhoto's different operating modes.

- ✦ Use the **Size control** to shrink or expand the size of the thumbnails displayed in the Viewing Area. Moving it all the way to the left will shrink the thumbnails down to tiny images, nearly impossible to discern one from another when you're in Import or Organize mode (or when you've moved to Share from one of those modes) and to "fill the Viewing Area" size when in Edit or Book mode. Moving the slider right zooms in when in Edit or Book mode and expands the thumbnails until you get to one per row in Import or Organize mode. Once again, the Share mode display inherits the characteristics of the previous mode.

Import mode tools

When you connect a compatible digital camera, iPhoto switches to Import mode if you haven't bothered to do so. The iPhoto tool panel display will resemble that shown in Figure 8-4. The camera type and contents will probably be different, but other than that, what you see is what you get.

Figure 8-4: These are iPhoto's camera import controls and status display.

From left to right, you'll see

- The make of attached digital camera and how many images it currently holds
- A frame which will, during import, display the current image's thumbnail
- A status bar displaying the progress of the current import above a line telling how many images remain to be imported
- The Import button which, when clicked, initiates the import process
- A check box telling iPhoto whether to erase the camera's memory (or memory card) when the import is complete

Organize mode tools

Shown in Figure 8-5, the Organize mode tool panel looks extremely easy to use, but can result in confusion until you learn its tricks, which we'll cover in the "Organizing Your Photos" section in Chapter 9. The keyword grid has fourteen user-settable keywords, five of which (Favorite, Family, Kids, Vacation, and Birthday) are presupplied, as well as two non-changeable categories (None and the checkmark).

Figure 8-5: iPhoto's keyword assignment/search grid and display control check boxes.

Edit mode tools

As we stated earlier, iPhoto's editing tools are no threat to Photoshop. iPhoto provides a minimal set of tools (shown in Figure 8-6) to perform the most common photo-editing tasks: cropping, adjusting brightness and contrast, red-eye elimination, and (sort of a bonus) converting your beautiful color photo to a classic black and white.

Figure 8-6: iPhoto's editing tools are a spartan but useful collection.

iPhoto's editing tool chest seems kind of empty, but does include the following useful tools:

- The **Constrain pop-up menu** establishes the proportions of a selection. For example, if you know that you're planning to print an 8×10 of your 2048×1536 image, some of the 2048 is going to have to go (1920×1536 works out to 10×8 at 192ppi).

- The **Crop** button is available when part of the photo is selected. Click it and, poof, your picture has been trimmed to just the selection.

- **Brightness** and **Contrast controls** are similar to the like-named controls on your TV set or computer monitor. Moving brightness to the right lightens your picture by moving the pixels closer to white, although light pixels move toward white at a faster rate than dark pixels. Similarly, turning brightness down makes the picture darker by darkening all the pixels, with the dark pixels moving toward black faster than the lighter pixels. Contrast moves dark toward black and light toward white, sharpening the demarcation between light and dark areas of your photo.

- **Red-Eye** reduction is a technique to eliminate the flash's reflection off the blood vessels in your subject's cornea. Was that clinical enough?

- **Black & White** converts your color photo to an old-fashioned black-and-white photo (really, grayscale). You see the Black & White effect throughout this book — all of our screen shots were in color when we submitted them, but they were converted to black-and-white for printing.

- iPhoto's Edit mode only shows one picture in the viewing area at a time. The **Previous** and **Next** buttons let you move from one picture to another.

Book mode tools

Book mode is where you design and lay out your coffee table books, which, for a relatively modest fee ($30 for a 10 page hardbound book, plus $3/page for additional pages), Apple's preferred bindery will print up and ship back to you. Figure 8-7 shows the Book mode toolbox.

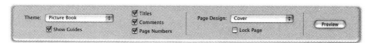

Figure 8-7: Use iPhoto's Book tools to design, layout, and preview a picture book.

The Book mode tools are:

- The **Theme pop-up list** lets you select one of the limited number (six at the time we're writing this) of book designs as your starting point.

- The **Show Guides check box** specifies whether light-blue guidelines are displayed while you're laying out your book. These guides delimit the editable areas on each page.
- The **Titles**, **Comments**, and **Page Numbers check boxes** tell iPhoto whether to include picture names and comments adjacent to each photo and whether page numbers should appear on each interior page of your book.
- The **Page Design pop-up list** shows the layout choices for pages of your chosen Theme. For example, the Yearbook theme allows up to 32 pictures with captions and comments per page, but the Portfolio theme only allows up to four photos with captions and comments per page.
- The **Lock Page check box** tells iPhoto not to reflow pictures onto or off of the chosen page if earlier pages have their design changed.
- The **Preview button** opens a window where you can move from page to page, seeing how your book will look.

Share mode tools

Share mode (Figure 8-8) is where you can actually do things with your photos other than viewing them in iPhoto. The first two buttons (Print and Slide Show) are available in the other modes, as well, via File➪Print and the Play button.

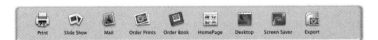

Figure 8-8: In Share mode, only six of the nine buttons actually let you share your photos with others. The other three let you use them outside of iPhoto.

The labeled buttons in the Share toolbox are:

- **Print** is self-explanatory. It presents iPhoto's Print dialog box so that you can print your photos on your Mac's printer.
- **Slide Show** asks you to verify your Slide Show settings (see the "Setting iPhoto Preferences" later in this chapter) and then plays your slide show.
- **Mail** creates a message in Apple's Mail application with your selected photos attached and, if you wish, resized for the convenience of your recipients (3-megapixel images are *really* big attachments, especially after they're encoded for e-mail transmission). See the "E-mailing Your Photos" section in Chapter 9.
- Think of the **Order Prints** button as an electronic Fotomat. Click it to order prints of your photos from Kodak. See the "Ordering Photos" section in Chapter 9.

✦ The **Order Book** button assembles your latest Book design and connects to Apple's Online Store to order one or more copies. Ordering books requires an Apple One-Click account, which is easy to create. See the section "Ordering Photos" in Chapter 9.

✦ Use the **HomePage** button to quickly create a Web page of your selected photos using your .Mac account (if you have one). Your design choices are limited, but it is a very quick way to get your page created and published. See the "Web Publishing Your Pictures on Your .Mac HomePage" section in Chapter 9.

✦ The **Desktop** button will use the selected photo (you can only have one selected) as your Desktop picture without you having to mess with System Preferences (until and unless you want to go back to a non-picture Desktop). See the "Using Your Photos on the Desktop" section in Chapter 9.

✦ Apple's OpenGL Screen Saver (provided with System Preferences) displays visually stunning screensavers. The **Screen Saver** button lets you select your pictures to use in one of the screen savers. See the "Using Your Photos on the Desktop" section in Chapter 9.

✦ Sort of a catch-all button, the **Export** button lets you export photos from the Library (possibly changing the name and format along the way), create a Web Page of your photos to publish somewhere other than your .Mac account, and save your current Slide Show as a QuickTime movie for distribution to friends or posting on the Internet. See Chapter 10 for a rundown of the Export button's three faces.

Setting iPhoto Preferences

All but the most single-purpose programs are incomplete without a Preferences dialog box where you can tailor an application's behavior to more closely match your way of working. To access the iPhoto Preferences dialog box (Figure 8-9), choose iPhoto⇨Preferences (⌘-Y).

The iPhoto Preferences fall into five categories and, in an unusual move by Apple programmers, there are no dividing lines or tabbed panels separating the preference groups. You can set preferences as follows:

✦ **Photos:** The controls in this group manage the presentation of photos in the Viewing Area.

- You can choose **Shadow** to display your photos with a faint drop-shadow (the default) or with a frame. If you choose **Frame**, the slider becomes active and you can set the frame's shade of gray anywhere between white and black.

- **Align to grid** keeps your photo thumbnails in an orderly row and column display. Supposedly, turning this off lets you rearrange the photos into a pattern of your choosing, but everything stays aligned to the grid when we turn it off.

- Normally, iPhoto displays your photos with the oldest at the top left, working across rows and down the scrollable pane to the newest. Clicking **Most recent at top** reverses this order.

Figure 8-9: The iPhoto Preferences dialog box crams a lot into one small window.

+ **Rotate photos** offers two choices, **Clockwise** and **Counter Clockwise** (the default). The button for the current preference is displayed to the right.

+ **Double-clicking photos opens them in** offers three choices:

    - **Edit View** is the default and is the same as clicking the Edit mode button.

    - **Separate Window**, as its name implies, opens the target image in its own window with the Edit mode controls in a toolbar, as shown in Figure 8-10.

    - If you click **Other**, then you can click the **Set** button and choose a more powerful editing application. Some Macs come with GraphicConverter (a very powerful shareware image editing and creation tool) and PixelNhance (an application focused on manipulating existing images), either of which make an excellent choice if you find iPhoto's editing tools inadequate. Then, of course, there is the expensive crème de la crème of photo editing tools: Adobe Photoshop (www.adobe.com).

+ The **Assign/Search uses** section specifies whether you use the Keywords array in the Organize toolbox or the Info area's Comments box when doing a search.

✦ The **Slide Show** area is where you specify the screen time of each image in your slide show, whether the slide show loops, and what background music to play during the show. These settings are in effect if you click the Play button on the iPhoto window; they are the default settings if you click the Slide Show button in the Share toolbox.

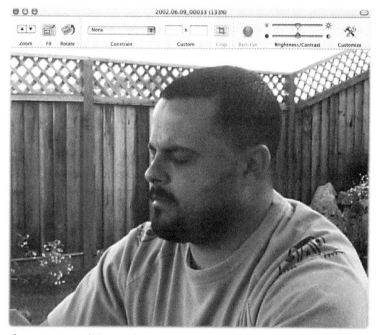

Figure 8-10: Editing a photo in its own window places the Edit mode controls in the window's toolbar.

Summary

In this chapter, you've learned a little about the history of digital photography, been introduced to the myriad features available and tradeoffs to consider when purchasing a digital camera, learned about the iPhoto window and its five modes, and perused the iPhoto Preferences window. In the next chapter, we'll show you how to utilize these iPhoto features and tools.

✦ ✦ ✦

CHAPTER 9

Getting Started with iPhoto

In This Chapter

Organizing your photos

Editing photos

Laying out books

Printing photos

Ordering photos

E-mailing your photos

Creating a slide show

Using your photos on the desktop

Web publishing photos on your iTools homepage

---

iPhoto is an easy-to-use, but still powerful photo collection organizer and manager. It can communicate with most current digital cameras. (See www.apple.com/iphoto/compatibility/ for a long, though still incomplete, list of compatible cameras.)

Utilizing iPhoto's tools you can organize, search, print, edit, and use your digital photos in myriad ways. Not only can you produce the traditional 4×6, 5×7, and 8×10 prints, but you can print contact sheets and greeting cards, lay out coffee table books and have them professionally printed and bound, or send your digital images to Kodak to be professionally printed.

You can use your pictures in a screen saver, a slide show (with background music), or place them on your desktop in place of the standard background. With just a few clicks, your photos can be on the Web to share with friends and family or sent as e-mail attachments.

You can also drag copies directly from your iPhoto window into your report for school, your inventory database, or just about any other document you're creating with a drag-and-drop savvy application (such as AppleWorks or Microsoft Office). Think of iPhoto as your one-stop art collection, because the images don't have to be photographs — any graphic in a compatible format can be stored and managed in iPhoto.

Importing Pictures

Your camera's memory is full, you have folders of photos you downloaded with Image Capture or the software that came with your digital camera before you got iPhoto, you have Kodak PhotoCDs full of pictures from your film camera, or you have the ever-present drawer or shoebox full of snapshots. Maybe all, or at least more than one, of these are true.

iPhoto handles the first three alternatives neatly, with no fuss or mess. If you have a digital image, the odds are that iPhoto can handle it. iPhoto will not, however, work with digital images in obscure or proprietary formats. Dennis, for example, has an old Casio digital camera in his collection that saves its pictures in Casio's proprietary CAM format. In a case like this, you're going to need an external tool such as GraphicConverter or the software that came with your uncooperative camera to convert the image to a supported format.

The loose snapshots, though, are going to have to be digitized. If you have a scanner, you could scan them and save the images on your hard disk. Alternatively, you could take them to your Kodak outlet or some other development house and have them scanned to CD. Once they're in digital form, you're ready to feed them to iPhoto.

Importing from a supported digital camera or equivalent

Using the USB connector, hook your camera up to your Mac and iPhoto will start up automatically in Import mode. You'll see information about your camera in the Import toolbox, including how many pictures it holds, as shown in Figure 9-1. Click the Import button and iPhoto will start importing the photos, displaying a thumbnail of the photo it is currently reading and telling you how many photos still await import.

Tip If your Mac doesn't recognize that a camera is connected and you know your camera is supported, try turning the camera off and then back on while it is connected.

iPhoto even makes it easy for you to erase the photos from your camera's memory or memory card. Just select the "Erase camera contents after transfer" check box, if you wish. Selecting this check box means that you never import the same picture(s) twice because you forgot to erase them the first time you imported them. If you're a very cautious and organized sort, though, you might want to leave this check box cleared and manually delete the pictures after you've verified that everything was imported and that you have made backups of the photos of particular interest.

When iPhoto finishes importing your pictures, it is even obliging enough to switch to Organize mode, as shown in Figure 9-2, displaying your Photo Library. (See "Organizing Your Photos" later in this chapter on how Organize mode works.)

Note If you are importing from a memory card in a memory card reader rather than a camera, you can switch to the Finder and locate the memory card as another disk at the Finder's Computer level. Double-click this icon and you can selectively delete or copy images from the card.

(a)

(b)

Figure 9-1: iPhoto's Import mode window, just waiting for you to click the Import button (a); iPhoto shows you what photo it's importing and how many remain (b).

Depending upon your camera, it might behave like a memory card and mount as a disk. If so, be sure to eject the camera or card using File ➪ Eject (⌘-E), dragging it to the Dock's Eject icon, or Control-clicking the camera's icon and choosing Eject from the contextual menu before disconnecting the camera or turning it off.

To iPhoto, a Kodak PhotoCD is just like a camera or memory card. Insert the CD with iPhoto running and click the Import mode's Import button. iPhoto will do the rest.

Note If iPhoto doesn't detect a compatible camera, memory card reader, or a PhotoCD, the Import button is disabled (dimmed) and you'll need to choose File ➪ Import or use drag-and-drop to get your images into iPhoto, as described in the next section.

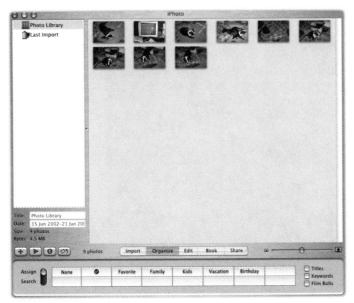

Figure 9-2: iPhoto assumes that you want to organize your newly imported photos.

Importing other digital images

You don't have to import your pictures directly from a camera. In fact, they don't have to be photographs at all. iPhoto will import images in a wide variety of formats: BMP, FlashPIX, GIF, JPG, MacPaint, PDF, PICT, PNG, PSD, SGI/Targa, or TIFF or anything else QuickTime reads.

 Even though iPhoto will import multipage PDF files, you can only see or work with the first page in iPhoto. You can still access the other pages using a separate program, like Adobe Acrobat or Photoshop, as described in the "Using an External Program for Photo Editing" section in Chapter 10. The same is true of multilayer TIFF files. All layers of multilayer Photoshop files are visible, though.

If you want to use iPhoto as a Clip Art Gallery, it will oblige. Similarly, if you want iPhoto to be the graphics scrapbook where you store the charts and images that you might need someday, go for it. With the keyword and comment capabilities (see the "Using the Organizational Tools" section later in this chapter), iPhoto can serve as a handy graphics document database and catalog.

You can add image files to iPhoto in two ways:

+ Choose File ⇨ Import.

    An Import Files dialog box appears. Navigate to the file or directory you want imported and click the Import button. You can use the Shift and ⌘ keys to select multiple files within the same directory, as shown in Figure 9-3. iPhoto will switch, temporarily, to Import mode and display the Import's progress, just as if you were importing from a camera.

Figure 9-3: You can select multiple items in the Import Photos dialog box.

+ Drag the images or folder of images from the Finder or another application that supports drag-and-drop, such as iView Media, GraphicConverter's Browser, or Photoshop's File Browser. Figure 9-4 shows an image being dragged from an iView Media catalog to iPhoto.

 Note iView Media, covered in Chapter 12, "Enhancing Your iPhoto Experience," overlaps iPhoto's organizational tools and, in many cases, surpasses them. While a superb graphics database, iView Media doesn't recognize cameras, has no editing tools other than rotation, and lacks most of iPhoto's sharing capabilities.

Organizing Your Photos

Regardless of how you add your photos and images to iPhoto, they all end up in the Photo Library. To be more precise, copies of every photo and image go into the Photo Library. This is an important distinction for two reasons:

1. More than double the hard disk space is consumed. Not only does iPhoto make an exact copy of the file, it creates a thumbnail image, and if you do any editing, it creates yet another copy beforehand and stores that as an "original" in case you decide to abandon your edits and revert to the original.

Figure 9-4: Drag pictures from other application documents to add them to iPhoto's Library.

2. Unless you erased (or had iPhoto erase) your camera's memory or memory card, the original file remains where it was. This is also true for any images you drag into iPhoto's window. This means that you always retain a backup in case you delete the image from iPhoto. This is helpful if, for example, you need to import an image into iPhoto to include in a book or slide show but have no further need of the image in your Library once that task is completed.

Your Photo Library will grow (and grow and grow). Before you know it, finding the photo you're looking for will become harder than finding the proverbial needle in a haystack. No one is going to stop you from scrolling randomly through your Photo Library looking for a particular photo or type of photo, but iPhoto's Organize mode provides a number of tools to help you group, annotate, and search for photos.

Tip   Hold down the Option key when scrolling to reduce the scroll speed and smooth out the presentation.

Using iPhoto's organizational tools

Your Photo Library is presented in one of two ways, as shown in Figure 9-5: by Film Roll or by Date. Before you start asking, "What's with this film roll business? I went digital so that I won't have to mess with film," we'll tell you. It's just a metaphor.

Every group of pictures you import, whether from a camera, Kodak PhotoCD, or by choosing File ⇨ Import, or dragging and dropping is grouped by iPhoto into an entity that it calls a Film Roll, which is date- and time-stamped for future reference. You can switch between these two presentations in two ways:

- ✦ Choose Edit ⇨ Arrange Photos ⇨ by Film Roll (Shift-⌘-F) or Edit ⇨ Arrange Photos ⇨ by Date (Shift-⌘-D).
- ✦ Select the Film Rolls check box at the bottom right of the iPhoto window to group by Film Roll (or clear the check box to display by date).

If you examine the Edit ⇨ Arrange by submenu, you'll see a third choice, Manually, but it's disabled unless you're working in an album (see the "Creating your own Albums" section later in this chapter).

The default ordering is "Honor your elders." In other words, if you're displaying Film Rolls, the first roll is at the top and the last roll added is at the bottom. Similarly, the oldest picture is at the top-left, continuing across the rows and down the scrollable pane until you get to the newest addition on the bottom-right. You can reverse this behavior by selecting "Most recent at top" in the iPhoto Preferences dialog box (iPhoto ⇨ Preferences or ⌘-Y).

Understanding the iPhoto Library's Structure

iPhoto creates the iPhoto Library in your Home directory's Pictures folder. You can move the iPhoto Library folder to another location as long as you create an alias to it, placed in the Pictures folder, and named iPhoto Library.

If you open the Photo Library folder, you'll see other folders:

- ✦ **Albums** contains data files denoting which pictures appear in which of your albums and how they're organized.
- ✦ **Folders identified by year**, which contain folders for the month (by number), which contain folders for the day of month their images were added to iPhoto.

Also in each of these day of month folders are folders named as follows:

- ✦ **Data**, which contains data files for each image in your Library, chock-full of all the information about each image: size, modification date, dimensions, keywords, and so forth.
- ✦ **Thumbs**, which contains the thumbnails for each image.
- ✦ **Originals**, which contains the original copies of any photos you've cropped or otherwise edited. This folder only exists if at least one image in that group has been edited.

While we appreciate that learning how iPhoto keeps track of things is interesting, we have one piece of strong advice: *Do Not Manipulate, Delete, Move, or Otherwise Edit These Files and Folders!* Doing so is a virtual guarantee that iPhoto won't be able to work with them and might even crash.

(a)

(b)

Figure 9-5: Your Photo Library can be displayed by roll (a) or by date (b).

We both prefer the Film Roll display. As Figure 9-6 shows, you can collapse or expand an individual roll's display by clicking the disclosure triangle to the left of the roll's name. That's a very good thing.

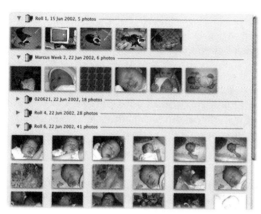

Figure 9-6: Use the disclosure triangle to hide a film roll's contents.

Tip By hiding rolls, you also speed iPhoto's scrolling and display. Once your Library has grown to significant size (even a couple hundred pictures is enough), you will really notice how much faster iPhoto responds if you collapse most of the rolls.

You can even arrange the Viewing pane's contents by Film Roll, without the disclosure triangles and lines. You can either select the Film Rolls check box and then clear it, which will impose the Film Roll sort and then leave it in place when the dividing lines go away; or, you can choose Edit ⇨ Arrange Photos ⇨ by Film Roll (Shift-⌘-F) and then clear the Film Rolls check box.

What's in a name?

The greatest annoyance in the iPhoto 1.0 release was that all photos, even those imported from your hard disk, had cryptic names and you were stuck with those names. iPhoto 1.1.1 (1.1 was released and withdrawn in a matter of just a few hours) removed, or at least lessened, the annoyance. Now, when you import files they retain their names. Of course, the name they come with from a camera probably won't be much better than the sequence naming iPhoto 1.0 used. (Names like DCP_0014 or MVC_011f aren't exactly descriptive.) To improve on the situation, Apple included editable titles via the Info pane. Select a photo or roll and you can change its name in the Info pane's Title text field.

You can even change the date of a photo or a roll. While this will almost never be necessary for photos you import from your camera, images you scan and import or obtain in other ways might not include valid date information. Similarly, a roll's date is the date and time you imported its images. If you have multiple memory cards, you might have imported the rolls out of order and this gives you a chance to fix the date/time to match when they were taken.

Note

Most digital cameras include what is called EXIF (EXchangeable Image Format) data (`www.pima.net/standards/it10/PIMA15740/exif.htm`). The EXIF record includes a wealth of information, including date and time shot, all of which depends upon your camera's clock being properly set.

Tell me all about it

iPhoto provides two ways of attaching information to your photos. One, Keywords, is pretty rigid and primarily useful for categorizing your photos. The other, Comments, is freewheeling and lets you describe the image.

Categorizing by keyword

That deceptive-looking 16-box grid in the Organize mode toolbox lets you assign zero or more categories to your photos. As you might surmise from the Assign/Search toggle switch, the whole purpose behind keywords is to make searching for specific groups of photos easier (see the "Searching your Photo Library" section later in this chapter). Apple starts you off with seven boxes filled in, but the first two (None and ✓) are immutable. The 14 remaining boxes are editable, as follows:

1. Make sure the toggle switch is set to Assign.
2. Choose Edit ⇨ Edit Keywords (⌘-K).

    The None box changes to say Done, the dividers between the cells thicken, and a blue border appears around the currently selected cell, which defaults to the first unassigned cell, as shown in Figure 9-7.

Figure 9-7: iPhoto assumes you want to assign a keyword to the first empty box.

3. If you wish to edit the keyword in an existing cell, select its text by double-clicking and edit as you would any other selected text. Otherwise, just enter the keyword you want to assign to this new cell.

Tip

Although iPhoto will allow you to assign long, multiword keywords to the boxes, they don't scroll and most of your label will wrap out of sight. You should probably limit keyword length to ten characters or so to keep the keyword visible.

4. Repeat Step 3 as often as desired, until you have the keyword collection you want.

5. Click the throbbing aqua Done box or choose Edit ⇨ Done Editing Keywords (⌘-K).

 Note If you've been using the Mac since before OS X, you might remember labeling items in the Finder. Well, keywords are a lot like the text labels that went with the colors. If you changed the text associated with a color, everything that was labeled with that color got the new text label. The 14 assignable keywords here behave similarly, the difference being that a photo can have more than one keyword assigned, but the Finder items can only have one label.

The ● keyword is reserved and the only really good use we can find for it is assigning a temporary keyword for photo selection via a Search (see the "Searching your Photo Library" section later in this chapter) when preparing to create a new album.

Assigning keywords to photos is very easy:

1. Select the photo or photos in the Viewing pane.
2. Click the boxes in the keywords grid to assign those keywords to the photos you've selected.
3. Repeat Steps 1 and 2 as desired for other photos.

Removing keywords from a photo is an almost identical process:

1. Select the photo or photos in the Viewing pane.

    The keywords assigned to those photos are highlighted in the grid.
2. Click the keyword you wish to remove from the photos.

When your photos have keywords assigned to them, selecting the Keywords check box will display each photo's keywords to the photo's right in the Viewing pane. The keyword list grows from the top down, as shown in Figure 9-8, with the exception of ●, which always appears as a mark in the bottom right corner of the photo.

Figure 9-8: Keywords appear as a list to the right of your photo when the Keywords check box is checked.

Do you wish to comment on this photo?

The old saying is that a picture is worth a thousand words. We don't know if that's true of all photos (it surely isn't of some of ours), but every photo has a story behind it. In fact, people have written notes on the backs of their photos for years, noting the names, locations, and people involved or telling how the photo came to be. iPhoto lets you tell your photo's story in the Info pane's Comments field, as shown in Figure 9-9. If the Comments field isn't visible, just click the circled-i (Info) button to make it so.

Figure 9-9: Write about your picture in the Comments field.

The Comments field doesn't scroll, but you can keep typing even after the cursor has disappeared from view. Alternatively, you can drag the handles (they look like small indentations) either above the Info pane or between the Album list and the Viewing pane to resize the panes, as shown in Figure 9-10.

With a simple Preferences change, you can replace the Keywords grid with a Comments text box. Unlike keywords, you can enter comments for only one photo at a time. You can, of course, copy and paste the same comment into the Comments text box for as many photos as you like, though it's a bit more work than assigning keywords to multiple photos.

Creating your own albums

One of the easiest ways to organize your photos is to put them in albums. iPhoto recognizes this and provides virtual photo albums. You don't have to mess with tape, glue, plastic protective sheets, mounting corners, extra pages, a pair of scissors, or a paper cutter. If you want the same photo to appear in more than one album, you don't even have to bother creating extra prints. iPhoto does all the bookwork for you by keeping pointers (like aliases) to an album's photos.

Figure 9-10: Drag the handles to resize the various iPhoto panes.

iPhoto makes it easy to create albums. Here's what you can do:

♦ Select a group of photos, either from the Viewing pane or from the Finder, and drag it to a blank area of the Album list.

iPhoto creates a new album with the name Album-1 (or whatever number you're up to) containing the selected photos and selects it in the Album list. Double-click the name to make it editable if you wish to rename the album.

♦ Click ⊕ to create a new album in the Album list.

iPhoto will display the New Album dialog box shown in Figure 9-11, asking you to give the album a name. (You're offered the very anonymous Album-n, where n is whatever number you're up to, as a default.) Name your album and you can now drag any photos you want to the album's name or icon in the Album list.

Figure 9-11: The New Album dialog box offers a very forgettable default name. You can surely choose a better one.

✦ Choose File ➪ New Album (⌘-N).

You're now exactly where you would be if you clicked ⊕. Proceed in the same way.

Adding photos to an album is as easy as dragging them to the album's name in the Album list, either from within iPhoto or from the Finder or another application. If the photos aren't dragged from the Photo Library or another album, iPhoto adds them to the Photo Library, creating a new Film Roll, while placing them in the album.

iPhoto doesn't know whether an image you're importing already exists in the Library. It assumes that anything you're importing is new, so you can easily end up with two or more copies of the same picture if you Import it more than once. That's why you should erase your camera's contents after you know the pictures are safely imported and why you should keep track of which files you've imported from your disk or a PhotoCD. Being conscientious in adding keywords and comments can also help you find photos if you're unsure whether a photo has already been imported, as you'll see in the "Searching your Photo Library" section, next.

Albums form the basis for your slide shows, Web pages, screen savers, and books as we discuss later in this chapter.

Searching your Photo Library

Visually scanning hundreds or thousands of thumbnails to find specific photos is, at best, a tedious, time-consuming, and error-prone process. Adding keywords and comments to your photos (as described in the "Tell me all about it" section earlier in this chapter) and then searching for the keyword or a text string using iPhoto's built-in database search will be much faster and more thorough. Of course, it does require that the data be there to be found.

Dennis recalls that when he was a very young programmer, he learned a very valuable lesson. There are "good lazy programmers" and "bad lazy programmers." Bad lazy programmers do very little overall design work and cut corners while writing their code, just to say they're done. Then, they have to spend a lot of time (usually, over and over again) fixing what isn't right, frequently creating new problems while fixing old ones. Being good lazy means that you are willing to do more work in the beginning to save you all that time and effort later. Working with a database — and iPhoto is definitely a database, among other things — offers you the same choice. Annotate your photos when adding them to the database and you'll easily find them when you want them; otherwise, you can laboriously pore through the thumbnails to find the photo(s) you seek.

Another way of looking at annotating/categorizing your photos is that you can pay iPhoto now, or you can pay it later. If you pay later, the interest charges mount up (rapidly) and the coin of the realm is your time.

iPhoto lets you search for matching keywords or for text in comments. Unfortunately, you have to invoke iPhoto ⇨ Preferences (⌘-Y) to specify which is to be searched and you can't combine the search types.

Take the following steps to search for photos that match one or more keywords:

1. Make sure that your Preferences state that Assign/Search uses Keywords.
2. Flip the Assign/Search toggle to Search.

   None changes to Show All in the Keyword grid.
3. Click a keyword to reduce the display to just photos with that keyword, as shown in Figure 9-12.
4. Click additional keywords to further reduce the photo display to just those photos matching all the selected keywords.

   You can click a selected keyword to remove it from the search set or click Show All to deselect all the selected search keywords.

These searches are sometimes called AND searches, meaning a photo has to match all the criteria to be included. Unfortunately, iPhoto doesn't provide an OR search (where matching any criterion would include the photo) — maybe if enough users request it, an OR search will show up in a future revision. We requested it at www.apple.com/macosx/feedback.

Setting your preferences (iPhoto ⇨ Preferences) to "Assign/Search uses: Comments" is actually a bit misleading. While the search will find matches in any photo's Comments field (Figure 9-13), it will also find matches for keywords, photo titles, and filenames (Figure 9-14).

In reality, iPhoto doesn't search for strings in a comment search, at least not in the traditional sense. The search more closely resembles a Sherlock Internet search, doing matches on each word individually. If you enter "baseball game" as the search string, iPhoto returns all photos that had both words anywhere in the searchable fields. For example, if a photo had "baseball" in the comments and you had a "Games" keyword assigned to it, iPhoto will display the photo as a match.

Since a Comments search also matches on keywords, you might consider it the more flexible search. (We know we do.) We find it annoying, though, that we have to switch our preferences to "Assign/Search uses: Keywords" in order to assign keywords and switch it back before we perform a search.

Removing photos from albums and the Library

There will come a day when you want to remove one or more photos from an album. In fact, if you take a lot of digital photos, you'll eventually want to remove photos from your Photo Library, just to speed iPhoto up.

(a)

(b)

Figure 9-12: Before clicking a keyword, everything is available (a); Clicking a keyword reduces the displayed photos to just those that have the selected keyword assigned (b).

(a)

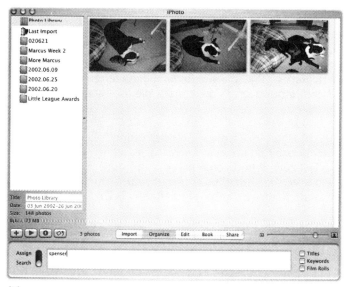

(b)

Figure 9-13: Before entering a search string, the Viewing pane shows everything (a); Entering a search string finds all the photos with that string in the Comments (b).

Figure 9-14: Searching Comments also finds matches in titles, filenames, and keywords.

Tip

We strongly recommend periodically archiving older photos to CD or some other medium, and then removing the photos from your Library. As an iPhoto Library fills up, performance degrades. Of all the wonderful things we can and do say about iPhoto, its speed and responsiveness don't make the list — and big Libraries only exacerbate the problem.

Removing photos from an album is a truly simple operation. Select the photo(s) you wish to delete and choose Edit ⇨ Clear or press the Delete key. (Del also works, if your keyboard has a Del key.) When you remove a photo from an album, iPhoto doesn't even ask whether you're sure. If you change your mind or delete a photo by mistake, select Edit ⇨ Undo Remove Photo From Album (⌘-Z).

Note

iPhoto's Undo commands are very literal and occasionally long-winded. They spell out exactly what you'll be undoing.

When you remove a photo from the Library, on the other hand, the action is not undoable and iPhoto will post an alert (Figure 9-15) that asks if you really want to remove the photo. It also informs you that the photo will also be removed from all albums. Other than the alert, though, the process is identical: Select the photos you want to remove and choose Edit ⇨ Clear or press Delete (or Del).

Figure 9-15: iPhoto asks for verification when deleting photos from the Library.

Making Adjustments to a Photo

iPhoto's editing tools are no threat to Photoshop, GraphicConverter, or any other dedicated image-editing application. The iPhoto editing tools are, however, the tools you'll probably need the most often.

Customizing the Edit Window's Toolbar

Just like the toolbar in a Finder or Mail window, the toolbar in iPhoto's separate Editing window is customizable. With an Edit window open, choose Window ⇨ Customize Toolbar to display the sheet shown in the figure below.

Customize the Edit toolbar using the objects on this sheet.

In addition to being able to remove, replace, or add buttons to the toolbar, you can choose whether the buttons display both Icon & Text, Icon Only, or Text Only in the Show popup menu. ⌘-clicking the lozenge button at the top-right of the Edit window, in the window's title bar, will cycle through the Show choices without you having to display the Customize sheet.

In general, whether you are editing in a separate window or editing in the iPhoto window's Edit mode, your tools are the same. There are some differences however, the first being that since you no longer have the size slider on the iPhoto window to zoom in or out when editing in a separate window, you'll find two Zoom buttons on the Edit window toolbar's left end. The up-arrow zooms in and the down-arrow zooms out.

Rotating an image

iPhoto assumes that all your photos are in landscape orientation. After all, there's no way for iPhoto to know you rotated your camera before shooting that picture of Uncle Joe and Aunt Betty. iPhoto doesn't even consider rotating a picture as an editing action and puts the Rotate button alongside the New Album, Play Slide Show, and Show Information buttons in the main window rather than in the Edit pane.

iPhoto's default rotation direction is counter-clockwise (the right edge becomes the top). You can change the rotation direction in iPhoto's Preferences or, if you only want to rotate an occasional picture clockwise, press the Option key while clicking the Rotate button when performing those rotations (or click Rotate three times).

Note The counter-clockwise default is an artifact of more people being right-handed than left. When a person rotates the camera for a shot, their tendency is to put the viewfinder on the same side as their dominant eye: for right-handed people that's usually the right eye. If you're left-handed (or tend to put the viewfinder on the left side of the camera when taking a portrait shot), you'll probably want to change the preference.

Cropping an image

Most digital cameras, like most computer monitors and TVs, have a 4:3 aspect ratio (well, at least they did until the advent of HDTV, Cinema Displays, Titanium Powerbooks, and the like). Some standard photo sizes are 4×6, 5×7, 8×10, and 11×14 and you'll notice that not one of those is a 4:3 ratio.

Note We've always considered it a little curious that photo sizes always list the smaller dimension first and monitor sizes (and aspect ratios) list the larger first.

There are three ways to fit a 4:3 image in a frame with a different aspect ratio:

- You can distort the picture by stretching or compressing in one dimension.

    iPhoto doesn't provide any tools to affect distortion, so if you want a fun-house mirror effect, you're going to have to employ an image-editing application like Photoshop.

◆ You can *letterbox* the picture, leaving a border along two edges.

Accomplishing this is simple, just tell iPhoto to print at the desired size and it will fit your picture into the frame. A 1280×960 photo printed to fit on 4×6 paper will leave a 1/3-inch border on the left and right.

◆ You can crop part of the picture so the aspect ratio is the same.

iPhoto makes cropping easy with Edit mode's Constrain pop-up menu. Choose the image size you want to finish with and perform your selection as shown in Figure 9-16. iPhoto will keep the selection's proportions correct. When you've slid the selection rectangle to surround the part of the picture you want kept, click the Crop button.

(a)   (b)

Figure 9-16: Choose 8×10 from the Constrain pop-up menu (a) and iPhoto's selection rectangle will maintain those proportions (b).

Cropping is also useful when you want to reduce a photo to show only your subject, eliminating distracting surroundings or backgrounds.

Caution

If you want to print the picture, be careful of cropping a picture too much unless you have a *really* high-resolution image to start with. Cropping a 2048×1536 image to 1500×1200 will make an 8×10 print of marginal quality; any lesser resolution and you'll have serious jaggies problems.

If your preferences are set so that double-clicking a photo opens it for editing in a separate window, you get one extra benefit. You can set a customized constraint, such as 3×5, by entering the values in the text boxes that show up between the Constrain pop-up menu and the Crop button.

Adjusting brightness and contrast

The brightness and contrast sliders behave just like the brightness and contrast controls on your TV set.

Increasing brightness moves all the pixels closer to white (light pixels move to white faster than dark pixels) and decreasing brightness moves all the pixels closer to black (dark pixels moving faster than light pixels). Figure 9-17 shows how a picture is altered when brightness is moved to the extreme settings.

Increasing contrast moves dark pixels toward black and light pixels toward white, resulting in greater discrimination between light and dark areas. Decreasing contrast moves dark and light pixels toward a midpoint (50 percent gray), dulling the picture. Using the same original image from Figure 9-17, Figure 9-18 demonstrates adjusting Contrast to its extreme settings.

Figure 9-17: The original image (a); maximum brightness (b); minimum brightness (c).

(a) (b)

Figure 9-18: Maximum contrast (a); Minimum contrast (b).

Removing red-eye from an image

How many times have you taken a photo, using your flash, and found the person dead-center in your picture looking as if red-hot coals had replaced their eyes? This phenomenon, called *red-eye*, is the result of your flash reflecting off the blood-red retinas at the back of your subject's eyes. The dimmer the room, the more open the subject's pupils and the more light reflected.

Here's how to remove the red-eye effect:

1. Zoom in so that you have a good view of the affected eye(s).
2. Select the eye and a significant amount of surrounding skin.

    The red-eye tool works by distinguishing red from almost-red in a comparison with normal skin tones, so the more facial skin in your selection the better (so long as the person isn't sporting a bright sunburn).
3. Click the Red-Eye tool.

    The Red-Eye tool converts the red pixels to black; now your subjects don't look like victims of demonic possession.

While this fix for red-eye is less than perfect (coal-black eyes are better than red, but not really realistic), you're better placed to avoid red-eye altogether if you use a flash that is separated from your camera by a few feet or if you use strong indoor or reflected light rather than a flash.

Converting to black-and-white

The screen shots and photos in this book were color when we submitted them. During the production process, they were converted to black-and-white for printing.

(Color is a lot more expensive to print than black-and-white.) If you're going to be duplicating your photos in a newsletter or on a copy machine, you're better off with using black-and-white images — then your copies will look like your originals.

iPhoto's Black & White button drains all the color out of your picture, reducing it to a grayscale image, commonly (and imprecisely) referred to as a black and white. We'd put a screen shot in here to show you what's going on, but Production would be converting the "Before" shot to black-and-white for printing and you wouldn't see any difference.

If you're editing a picture in its own window (iPhoto ➪ Preferences, "Double-clicking photos opens them in: Separate Window"), the Black & White button will be called B&W and it won't be present on the default toolbar. You'll need to click the Customize button and add B&W you wish to employ it.

Laying Out Books

One thing that sets iPhoto apart from other photo organizers is that you can take one of your iPhoto albums and, with just a few clicks and a credit card, order a hard-bound book of your photos, professionally printed on acid-free glossy paper. We know this has to be a cool feature because when Steve Jobs announced it at Macworld in January 2002, he was clearly in awe (or an even better actor than many award-winners).

While we're yet to be convinced that producing coffee table books of your photos is anything but a niche market today, the potential is clear. A well-designed, hardbound wedding album, baby album, or the like is a much more convenient and attractive gift or keepsake than the traditional "pasted-in photos" albums. They're even nicer than the vacation flipbook albums memorializing your first visit to the Australian outback. They're also a convenient way to create yearbooks, whether from a school class or to tell the story of a Little League team's season.

We'll cover the actual ordering process later in this chapter in the "Ordering photos: Coffee table books" section, but will note here the cost of these books: $30 for the first 10 pages (or fraction thereof) and $3 for each subsequent page. Each page in a book is 9 by 11.5 inches.

Now, let's discuss the layout process.

Putting together your album

The first thing you'll notice is that iPhoto won't let you switch to Book mode unless you have an album selected (Figure 9-19). Everything you do in iPhoto's Book mode is tied to the album, and changes in the order of photos in the book are reflected back to the order of the photos in your album.

Figure 9-19: iPhoto's Book mode requires an album for its content.

Before you enter Book mode, though, identify the photo you want on the book's cover and place it first (if it's not already there) in the album because iPhoto won't let you change the cover photo in Book mode (you'd have to return to Organize mode to do so).

iPhoto offers six *themes* (book design templates), only two of which will place more than four photos on a page. This has an upside: You won't be reducing the size of your photos to the point where they're hard to see and lose their impact. On the downside: You'll burn up your ten pages quickly and go into the $3/page overflow. Even four photos on a page is a bit crowded, so you're probably going to end up with only about two dozen photos in a 10-page book (not including the photo on the cover), unless you have a lower-resolution camera. iPhoto will put low-resolution warnings on any photo that doesn't have enough pixels to print well, which pretty much means that if there's only one photo on the page, it should be at least a 2-megapixel photo (and 3 megapixels is a lot better). If you have a 1-megapixel digital camera, you're probably not going to be thrilled with the Picture Book theme if you ever employ the one-photo-per-page design option.

> **Note** iPhoto's themes all expect photos with a 4:3 aspect ratio. If you've cropped your figures to a different aspect ratio, you should revert them to their original condition or crop again back to a 4:3 ratio. If, like Dennis's Kodak DX3500, your camera creates photos with a different aspect ratio, you're going to need to crop them to 4:3 or have your book look bad. If you're a bit adept at using Apple's Interface Builder and editing XML, though, you can work around this.

Although you can reorder most of the photos in Book mode, it is a lot easier to set the photo sequence in Organize mode. Books are laid out horizontally (they're wider than they are tall), which is great for the typical landscape orientation photo when you're placing one, three, or four per page. However, you might consider saving grouping any portrait-orientation shots for two-per-page presentation. Figure 9-20 shows two portrait photos on a page at the top and two landscape photos on a page at the bottom (using the Picture Book theme).

Figure 9-20: Two portrait pictures (top) fill a landscape page better than two landscape photos (bottom).

Choosing a theme

Once you have your album populated and ordered the way you want it, it's time to actually build the book. Click the Book button and iPhoto's window will switch to that shown in Figure 9-21 (except that your pictures will be used). By default, iPhoto will use the album name as the title on your book's cover page, but you can change that, if you wish.

The Viewing pane is now divided into two parts, an editing pane and a horizontally scrolling list of numbered page thumbnails. Pay attention to those numbers, because they tell you how many pages your book is going to be, which tells you how big a dent the book will make in your credit card.

Chapter 9 ✦ Getting Started with iPhoto   161

Figure 9-21: The Viewing pane splits into two parts when you enter Book mode.

Before you go any further, decide which of iPhoto's six themes you want to use. You can always change themes later, but that change will cost you any text, captions, and other design work you've done.

Tip If you want to try out a different theme after you've done some work, duplicate the album and try the theme out on the duplicate. If you like the new theme, you can switch between albums and copy/paste the text rather than recreating it from scratch. If you decide that your first choice was better, you can go back to that.

Here are iPhoto's six canned themes:

✦ **Catalog:** Although well laid out for a product catalog, this is probably a bit expensive for just about any product line unless you're an exclusive jeweler or furrier. It's probably not an original idea, but Dennis chose this theme for an insurance inventory. Catalog offers one, four, or eight photos per page, with accompanying product name and large description boxes for each photo. In this case, we recommend landscape photos for the one-per-page and eight-per-page choices and portrait for the four-per-page design.

✦ **Classic:** A simple and aptly named design, Classic focuses on the photo, with page designs for one, two, three, or four photos per page with small name and description boxes beneath the photos. One advantage of this theme is that even the one-photo-per-page design will accommodate a 1280×960 (1-megapixel) image without a low-resolution warning.

✦ **Picture Book:** An aptly named theme, the only text allowed in this book is on pages with Cover or Introduction (text-only) designs. With proper orientation choices, the picture pages are *full-bleed* (print from edge to edge), providing a striking presentation on each of the one-, two-, three-, and four-per-page designs.

✦ **Portfolio**: Resembling a model's or artist's portfolio of work, this theme provides for full-bleed printing on the right side of each page, with the left side reserved for titles and commentary (or white space). Portfolio offers one-, two-, three-, and four-per-page designs.

✦ **Story Book**: We don't know where this design got its name, other than the fact that every page has a large rectangular text box at the bottom or along the right edge where you can write a story about the one to three pictures on that page. If the text flowed from page to page, the name might be more appropriate.
No photo is square to the page and when two or more photos are on a page, they overlap slightly.

✦ **Year Book**: Allowing up to 32 photos per page, the Yearbook theme can cram many small pictures into a minimal number of pages. The text box for each photo is small, especially considering the font size used (11.8 points), so you have a very limited number of characters available before iPhoto puts a warning triangle on your caption. At 32 photos per page, you only get a Titles box. The Year Book theme is aptly named, serving well for a school or class yearbook.

As you investigate the different themes' suitability for your book, you'll also notice that you still have a lot of design work ahead of you, arranging the photos so that they show to best advantage.

Designing your pages

Once you've selected your photos and the theme, it's time to get down to the real work: laying out the design. Always keep in mind that iPhoto books are a sequence of photos, flowing from one to the next just as they appear in the Organize mode's Viewing pane.

When you move a photo in Organize mode, it induces a ripple effect on your book's pages. Suppose, for example, that your first page has three photos, your second page has one photo, and your third page has two photos (we're going to ignore subsequent pages, but you'll get the idea). If you were to go into Organize mode and move the photo that is on page 2 so that it immediately follows your cover photo and then switch back to Book mode, your page design sequence will remain the same, but the photo on page 2 will now be the one which was previously the third photo on page 1. On the other hand, if you were to drag page 2 to precede page 1, you would get the same sequence of photos, but will not affect which photos are grouped on a page.

Every page you create poses three questions:

✦ How many photos do you want on the page?

✦ What text, if any, do you want on the page?

✦ How do you want the text formatted?

The first photo of any album will be your Cover photo. iPhoto won't let you move the Cover page, so if you want a different photo there, switch to Organize mode and move the photo you want to the top-left of the album's Viewing pane. The Cover photo will appear, nicely centered, on your printed book's linen cover (see the "Ordering Photos: Coffee table books" section later in this chapter to learn about specifying your cover's color). iPhoto places the album name as your book's default title, as shown in Figure 9-22. You can edit the title, if you wish. There's also a second text field for a subtitle.

Note We don't know why the subtitle field uses neither the album's, nor the cover photo's comment as a default as is the case with other page designs, if you have the Comments check box selected.

Figure 9-22: The book's cover uses the album name as the default title.

iPhoto's themes each have their own set of page designs, but these page designs fall into four general categories, as follows:

- ✦ **Cover:** The first page of your book must have the Cover design, but you can apply the cover design to internal pages as well. This can be handy if you would like to use the Cover design to introduce chapters.

- ✦ **Introduction:** With Story Book the sole exception, this is a text-only page with two text boxes. (Story Book also has two text boxes, but includes three photos.)

  iPhoto starts you out with the album name in one box and your long name (the one the Mac knows you by) with the month and year the pictures were taken in the other box. Feel free (please!) to replace this text with something more appropriate.

+ **One, Two, ... (number of photos per page):** iPhoto will place the specified number of photos on the page, but they will be arranged according to iPhoto's programmed sense of aesthetics. You can, with a little experimentation, determine how iPhoto will arrange things. For example, refer to Figure 9-20, our earlier case of two portrait photos versus two landscape photos. Similarly, when displaying three photos per page, you will often get superior results (depending upon the theme and the order in which the photos occur) with one portrait and two landscape prints as shown in Figure 9-23.

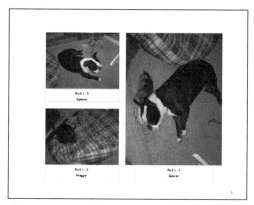

Figure 9-23: With three photos per page, one portrait and two landscapes are often an effective combination.

+ **End:** This design exists only in the Story Book theme and has one photo, and that photo is partway off the page.

As you change the number of photos on a page, that change also affects which photos are on subsequent pages — another ripple effect. The ripple can be particularly annoying if you've already designed one of the later pages and had it just the way you wanted it, only to see your work go *poof*. The solution to this dilemma is the Lock Page check box. Once you have a page exactly the way you want it, select the page and select the Lock Page check box. If you lock a page, the thumbnail will sprout a small lock icon in the lower-right corner, as shown in Figure 9-24.

Figure 9-24: Locked pages display a padlock icon in their thumbnail's lower-right corner.

There are a few "gotchas" associated with locking a page:

- ✦ If, at some future time, you decide you want to make a change to the page design, you have to unlock it, possibly resulting in a wild cascade of changes as iPhoto realigns everything according to the theme's priorities. One way to avoid this cascade is to temporarily lock the preceding page before unlocking the one you want to modify.

- ✦ Changes to picture order you make in Organize mode won't be reflected on the locked page. It is, essentially, a static item and all the other photos flow around it.

- ✦ Changing themes will remove the lock and all your other design work. Invoking Edit ➪ Undo will restore your designs, but the lock will still be gone.

The smallest book you create will have ten single-sided pages, even if some of them are blank. You're paying for a minimum of ten pages and, by George, Apple's going to make sure you get those ten pages (but they will warn you first that some pages will be bereft of photos). The largest book available has 50 pages — and costs you $147! If you try to produce a book with more than 50 pages, you won't be allowed to have it printed. You should make these limits part of your design and layout process. Of course, if you're willing to pay for it, you really can get more than 50 pages printed, just split your book into volumes like the *Encyclopedia Britannica*, and pay accordingly.

Adding page numbers to your book

The three check boxes beside the Theme pop-up menu control which elements other than your photos show up on your book's pages. The easiest to deal with is Page Numbers, which are printed in the bottom-right corner of each page. Take them out or leave them in, depending how you feel about having numbered pages. Don't worry, though, if the page number location and a photo coincide — the photo wins, hiding the page number.

Adding titles and comments

Most numbered page designs allow accompanying each photo with two text boxes, whose appearance are predicated upon selecting the Titles and Comments check boxes. In other words, if you want to place text in the boxes, you have to select Titles for the first field and Comments for the second — selecting just one displays just that one field. As shown in Figure 9-25, some designs can look really strange if you don't have the text, because iPhoto's themes don't use the space where the text would be to enlarge the photos' display. iPhoto puts the photo's title in the first field and any comments you've added to the photo in the second field, but you're welcome to edit, replace, or delete those entries as you wish.

Some themes and page designs have rather small boxes for Comments and, if your text overflows, iPhoto will cut it off and display the ubiquitous exclamation point in a yellow triangle Caution icon to make sure you're aware of that fact. You'll probably want to edit that text before you have your book printed.

(a)

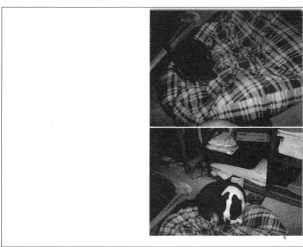

(b)

Figure 9-25: A Portfolio "Two" page with Titles and Comments on (a); The same page with Titles and Comments turned off (b).

Spellchecking your book

iPhoto even includes an interface to OS X's Spellchecker, which is a good thing since iPhoto deviates from standard OS X application behavior by not including a Services submenu in the iPhoto application's menu. There are three ways to check your spelling in iPhoto and, with what you're going to pay to have the book produced, you really don't want any spelling errors making you look foolish.

- Edit ➪ Spelling ➪ Spelling will check the spelling in whatever text block contains the cursor. The keyboard shortcut for this is ⌘-: (yes, normally you would see this marked as Shift-⌘-;).

- Edit ➪ Spelling ➪ Check Spelling (⌘-;) will check the current selection. If there is no selected text, the current text block is checked, just as if you had chosen Edit ➪ Spelling ➪ Spelling.

- Edit ➪ Spelling ➪ Check Spelling As You Type is a toggle. When this item is checked in the Edit ➪ Spelling submenu, the spellchecker will follow along as you type and, interactively, help you correct your spelling as you work.

You can also invoke any of the three spelling choices by Control-clicking in a text box and choosing from the contextual menu's Spelling submenu.

iPhoto's Funny Font Handling

iPhoto's treatment of fonts is different from what we've all come to expect in a Mac application. You cannot change the font family or typeface or apply a bold or italic style to a single character or word — all changes of this type affect all the text in that field and, in the case of books, in all the fields of that type, as shown in the accompanying figure.

Change one word's font and you change the fonts for that whole field and all like fields.

Adding to this global font change property, iPhoto also teases you in the Font panel (Edit ➪ Font ➪ Show Fonts, or ⌘-T). It shows you the Sizes display, lets you edit the Sizes text box entry, and then rejects your change. Like the original Model T Ford's approach to color ("You can have any color you want, so long as it's black") iPhoto's approach to font sizes in books is, "You can print in any size you want, so long as it is the one we chose for this theme."

Words that are not in the OS X dictionary or in your personal learned words list sprout a red dotted underline. Figure 9-26 shows the standard Spelling dialog where you can correct your errors, tell the spellchecker to ignore a word in the future, or add the word to your learned words list.

The learned words list is in your Home folder's Library/Spelling folder in a file named for the language you're using. For example, mine (and probably, yours) is in ~/Library/Spelling/English.

Figure 9-26: OS X's spellchecker is on hand to help you catch typos in your book.

If, like Dennis, your spelling errors generally fall into the category of transposed letters that leave a real word ("filed" rather than "field" is one of his personal gotchas), iPhoto's contextual menu can come in handy. Control-click in a text block and choose Speech ⇨ Start Speaking, as shown in Figure 9-27, to have the Mac read your text back to you. Dennis finds the available computer voices (System Preferences ⇨ Speech ⇨ Text to Speech tab) annoying, but a lot of people find them cute, entertaining, or useful. At least you have the option.

Figure 9-27: The contextual menu gives you the option of having the Mac read your text to you.

We're somewhat relieved to see that iPhoto hasn't ignored contextual menus completely. Maybe more will show up in future revisions.

Previewing your book

Once you are reasonably sure you have the book you want, it's time to double-check. You can preview your book on-screen by clicking the Preview button at the right end of Book mode's toolbox or by double-clicking one of the thumbnails. iPhoto will present a preview window, shown in Figure 9-28, with a current page text box at the top left, flanked by previous and next page arrow buttons. Type a page number in the text box to go to a specific page if you don't like clicking the buttons repeatedly (page 0 is the cover). The Show Guides check box determines whether thin blue lines surround the text fields.

Figure 9-28: You can preview your book onscreen.

As you can see, the default window size makes the text well-nigh unreadable. Click the zoom (green gumdrop) button to make the window grow to maximum size so that you get a reasonable picture of the text as well.

 Caution There's a bug we hope Apple fixes by the time you're reading this. Trying to invoke the Spelling Checker or Speech from the Preview window sometimes causes iPhoto to crash (Unexpectedly Quit).

Although it won't have the fancy linen cover or the acid-free glossy paper (unless you decide to splurge), you can print your book on a color inkjet or, if you have one, a color laser printer to get a really good idea of how your book will look. Just choose File ⇨ Print (⌘-P), choose your printer if it isn't already chosen, and click Print. Alternatively, you can click the Print dialog's Preview button to generate a temporary PDF file, which will open in the Preview utility. By choosing Preview's File ⇨ Save As PDF command, you can save the PDF file for further review or just to send off to others.

Note Preview will display the pages rotated 90 degrees clockwise (the top will be along the right edge). You can open the PDF in Adobe's Acrobat Reader and choose View ➪ Rotate Counterclockwise to see it as it is meant to be seen.

When you're really sure that you want to send the book off to be printed and bound, with your credit card charged, check out the "Ordering Photos: Coffee table books" section later in this chapter.

Printing Photos

We can almost guarantee the time will arrive when you need a printed copy of one or more of your photos. Web pages and e-mail are nice, but Grandma wants an 8×10 of Junior's picture to put on the mantle, a wallet-size to carry around and show her friends, and a 4×6 to put in the family photo album, and you don't dare disappoint Grandma!

Of course, you could just use the easy iPhoto-Internet interface to order prints from Kodak (see the "Ordering Photos: Prints" section later in this chapter) and, if you don't have a color printer or just don't feel like a do-it-yourself type, that's certainly a reasonable way to go.

Preparing to print

With an appropriate color printer and photo quality paper, you can get a print just as good as the ones you order from Kodak. There are fine inkjet printers available for well under $100, but they typically only use a four-color cartridge. While the output quality of these printers is usually quite good, if you want to challenge the professionals you'll need a printer with a six-color cartridge (such as an Epson Stylus Photo 780).

 Note Many of these printers are quite inexpensive. That's because inkjet printer manufacturers have learned the lesson taught by Gillette and Schick in their razor business: You can just about give away the carrier, the profit is in the consumables. If you're paying retail, it can cost $60 or more just to replace both the black and color cartridges in an inkjet printer that only cost you $59 or $79 to begin with. And, just so you know, printing color photos on glossy photo paper will go through ink cartridges like a '65 Caddy goes through gasoline.

There are two things you need to do if you want quality inkjet photo printouts:

✦ Use the right paper and tell your printer driver what kind of paper you're using and that you are going for quality rather than speed.

No matter how much you try, you're not going to get a decent photo on typical 20# bond typing paper. Paper like this just absorbs the ink and you get a dull, smeared look. Glossy paper made specifically for photo printing, such as

Hewlett-Packard's PhotoSmart, Kodak's Inkjet Photo, or Epson's Glossy Photo, is the ticket. This paper is expensive, running as high as $1 per sheet, and with the amount of ink you'll use for an 8×10, your photos might cost a little over $2 each on average, but that is only half as much as an 8×10 from Kodak ($3.99 at this writing). If you can get a good buy on your paper and ink cartridges, you'll actually be under half the cost. (Dennis buys his at Costco for about 60 percent of list.)

But, using the right paper doesn't do any good unless you let the printer driver know about it. In your Print dialog (File ➪ Print or click the Print button in Share mode), there's a button labeled Advanced Settings. Click it to access OS X's standard Print dialog for your printer and, in the pop-up menu that says Copies & Pages, choose Advanced Settings. Use the controls (they might be pop-up menus or radio buttons, depending upon your printer model) to let the printer driver know what kind of paper you're using and that you want the highest quality setting.

✦ Don't try to print a photo larger than its resolution will support.

Inkjet printers do their best work if they can work with photos that are between 220 pixels per inch and 300 pixels per inch. This is a separate consideration from how finely the printer can spray the ink. If the photo is 600 dpi and your printer can print 720 dpi, the picture won't look any better than if the photo was 300 dpi and you printed at 720 dpi unless you put it under a really good magnifying glass and had some fine detail to compare. In other words, bumping the photo's resolution above 300 dpi doesn't gain a *perceptible* advantage. Lower photo resolutions, though, can have a significant, visible, negative effect. Having written that, we admit that sometimes you get better results in practice than theory would indicate. For example, using the Epson Stylus Photo 780, we've gotten superb 8×10 prints from 180 dpi originals (1800×1640) and even some 1-megapixel (1280×960) photos. A lot depends upon the original photo's clarity and just how much detail the JPEG compression loses.

Many people will advise you to print draft copies on regular paper "to see how things look." We don't share that philosophy. The process uses a lot of expensive color ink and the results aren't indicative of what you'll produce with good paper and the proper settings — prints that look muddy and dull when printed on plain paper often turn out clean and crisp when printed at 720 (or 1440) dpi on glossy photo paper. What you see on your screen will be a better indicator of how the final print will appear than a plain paper draft.

Printing from iPhoto

Select the photo or photos you want printed and choose File ➪ Print or, in Share mode, click the Print button. iPhoto makes the actual printing process easier than most applications with a customized printing dialog box, shown in Figure 9-29. iPhoto displays a preview of what your first page will look like on the left.

Figure 9-29: iPhoto presents a custom Print dialog box.

Choose your printer from the Printer pop-up menu, if it isn't already displayed. Choose your paper and print quality combination from the Presets pop-up menu, if iPhoto offers choices for your printer. Strangely, the Epson Stylus 777 printer driver offers quite a few presets, while the Epson Stylus Photo 780 offers only Standard. Finally, in the Style section, specify what you want to print and how you want things laid out. iPhoto offers four styles:

✦ The **Contact Sheet** prints out a photo array. You can specify from one to eight photos per row. The more photos per row, obviously, the smaller the prints, as shown in Figure 9-30. Depending upon the printable area your printer supports, you can have up to 104 prints per page (13 rows of 8 photos) or 112 prints per page (14 rows of 8 photos). In fact, if your printer supports it and you choose to use 4×6 paper, you can get 15 rows of 8 really tiny pictures on a single sheet. If you select multiple photos, you will get one copy of each laid out in the array. If only one photo is selected, you will get one full page containing multiple prints of that photo — a pretty decent shortcut to printing multiple wallet-size copies. When multiple photos are selected, the Save Paper check box is enabled, allowing you to print closer to the edge of the paper.

Figure 9-30: The Contact Sheet can be used to fill a page with the same photo.

✦ **Full Page** printing is pretty self-explanatory. Choosing Full Page will rotate each selected picture and enlarge or reduce it to fill a page (subject to the margin, which you can set, up to 1 inch on each side). Figure 9-31 shows the Full Page selection.

Figure 9-31: Full Page printing fills the printable area, less any margins you set.

✦ Choosing **Greeting Card** tells iPhoto to rotate and resize your photo(s) to fill either a quarter (Double-fold) or half page (Single-fold), allowing you to fold your printout into a greeting card. Figure 9-32 shows the Greeting Card choice. This choice's name is a bit misleading, since you still have to add your message to the card, either in another program or by hand.

✦ Certain photo sizes are considered standard. iPhoto caters to three of these sizes (4×6, 5×7, and 8×10) with the **Standard Prints** style as shown in Figure 9-33. When more than one photo is selected (and more than one at the size selected will fit on a page), the One photo per page check box is enabled, allowing you to restrict printing to one photo per page, centered on the page.

Figure 9-32: All set to add your message and fold into a greeting card.

Figure 9-33: You can print standard photo sizes, all ready for trimming.

While making many things easier, iPhoto also makes a few printing operations more confusing by offering a Page Setup dialog and then ignoring some of the settings you make, such as print orientation. The one setting that iPhoto does honor from Page Setup is the paper size. One thing we find particularly annoying, though, is that iPhoto says that it can't fit a 4×6 print on 4×6 Photo paper, as sold by Epson and Hewlett-Packard. Fortunately, there is a way around that: Choose Full Page rather than Standard Prints as your style after you've selected one of these paper sizes.

Tip If the colors in your printouts look way off, click the Print dialog's Advanced Options button and, in the OS X Print dialog, choose Color Management from the unlabeled pop-up menu. Click the ColorSync radio button if it isn't already selected.

The Preview box on the Print dialog's left side can give you a rough idea of what your printout's first page will look like, but it won't tell you anything about subsequent pages, including whether there are low-resolution warnings on any of those photos. Fortunately, as with all good OS X programs, you can "print" to a PDF file by clicking the Print dialog's Preview button. iPhoto will create a temporary PDF file of your entire print job and open it for you with the OS X Preview utility (where you can save the PDF file, if you wish).

Ordering Photos

Whether you want copies of specific photos or a ready-made album, iPhoto makes it easy. Apple has established a relationship with Kodak that lets you order prints of your photos and, as we saw earlier in this chapter in the "Laying Out Books" section, you can assemble your own photo albums and, as we describe below, have them professionally printed and bound. The only limitation upon this feature is that, at least so far, this service is only available in North America.

Prints

If you don't have an appropriate printer, or you just don't want to hassle with buying and loading expensive special paper and then trimming the prints, you can order prints from Kodak with just an Internet connection, a few clicks of the mouse, and a credit card, as follows:

1. Make sure you have an active Internet connection
2. Select the photos you want printed.

    You can select an album and have its contents printed or select individual photos for printing.

3. Enter Share mode and click the Order Prints button.

   Your Mac will (probably) ask whether it is okay to open an item in your Keychain. This is where your One-Click settings are stored and they are necessary to the ordering process. If you haven't established a One-Click account, you'll need to do so before you can order.

   iPhoto will display the Order Prints dialog box, as shown in Figure 9-34.

Figure 9-34: iPhoto presents the Kodak Print Service's Order Prints dialog box.

4. You can specify that you want a set number of 4×6 and/or 5×7 prints of every selected photo using the two quantity boxes at the top-right of the dialog. If you want varying quantities and sizes of the different prints, use the quantity boxes for the desired sizes of each photo.

   Notice that iPhoto will display low-resolution warnings next to any sizes that will not print well.

   Once you have all your quantities filled in, check to see what the damages are and, if you still want to place the order, click the Buy Now With 1-Click button. iPhoto will transfer the photos to Kodak over your Internet connection and they'll process the order and charge your credit card. You'll see an alert similar to the one in Figure 9-35 telling you that your order has been received. You'll also receive an e-mail from Apple confirming and thanking you for the order.

Having Kodak print your photos is definitely convenient and not too much more expensive than printing the photos yourself, except on small orders where the shipping charges really inflate the per-print cost. Of course, if you're having them sent to Grandma, you don't have to find a photo mailer and put stamps on it, so the incremental cost is not too bad. Where Kodak really shines, if your camera can produce a high-enough resolution image, is printing really large photos — the 16×20s and the 20×30s that you frame and hang on the living room wall, but which you can't print out on most inkjet printers.

Figure 9-35: Your order's been placed; now you wait for the prints to show up.

Resolving Resolutions

Whether you're printing the photos yourself, ordering from Kodak, or having a book printed by Apple's designated bindery, there are some basic guidelines you should follow to avoid the yellow triangle warning.

According to Kodak's Ofoto Web site (www.ofoto.com/PhotoTipsDigital.jsp), use the following reference table:

Print Size	*Minimum Resolution*
Wallet-size (2"×3")	320×240
4"×6"	640×480
5"×7"	1024×768
8"×10"	1536×1024
16"×20"	1600×1200
20"×30"	1600×1200

Yes, we're surprised by the recommendations for 16×20s and 20×30s as well, although that makes Dennis's Kodak DX3500 (1800×1200 resolution) look like a better purchasing decision.

At any rate, those recommendations are *minimums*. Any resolution less than those in the list will prompt you with a low-resolution warning flag when laying out a book or printing.

You should also be aware that edges of your photos will be cropped if the aspect ratios don't match. Ofoto calls this process Zoom & Trim. First they enlarge (Zoom) the photo so that it completely covers the print area, then they crop (Trim) any overflow.

Coffee table books

You've selected your album, gone into Book mode, created the book you want printed and bound, now what? iPhoto considers ordering a book to be a Sharing experience, so click the Share button and then click the Order Book button in Share mode's tools panel, making sure that you have an active Internet connection beforehand. If you're not connected, iPhoto won't proceed.

iPhoto will spin the cursor for a while (how long depends upon the length of your book and the speed of your Mac) while it converts your book into something it can send over the Internet. When iPhoto's ready, you'll see a screen similar to the one in Figure 9-36.

Figure 9-36: The Order Book dialog box will tell you the basic cost, but you have to enable 1-Click Ordering to place the order.

Note

There are two things about which iPhoto might warn you here. The first is about the presence of any low-resolution warnings still in your book. You can either go back and fix those problems or tell iPhoto to order the book anyway, but if you do so, be prepared for some blotchy prints. The second is if your book has fewer than ten pages. In this situation, you can either return to Book mode and modify the layout or Organize mode and add more photos to fill up the remaining pages, or just tell iPhoto to have them print the book with some blank pages.

If you haven't created an Apple ID and enabled 1-Click ordering, that lower-right button will be as shown. Once you have 1-Click ordering enabled, the Tax and Shipping charges will fill in, and the buttons along the bottom will enable (with some changes) as shown in Figure 9-37.

Creating an Apple ID is easy. Your ID is just your e-mail address, with a password you create. The password must be at least eight characters long and at least one must be nonalphabetic. In case you forget your password at some future time, Apple gets two questions and answers from you to use for verification purposes so that you might create a new password for your account.

Answer a few more questions: credit card number and expiration date, billing address, one or more named shipping addresses and whether you prefer standard or expedited (faster, but more expensive) shipping.

Note   Although the offer might not last forever, while we're writing this material Apple is offering a free ten-print (4×6s) order when you first activate your 1-Click account.

Choose a color from the Cover Color pop-up menu. If you want more than one copy of the book, adjust the quantity in the text box or by clicking the up or down arrows next to it. Click the Buy Now With 1-Click button when you're ready to go.

Figure 9-37: Once you have an account, all the gory pricing and shipping details are revealed.

Now, just sit back and wait for FedEx to deliver your book(s).

Note   Dennis found the book both very nice and a little disappointing. The binding is excellent, the acid-free paper looks, feels, and even smells nice (or maybe that's the linen cover). The quality of the printout is pretty good, but nowhere near comparable to what you get when you order Kodak prints. Actually, side-by-side, the prints in the book don't look quite as good as those he gets from his Epson 780 Stylus Photo inkjet printer on glossy photo quality paper.

Apple doesn't do the printing/binding themselves; they outsource this work. They won't acknowledge which company actually does the work, but the most common guess is MyPublisher.com. You might want to check out the MyPublisher.com Web site, because they have a lot more themes than those in iPhoto (including do-it-yourself); however, you don't have the easy iPhoto interface to use while laying out your book.

E-mailing Your Photos

There are some situations where you're going to have to order prints or print them yourself and mail them (can you say, "Grandma?"), but other than those cases, you'll find e-mail the faster, more convenient way to distribute your photos. One e-mail message can send the photos to dozens of relatives, saving you not just the printing costs, but the photo mailers and the postage.

If you use OS X's Mail application as your mail client, you're just a click or two away from sending your photos to friends and family. Plus, with the addition of a freeware utility named iPhoto Mailer Patcher (self-described as a hack and available at `homepage.mac.com/jacksim/software/`), you can do the same with Entourage, Eudora, Mailsmith, PowerMail, or QuickMail Pro.

iPhoto, while not a scriptable application, invokes AppleScripts to communicate with Mail. What the iPhoto Mailer Patcher does is rename the script in iPhoto's package and install a replacement script that invokes your mail client of choice. The patcher also replaces the picture used for the button in iPhoto's Share tools panel.

Follow these steps to send photos to others via e-mail:

1. Select the photo(s) you wish to send.
2. Enter Share mode (if you're not already there) by clicking the Share button.
3. Click the Mail button in the Share toolbox.

   If you forgot to select any photos, iPhoto will display an alert telling you to do so and try again. Otherwise, iPhoto will display the dialog shown in Figure 9-38. Below the Size pop-up menu, iPhoto tells you how many photos you've selected to e-mail and how much disk space they use. Be aware that the size of the photo message will be substantially larger since Mail will have to encode the images for transmission over the Internet. The encoding will typically add 30 to 50 percent to the size of a binary file like a photo. If your recipients are using a dialup Internet connection (as opposed to broadband, like cable or DSL), they'll appreciate you keeping your messages as small as possible. iPhoto offers a little assistance here, as well, with the Size pop-up menu.

Figure 9-38: The Mail Photo dialog box lets you set parameters for the mail message and resize the image(s) for quicker transmission.

4. Choose an image size from the Size pop-up menu.

   A typical 2-megapixel image is over one-half megabyte in size and will approach three-quarter megabytes when encoded. Attach four of these pictures and you're quickly looking at a mail message of 3MB that will take 10 to 15 minutes to upload on a dialup and 10 to 15 minutes to download using a dialup connection — all for photos too large to fit on a standard computer screen in the first place. Reduce them to 640×480 and you'll cut the size by over 75 percent, saving everyone involved some time and your recipients will be able to view your photos without resizing.

5. Select the Titles and/or Comments check box if you want Mail to include the photos' Title and Comments information in the body of your e-mail message.

   If only a single photo is being sent, selecting the Titles check box will make the photo's title the e-mail message's Subject.

6. Click Compose.

   iPhoto now goes to work, resizing the photos (if requested) and converting them to JPEG images (if they weren't already). It then sends a series of AppleEvent messages to launch Mail, if it isn't already running, and to tell Mail how to compose the message and what photo files to attach.

7. Address your messages in Mail and click Send.

Most e-mail boxes (such as the wonderful mac.com addresses available via .Mac) have size limitations — mac.com mailboxes are "full" when they contain 15MB. Think of the mailbox as your checking account and the 15MB as your overdraft protection. If an incoming message would put your mailbox over the limit, it and subsequent messages "bounce" like bad checks until you free up enough space. So, be considerate of others and keep the message sizes manageable.

If you don't want iPhoto to convert the photo to JPEG (you might be sending a PDF, a TIFF, or a Photoshop PSD file that you want to have arrive intact), don't use Share's Mail button. Launch your mail client and drag the photo(s) from iPhoto to the message window (Mail), Enclosure tab (Mailsmith), or whatever place your mail client uses to indicate attached files.

Publishing Your Pictures on Your .Mac HomePage

Creating a Web page of your photos and sending a simple message telling your friends and relatives where they can check out your latest offerings is actually far more versatile than sending a large group of recipients photos via e-mail. You don't have to restrict the number of photos so that everything will fit in their mailboxes and you can post as many as you want, within the limits of what your Web server allows. The easiest way to post your photos on the Web is using an iTools account.

Note If you don't have a .mac account, by all means get one. They're only $100 a year, they provide 100MB of storage for your Web pages and assorted other items, and they provide a conduit for obtaining all sorts of OS X software. Just go to www.mac.com and follow the simple directions or pick up a copy of the *Macworld Mac OS X Bible* or *Mac OS X for Dummies* (John Wiley & Sons, Inc.) and read all about it in there.

Assuming that you have an active Internet connection, iPhoto makes creating an iTools HomePage almost effortless. If you aren't connected, establish a connection and follow along:

1. Select the photos (or album) you wish to publish.
2. If you're not already in Share mode, click the Share button.
3. Click the HomePage button in the Share toolbox.

   iPhoto will connect to the iTools Web pages and display a Publish HomePage dialog box similar to the one in Figure 9-39. We say "similar" because the frame styles and page layouts are subject to change and enhancement and your photos, not Dennis's canine collection, will be displayed.

4. Select and edit any of the text on the page that you wish, be it the page name, description block, or any/all of the photo names. Though not documented, there appears to be a 40-character limitation on photo captions.

Note Apple puts a little ad at the bottom of your page telling your visitors that the page was "Made with Apple iTools." Although you can't remove that logo here, you can (after publishing the page) mount your iDisk and edit the HTML file iPhoto placed in your Sites folder to remove it, assuming you have some familiarity with HTML. We'll cover this topic in Chapter 10, "Going Further with iPhoto."

Figure 9-39: The Publish HomePage dialog box, ready for you to customize your page.

5. Select a frame style for your thumbnails.

6. Click Publish when you're ready.

    iPhoto will upload the photos and thumbnails to your iTools account. The photos and thumbnails will be in the Pictures folder and the HTML file, named PhotoAlbum1.html, will be in your Sites folder. If you already have a PhotoAlbum1.html, this will be PhotoAlbum2.html, and so on. When the upload is completed, iPhoto will ask whether you want to check your work, as shown in Figure 9-40.

Figure 9-40: iPhoto tells you you're done and asks whether you want to visit your new page.

 Caution If you already have pages other than those managed by Apple's HomePage tools published in your iTools account, do *not* publish the page in this manner unless you're willing to have your index.html file wiped out. iPhoto doesn't add the page to existing index.html files it doesn't manage, it replaces those index files with a new one that points to the PhotoAlbum collections.

Assuming that you clicked the Visit Page Now button, you'll see your handiwork, as Dennis did in Figure 9-41.

Clicking a thumbnail will display an enlarged copy of the photo, nicely placed in a Slide Show window (Figure 9-42). The Slide Show loops; if you're looking at the first picture on the page and click the left-pointing arrow button, you'll be taken to the last photo on the page, and vice versa.

If iPhoto's subset of the iTools page designs don't satisfy your aesthetic sense, you can follow a more hands-on path to creating an iTools photo HomePage, as follows:

1. Open your iDisk in the Finder (Go ⇨ iDisk or Option-⌘-I).

2. Create a new folder inside your iDisk's Pictures folder.

3. Drag the photos from iPhoto's Viewing pane to the folder you created in Step 2.

4. Start your Web browser and go to www.mac.com and log in.

 Caution Some browsers don't interact well with the HomePage functions. If you're having problems, you might want to switch (temporarily) to Internet Explorer.

5. Click the HomePage button on the .mac Web page.

Figure 9-41: The finished Web page, displayed in Internet Explorer.

Figure 9-42: Click on a thumbnail to see an enlarged version of the photo in a slide show window.

6. Click the Create a Page panel's Photo Album tab and select from the wide theme selection available (16 at the time we're writing this).

   You can also find Photo Album styles on some of the other tabs, such as Personal and Education.

7. When you click a theme, HomePage will ask you to identify the folder containing your pictures. You did perform Steps 2 and 3, didn't you? Select the folder in the list and click Choose.

   iTools now displays an "Edit your page" window. Click "Edit changes to Preview."

8. Click the Edit button and perform any editing you desire, eliminating or replacing the placeholder text and, if you wish, changing the photo captions from the filename default.

9. Click Preview when done to check your work.

10. Assuming that you like what you see in the Preview, click the Publish button and HomePage will create your page and offer to send iCards announcing it to people you specify. You can click on the link to check it out or go back into HomePage to create more Web pages by clicking the Return to HomePage button.

You can password-protect individual sites created by HomePage and group your HomePage sites into categories using the HomePage tools.

If this level of control is still insufficient, check out the "Creating Custom Web Pages" section in Chapter 10.

Creating a Slide Show

Photo slide shows have a long history, from the tedious vacation slides your grandparents projected onto a pull-down screen (or a wall) to the even more boring, but more high-tech, presentations you'll see if you ever attend a time-share sales pitch. But slide shows don't have to be boring. With iPhoto you can group your slides and set the show to music. Dennis's friends, Joseph and Tammy, had a baby boy just before Dennis started working on these chapters. (You see a number of Marcus's pictures in the book.) Naturally, lots of photos were taken by parents, grandparents, and friends and Dennis used iPhoto to create albums of the best photos for slide shows, each with its own "baby" background music (Nat King Cole's renditions of "Yes Sir, That's My Baby" and "Too Marvelous for Words," "Pretty Little Baby" by Connie Francis, and many others). Then, using iPhoto's Share mode, he exported the slide shows to QuickTime (see the "Sharing a Slide Show" section in Chapter 10) and using Toast Titanium burnt them to VideoCD. The young parents loved the gift.

Not only can iPhoto create slide shows, but it can play them right on your Mac, full-screen, in living color and stereophonic sound.

Playing a slide show

If you're happy with your Slide Show Music preference, all you have to do is click the iPhoto window's "Play the slide show" button to have your screen go completely black, the music start to play, and your selected photos or album to fade in and then start cross-fading from one to the next at 2 second intervals (or whatever you changed your Slide Show: Play each slide for *n* seconds setting to be).

iPhoto has a precedence it follows to determine which photos are shown in a slide show. If no photos are selected, all the photos in the Viewing pane (even if there is just one) are shown in sequence. If a single photo is selected, the show starts with that photo and proceeds to the end of the Viewing pane before looping back to the beginning. If multiple photos are selected, they are the only ones displayed in the slide show.

The shorter the play time for each slide, the less visible the cross-fade transition will be.

Other than presenting photos that will actually interest your audience, appropriate background music does more to make a slide show pleasurable than anything else. Apple seeds the pot with two classical classics: Bach's *Minuet in G* and *Jesu, Joy of Man's Desiring*. You can add any AIFF, MP3, or WAV files you have to the list. Your iTunes Library can be a great source and you can find more music on the Internet, both on the Web and in Internet newsgroups (Usenet). Check out the iTunes chapters (3 through 5, in particular) for tips on where to find music and how to get it on your Mac. To add a song to the list:

1. Choose iPhoto ⇨ Preferences (⌘-Y).
2. From the Slide Show: Music pop-up menu, choose Other.

   iPhoto will display an Open dialog box, conveniently defaulted to looking in your iTunes Music folder.

3. Navigate in the Open dialog to locate the song you want and click Open.

   This adds the song to the Music pop-up menu. If, at some future time, you wish to remove it from the pop-up menu, choose Edit List and, in the sheet that appears, select the song and click Delete.

Don't delete Minuet in G or iPhoto will keep resetting your Music choice to None. This is a bug. Hopefully, Apple will fix this anomaly before you read this material, but just in case . . .

You can also enter Share mode and click the Slide Show button to present the Slide Show Settings dialog box (Figure 9-43). From this dialog box you can set all the Slide Show preferences.

Figure 9-43: The Slide Show Settings dialog gives you access to all the Slide Show preferences.

Controlling your slide show

Although you don't have enough control to set different timings or transitions for your slides, iPhoto does give you some control over the presentation:

- Pressing the Space Bar pauses the slide show until you press Space again.

    A small Pause or Play indicator appears briefly in the lower-right corner of your screen. Even though the slides don't advance while you're paused, the music plays on.

- Pressing the left-arrow (←) or right-arrow (→) keys will disable the slide show's automatic advance timing putting you in manual control. You now advance (→) or move backward (←) at your own pace. Once again, the music plays on.

    If you want to resume automatic advance timing, press Space.

- You can temporarily speed up or slow down slide advancement by pressing the up-arrow (↑) or down-arrow (↓) keys, respectively.

    One slide per second seems to be as fast as you can make iPhoto move. Maybe someday, with faster processors and hard disks, iPhoto will be able to advance fast enough to make a slide show into a smooth animation.

- Clicking the mouse or pressing any key other than Space or the arrow keys will terminate the slide show.

If you want the best visual results from your slide show, make all your photos the same size. Your screen resolution is a great choice, especially if you want the pictures to completely fill the screen and to avoid any letterboxing effect. By making them the same size and orientation, you avoid changing the display area in which the photos appear and this makes the transitions more effective. Additionally, if your photo's aspect ratio is different from your monitor's aspect ratio, you'll experience letterboxing.

Using Your Photos on the Desktop

We're not really certain why the Desktop and Screen Saver choices are listed as Share options (except that they don't fit any better anywhere else). After all, using a photo as your Desktop Picture isn't sharing it with anyone, at least anyone other than yourself. The same holds true of using your photos as your Screen Saver.

Having puzzled over the why, we can say that we're very glad the options exist and won't quibble about their placement.

Desktop pictures

Since the beginning of the Mac, users have loved to plaster a picture on their screen to replace the patterned (or solid) background Apple provides as a default. A clever young programmer named Clay Maeckel achieved some measure of fame with his shareware DeskPict utility, making desktop pictures available to the Mac masses. With OS 8, Apple finally made desktop pictures a part of the new Appearance Manager and blessed them as a supported feature of the Mac OS. In Mac OS X, you have a Desktop System Preferences panel where you can set your Desktop picture and you can even specify background pictures for individual Finder windows.

The point of all this is that many people like to wallpaper their desktop with photographs of friends, family, pets, or cool scenery. iPhoto gives you two-click access to setting any photo in your Photo Library as your Desktop picture:

1. Click to select the photo you want to use.
2. In Share mode, click the Desktop icon in the toolbox.

    (Okay, if you weren't already in Share mode, it's three clicks.)

That's all there is to it. Your selected photo is now your Desktop picture, as shown in Figure 9-44. It's even a good reason to keep your Desktop tidy, hiding applications you aren't using and not leaving files and folders scattered around the Desktop.

You can change to any other photo just by following the above steps, but if you want to go back to a boring desktop pattern, you'll have to access the Desktop System Preferences panel and set it there, as shown in Figure 9-45.

Screen savers

In the old days of black-and-white computer displays (cathode-ray tubes or CRTs), leaving your screen on for long periods would result in a ghost of the static image being burned into the screen. Dennis remembers being able to see the menu bar on his Mac Plus (1986), even when the computer was turned off. In response to this situation, various clever individuals came up with screen savers for the Mac, the most famous of these being the After Dark "Flying Toasters" from Berkeley Systems.

With modern color CRTs and, even more so, with today's LCD screens, burn-in is not a problem. Regardless, screen savers are more popular than ever as they entertain, display messages, or just hide what's on the screen while you're away from the computer.

Figure 9-44: Bob (sans his trademark shades) and family posing in front of an Eskimo totem while on vacation makes a great desktop picture.

Figure 9-45: Choose a collection from the Collections pop-up menu and then select a dull replacement as your photographic backdrop.

Recognizing that folks like screen savers, and probably to show off OpenGL technology, Apple includes a Screen Saver with OS X and places your interaction with it in System Preferences.

In addition to the static displays, animated icons, and other variations on traditional screen savers, Apple includes some themed photo slide shows: beach scenes, stellar displays, and forest scenes. But these photo collections don't just transition from one still image to the next, they move slowly toward or away from you before cross-fading to the next image.

iPhoto makes it easy to use your own photos as a screen saver:

1. Collect the photos you want to use into an album.
2. Switch to Share mode and click the Screen Saver toolbox icon.

   iPhoto will display the Screen Saver dialog box shown in Figure 9-46.

Figure 9-46: Choose your album in the Screen Saver dialog box.

3. If your preferred album isn't already selected in the Use pop-up menu, choose it.
4. Click the Preferences button to display the Screen Saver System Preferences panel, where you can check out your handiwork, as shown in Figure 9-47.

Figure 9-47: Preview your screen saver in System Preferences.

5. If you like what you've created, Quit from System Preferences and click OK in iPhoto's Screen Saver dialog.

Now, when the OS X screen saver kicks in, you'll see your photos.

Tip

Two tips here, actually. First, use landscape photos for your screen saver because portrait photos will be rotated to landscape orientation by the software before being displayed. Second, try to make sure the resolution of your photos is at least that of your monitor to avoid the jaggies and blurry pictures as the screen saver scales them to fill (or more than fill) the screen.

Summary

We covered a lot of ground in this chapter. You learned how iPhoto structures and manages your Photo Library. You also saw how to import pictures whether from camera, disk, or Kodak PhotoCD (sometimes called PictureCD) and perform minor editing. Additionally, you learned to create your own albums and use them to create books, slide shows, and screen savers. We covered printing your own photos as well as ordering prints from Kodak and linen-bound books from Apple. You also saw how to send your photos via e-mail and use a photo as your Desktop picture with a single button click.

✦ ✦ ✦

Getting Advanced with iPhoto

In This Chapter

Exporting your photos

Sharing a slide show

Creating custom Web pages

Using an external program for photo editing

Plugging in to iPhoto

As we saw in the last chapter, iPhoto provides a good return with minimal effort. But there's still much more you can do, much of which you'll find via the File ⇨ Export (⌘-E) command, and the Share button that was mentioned, but not discussed, in the "Export" section in Chapter 9.

- ✦ If you want to create photo album Web pages on a Web site other than your .Mac site, or if you don't care for the limited selection of .Mac HomePage photo album themes, don't worry—iPhoto makes it simple to export your pictures as Web pages you can tweak to your heart's content.

- ✦ If you want to make a slide show for other folks, iPhoto teams up with QuickTime and, voila—a QuickTime movie slide show you can put on the Web, burn to a CD, or e-mail to anyone, anywhere.

- ✦ If you want copies of photos in your Library, for any reason whatsoever, iPhoto exports to most popular graphic file formats.

Do you need more powerful tools than iPhoto offers to edit your photos? That's no problem either. As long as iPhoto knows what program you prefer, double-clicking any thumbnail will open the photo in your preferred program. iPhoto will even let you undo the editing session as well as keep an original copy if you choose to Revert at a later time.

Finally, iPhoto has an extensible plug-in architecture, so third-party developers can provide additional iPhoto functionality such as exporting to Roxio's Toast Titanium or a dedicated Web site creation tool like PhotoToWeb.

Exporting Your Photos

iPhoto may be the perfect tool for collecting, organizing, and otherwise managing your collection of digital images, but it probably isn't the only program you will use with your pictures. After all, you can't easily create a newsletter, a business presentation, a montage, or a million other things that have pictures in them using iPhoto.

And often when you share images with others, they want you to supply the files in a specific file format. For example, the pictures in this book have to be TIFF files; the files Bob submits to his editor at www.osxfaq.com for use online have to be .jpg files, and so on.

Tip   One way to avoid the issue of file formats is to drag the photo from iPhoto to another application's document window and hope it works. AppleWorks, Microsoft Word, Microsoft Powerpoint, InDesign, and many other programs offer graphics tools that work on drag-and-dropped images. But we digress.

The File Export tab (shown in Figure 10-1) appears when you click the Share mode's Export button or choose File ➪ Export (⌘-E).

Figure 10-1: Export your photos for use in other programs via Export Images' File Export tab.

The Format pop-up menu gives you four choices:

- **Original** tells iPhoto to export it in whatever format you imported: JPEG, PSD, PDF, TIFF, etc.
- **JPG** tells iPhoto to convert any files in a different format to JPEG as they're exported.
- **TIFF** tells iPhoto to convert any non-TIFF files to TIFF as they're exported.

  iPhoto saves TIFF files as a multipage TIFF, with the thumbnail saved as the second page. TIFF files tend to be much larger than the other formats because they are not compressed. Even though compression is available in the TIFF standard, many applications, particularly on the Windows platform, do not recognize compressed TIFFs.

✦ **PNG**, for Portable Network Graphics, is one of the three standard graphics formats recognized by Web browsers, at least those released in the past couple of years. PNG actually comes in two variants, PNG-8 and PNG-24. PNG-24 is the one used by iPhoto since PNG-8, like GIF, only supports 256 colors and PNG-24 supports millions of colors. Although PNG doesn't compress as much as JPEG, it does so losslessly, resulting in TIFF-quality images at much smaller file sizes.

The Name box gives you a choice between using the name that the photo started with, usually something cryptic from your camera like DVC-0013, or the (hopefully less cryptic) title you assigned it in iPhoto.

The Size box also gives you two choices. You can either export the file at its actual size (Full-size images) or you can scale it so that it fits within a rectangle of your definition.

Even though iPhoto labels the boxes with a (w) and (h) for width and height, they don't really mean it. The (w) actually means "long edge" and the (h) means "short edge." For example, if you set the boxes to 640 and 480, respectively, and export a portrait photo that is 960×1280, the resulting photo, when opened in another application will be 480 pixels wide and 640 pixels tall.

If your photos and the rectangle you describe do not have the same aspect ratio, iPhoto will scale the image so that it completely fits within the rectangle but will not fill it. This effect is called *letterboxing*—you see it on TV whenever a widescreen movie is shown. (The black stripes above and below the picture are the letterbox effect.)

Sharing a Slide Show

When you choose File ➪ Export or click Share mode's Export button, the Export Images dialog box appears and its rightmost tab, shown in Figure 10-2, is QuickTime(tm). Although the tab's name doesn't make it obvious, this tab's raison d'etre is exporting slide shows.

Exporting a slide show means turning your slide show into a movie. Apple, not surprisingly, chose their QuickTime technology—available for both Mac and Windows—as the means to this useful end.

Consider adding a title screen and possibly other narrative screens. Since iPhoto will happily import a number of different formats, you can use AppleWorks, Photoshop, GraphicConverter, or other programs to create and save text or other nonphotographic images, then import the files into iPhoto, as described in the "Importing Pictures" section in Chapter 9.

Figure 10-2: As far as iPhoto's Export is concerned, QuickTime and Slide Show are synonymous.

Before you export a slide show, make certain any title or narrative screens are in the proper position in the slide show's album, and check one more time that everything looks just the way you want it to look. Refer to "Creating a Slide Show" in Chapter 9 if you need help.

Caution

Be sure to look at the Export Images dialog's lower left corner (as shown in Figure 10-2) to see how many photos are going to be in your movie. There is a subtle difference between the way slide shows work inside iPhoto and the way iPhoto exports slide shows, and in this case, if you don't know, it could hurt you. If you select just one photo in an album and then play the slide show within iPhoto, the selected photo is the starting point for the show and the show includes all the photos in the album. On the other hand, if you select just one photo in an album and export the slide show, the slide show includes just that one photo. So, if you want a slide show to start with a specific photo and include all the photos in the album, reorder the photos to put the selected photo first and then export the entire album as your slide show.

Click the QuickTime tab, and then in the QuickTime's Images box, specify the dimensions for your movie. The default, 640×480, is generally considered a great compromise size between compatibility with older systems and maintaining image detail. Those dimensions also make the file small enough for comfortable play from CD (assuming that you don't put too many pictures in the slide show), particularly on older hardware with 1× or 2× speed CD-ROM drives.

If you want to post the movie on the Web (see the "Putting Your Movie on the Web" section in Chapter 15), even 640×480 may even be too large.

Unlike exporting files, as described in "Exporting Photos" earlier in this chapter, Width and Height mean what they say here. Not only will any photos with a different aspect ratio receive a letterbox effect on playback, but portrait orientation photos will be reduced in size to fit within the height limit, as shown in Figure 10-3.

Figure 10-3: Portrait photos really shrink when displayed in a landscape slide show.

Mixing landscape and portrait photos will result in letterboxing, but if you are willing to have all your photos letterboxed with each photo at the same resolution, set the rectangles dimensions as square (such as 640×640). Be aware, though, that this will increase the size of the QuickTime movie.

You can also set the duration of each photo's display in the Images box. By default, iPhoto uses the duration set in your preferences (iPhoto ⇨ Preferences). Unlike the on-screen slide show, though, you can set durations in fractions of a second rather than just full seconds. Unfortunately, you are still limited to a maximum of 60 seconds per slide, but you can set the duration as low as 0.01 seconds. The only reasons we can see for setting a duration that low is if you have thousands of similar pictures and are trying to perform animation or embed subliminal messages, although there are easier ways to do this. Besides, values less than one second get treated as one second when you export your movie.

The Background box controls what you see behind your photos. If all your photos are the same orientation and have the same aspect ratio as the Width and Height set above, you're never going to be aware of the background. However, if any letterboxing occurs, the background (which defaults to Black) will fill the margins.

Click the color preview box next to the word Color to display the Colors dialog box (Figure 10-4).

Figure 10-4: You can set your background color using the Colors dialog box.

Initially, the Colors dialog box displays the color wheel, where you adjust the colors available by raising or lowering the slider on the right and selecting your color by moving the square inside the circle. Besides the Color Wheel button, along the dialog's top are Color Sliders, Color Palettes, and Image Palettes buttons, each of which provides access to a different mode of color selection. (If you're running Mac OS X 10.2 or later, you'll also see a Crayons button.) Find the color picker that you feel comfortable with (Dennis prefers the color sliders) and set your background color.

If you would rather have a picture for your background, such as the swirling Aqua Blue that OS X uses for a default Desktop background, click the Image radio button (Figure 10-2) and navigate to the picture you want to use.

> **Tip** The OS X galleries of desktop pictures are in /Library/Desktop Pictures.

The Music box (Figure 10-2) has just one check box and it determines whether your slide show has a sound track. If you select it, the song set in your iPhoto preferences will be used. You are now ready to export your movie. Click the Export button and iPhoto will ask you to name the movie (it will add the .mov extension for you). By default, iPhoto offers to save the movie to your Movies folder, but you can choose any location. Depending on the number of pictures, their size, and the speed of your Mac, the Export process could take a while, so iPhoto displays a progress bar while rendering and saving your movie.

And that's all. Double-click the movie to view it in QuickTime Player.

Creating Custom Web Pages

Don't get us wrong, we think that using iPhoto's or Apple's .Mac HomePage software, as described in the "Web Publishing Your Photos on Your .Mac HomePage" section in Chapter 9, is a great way to post attractive and functional photo albums. But, you are limited to the designs that HomePage provides and the structure it imposes. It is difficult to build and maintain a comprehensive Web site, of which your photo albums are just one part, using HomePage tools (not impossible, just difficult). Additionally, if you have Web space with your ISP, school, or business that you're trying to use, HomePage-built pages won't do you much good.

iPhoto caters to the do-it-yourselfer with the (you guessed it) Export Images dialog's Web Page tab. As with most options, you gain some things and you lose some things. The main things you lose are the nice themes and some of the fancy designs. What you gain are flexibility of design and control over your page's presentation. The Export Images Web Page tab is shown in Figure 10-5.

Figure 10-5: Control your photo album's presentation with the Web Page tab.

As you can see, the Web Page tab contains three sections, as follows:

- The **Page** box manages the settings which describe your page as an entity.
  - In the **Title** field you can specify what you want to have appear in the browser window's title bar and, centered in large bold letters, at the top of your page.
  - The **Columns** and **Rows** fields are where you specify how many thumbnails you want to have in each row on your page and how many rows before iPhoto generates a second, linked page. iPhoto tells you, to the right of the text boxes, how many pages your configuration will create.

It's a good idea to limit the number of images on a page, both to minimize scrolling by your page's visitors and to decrease the time needed for them to load a page into their browser, even at only 12KB each, 30 to 40 thumbnails can take a while to download on a dialup connection. iPhoto's default setting is to display ten rows of three thumbnails, but we feel that is too many, especially if your visitors are likely to be dialup users or are using older computers (or WebTV) where they would have to do a lot of scrolling and the page would take a long time to load. Three rows of two thumbnails will fit in most browser windows without any scrolling. More rows will involve vertical scrolling, which seems to annoy visitors less than horizontal scrolling.

- The **Background** option is where you specify a background color or image for your Web page. The default is a solid white background.

Clicking in the color preview box next to **Color** presents the Cocoa Colors dialog box, where you can use one of the Cocoa color pickers to specify your background color, as described in the "Sharing a Slide Show" section earlier in this chapter.

Clicking the **Image** radio button enables the Set button. Click it to present an Open dialog box you can navigate to find the background picture you wish to use. The image will be tiled, as shown in Figure 10-6, to fill the window as you scroll.

Figure 10-6: A small, faint GIF image can be a nice background wallpaper for your photo album pages.

- **The Thumbnail** box is where you specify the maximum dimensions for the thumbnails your page will display.

  Once again, the words "Width" and "Height" are misleading. iPhoto exchanges their meanings for portrait orientation photos.

- **The Image** box is where you specify the maximum dimensions on your photos. These photos are what your page's visitors see when they click on one of the thumbnails. Select the "Show title" check box if you want the photo's title to be displayed, centered beneath each thumbnail and left-justified beneath each photo.

Unless you have selected a photo or group of photos, iPhoto assumes you wish to export the current album (or your entire Photo Library). Unlike Web pages created with the HomePage tools, exported Web pages do not limit the number of photos you can use. iPhoto will generate another page each time the grid you specified in the Rows and Columns fields fills up.

When you have everything the way you want it, click the Export Images dialog's Export button. iPhoto will present a sheet asking where you want the pages placed. By default, iPhoto will suggest your Home folder's Sites folder. Unless you wish to replace the contents of the Sites folder or whatever folder is currently displayed, we recommend that you click the New Folder button and name a new repository. Click OK and iPhoto will start creating your Web pages.

After iPhoto is finished, you can check out what you and iPhoto created. In the Finder, navigate to the folder where you created your Web page and you should find the following items:

- A folder named Images, which contains each of your photos, scaled as you specified in the Image area and numbered starting from zero (0). If you specified a background image in the Page area, it will be numbered 99999 and will be converted to a JPEG.

- A file, index.html, that is the first page of your photo album.

- Files named Page1.html, Page2.html, etc. These are the additional pages iPhoto generates each time your thumbnail array fills up. The file, Page1.html, corresponds to the Page 2 link on your Web pages. Page2.html corresponds to Page 3, and so forth.

- A folder named Pages, which contains the HTML files a browser will load when your visitor clicks on a thumbnail. These files are named Image0.html, Image1.html, and so forth, corresponding to the photos in the Images folder.

- A folder named Thumbnails, which contains numbered JPEG files: 0.jpg, 1.jpg, 2.jpg, and so on, corresponding to the photos in the Images folder. The various Page.html files display these thumbnails.

Tip You can now preview your work by opening the index.html file with your browser.

A (Very) Brief Overview of iPhoto's HTML

We're not going to teach you how to create pages from scratch or do anything fancy with Java or JavaScript. What we are going to do is show you the HTML of a typical iPhoto-generated Web page and what the various *tags* (HTML directives) and *attributes* (tag options) mean.

With a plain text editor such as BBEdit or TextEdit (if you turn off Rich Text) you can edit these files, changing the appearance, or adding functionality. Dennis uses BBEdit (www.barebones.com), which comes with excellent HTML reference material. If you're a more visual sort, you could load the page into a graphical page editor, such as Freeway (www.softpress.com) or WebDesign (www.ragesw.com) to make your changes. If you check Version Tracker for HTML editors, you'll find a large number available, many of them freeware or shareware. If you own Microsoft Word X, you can even do your page editing with it if you click the Save only display information radio button in Word's Save As Web Page dialog box (also with AppleWorks, but its HTML support isn't nearly as complete).

The following HTML was generated by iPhoto:

```
<!DOCTYPE HTML PUBLIC "-//W3C//DTD HTML 4.01 Transitional//EN">
<html>
 <head>
  <meta http-equiv="Content-Type" content="text/html; charset=utf-8">
  <title>
  Spenser &amp; Maggie
  </title>
 </head>
 <body background="Images/99999.jpg">
  <h2 align="center">
  Spenser &amp; Maggie
  </h2>
  <a href="index.html">
  Page 1
  </a>
   | 
  Page 2
  <table cellspacing="2" width="100%" cellpadding="2">
   <tr>
    <td align="center" width="50%">
     <a href="Pages/Image8.html">
      <img src="Thumbnails/8.jpg" alt="Spenser" width="240" height="160">
     </a>
     <br>Spenser
    </td>
    <td align="center" width="50%">
```

```
        <a href="Pages/Image9.html">
          <img src="Thumbnails/9.jpg" alt="Twosome" width="239" height="180">
        </a>
        <br>Twosome
      </td>
    </tr>
  </table>
 </body>
</html>
```

HTML tags are enclosed in angle brackets (< and >) and the values assigned to attributes are enclosed in double quotes.

Most tags consist of a start tag and an end tag. The end tag will be a slash (/) followed by the start tag's name. Some tags, those that don't apply to a block of data, such as insert a horizontal line (`<hr>`), insert a line break (`<br>`), or display this picture (`<img>`), don't take an end tag.

The first line is a comment, specifying what HTML revision is being used for the document, in this case 4.01. The next line, `<html>`, signifies the beginning of the HTML, describing the page a browser should render. The lines between `<head>` and `</head>` (start and end of header information), include the title for the page and any metainformation that might be of interest to browsers or search engines.

The actual page contents start with the `<body>` line and end with the `</body>` line. The body line tells the browser to find a background image named `99999.jpg` in the Images subdirectory of the directory holding the page's HTML file.

The page's heading, Spenser & Maggie, is to be centered horizontally and displayed in the second largest heading style. Certain characters, such as the ampersand, have special meaning in HTML and must be described with a name, in this case `&amp;`.

The next tag, called an *anchor* tag, tells the browser that Page 1 is a link and that, when clicked, the file `index.html` should be loaded.

At this point, iPhoto generated an HTML table, each cell of which contains a thumbnail. The `cellspacing="2"` attribute tells the browser to keep a 2-pixel border around each cell and `cellpadding="2"` says to keep a 2-pixel margin between the cell's border and the cell's contents. The `width="100%"` attribute tells the browser to fill the window horizontally with the table.

The `<tr>` tag tells the browser that a new row is starting. The table datum (`<td>`) or cell tag tells the browser that the enclosed information should be placed in a table cell and that it should be centered, with the cell's width being 50 percent of the table's width. The anchor tag surrounding the image (`img`) tag tells the browser that the thumbnail specified in the `img` tag is a hyperlink and which page to load when the link is clicked.

Now, all you have to do is upload them to your Web server (even the Sites folder on your iDisk), which will probably involve using an FTP client like Interarchy or Fetch. Since each Web server is a bit different, get the particulars for your situation from your ISP. Alternatively, if you have a relatively fast, always-on Internet connection, such as a cable modem or DSL, you could use OS X's built-in Web Sharing, as follows:

1. Make certain that you have the pages in your Sites folder hierarchy.
2. Open System Preferences and select the Sharing Preferences pane.
3. Turn on Web Sharing by clicking its Start button.

   Write down the IP address that appears under Network Identity. This is the first part of the URL people will need to enter in order that they might access your Web pages.

4. Assuming that the IP address in Step 3 was 10.10.10.1, that the pages are in a folder named MyPages, and that your short login ID is drc (that's Dennis's), you can let folks know that your new pages are available at `http://10.10.10.1/~drc/MyPages/`. Make sure they don't forget that last /.

iPhoto's HTML is straightforward and the pages it generates aren't very fancy. If you're accustomed to editing HTML, you can add all sorts of bells and whistles to the pages iPhoto generates. Fortunately, iPhoto is extensible via plug-ins, as we discuss later in this chapter (see the "Plugging in to iPhoto" section) and there is a very nice, free plug-in named BetterHTMLExport (`www.droolingcat.com`) that adds a Better Web Page tab to the Export Images dialog for those of you who want something a little nicer but don't want to soil your hands actually editing the HTML.

Using an External Program for Photo Editing

iPhoto's editing tools are quite minimal. You can crop, adjust brightness and contrast, convert a color picture to black-and-white, and eliminate red-eye. After that, your editing toolbox is empty.

There is a wide variety of image editing applications you might use. For example, many desktop Macs come with licenses for Lemke Software's shareware GraphicConverter (`www.lemkesoft.com`) and Caffeine Software's free PixelNHance (`www.caffeinesoft.com`). Although Dennis considers GraphicConverter the best $35 he ever spent on software, the royal flush of photo editing programs is Adobe's Photoshop (version 7 is OS X-native), at almost 20 times the price of GraphicConverter. Photoshop Elements 2.0, at a list price of $99 is another excellent bargain, giving you all but the very high-end Photoshop features in an affordable package. Another very powerful and interesting image editor is TIFFany3, also from Caffeine Software.

As you learned in the "Setting iPhoto Preferences" section in Chapter 8, you can tell iPhoto to send images to another application when you double-click the thumbnail. Using Photoshop or another external editor enables you to perform such tasks as removing scratches, eliminating shadows, adding distortions, correcting color, sharpening blurry edges (we told you to use a tripod), and adding objects to your image. In short, you can do (almost) all the cool things you see people do with computer editing software on TV shows (such as *24, The Agency,* and so forth) and in the movies (although not as easily as these fictional characters do it).

If you're asking, "Why can't I just drag the thumbnail to the application icon of any editor I want?" the answer is, "You can, but then iPhoto won't know about the changes, won't update the thumbnail and, if you hadn't edited it previously in iPhoto, you won't be able to Revert to Original."

One of the nicest things about designating an external program as your editor for double-clicked photos is that you still have Edit mode for when iPhoto's tools suffice. Additionally, if you press Option while double-clicking, iPhoto reverses the precedence and uses its own editing tools.

Plugging in to iPhoto

iPhoto, like iTunes, iMovie, and iDVD, provides a lot of functionality in a simple, straightforward interface. But Apple realizes that a significant minority of their users are going to want more, or slightly different, functionality than the basic program provides. Back in 1986, Apple introduced HyperCard and, realizing that people were going to want to do more with it than was possible out of the box, they included the XCMD interface so that users could extend HyperCard's power and flexibility. The plug-ins you see for today's Web browsers that enable you to view PDF files and Flash animations or watch QuickTime movies on a Web page perform the same function. Apple provides a similar plug-in architecture for iPhoto.

Think of iPhoto as the software equivalent of an iMac. Other than hooking up a printer (or, obviously, temporarily connecting their digital camera), most people rarely add anything to their iMac's hardware configuration. However, USB and FireWire ports are present so that you can plug in scanners, floppy disk drives, Zip drives, and a myriad of other devices. Any one of these would make the iMac larger and more expensive for everyone if they were part of the standard package. Most people will never add anything to their basic iPhoto configuration, but if you want to do so, the capability is present via the plug-in architecture.

At the time we're writing this, iPhoto is still relatively new and, since it does so much so well, only a few plug-ins have appeared. Here are some that we like a lot:

✦ **BetterHTMLExport** (www.droolingcat.com) significantly outshines iPhoto's basic Web Page export, adding the following features:

- Not just titles, but also comments on both the thumbnail pages and the image pages
- Previous and Next links on the image pages so that your visitors don't have to return to the thumbnail page to view another full-size image

- Optional links on each thumbnail and image page so that you can easily integrate your photo album into a larger Web site
- The option of exporting the original image rather than a scaled-down JPEG
- Navigation link placement placed under your control rather than fixed to the top-left of each thumbnail page
- A templates mechanism, allowing you to design an overall "look" for your pages (A few examples are included with the software.)

✦ **iPhoto Toast Export Plug-in** (www.elgato.com) adds something that we were amazed to see missing from iPhoto — the ability to burn CDs directly from the application, just as you can burn CDs from iTunes.

Admittedly, this plug-in requires Toast Titanium, but as we frequently mention, Roxio's Toast Titanium is one piece of software we both think you should own if you're planning to burn many discs.

✦ **iPhoto to OmniGraffle Album Export** (www.omnigroup.com) lets you export photos directly from iPhoto into OmniGraffle albums.

OmniGraffle is an excellent diagramming tool, great for laying out organization charts, family trees, and timelines.

iPhoto, like most Mac OS X applications, is really a folder masquerading as a single application file. If you control-click the iPhoto icon (in the Finder), one of the contextual menu options is Show Package Contents. Choosing this opens the disguised folder in a new Finder window and you can now burrow down to see all the folders and files that make up your application. One of the folders in iPhoto's Contents folder is named PlugIns and is the repository for both the plug-ins that came with iPhoto and any you add.

Obviously, adding plug-ins by digging into the application package is somewhat less than elegant and not what one expects from Apple. Rest assured, Apple has provided an easier way to add (and remove) plug-ins:

Note

In Mac OS X, 10.2, Apple changed the menu item from Show Info to Get Info. They also eliminated the popup menu, going to expandable panes at the bottom of the dialog box instead. We're using the 10.1 terminology and dialog box here. If you're running 10.2, adjust accordingly.

1. With iPhoto not running, select the iPhoto icon in the Finder and choose File ➪ Show Info (⌘-I) or control-click the iPhoto icon and choose Show Info from the contextual menu.

2. In the iPhoto Info window, choose Plugins from the pop-up menu as shown in Figure 10-7. (It's the Plug-ins section in OS X, 10.2.)

The currently installed plug-ins appear. The default installation of plug-ins is shown in Figure 10-8.

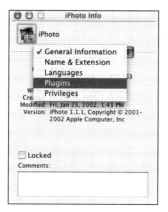

Figure 10-7: Select the Show Info dialog's Plugins pane.

Figure 10-8: iPhoto's preinstalled plug-ins collection.

3. Click the Add button.

   An Open-style dialog named Add appears. Navigate to the folder for the plug-in you want to install, as shown in Figure 10-9 and click Choose.

   Your plug-in is now installed, as shown in Figure 10-10.

 Sometimes, the plug-in doesn't show up right away in the list and you have to close the iPhoto Info window, reopen it, and choose Plugins again. Hopefully, this bug will be fixed by the time you read this material.

The next time you choose File ⇨ Export (⌘-E) or click Share mode's Export button, you'll see your plug-in as yet another tab in the Export Images dialog box, as shown in Figure 10-11.

Figure 10-9: Find the plug-in you want installed.

Figure 10-10: Your newly installed plug-in has joined the club.

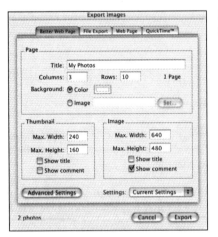

Figure 10-11: The new plug-in's tab shows up in the Export Images dialog box.

We used BetterHTMLExport as our example. At first glance, you might not notice much difference between the Web Page tab that iPhoto provides and the Better Web Page tab. There are two new "Show comment" check boxes, an Advanced Settings button, and a Current Settings pop-up list. Clicking the Advanced Settings button exposes a lot of new functionality, as shown in Figure 10-12.

Figure 10-12: The Better Web Page's Advanced Settings sheet gives you a lot of options.

Removing a plug-in is just as easy. Select it in the list and click the Remove button. You can also disable a plug-in by clearing the check box next to its name. This eliminates its tab in iPhoto, but leaves it installed if you might want to use it at a later date.

Since we expect that more plug-ins will appear as iPhoto gains wider usage, the Export Images dialog box is going to get really crowded. Disabling a few plug-ins that you use only occasionally, without having to remove and later reinstall them, is a great way to simplify the row of tabs you'll see in the Export Images dialog box.

Summary

In this chapter you saw how to export your files, slide shows, and Web pages. You also learned some advantages of using a dedicated graphics editing program with iPhoto. Finally, you learned how to extend iPhoto's capabilities with plug-ins and reviewed a few of the currently available plug-ins.

✦ ✦ ✦

More iPhoto Tips, Tricks, and Techniques

CHAPTER 11

✦ ✦ ✦ ✦

In This Chapter

Inside an iPhoto Library

Managing your iPhoto Library

Taking better pictures

✦ ✦ ✦ ✦

We managed to use up most of our iPhoto keyboard shortcut tips in the last two chapters, but that's okay. The really good iPhoto tips involve planning, preparation, and organization. In fact, some of them don't even require iPhoto — they revolve around shooting the best shots you can, which will, in turn, give you something really good to work with in iPhoto.

In addition to these basic tips on taking snapshots, in this chapter we delve into how iPhoto stores and organizes your collection of digital images.

Inside an iPhoto Library

At heart, iPhoto is a database for pictures, with special tools for displaying, editing, printing, and sharing its contents. In fact, it is a relational database in which album files contain pointers into the *central store* (main database), thus eliminating redundant copies of those wonderful snapshots you want included in multiple albums. Further, the central store is divided into multiple files in nested folders, with the actual pictures stored four levels deep.

Figure 11-1 shows one of Dennis's iPhoto databases, in a Finder list view. You can see that the actual pictures are in a numbered folder, within another numbered folder, inside yet another numbered folder at the iPhoto Library folder's top level. This top-level numbered folder is the year. Within a year folder are numbered folders corresponding to months. Inside those are numbered folders for the days of the month, where you will find your pictures along with a few more folders. iPhoto uses the creation date for pictures you add from the Finder and the camera-supplied date data to distribute camera-imported pictures into the various folders.

Figure 11-1: iPhoto organizes your photos by year, month, and day.

Caution   Do not, under any circumstances, move, rename, or otherwise mess with the files and organization in your iPhoto Library hierarchy. We're presenting this information for two reasons: So you can write AppleScripts that will copy pictures and albums into other applications, since iPhoto is not yet scriptable; and so that you will have an understanding of what iPhoto is doing behind the scenes — knowledge is power. If you do abuse that power, don't hold us responsible — you have been warned!

Nestled in a day-of-month folder with your pictures are a few folders, as follows:

✦ **Thumbs** contains thumbnail images of your various pictures, but you won't recognize them from their names. All you'll see for names are a number (followed by a .jpg extension if you've set your Finder preferences to show filename extensions).

When iPhoto first appeared, you couldn't name your pictures. iPhoto assigned them sequential numbers and that was that. Internally, iPhoto still assigns the pictures numbers and that's how it deals with them, the names are just for your benefit.

✦ **Data** is where iPhoto stores the information about what you've named the photos as well as other attributes, such as whether the photo has been rotated, edited, and so forth.

✦ **Originals** might or might not be present. If you have edited any of the photos in this day's folder, you'll see an Originals folder and it will contain the (surprise) original, preediting, image. This is how iPhoto lets you revert to original if you don't like the editing you've done, by keeping a spare copy available. The downside is the extra disk space consumed keeping that copy around.

Located with your year folders at the top of your iPhoto Library hierarchy is the Albums folder. Nestled snugly within the Albums folder you'll find more folders, each bearing the name of one of your iPhoto albums and accompanied by a data file of the same name with `-data` appended. The folders contain aliases to each of the album's photos, and the data files tell iPhoto how they're arranged and other album-specific information, such as any book theme settings or slideshow settings.

Also at the iPhoto Library's top-level are three more files: Dir.data, Library.data, and Library.cache, which iPhoto uses to manage your photo collection and load your Library.

Managing Your iPhoto Library

You've undoubtedly noticed by now that for all iPhoto's wonderful features and ease-of-use, iPhoto doesn't count speedy performance among its attributes. As your iPhoto Library grows, iPhoto gets even slower. Lots of memory, a fast hard disk, and a speedy processor all help, but only to a point. The main thing you can do to minimize your wait time is to cull photos from your Library when you're done with them. Back them off to Zip or CD and eliminate them from the Library. Chapter 12, "Enhancing Your iPhoto Experience," lists some software (and hardware) you can use to help keep your Library's size under control.

Unless you have a superb memory, your Library will rapidly grow to the point where you'll have trouble remembering just where that special photograph is located. As we noted in the "Searching Your Photo Library" section in Chapter 9, naming and adding comments to your photos when you import them will save you scads of time later on. Although Keywords are convenient, all they do is categorize your photos into (up to) 14 categories. By all means, apply keywords to your photos if you wish, but the real strength of iPhoto's searching comes from setting your iPhoto Assign/Search uses preference to Comments when you're trying to find something. Not only will it find keywords, it will find matches on the title or any text in the Comments fields.

Note Okay, so the previous paragraph repeats information from Chapter 9. Some tips bear repeating and this is one we think falls into that category.

Taking Better Pictures

This topic could easily fill a book of its own, and it has, many times over. We even recommend few good books for your consideration in Chapter 12, "Enhancing Your iPhoto Experience."

We're not going to challenge those tomes, but we are going to cover a few basics that will get you off on the right foot (or the left, if you're a southpaw).

Photo composition

Unless you're just clicking the button, most photos you take will have a subject. That subject will often be surrounded with extraneous items, called the background. How you position your subject relative to the background and how you take advantage of the background to focus attention on your subject is part of the art of composition.

Split things into thirds

Contrary to what you might think, the exact center of a picture is seldom the right place for your subject. Think of your picture as a tic-tac-toe board, divided into thirds both horizontally and vertically. When you have, for example, a portrait shot, try to position your subject's eye line on the line separating the upper and middle thirds. As you can see in Figures 11-2 and 11-3, positioning the subject's face in a landscape shot at the intersection points (Figure 11-2) is very effective in making their face the eye-catcher. Alternatively (Figure 11-3), positioning the subject in the exact center of the frame reduces the impact and allows background items to capture your viewers' attention.

Figure 11-2: Dividing lines and intersection points provide good positioning for your subjects.

Figure 11-3: Unless it's a close-up, your subject can disappear if centered in the frame.

Don't let the background overwhelm your subject

The more objects in your photograph, the more likely that your subject will fade into the background. Don't distract your viewer with nonessentials.

Some things to avoid (besides somebody holding up two fingers behind your subject's head) are poles, wires, signs and signposts, tree trunks, and fence lines. We all have a tendency toward tunnel vision when framing a shot in our viewfinder. Making an effort to check the edges and corners for these distractions is a good habit to acquire. The closer to your subject these objects are, the clearer and more distracting they'll be. Figure 11-4 is a good example of bad positioning because the base of the fan on the left distracts the viewer's eye from the subject.

Figure 11-4: The base of that fan distracts the viewer's eye.

Ideally, your background should be composed of soft tones and indistinct shapes. The subtler it is, the more your subject will stand out and the better your picture will be.

How close can you get?

Until the edges of the picture start lopping off parts of your subject, you can probably get closer and take a better picture. Figure 11-5 shows a close-up on the left and a more distant shot on the right, showing clearly how much more compelling a close-up is.

(a)   (b)

Figure 11-5: A close-up of Maggie (a); a less effective shot taken from a few feet further away (b).

 Getting up close has a beneficial side effect. Since you have less wasted background to crop out, you have a higher effective resolution and you'll get better prints when you print them, send them off to Kodak, or include them in your coffee-table book.

Let's look at things another way

The angle at which you take your photos can have tremendous impact. If you were to take a photo of Shaquille O'Neal from ground level, you'd be emphasizing his height in a way that just wouldn't come across if you stood on a chair to shoot him at eye-level.

Conversely, if you're trying to give a clear picture of a football play, you're well-advised to shoot it from an elevated position, say a press box. Those "blimp" shots you see during Bowl Game telecasts have impact for just this reason.

Take pictures of a stationary subject from as many perspectives as possible. We will bet that the results surprise you and that your favorites will come from nontraditional angles.

Make use of your camera's capabilities

If you own something a little better than a simple point-and-shoot digital camera, you could well have the tools to take stop-action shots and create some other special effects that we'll describe in the next few paragraphs.

Freeze that shot

The secret to getting a good stop-action photo is being able to control your shutter speed and your lens aperture. The shutter has to open and close very quickly to freeze the action. However, if the shutter isn't open for very long, less light gets in and you're likely to end up with a dark picture. That's why you want the aperture larger than normal — to get the same amount of light in that you would with a slower shutter speed.

How you achieve this feat, assuming that your camera even supports it, varies from camera to camera. Some call it *shutter priority mode*, others call it *time value* and you can find them on a switch or dial. With others, you have to hunt through the camera's menu system to find your feature.

In any case, turn on shutter priority mode and set your shutter speed to a very short time, like a millisecond (1/1000th of a second) and let the camera take care of adjusting the aperture.

Make your subject stand out

Backgrounds should be just that, something subtle that accentuates your subject. In most professional photos the backgrounds are indistinct and sometimes even hazy. You, too, can achieve this effect by controlling the focus and aperture. Use your optical zoom to make your subject stand out more and, if you have a manual aperture control, use a large opening (like f-2.8) while focusing on your subject. Additionally, the further you can separate your subject from the background, the better.

Avoid the flash

Natural lighting is best, but failing that, you should try to use lighting that is slightly away from the camera. Not only will the flash occasionally result in red-eye, but you have no control over shadowing. By positioning lights at different angles, you can eliminate shadows created by facial features and uneven surfaces.

Bob often tapes a small piece of white cardboard to the left or right of the flash on his camera to achieve different types of flash lighting effects. It's low tech but changing the amount and angle of flash can make a huge difference in a shot. Give it a try.

Summary

In this chapter, you learned how iPhoto stores your pictures, that large libraries can force iPhoto to a crawl, and that even just a few techniques can help you take better pictures.

✦ ✦ ✦

Enhancing Your iPhoto Experience

In This Chapter

Hardware purchases to consider

Software acquisitions to consider

There's an old saying that goes, "a picture is worth a thousand words." We disagree. We'd say, "a good picture is worth much more than a thousand words; a lousy picture is worth much less."

Creating a good digital picture is the result of many things: good equipment, good software, good technique, and good subject matter are paramount among those. We can't help you with the last of these, nor can we help much with technique.

Note If you're interested in learning more, try the *Digital Photography Handbook* by Mark Chambers (Wiley Publishing, Inc.), a handy guide to digital photography technique. It's somewhat biased toward Hewlett-Packard equipment, but still covers style, composition, and technique nicely.

You're starting with good equipment and software — a Mac, Mac OS X, and iPhoto. But even a Mac running OS X and iPhoto can't make a silk purse out of a sow's ear. Fortunately, there are accessories for your camera that may help you capture better pictures in the first place. And, there is also hardware and software that can help iPhoto produce great results from your photos.

Hardware to Consider

Some of the items we're going to suggest might seem like "no-brainers"—items you'd expect to buy (like a digital camera or a color printer), but we're going to tell you some of the things you should be considering when you make that purchase. Other items might not be so obvious, at least until we mention them.

Digital camera

Although iPhoto will work with most digital images, such as scanned photos (see the "Scanner" section later in this chapter) or photos imported from a Kodak PictureCD, for example, a compatible digital camera and iPhoto make a dynamite combination. You can import your photos, erase the camera's memory (or stick in another memory card) and just keep shooting.

Most digital cameras have LCD screens that show you what your picture looks like right after you take it. That means no more waiting until they're developed to see whether you got the shot. If you don't like the Grand Canyon shot you just took, erase it and take another. If you chopped your husband's head off at the hairline, just do it over (unless that's what you *really* wanted to do).

We covered resolutions, aspect ratios, battery life, and memory capacity in the "Choosing a Digital Camera" section in Chapter 8, "Introducing iPhoto." There are additional factors to consider, though, in choosing a digital camera, just as when you purchase a film camera.

- ✦ A camera's weight, size, and shape will impact how willing you are to carry it around and have it available when those interesting shots appear. If it's too bulky or too heavy, you won't be able to carry it around in your shirt or coat pocket. Too small, and you'll have problems using it comfortably as you contort your fingers to click the shutter release without blocking the flash or lens.

- ✦ Don't be misled by digital zoom features. All digital zoom does is enlarge the pixels, resulting in a lower effective resolution. Optical zoom, on the other hand, is like a magnifying glass. You get your magnified image without losing resolution.

- ✦ Assuming that you're willing to put up with a little extra size, an LCD flip screen can be a great boon. By angling the screen, you can hold the camera down low or up high and still see what's framed in your shot. You can even position it to see yourself in the shot, for those self-portrait efforts.

- ✦ Manual controls get you out of the digital Instamatic equivalent's world and into that of professional Nikons and Leicas. The big three features here all deal with *aperture* (how wide the shutter opens when you take a shot) and *shutter speed* (how fast the shutter opens and closes):
    - Aperture priority mode lets you control aperture.
    - Shutter priority mode lets you control shutter speed.
    - Manual mode lets you adjust aperture and shutter speed independently.

- ✦ Some cameras offer you the digital equivalent of different film speeds. You can choose a faster film speed, often labeled ISO, such as 200 or 400, when you are working with more light. Doubling the ISO rating (say from 100 to 200) means that you can get the same exposure with one less F-stop on the lens.

- Burst mode lets you operate like the fashion photographers you see in movies and on TV, snapping picture after picture as if the camera were a machine gun. When you take multiple photos rapidly, you can choose the best of many similar shots as your final effort. The trick here is to get a camera with a large memory buffer, because memory cards are s-l-o-w. There is no way to write the data to a SmartMedia or CompactFlash card fast enough to keep up—the data has to be stored in the camera's fast RAM and downloaded to the memory card as time permits.

- The last two features we'll mention, sliding lens covers and attachable lenses/filters, are pretty much mutually exclusive.

  Detachable lens covers are a royal pain. More than one professional, to say nothing of legions of hobbyists, have snapped pictures while forgetting to remove the lens cap. And, when you do remove the lens cap, it frequently gets lost or, if attached by a cord, flops around getting in the way. This makes the automatic, sliding lens cover integral to most point-and-shoot models quite attractive.

  Attachable lenses and filters, on the other hand, typically have to be threaded onto your camera. The finer the threads, the harder it is to attach things and the easier it is to mess up the threads. However, having the capability to use a telephoto or wide-angle lens or attach various lens filters lets you take a wider variety of pictures under varying conditions. See the "Lenses and filters" section later in this chapter.

All the major camera manufacturers (Sony, Nikon, Canon, Leica, Minolta, Olympus, etc.), as well as a plethora of companies that you might not ordinarily associate with cameras (Hewlett-Packard, Epson, Logitech, and Toshiba), are competing for your digital camera business. Every year, more and more powerful and feature-rich digital cameras become available at the same or lower prices as the previous year's models. Like buying a computer, figure out how much you need, add a little bit more for growth, close your eyes, and dive on in. If you're waiting for the absolute best deal, you'll never actually *buy* a camera because something better is always coming along and the price (at least on existing models) is always coming down.

Scanner

Until Apple shipped OS X, 10.2 (Jaguar), scanners were the forgotten stepchildren in the Mac's family of supported hardware. Now, with Image Capture recognizing USB-connected scanners, you can easily connect compatible scanners and scan in your loose photos.

Epson, Hewlett-Packard, UMAX, Canon, and many other companies offer a wide variety of scanners, ranging in price from well under $100 to over $1000. You probably won't need anything more than 300 dpi resolution to scan your photos for use with iPhoto. After all, at 300 dpi, a 4×6 print is 1200×1800 resolution (2.2 megapixels, the way Kodak advertises their DX3500 and DX3600 models). Since even most inexpensive scanners will give 600 dpi or better resolution, even a wallet-size photo (2×3) can be treated like a 2-or-more-megapixel image, and that means you'll get a good print even when blown up to 8×10.

The major thing to look for in a scanner is its *optical resolution*, which is the resolution at which it really scans. The *interpolated resolution* is the scanner's equivalent of a camera's digital zoom — the scanner approximates the pixels in between the ones it actually scans. With scanners under $100, like the Epson Perfection 1250U, providing 1200×2400 dpi optical resolution, your scanning needs can be satisfied at budget prices.

If you're interested, that Epson 1250U has an interpolated resolution of 9600 dpi.

Be aware that the higher you set the scanning resolution, the more disk space your image will consume. A 4×6 photo scanned at 1200 dpi can require dozens of megabytes, depending upon the bit-depth (i.e., the number of colors).

Another feature to look for when purchasing in a scanner is a *slide adapter*, a small case for holding photographic slides. If you have a collection of slides from your film camera days, this attachment is a must, assuming you want to digitize your collection. A slide adapter works by projecting the scanner's light through the adapter, off the internal mirror, and then through the slide — in short, you are using your scanner and the adapter as a slide projector so that the slide's image will appear to the scanner as if it were reading a piece of paper.

Burning drive

Yes, we're pounding this point home again. Digital photos take up a lot of disk space. Your iPhoto Library is going to get really large and slow iPhoto down. Eventually, you're going to want to remove old photos from iPhoto, but you probably don't want to consign them to the bit-bucket (a digital wastebasket). After all, they're memories and you might want to look at them again some day — maybe to embarrass your kids when their teenage friends drop by.

Backing your digital photos up to CD or DVD is a compact and convenient archival method and allows you to free up the space they used. To accomplish this, though, requires a CD or DVD burner. Most Macs come with one these days, but if yours doesn't, you might consider getting an external burner.

We recommend that you avoid USB burners — they're very slow and not that much less expensive than the much faster FireWire drives we see for $175 and up.

Tripods

Have you ever noticed that when professional photographers set up a studio shot or just about any other posed photo, their camera is on a tripod? There's a reason for that — it stabilizes the camera so that nothing, including you clicking the shutter release, moves the camera or blurs the photo. The camera's shutter isn't open very long, but if the camera moves while it's open, a blurred (or worse) shot will result.

The standard rule for tripods is based on use with a 35mm camera. The rule states that you need to use a tripod any time the shutter speed is slower than the reciprocal of the lens focal-length (in inches). Thus, if the lens focal length were 5 inches, you would need a 1/5 second shutter speed. Most digital cameras have lenses equivalent to a 35mm film camera, so the rule applies.

This rule has a couple of addenda. One is that you should use a tripod whenever it is dark. The other is that you should use a tripod whenever you plan to have enlargements made. (Enlarging an image exaggerates any camera jitter effect.)

You'll find literally dozens of tripod brands and sizes available. Although you'll probably find your best prices on the Internet, buying a tripod without handling it is an iffy proposition. Knowing how much they weigh and how easily they are to set up and break down is critical. If the tripod is awkward to use or carry, you won't use it and then it's just money down the sewer.

 A mini tripod is also a handy accessory. Dennis keeps one to use with indoor shots where he can set it on a counter or table.

When you look at tripods, consider how small they are collapsed and how tall they are when extended. A tripod that extends to only 45" is probably going to be very uncomfortable for most adults to use (unless you have a flip-out LCD on your camera). Dennis is only 5'5" and finds any tripod shorter than 58" uncomfortable to use from a standing position. You should also consider the degrees of flexibility in the tripod's *pan head*, the little swivel stand to which you attach your camera. For example, if the pan head will rotate on all three axes, you can get portrait orientation shots in addition to panning horizontally and vertically.

Lenses and filters

You've probably all encountered the terms *wide angle lens* and *telephoto lens*. What these terms reference is the angle captured when you take a photo. For a typical 35mm camera, you have a standard focal length of 50mm, as shown in Figure 12-1. This approximates the 46-degree angle subtended by the human eye.

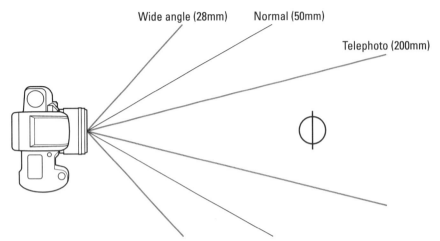

Figure 12-1: The human eye and a standard lens capture a 46-degree field of view.

A wide-angle 35mm lens has a focal length between 24mm and 35mm, and a telephoto lens has a focal length between 80mm and 300mm. One way to think of this is as zooming in (telephoto) and zooming out (wide-angle).

Focal lengths less than 20mm are called *super wide angle* and those greater than 300mm are called *super telephoto*.

If your camera supports attachable lenses and filters, you'll be able to take much better long-distance and close-up shots using telephoto and wide-angle lenses than using your camera's zoom feature — particularly if it is a digital zoom. Many digital cameras experience *barrel distortion* when shooting wide-angle shots using their zoom capabilities. A shot shows barrel distortion when the image center is spherized (rounded). For those of you who have used Photoshop or Photoshop Elements, the Spherize Filter produces the same effect.

Filters are used to, well, filter certain wavelengths of light entering your lens or to change the angle at which the light enters. For example, you can filter ultraviolet light with a UV filter and reduce haziness. Similarly, a neutral density filter would be used in bright to very bright conditions, in effect, becoming sunglasses for your camera. A polarization filter changes the angle of light, reducing glare. This makes polarization filters especially useful on sunny days in the snow or at the beach.

Color printer

This is another recommendation in the of-course category. If you never want a printed copy of your photos (or if you send them all off to Kodak for professional printing), the color printer won't be necessary. However, we print a lot of our photos out, even if just in contact sheets. We also use our photos in other documents, such as letters written in AppleWorks or Word, and Kodak doesn't print those.

Nor do they print the greeting card formats iPhoto offers. (Personalized birthday cards are great.)

What do you look for in a color printer?

Obviously price is one consideration. The initial cost of a color inkjet can be very deceiving, though. As we mentioned in Chapter 9, "Getting Started with iPhoto," the consumables are where the printer manufacturers make the money. Somehow, it just feels odd to spend $40 ($20 each for the black and color cartridges) every couple of weeks to refill a printer that only cost $79 to begin with, but if you're using the printer to print photos, it's not that bad a deal.

Consider that, at high quality on glossy photo paper, you get approximately 30 prints per cartridge at 8×10, with each cartridge costing about $20. With glossy photo paper costing between 50 cents and a dollar a sheet, an 8×10 ends up costing less than $2 (closer to $1.50, actually). This beats by quite a bit the $3.99 plus tax and shipping that you'd pay to have Kodak do the job (less than half-price).

Another consideration is color fidelity and print quality. Although most of the better color inkjets (Epson, H-P, LexMark, and Canon) print good photos with their standard four-color printers, the six-color printers produce better, crisper prints. Some of these printers require replacing the entire cartridge when one color runs out, some of the newer printers have separate cartridges for each color. Adding up the costs of the individual color cartridges will result in a higher price than that of one of the combined color cartridges, making this an unattractive alternative if your photos tend to deplete all colors somewhat evenly. However, if you tend to empty one inkwell faster than the others (maybe you use a lot of blue printing ocean and sky), the separate cartridge approach can be quite attractive. You need to analyze your usage to determine which printer style suits you best.

Another consideration might be whether the printer supports wide format printing. If you plan to produce many large prints, a wide printer can come in really handy. Dennis has a couple of 11×17 prints that he really likes from an Epson 1200.

Remember, there's no right printer for everyone. Pick the features you want and see what you can find with those features in your price range.

Software Acquisitions to Consider

iPhoto does most things really well, but there are a few gaps in its feature set. For example, it is the only one of the four major iApps that doesn't have a burn-to-disk feature. Although the 1.1.1 upgrade added Comments and user-assigned names for your photos, iPhoto still isn't a full-featured image database. Similarly, as we discussed in the "Using an External Program for Photo Editing" section in Chapter 10, iPhoto's image-editing tools are good but minimal. Additionally, iPhoto can really slow down when your Photo Library gets large. All of these shortcomings can be addressed with various software products, while still letting you take advantage of iPhoto's many best-of-breed features.

Toast 5 Titanium

Roxio's ever-valuable product, Toast 5 Titanium, is once again number one on our recommendation list. With the addition of the iPhoto 1.1.1 Toast Export plug-in (see the "Plugging into iPhoto" section in Chapter 10) you have a quick and easy method of archiving photos and albums.

One of the programs that comes with Toast is iView Media, a powerful image database application, which we'll be covering in our next recommendation.

A great feature of Toast, though, is that you can use it to burn VideoCDs, discs that play in most set top DVD players, and provide VHS-quality video. You can drag any QuickTime movie, such as an exported slide show, onto Toast's VideoCD window and it will convert the movie to a VCD-compatible MPEG-1 file, all ready to be burned and enjoyed on your TV set. Using inexpensive CD-R media, you can share slide shows of your kids with their grandparents, of your vacation with friends and relatives, or your presentation with customers or coworkers.

iView Media/iView MediaPro

iView Media is an organizational tool for images, movies, sounds, fonts, and other media files (including Web pages, AppleWorks documents, and many page layout documents). You import media into a *catalog*, iView's term for a multimedia database, as shown in Figure 12-2. iView only imports disk files, it doesn't recognize attached cameras or scanners unless you upgrade to the iView MediaPro product.

Note iView MediaPro adds one nice option in its Import from Camera dialog box: embedding a ColorSync profile into each image. ColorSync profiles make color-matching from screen to printer accurate.

With iView Media or MediaPro, you can archive your photos on CD, freeing up disk space, and when you want to access them, the program will tell you which CD to insert. From here on, we're just going to write "the iView programs" when we mean either Media or Media Pro.

iPhoto's Comments feature is nice, but the iView programs support IPTC (International Press and Telecommunications Council) tags, a standard for annotating news data and graphic files, as well as recorded voice annotations, and 16 user-defined fields.

Figure 12-2: The iView catalog is like the iPhoto Library (on steroids).

iView's Slide Shows are more flexible than iPhoto's. You can set differing durations and transitions for individual slides, a feature unavailable in iPhoto.

When you create Web pages from your iView catalog, you have a template-driven exporter at your command, similar to those offered by the BetterHTMLExport plug-in (see the "Plugging in to iPhoto" section in Chapter 10) from Drooling Cat.

iView also has a built-in Backup utility for use with removable disks, such as the Zip, or onto CD-R media using Toast or OS X's built-in Disc Burner.

They're still not Photoshop, but the iView programs offer Sharpness; Hue Saturation & Lightness; Color Correction; and Invert (essentially creating a negative from a positive, or vice versa) tools to those available in iPhoto but don't include Red-Eye correction. In addition to Revert to Original, the iView programs have a Version Control feature, letting you go back to any earlier saved version of an image.

If you're willing to forsake iPhoto's easy printing interface and deal with all the issues yourself, the iView programs offer template-driven printing, which will let you define and print not just greeting cards, but CD jewel cases, Zip cases, and so forth.

The iView programs are very powerful, but lack much of iPhoto's ease of use. Also, you don't get the nice interface to Kodak prints or hardbound photo books present in iPhoto. Our primary photo use of iView is as an intermediate step between iPhoto and archiving the pictures. Another use is when we're trying to keep a project together (fonts, word processing documents, EPS or Illustrator files, and photos).

Adobe Photoshop 7/Photoshop Elements

Photoshop is the standard against which all other photo-editing programs are measured. With a complex, palette-filled interface (shown in Figure 12-3), Photoshop 7 is not considered an easy program for the new or occasional user. It is, most definitely, a tool targeted at the power user, and priced to match at $609 (list) or $149 for those upgrading from an earlier version.

Photoshop Elements 2 (list price $99) retains much of Photoshop's palette-heavy interface and adds a few consumer-friendly options, such as the Quick Fix dialog box that lets you remove red-eye as well as adjust lighting, contrast, color, and focus quickly.

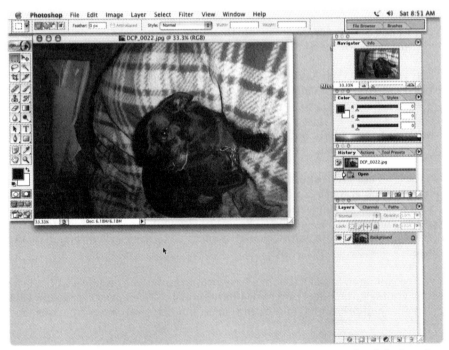

Figure 12-3: Photoshop offers palettes galore (and these are just the default set).

Not only do the Photoshop products offer an incredibly rich editing environment, they also give you access to some really nice printing options. One of our favorites is the Picture Package, as shown in Figure 12-4. One 8.5×11 sheet of glossy photo paper filled with copies of your photo at the same or different sizes, just like the sheets you get when you order a photo package of your kid's school pictures.

Photoshop is such a complex product, with so many features and capabilities, that books much larger than this one are devoted to it. Check out the *Photoshop 7 Bible* by Deke McClelland (Wiley Publishing, Inc.) for tons of info. You can download a trial version of Photoshop from Adobe's Web site at `www.adobe.com/products/photoshop/main.html`.

GraphicConverter

Considered by many (we're among them) to be one of the best shareware programs ($35) around, GraphicConverter is bundled on many PowerMac systems just as AppleWorks is bundled on iMacs. As you might surmise from the name, GraphicConverter started out as an application to convert between the various graphic formats — there are literally hundreds of them. With the addition of painting and bitmap editing features as well as a very handy browser (shown in Figure 12-5), GraphicConverter can stand on its own as a powerful photo-editing tool.

Just double-click any thumbnail in the browser and an editing window will open for that picture, as shown in Figure 12-6.

Figure 12-4: Get multiple prints in varying sizes on one sheet with Photoshop's Picture Package.

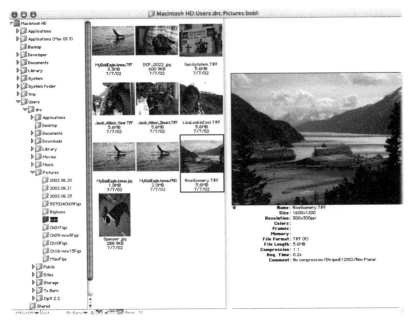

Figure 12-5: GraphicConverter's browser lets you move from image to image, wherever they are on your Mac.

Additionally, GraphicConverter has a rich AppleScript dictionary, allowing you to build programs to do multiple, complex operations on photos or groups of photos.

iPhoto Library Manager

Brian Webster (http://homepage.mac.com/bwebster) offers a wonderful freeware utility name iPhoto Library Manager. As the name implies, you can create multiple iPhoto Libraries and, using the iPhoto Library Manager, specify which is to be used the next time you open iPhoto. In addition to being able to store your photo libraries other places than your Pictures folder, iPhoto Library Manager will also set up the permissions on your photo libraries so that they might be shared with other users on your Mac.

iPhoto Librarian

A similar concept to the iPhoto Library Manager, Scott Schroeder's freeware offering from Scruffy Software (http://homepage.mac.com/scrufmeister), iPhoto Librarian lets you maintain multiple, separate Photo Libraries or even just one, if you want it somewhere other than your Pictures folder. Written in AppleScript, you double-click it and it asks whether you want to use the Default Photo Library or a different one (Other). Select your Photo Library of choice and iPhoto Librarian will launch iPhoto with your selected library.

Figure 12-6: GraphicConverter's editing environment is accessible from the browser.

SmartSound MovieMaestro

The biggest problem we have with the soundtrack feature on iPhoto slide shows is synchronizing things so that the music doesn't seem to just cut off when we get to the last slide. We also find the Preferences interface to add new songs to the pop-up menu a bit cumbersome.

Although SmartSound's MovieMaestro (www.smartsound.com) doesn't completely resolve our second annoyance, it makes a good first step. Once we've created a soundtrack, we just choose File ➪ Save Sound and pick Soundtrack to iPhoto from the Save dialog's pop-up list. The next time we open iPhoto, the soundtrack is there in the pop-up list, ready for selection.

MovieMaestro's *raison d'être* is scoring movies. If you export your slide show, you can use MovieMaestro to create precisely timed, customized soundtracks for your slide show movie, as follows:

1. In iPhoto, export your slide show, making sure that the "Add currently selected music to movie" check box is cleared, as shown in Figure 12-7. Click Export and, in the Save sheet that appears, name your movie and tell iPhoto where to save it (your Movies folder is the default).

Figure 12-7: Start out with a silent slide show.

2. In MovieMaestro, select "Create music for a movie," as shown in Figure 12-8.

Figure 12-8: Tell MovieMaestro that you're going to score an existing movie.

3. Locate your movie and click Open.
4. Click Add Music and select the music you want your slide show to use.

   The music block is added to MovieMaestro's timeline, as shown in Figure 12-9, set to your slide show's length. Optionally, select a different variation.

5. Click Save Sound.
6. From the Save Soundtrack dialog's Save pop-up menu, choose Movie and Soundtrack as shown in Figure 12-10, and click Save.

Chapter 12 ✦ Enhancing Your iPhoto Experience   233

Figure 12-9: The music appears in MovieMaestro's timeline.

Figure 12-10: Save the movie and soundtrack together.

You're done. Your QuickTime movie now has a score, matching in length.

MovieMaestro is a neat product for scoring movies and we'll be mentioning it again in Chapter 17, "Enhancing Your iMovie Experience," when we tell you some of the things you can do to add high-quality soundtracks to your iMovies. If you outgrow MovieMaestro, its big brother, SonicFire Pro does even more, but requires more effort on your part.

Educational Web sites

In addition to the Web sites we've mentioned in previous chapters, we'd like to add a couple here for your consideration.

Digital Photography Review (`www.dpreview.com`) is an excellent reference to all sorts of topics relating to digital photography. Between its Glossary, News, Learn, and Forum sections, you're almost certain to find answers or guidance when you have questions. Besides, learning about this stuff can be fun.

Although slanted toward Canon equipment, EF Lens 101 (`www.usa.canon.com/eflenses/lens101`) includes a wealth of information on lenses and a great, illustrated glossary of photo terminology.

Summary

In this chapter you learned about some things you can purchase to help you take better photos, bring old photos and slides into iPhoto, and archive photos from iPhoto, freeing up space and improving performance.

On the software side, you saw programs that significantly enhance your photo editing options, printing options, and library management. Additionally, you encountered MovieMaestro, which helps with scoring your slide shows and the ever-useful Toast Titanium for backing up your Photo Library and burning slide shows to VideoCD.

Finally, you learned about a couple of Web sites to check when you have specific questions about photography, digital or otherwise, or if you just want to learn more about photography and lenses.

✦ ✦ ✦

iMovie

iMovie

PART IV

In This Part

Chapter 13
Introducing iMovie

Chapter 14
Getting Started with iMovie

Chapter 15
Getting Advanced with iMovie

Chapter 16
More iMovie Tips, Tricks, and Techniques

Chapter 17
Enhancing your iMovie Experience

Introducing iMovie

CHAPTER 13

In This Chapter

Discovering digital video

Gathering the bare essentials

Exploring the iMovie window

Setting iMovie preferences

Some applications just scream **Breakthrough**! MacPaint was the first one on the Mac, capturing hearts and piquing imaginations. Soon thereafter came the LaserWriter-PageMaker combination, and HyperCard.

Today, iMovie — at least in our humble opinion — is yet another breakthrough from Apple.

The first time Dennis sat down with iMovie and created something viewable and entertaining from a collage of typically disjointed home movies, he felt an excitement that he hadn't experienced with computers since the first time he sat down with a 128K Mac and MacPaint in 1984. Bob, who was still producing television commercials in Los Angeles in 1984, says he's been waiting almost 20 years for the ability to edit "near-broadcast quality" video on his Mac at a price he can afford.

Well over two years later there still isn't an application for Windows that can hold a candle to iMovie in either ease-of-use or bang for the buck. Microsoft's Movie Maker is, at best, a pale imitation; other Windows programs that do the things iMovie does cost more and aren't as easy to use.

Discovering Digital Video

When we were growing up, our parents and grandparents were big on creating home movies (and compiling albums and boxes of still photos and slides). There wasn't a birthday party, trip to the zoo, or Little League game that didn't see one or more of them jostling for position with their movie camera, generally with portable lighting attached. Cameras using 8mm and 16mm film were state of the art for the home videophile, just as they had been for our grandfathers back when our parents were young. It wasn't until the late 1970s that home videotaping came into vogue, concurrent with the introduction and battle between Betamax (a.k.a. Beta) and VHS.

In spite of these advances, the technology was still analog, though. Silver-based film was replaced by tape, and bulb-based projectors were replaced with VCRs.

> **Note** In contrast to your parents'—and perhaps your own—ancient VCRs, iMovie uses higher-quality digital video, often referred to as "DV."

Things went on like that, with little change beyond variations in tape size (VHS, VHS-C, and Hi8), for about a quarter century. Then, in the late 1990s, Apple (and a few others, including Sony) introduced a new technology called FireWire, (also known as IEEE 1394 and iLink), and several vendors (including Canon, Sony, and Panasonic) introduced new digital camcorders designed to use FireWire to transfer video from camcorder to computer. This put analog video gear on the endangered species list—in a few more years analog will seem as quaint as 8mm film or vinyl "high-fidelity" records seem to us today.

Professional filmmakers have been using custom-configured Macs and other computers to edit video for years, but until FireWire and digital camcorders came along, these systems required lots of additional (and very expensive) hardware and software add-ons. ($100,000+ configurations were not uncommon.)

All that has changed. Ever since Apple began to include FireWire and iMovie on all their computers and the price of digital camcorders dropped below $500 (though most are still priced higher), the cost-of-entry for home users has become so affordable that almost anyone with the desire can now make a movie.

How affordable? Today you can get a basic iMac for around $800 and an inexpensive digital camcorder for under $500. So today you can get started with digital video for around $1300. To put that in perspective, Dennis's first VCR, which he bought in 1977, cost about the same as today's entry-level iMac. (And don't forget that the dollar was supposedly worth more then.)

Of course, most people will want more than the bare minimum system, but compared to prices just a few years ago, it will still be affordable. And don't forget: Your Mac can do more than just edit and play video, (unlike the projectors, splice blocks, razor blades, and film processing from days of yore).

Proliferating formats

When home VCRs first appeared, a battle ensued between two available formats, VHS and Beta.

> **Note** Some would say the battle was between Sony, almost the sole supplier of Beta format VCRs, and the hundreds of manufacturers who offered VHS. We say, "almost," because Sony did license a few other companies, such as Toshiba and Sanyo, to manufacture and sell Beta VCRs.

VHS was decidedly inferior to Beta in quality, but it had some things Beta did not—it was offered by a wide variety of vendors, it cost less, and it offered more storage per tape. Beta's quality advantage wasn't nearly enough to overcome these factors and VHS soon won the war.

Today we're experiencing a similar situation in digital video. There are multiple formats including DVD (Digital Video Disc or Digital Versatile Disk, depending on who you ask), VCD (Video Compact Disc), SVCD (Super Video Compact Disc), and variants of all three. Toss in upcoming MPEG-4-based formats and the field gets even more crowded.

DVD is the clear quality champion and you'll see blockbuster movies (and less well-known ones as well) for sale and rent on DVD at your neighborhood, well, Blockbuster Video. In the United States you'll be hard-pressed to find commercial VCDs and SVCDs for sale. But this isn't true in Asia and Europe, where VCDs and SVCDs are quite common, and in many cases, even more available than DVD. There are many reasons for this, but here are the two biggest:

✦ If you're a conspiracy theorist, you believe that the major movie studios have used their near-monopoly power to keep VCDs and SVCDs out of circulation in the United States.

✦ DVD media costs a lot more than CD media, even when you compare them per minute of video.

We'll talk about DVD in great detail in Part V, "iDVD." If you want to know more about VCD and SVCD, check out Chapter 15, "Advanced iMoviemaking," and Chapter 16, "More iMovie Tips, Tricks, and Techniques."

Video compression

If you've looked at QuickTime in any detail, you've seen that it performs its magic of reducing the transfer rate of around 200MB/minute down to something you can watch enjoyably on a computer, and the resulting files take up a tiny fraction of the space for that same minute. It's all done with software called a *codec* (compressor-decompressor), with names like Sorenson, CinePak, Animation, and a slew of others.

Video compression is achieved by eliminating redundant or (hopefully) unnecessary data from both the video frames and the audio track. In fact, if you merely encode a digital video file's audio track as MP3 and create a JPEG image from each frame, the resulting file would be considerably smaller than the original.

Video codecs are even more efficient than audio codecs, eliminating information that doesn't change from frame to frame and performing other tricks. Consider this: A VCD-compliant MPEG-1 encoded file will be roughly 5 percent the size of the original DV stream! And even with all that compression and space saving, you still end up with VHS-quality video.

Gathering the Bare Essentials

Okay, we're really going to talk about the essentials for normal use, such as a digital camcorder or analog-to-digital FireWire converter; you'll need one or the other to move your video between your camcorder and your Mac.

You could use iMovie without such gear to create slide shows with transitions, music, and special effects, and if you don't have access to a camcorder or analog-to-digital converter (for importing analog video such as VHS or Beta), you can still have some fun with iMovie. But trust us, it gets boring real fast and you will barely scratch the surface of iMovie's capabilities.

What your Mac needs

Simply put, your Mac needs to meet certain minimum requirements to make productive use of iMovie. The following list describes what is necessary in either MacOS X or MacOS 9 but, as usual, we're going to focus on OS X.

- ✦ **iMovie 2:** Okay, this one is obvious. It ships with every Macintosh currently manufactured by Apple, is included in the box with retail copies of MacOS X (10.1 and later), and (at least currently) is available for free download from your iDisk's Software folder.

- ✦ **A ton of free disk space:** This is critical — raw digital video consumes over 200MB of disk space per minute. So ten minutes of video will take up better than 2GB of disk space. We feel that anything less than 10GB of free disk space will be uncomfortable. In fact, Dennis keeps a 30GB disk dedicated to iMovie projects and Bob has three 60GB FireWire hard drives he uses primarily for video.

- ✦ **FireWire:** This is almost a no-brainer, but some older OS X-capable machines don't have it. If that describes your Mac, get a FireWire PCI card. If you have one of the early iBooks, one of the pre-FireWire iMacs, or the like and can't upgrade to FireWire, you won't be able to import or export your video footage.

- ✦ **Memory:** As with anything else, the more RAM you have in your Mac, the better. While iMovie can and will run in a 128MB OS X machine, it will often be slow, especially if other programs or processes are running. We suggest at least 384MB (more is better) of RAM to work efficiently with digital video.

What you need to connect to your Mac

We've already mentioned two possible input devices: digital camcorders and analog-to-digital converters. You'll need a FireWire cable to connect your input device to your Mac, but Apple was prepared for you and includes a 4-pin to 6-pin

FireWire cable with each iMovie-capable Mac. This special cable, shown in Figure 13-1, has the normal (6-pin) FireWire connector to plug into your Mac and the smaller (4-pin) connector that almost every digital camcorder accepts.

Figure 13-1: The Mac gets the normal FireWire connector (far left); the camera gets the smaller connector. The FireWire logo is shown on the right.

Depending upon your camera model, the FireWire connector could be listed under a different name. On some models, it is called IEEE-1394, which is the name of the Institute of Electrical and Electronics Engineers standards document implemented in FireWire. On other models (Sonys, for example), it will be called i.Link, which is Sony's trademarked name for their implementation. FireWire is Apple's trademark name, which they have licensed for free to the 1394 Trade Organization, along with the FireWire logo and symbol.

Okay, we know you're about to ask (if you haven't already) what we mean by an analog-to-digital converter. Also known as *bridges* or *ADCs*, they are electronic devices that convert an analog stream of data to a digital stream and vice versa. Since iMovie can only deal with DV Streams as video input, whatever feeds it must provide a DV Stream, just as a digital camcorder would. The two most popular of these bridges are the Dazzle Hollywood DV Bridge (www.dazzle.com/products/hw_bridge.html) and the Formac Studio DV/TV (www.formac.com). If you can still find a Sony DVMC-DA2, it will also work, although Sony discontinued this product (which we think is a crying shame). The Formac Studio is more expensive than the Dazzle Hollywood, but it includes a 125-channel TV tuner, so you could actually use your Mac as a digital VCR and record TV shows to disk, although DV Stream format makes for some really large files at better than 200MB/minute. Figure 13-2 shows pictures of the Dazzle and Formac devices.

Virtually every digital camcorder includes analog inputs, allowing them to act as pseudo analog-to-digital converters. Connect an analog source (a camcorder or VCR) to the analog inputs and transfer your analog footage to DV tape. Once you've done that you can import the newly recorded DV footage to iMovie via FireWire.

(a)

Photo courtesy of SCM Microsystems

(b)

Figure 13-2: The Dazzle Hollywood DV Bridge (a); The Formac Studio (b).

Although it isn't 100 percent necessary, we would strongly recommend that you upgrade your QuickTime version to QuickTime Pro as well. Having QuickTime Pro allows you to edit the QuickTime movies that you export from iMovie, even adding some special effects such as transparency. QT Pro (as it is often abbreviated) also lets you perform far more format conversions than the basic QuickTime installation and lets you present your movies full-screen.

Another not-quite-100 percent add-on (but close) is a CD burner and a copy of Roxio's excellent Toast Titanium. Most current Macs include some sort of burner, but if yours doesn't then we strongly recommend getting one as a way to save your finished and exported movies. One of the nicest benefits of Toast Titanium, in addition to being faster for burning your CDs (a lot less "preparation" than Mac OS's built-in CD burning), is that Roxio includes a VideoCD-compatible export option that will let you play your movies on many set top DVD players. We discuss this in detail in Chapter 15. Of course, if your Mac is equipped with a SuperDrive, you also have iDVD 2 (which we cover in Part V of this book) and can burn DVDs, but DVD-R media is a lot more expensive than CD-Rs.

Jargon break

We'll be using a few terms here that were discussed in Chapter 2, but we want to make sure you understand them before we move on.

- ✦ **Clips** are the segments of a movie as they are stored on your disk.
- ✦ **Frames** are the smallest increment of duration used in iMovie. If you're dealing with NTSC (United States and Japan) video, there are 30 frames per second and with PAL video (just about everywhere else) there are 25 frames per second.

 Actually, NTSC video has 29.97 frames per second, but we're going to round things off for the sake of simplicity.

- ✦ **Tracks** are a stream of video or audio. Although QuickTime supports tracks of other types, like text, iMovie only works with video and audio (you get one of the former and two of the latter).

Exploring the iMovie Window

We know that Steve Jobs probably doesn't want to hear this, but there is one thing about iMovie that feels un-Mac-like: The iMovie window takes over your entire screen, as shown in Figure 13-3. You can't see your Desktop or anything else; even the Dock gets hidden, although you can pop it back into view by moving the cursor to where the Dock should be.

Figure 13-3: iMovie's window is as big as your screen.

One nice thing iMovie does for you is to remember the last project (what iMovie calls a movie) you worked on. If that project is still available, iMovie opens it automatically when launched.

In addition to a lot of striped background, iMovie's window consists of four main areas:

- **Monitor:** It looks like a TV screen with some VCR controls beneath it.
- **Shelf:** It's both a clip storage location and the control center for adding iMovie special effects.
- **Clip viewer/Timeline viewer:** These two tabs are where you do your actual movie composition.

✦ **Status area:** This is where iMovie places its internal trash receptacle and displays how much is in it and how much free space remains on your iMovie project's disk.

In the next few pages, we'll begin to explore these areas; we'll explore them in excruciating detail in Chapters 14 and 15.

Viewing the monitor

The monitor is more than just where you view your clips or movies. It is also where you do much of the actual editing and deleting of clip segments. The monitor is also where you preview and import footage from your (connected) digital camcorder.

Figure 13-4 displays two views of the monitor, one in Camera mode, the other in Clip Viewing mode. You won't see a lot of difference between them, except that the little toggle switch changes position and the Import button in Camera Mode changes to a scrubber bar in the Clip Viewing mode.

As you can see from Figure 13-4, the two modes have many items in common:

✦ **Screen:** Like the screen on your TV monitor, this is where clips or tapes play.

Note When in Camera mode with nothing playing, the screen will be blue and display whether or not a camera is connected and, if one is, where the tape is positioned in hours, minutes, seconds, and frames.

✦ **Rewind:** Just like on a VCR or a cassette player, this rewinds the tape or reverses direction of play in a tape or clip.

✦ **Fast Forward:** Again, just like on a VCR, this button advances the tape or moves through a clip at a faster rate.

✦ **Play:** Click it to start playing a clip or tape. When in Clip Viewing mode, you click it again to stop play. In Camera mode, you can also click it to stop play, even though you have a separate Stop button (see below).

✦ **Volume:** In Camera mode, you use this to control the level of sound input. When viewing clips, this control sets the sound output level.

✦ **Toggle Switch:** This two-position switch is where you tell iMovie that you want to work with the camera or with clips. Slide it to the little camera icon with the DV superimposed to make your FireWire-connected camera your input source or move it to the film strip icon to tell iMovie you're going to work with clips.

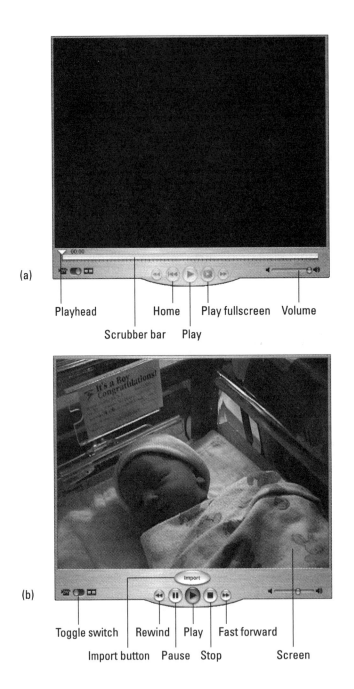

Figure 13-4: Monitor's Clip Viewing mode (a); Monitor's Camera mode (b).

Monitor items specific to Clip Viewing mode are as follows:

- **Home:** This button moves you to the beginning of the clip or sequence of selected clips.
- **Play Full Screen:** This little button, which is supposed to represent a "Play" arrowhead against a full screen backdrop, tells iMovie to fill your screen rather than just the monitor's miniscreen with your movie. Click anywhere onscreen while the clip is playing to return to the normal iMovie window.
- **Scrubber bar:** This aqua-colored bar with all the tick marks below it represents the length of your selected clip(s).
- **Playhead:** This down-pointing white arrowhead with the time indicator to its right moves along the scrubber bar to indicate your relative position in the clip(s) and the absolute position, timewise, within the clip(s).

Camera mode has a few other specialty items:

- **Import:** Clicking this button tells iMovie to start retrieving data from your camera and storing it on your disk.
- **Pause:** Click this button to pause your camera. The current frame will continue to display in the monitor screen.
- **Stop:** Click this button to halt the play or import process.

Seeing what's on the shelf

The upper-right portion of the iMovie window is a veritable cornucopia of functions called the shelf, and what appears on the shelf depends upon which of the buttons along its bottom is selected. When iMovie first launches, you see the shelf as shown in Figure 13-5.

Each of the buttons invokes a different display and we're going to show you each of them here. Full coverage of their functionality will come your way in Chapters 14 and 15.

Clips

Most of the time, the shelf will probably look like Figure 13-5. Each of those little squares can hold one clip, has an editable name at its bottom, and displays the length of the clip in the upper left. The image in the middle represents the first frame of the clip.

When you select a clip, its frame turns orange instead of white (although, being OS X, we would really expect to see it turn blue).

Figure 13-5: The shelf, in its clip-holding persona (with one clip).

 Unless you change the default preferences (see the "Managing your import preferences" section later in this chapter), the clip viewer is where imported camcorder footage always appears.

Transitions

Clicking the Transitions button alters the shelf's appearance, as shown in Figure 13-6. This is where you apply transition effects to clips, hopefully to the betterment of your movie. Check out the "Transitioning between clips" section in Chapter 14 for the lowdown on how this all works.

Titles

If you want to add credits or other text to your movie, this is the place. The shelf's Titles view, shown in Figure 13-7, gives you a wide range of titling and subtitling options. See the "Adding text" section in Chapter 15 for the lowdown on titling.

Effects

Special effects are what sell a lot of big-budget films, but the effects you employ from the shelf view (Figure 13-8) don't involve blowing up any trains, making people fly through the air, or morphing from one face to another. These effects are adjustments to coloring, lighting, and so forth in your clips and we'll tell you all about them in the "Applying visual effects" section in Chapter 15.

Figure 13-6: Select Transitions to apply special effects to your clips.

Figure 13-7: Add text titles and subtitles to your clips here.

Figure 13-8: Apply visual effects here.

Audio

Narrations, background music, voice-overs, and the like can enhance many movies. iMovie provides the tools for all this in the shelf's Audio view, as shown in Figure 13-9. We'll fill you in on all the details in the "Adding Sound Effects" and "Adding Narration and Background Music" sections in Chapter 15.

The clip viewer

Stretching across the bottom of iMovie's window is a double-duty pane: the clip viewer/timeline viewer. The clip viewer (Figure 13-10) is where you assemble your movie and apply the effects, transitions, and titling introduced in the previous section.

You can recognize the clip viewer by the eye on its tab. All the clips in your movie appear in sequence along the viewer, as do the effects applied. (There's a transition applied between the two clips in Figure 13-10.) The name of your movie and its total length are displayed along the tab border at the top left, as well as whether your movie is NTSC or PAL format.

If a clip is selected, its name will appear in the center of the top tab border, along with other information, such as the date and time recorded and the clip's length. When you select multiple clips in the viewer, you only get to see that the selection comprises "<Multiple>" clips and what their total duration is.

Figure 13-9: iMovie even includes a small audio recording studio.

Figure 13-10: The clip viewer is where you assemble your movie and apply special effects.

The timeline viewer

Recognizable by its analog clock face, the timeline viewer (see Figure 13-11) is one of iMovie's most powerful tools. Many of iMovie's best special visual effects, including fast- and slow-motion, can only be added in the timeline viewer.

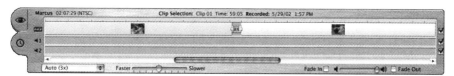

Figure 13-11: Use the timeline to view the different tracks of your movie.

Use the timeline viewer to see what is happening when in your movie, to edit and manage the video track and two audio tracks, and control the movie's speed and volume.

Unlike the clip viewer, where all clips take the same amount of space, every clip appears in a time-proportional bar in the timeline viewer's video track.

The pop-up menu at the lower left of the timeline viewer (it says "Auto (3x)" in Figure 13-11) controls absolutely nothing in your movie, just the magnification used to view the timeline. It's called the timeline zoom pop-up menu and you'll find it quite handy when you have really short clips or a really long movie. Setting it to 1x causes your entire timeline to fit in the viewer without activating the horizontal scroll bar.

In Chapter 15, we'll show you all of the timeline viewer's features, but your imagination is the only limitation on how you use these features. The timeline viewer is one of iMovie's most underrated features.

Status indicators

iMovie reserves a little bit of space between the shelf and the clip/timeline viewer in order to keep you informed about how much data you've discarded but not yet erased (the iMovie Trash) and how much disk space you have left (the Free Space status bar). Figure 13-12 shows these status indicators.

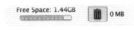

Figure 13-12: The Free Space gauge (left) and the iMovie Trash (right) keep you informed about when you're running out of disk space and how much space you can free up.

The iMovie Trash

iMovie maintains its own Trash for discarded clips and clip segments. Similar to the Mac's Trash, the contents aren't really gone until you empty the Trash. Unlike the Mac's Trash, though, you can't open the iMovie Trash and directly retrieve the clip you want. You have to choose Edit ⇨ Undo (⌘-Z) as many times as necessary to get back to where you were when you deleted the clip.

Tip

iMovie allows 99 levels of Undo, which should be more than adequate in most cases. The downside is that you'll then have to manually redo each operation after the deletion that you want redone. The conclusion we can draw from this is that we shouldn't throw clips in the Trash until we're really sure that we don't need them any longer. Stick them on the shelf, maybe scrolled down to the bottom, if you just want to get them out of the way.

There is one sure way other than quitting from iMovie or changing projects to eliminate your ability to choose Edit ⇨ Undo. That guaranteed undo-killer is to Empty the iMovie Trash. Assuming that you have enough disk space (see the "What your

Mac needs" section earlier in this chapter), we strongly recommend that you not empty iMovie's Trash until you're finished working on your project.

One really nice thing about iMovie's Trash, though, is that you can see at a glance how much material is in it. iMovie displays how much it is holding just to the right of the Trash icon.

The Free Space status bar

The handy little thermometer to the left of the iMovie Trash tells you how much free space remains on the disk holding your iMovie project. It's even color-coded to give you a warning when space gets really tight.

- ✦ **Green:** You have more than 400MB of free space left. In other words, you can import about two minutes of video or more.
- ✦ **Yellow:** You have at least 200MB, but less than 400MB left. You should consider freeing up some disk space.
- ✦ **Red:** Okay, things are getting really tight. You're down to less than 200MB. You really need to start doing some housekeeping. Emptying the Trash might be a good start.

Apple claims that DV footage takes about 220MB per minute, other sources claim 200MB per minute or 210MB per minutes. In any event, that's a lot of space disappearing rather quickly when you're importing video from your camera, creating clips out of still photos, or otherwise adding clips to your project.

At 100MB, iMovie will toss an alert up on the screen beseeching you to start clearing some space. When you get down to 50MB or so, iMovie won't let you import any more footage until you free up some space.

Tip

We weren't kidding when we said that lots of free space is a must when you're working with iMovie and digital video. While not everyone can afford to do so, investing in a large, fast secondary hard disk and dedicating it to iMovie projects is a very good idea. One problem with keeping your iMovie project on your startup disk is that this is also the disk that your Mac uses for virtual memory. If you have other programs running, it is possible that they will get swapped out to disk and the System will start taking disk space that iMovie is going to want. Of course, you could just not run other programs (like your e-mail program) while iMovie is running, but what's the fun in that?

Setting iMovie Preferences

We hope you're not tired of tabbed dialog boxes yet, because iMovie's Preferences dialog box presents you with four tabs: Import, Playback, Views, and Advanced. Fortunately, each tab contains only a few items, each of which can be quite useful.

Managing your Import preferences

The Import tab (Figure 13-13) deals with clips you bring in from a digital camcorder and still clips you create by importing a graphic file.

The "Automatically start new clip at scene break" check box takes advantage of the fact that digital camcorders signal the start and end of a recording session (a scene). When this box is selected, a new clip will be created when a start signal is detected. Starting a new clip at a scene break is the default setting.

Use the "Imported Clips Go To" radio buttons to specify whether imported footage should land on the shelf or go directly to the clip viewer. The shelf is the default location. Unless you know that you want everything to be in the clip viewer, in sequence, and without deleting any footage, we don't see a reason to change this preference.

The "Still Clips are __ seconds by default" option is initially set to 5 seconds. This is one setting we usually change for a couple of reasons. A 5-second still clip takes up about 17MB and, if we're inserting a still in the middle of a movie, it's generally for a transition effect (see the "Transitioning between clips" section in Chapter 15) and we only need it present for about 2 or 3 seconds. Your usage might be different and 5 seconds is not a bad duration for a slide show.

Figure 13-13: The Import tab displaying the iMovie default settings.

Selecting your Playback Preference

As you can see in Figure 13-14, there is only one Playback preference to set and that is whether iMovie should trade smoother motion for a sharper picture or vice versa when previewing your movie on the computer screen. Just so you don't get nervous, Apple puts in a little preamble telling you that this preference has absolutely no effect on video you export either back to the camera or to QuickTime. The default setting is for a sharper picture (Better Image) and that's a good choice unless slightly jerky motion grates on your nerves.

Figure 13-14: Choose between seeing all the frames and seeing sharp images in a subset of the frames.

 It has been our experience that this option only has a bearing on slower Macs (if you can call 500MHz slow). On a G4/800 iMac and a G4/667 PowerBook, neither of us noticed any jerkiness with Better Image selected, nor did we notice any loss of clarity when Smoother Motion was selected.

Viewing your Views preferences

The first thing we've got to tell you is that we would have named this tab differently. To us, this is the Timeline tab, because that's what it controls: how things look in the timeline viewer. There are four check boxes on the Views tab, as pictured in Figure 13-15.

Figure 13-15: Control the timeline viewer's display with the Views tab.

- ✦ **Show Thumbnails in Timeline** is selected by default. Turn it off if you don't like the little picture in the middle of each duration bar.
- ✦ **Use Short Time Codes** is also selected by default. This means that only as much of a time code (minimum being seconds and frames) as is necessary will be displayed. Turning it off will add the minutes field, even if it is not needed.
- ✦ **Show More Details** is cleared. If you want to see the clip names and durations in the Timeline, select this check box.
- ✦ **Show Locked Audio Only When Selected** is also off by default. Enabling this option will hide the fact that an audio clip is locked unless it is selected.

Moving up to Advanced preferences

The Advanced tab was definitely named correctly. Although there are only three check boxes (see Figure 13-16), each of them enables some very cool features.

Figure 13-16: The Advanced tab affects your camera and the Advanced menu.

- **Extract Audio in Paste Over** enables a really cool effect. You can paste a length of video over an existing track, retaining the audio from the footage you're replacing. This can come in really handy when you want to perform an intercut (we'll describe that in Chapter 16).

- **Filter Audio from Camera** tells iMovie to capture the audio when importing. One thing we know for sure, clearing this check box makes iMovie beep when we try to import from our cameras.

- **Video Playthrough to Camera** should be selected if you want iMovie to play your movie on both the Mac's screen and on your camera's screen.

The Video Playthrough to Camera option gives you a really cool capability. You can use your digital camcorder as a *pass-through device* (a digital to analog converter) and record your movie directly on a VCR or play it on a TV set. Just follow these steps:

1. Make sure that your camera is still connected via FireWire to your Mac and that Video Playthrough to Camera is selected in Advanced preferences.

2. Connect the AV-out port(s) on your camera to the red-white-and-yellow composite video connectors (they're often called RCA connectors) on your VCR or TV set (assuming that your TV set has RCA connectors for audio and video input).

You're in even better shape if your camcorder and VCR or TV have S-Video connectors. In that case, don't connect the yellow (video channel) connector to the VCR/TV, connect the S-Video cable instead. You'll get a better quality picture.

3. Set the VCR or TV to the appropriate input setting.

4. Play your movie in iMovie and watch it on your TV or tape it on your VCR.

Now, you know what your movie will look like when folks watch it on TV and you can create a videotape without what is called *generational signal loss*, which is why you lose quality with each copy of a copy when you use analog tape.

Summary

In this chapter you learned a little about the evolution of home movies, from the film cameras and projectors of the mid-20th century, through the VCR era of the '80s and '90s, to today's digital era. You've also been introduced to the iMovie screen's many parts and faces, as well as iMovie's Preferences tabs. The next few chapters delve more deeply into all these tools.

✦ ✦ ✦

Getting Started with iMovie

In This Chapter

Acquiring video from a digital camcorder

Working with clips

Importing images

Exporting your video

We had a big decision to make about this section: Should we spend 50 to 100 pages telling you about composition, lighting, choosing a camcorder, and so forth? Or should we hit the high points of technique but focus on iMovie?

As you might guess, we're focusing on iMovie. Those peripheral issues, such as how to actually create footage you'd want to use in iMovie, can be found mostly in Appendix A's "What Do I Need for iMovie?" section. Some related topics, though, appear in this chapter (and in Chapter 15, "Advanced iMovieMaking," and Chapter 17, "Enhancing your iMovie Experience") and in sidebars. So, if you're the sort who normally skips sidebar material, you might want to rethink that position in these chapters.

Because we didn't want to distract from the fun stuff by adding a lot of non-iMovie details in this chapter, we're going to assume you have a compatible digital camcorder, know how to use it, and how to light scenes, frame shots, and record usable sound in the field.

Acquiring Video from a Digital Camcorder

The first thing that iMovie needs is video footage. If you don't have any pictures or video, you don't have anything to watch or anything with which to work. The intended (and most common) source of iMovie footage is from a digital camcorder.

Connecting your camcorder

In the last chapter we showed you a picture of two FireWire connectors, a big one (six-pin) and a small one (four-pin). Most of you should have received a cable with these two connectors in the box when you purchased your Mac. Sometimes, you'll also get one with your camcorder, but if you didn't get a cable like this you're going to need to go out and buy one. Remember, it's called a 6-pin to 4-pin FireWire cable (it might be labeled IEEE-1394 or i.Link, instead of FireWire). Don't confuse it with a 6-pin to 4-pin USB cable or either of the two alternative (6-pin to 6-pin or 4-pin to 4-pin) FireWire cables. Just to make sure that you have its appearance firmly in mind, we're going to show you the connectors again in Figure 14-1.

Figure 14-1: The FireWire connectors needed to hook your camcorder to your Mac.

The smaller square (4-pin) connector should be inserted in your camcorder's FireWire port, which is very likely to be labeled IEEE-1394, i.Link, or DV in/out rather than FireWire. All these terms mean the same thing. The larger wide (6-pin) end should be inserted in one of your Mac's FireWire ports. The FireWire ports sport the FireWire logo shown in Figure 14-2.

Sometimes, if you connect the camera to another FireWire device rather than directly to your Mac, you can cause OS X to think that you've disconnected an external FireWire drive. We haven't heard of this happening when the connection is directly to the Mac. If you experience a drive being dismounted when you connect your camcorder (or some other FireWire device, like an iPod), power the drive down and then restart it so that OS X will get a signal to mount it back on your Desktop. You should probably run Disk Utility's First Aid tool to make sure that your disk and its contents are okay.

Once the cable is connected at both ends, turn your camcorder on to its VCR (or VTR or Playback) setting rather than its Camera setting (we'll just call it the VTR mode from now on). You've probably already figured this out, but we'll tell you anyway, just in case: Don't run your camcorder on battery power while uploading to and downloading from iMovie. For one thing, running from battery will drain the battery. For another, you'd really hate to have the camcorder shut down for lack of a charge in the middle of an upload or download.

Figure 14-2: Insert the four-pin connector (left) into your camcorder and the six-pin connector (right) into the FireWire port on your Mac.

 Tip   Another real battery drain is using the camcorder's LCD display. That's really a shame, because the LCD is usually a lot easier to see and use than a viewfinder. If you're running low on battery power or think you might be pushing your battery's limits later in your filming session, try to make do with the viewfinder.

Starting iMovie

The next step on the road to making your movie is to launch iMovie (kinda obvious, right?), which is probably in your Mac's Applications folder. Just click the Applications icon in a Finder window toolbar and look for iMovie. If you're going to use iMovie a lot, you might want to put iMovie's icon in your Dock as a (semi)permanent fixture, just like Apple did with iTunes and now (Mac OS X 10.2) does with iMovie, iPhoto, and iDVD. To do this, drag iMovie's icon to the spot in the Dock where you want the iMovie icon to be and let go. We keep ours between iTunes and iPhoto, as shown in Figure 14-3. From now on, all you have to do is click on the iMovie icon in the Dock to launch iMovie.

Figure 14-3: If you use iMovie a lot, you should consider keeping it in the Dock.

However you choose to launch iMovie, the first time it starts up you'll see a screen similar to the one in Figure 14-4. Since you don't already have a project to open (this is your first time, right?) click the New Project button and iMovie will present the Create New Project dialog box shown in Figure 14-5. By default, iMovie will offer to name it <your name>'s Movie, obtaining your name from your OS X login account (and omitting the brackets).

As much as we love iMovie (and we *really* do), it isn't without a few minor annoyances and the Create New Project dialog you see in Figure 14-5 is one of them. First, we don't like Save dialog boxes that have the column browser hidden. Second, the name offered is the same regardless of whether there is already a project with that name in Documents, which means that you will get an alert telling you to choose another name because there's already a folder with that name. This ties back to having the browser hidden, since you can't see what names are already taken. Make it second nature to click the Reveal Browser button to the right of the Where pop-up menu.

Figure 14-4: Welcome to iMovie. Watch it's little movie and choose your poison.

Figure 14-5: iMovie's rather plain Create New Project window.

 Tip

If you're fortunate enough to have a second internal hard disk with a lot of free space that you can use for iMovie, we recommend that you save your projects there. Keep that disk in your Favorites so that you can select it directly from the Where pop-up menu in the Create New Project dialog box. A little later, we'll tell you why we specify an internal hard disk.

Okay, you now have a new project going as shown in Figure 14-6. Isn't that an empty, boring sight?

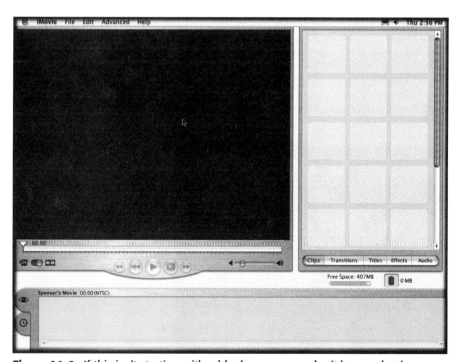

Figure 14-6: If this isn't starting with a blank canvas, we don't know what is.

If you haven't already done so, check out the "Exploring the iMovie Window" section in Chapter 13 to learn what all these screen areas are for.

iMovie will run in an 800×600 screen, but your shelf will be small (though scrollable) and everything will be crowded together. iMovie's window is designed to look best and be most functional at 1024×768 resolution. If you have one of Apple's beautiful 17" Studio Display LCDs or (drool) a Cinema Display, you're going to see a lot of blank space between the different areas.

Importing the video

If your camera is turned on and connected, the monitor should have a blue screen with the words Camera Connected centered horizontally and about 1/3 of the way down in white, with an empty timer display in the upper right, as shown in Figure 14-7. If you don't see a blue screen, check to make sure that the toggle switch (lower left) is in the DV position. iMovie will switch to DV automatically when it senses a camera being turned on. If, instead of saying "Camera Connected" iMovie tells you "Camera Disconnected," you should check your cable connections to make sure that the connectors are fully inserted and check your camera to verify that it is turned on in its VTR setting. If you still don't see "Camera Connected," try turning the camera off and back on. Finally, if that fails, check at `www.apple.com/imovie` to verify that your camera is one that iMovie supports.

You can also import video from disk files and, with a little work spent converting formats, from formats other than DV streams. We'll cover that in detail in Chapter 15, "Enhancing Your iMovie Experience."

Figure 14-7: iMovie sees your camera and is ready for you to start importing.

Controlling your camera with iMovie

One thing we really don't enjoy is trying to manipulate the tiny membrane-style controls on our video camera with our fingernails when we want to rewind, fast forward, play, or stop the camera. We've even gotten to the point where we connect the camera in iMovie just to use its much easier controls to review our clips (and the bigger screen ain't bad, either).

We've watched and tried two different approaches to importing video. The first way is to just click the Import button and let iMovie import everything to disk, after which we go back and select the footage we want, discarding the rest. The second method is a little more work upfront, but doesn't fill our disk with nearly so much wasted footage.

Tip By the way, if you don't have wasted footage, you probably didn't start shooting quickly enough or you stopped shooting too soon in at least some scenes. That's one reason professionals start shooting with that clapboard in view before the scene starts. They're making sure that they don't miss the beginning. They also shoot a couple of seconds after the director yells, "Cut," to make sure they don't lop off the ending.

You should recall the Import Preference setting that tells iMovie to create new clips at scene breaks (see the "Setting Your iMovie Preferences" section in Chapter 13). With this on, iMovie starts a new clip each time the camcorder signals that a recording session started (in other words, each time the camera switched to Record or Pause was turned off).

Note Scene changes aren't the only time iMovie will automatically start new clips. You'll also get a new clip after just short of 10 minutes of video, because iMovie won't allow a single clip to be larger than 2GB on disk.

Experience has taught us that what looks like more work isn't always. Professional filmmakers always shoot a lot more footage than they're going to need, just to make sure that they have everything they want. We suggest you follow their example. One of the corollaries to this approach is that you'll want to import manually rather than in bulk. This isn't actually as much work as it seems and it tends to use up a lot less disk space. Proceed as follows:

1. Using the Play, Rewind, and Fast Forward buttons, position the tape to just before the footage you want.
2. Click Play.
3. When the tape starts running and you see the footage you want, click Import. The Import button will turn blue, a new clip appears on the shelf, and the clip's time code starts increasing.

Tip Pressing the spacebar is the same as clicking Import.

4. When the footage you want is complete, click Import (or press Space) again. The Import button loses its blue coloring and the footage stops importing. However, the tape continues to play until you click the Stop or Play buttons.

Repeat these steps (or just 3 & 4 if you leave the tape playing) until you've imported all the footage you want.

Tip You might consider disabling the Importing preference that creates a new clip at scene breaks when manually importing if you know you have multiple scenes you wish brought in as one item. In general we leave it enabled, but there are situations where we disable it for a session.

Knowing your timecodes

While it is possible an iMovie-compatible digital camcorder exists that doesn't keep a running *timecode*, we haven't seen one or heard of it. You've seen the little timer running in the upper-right corner (usually) while you're taping—that's the timecode. You also see it in iMovie when you're controlling the camera, as shown in Figure 14-8.

Tip Keep track of the timecodes for important scenes when you're recording and you'll find it much easier to locate the scenes you want when it's time to import your video. Just fast forward (or rewind) the tape to the noted timecode and you're ready to start importing.

Figure 14-8: Finding your scene is a lot easier when you can tell time.

Tip There is one precaution you should take when you rely on timecodes. You should prepare the tape, which is called *blackstriping*. To blackstripe a tape, just record the length of it with the lens cap on. This will write black to the entire tape, but your camera will record the timecodes for the entire tape. Now, no matter if you forward over a stretch of tape, the timecodes will still be continuous.

If you forget to blackstripe a tape, you can get around that in a few (awkward) ways. The first is to import everything from the tape (with New Clip at Scene Break enabled), blackstripe the tape, and then write everything back out. A second method would involve using two digital camcorders and copying from one to the other. You'll need a 4-pin to 4-pin FireWire cable for this, unless you're willing to lose quality by making an analog copy.

Working with Clips

Okay, you've imported your video and have a slew of clips sitting on the shelf. Now, the real fun (and work) begins: you get to start constructing your movie. Selecting clips on the shelf is about the most basic action you can perform on them, but it starts a chain of events in iMovie. First, iMovie will switch into Edit mode (the toggle moves from DV to the filmstrip icon), and the beginning of the first selected clip appears in the monitor.

Note When you select a clip, its border turns yellow. You can select multiple clips by holding down the Shift key and clicking on the additional clips.

You need to select clips before you can edit them, add them to the timeline viewer, or delete them (by dragging them to iMovie's Trash icon). Okay, we just told you how to delete a clip as well.

Caution It is tempting, when the Trash icon tells you how many megabytes (or gigabytes) are deleted, to empty the Trash (File ⇨ Empty Trash). Be careful here! Not only does emptying iMovie's trash make the clips unrecoverable (unless you want to reimport them), but it wipes out iMovie's undo stack, so you can no longer undo the last actions you performed, even if they had nothing to do with the clips you deleted. iMovie will warn you, but we all know that confirmation dialogs are often OK'd without our actually reading them.

Renaming clips

We don't know about you, but names like Clip 3 don't tell us a whole lot about what the scene is. More than that, the thumbnail image you see (called the *poster frame*) in the clip often won't tell you enough about the clip for you to tell what the clip is about. For example, if you're filming your daughter's birthday party, how do you tell one clip from another when they all start out with a close-up of your little girl?

iMovie gives you a simple solution to this problem. You get to rename your clips. If you've used the AppleWorks 6 Presentations module, you will already know how to do this, because the process is the same as renaming slides. For the rest of you, just follow the steps:

1. Select a clip and click in the name area to make it ready for editing as shown in Figure 14-9.

Figure 14-9: A clip that's ready to be given a useful name.

2. Type a new name. You'll want to keep the names short, though, because only about ten characters will be visible and longer names will have some of the first ten replaced with ellipses.

Well, that was pretty easy, wasn't it? Now, repeat the process for each of the clips you're going to use so that you can recognize them.

Editing clips

It is an extremely rare and simple movie that won't require some editing. For example, you may want to remove unnecessary footage, such as a few extra frames at the start or end of a clip, or split a clip into two or more pieces so you can insert some other footage into the middle.

We saw in Chapter 13 that the monitor's control buttons are a little different when you're in Edit mode. That's because they no longer have anything to do with your camera, they control how you view and work with your clips.

You can edit a clip on the shelf or in the clip viewer, but if you want to edit a sequence of clips, they have to be selected in the clip viewer.

The scrubber bar is your friend

That little blue bar (Figure 14-10) between the monitor's screen and buttons is going to be just about your most powerful tool when editing clips. With it, you position within a clip or select part of a clip.

The tick marks below the scrubber bar don't actually tell you anything other than where you are within a clip or group of clips, relative to the total length. In other words, you have the same number of ticks (67) under a 3-second clip as you do under a 7-minute clip. Don't ask us where they came up with 67 as the number to use, either. (In iMovie 1, there were 123 ticks under the scrubber bar at 1024×768 resolution.)

Another Way to Rename Clips

There's another way to rename clips. Choose File ➪ Get Clip Info (Shift-⌘-I) or double-click the clip to display the Clip Info dialog box shown here:

Among other things, you can rename clips in the Clip Info dialog box.

Just as in a Finder or iTunes Info window, just select the part of the name you wish to change and start typing.

The Clip Info window provides a bit more information, though, that can come in handy. After you've renamed a clip, the actual file on disk still has the original name. If you want to use the clip in another movie, you're going to need to know the name of the disk file, and this is where you can find it. If you're curious as to how big the file is, you can see that information as well.

Finally, while you can use transitions to fade video out or in, fading the audio is done here. So, if you want your audio to fade to a whisper at the end of a clip, this is where you tell iMovie how gradual or abrupt you want the fade to be. Similarly, if you want the audio to increase in volume at the clip's start, you do that and specify how long it should take here as well.

Figure 14-10: Use the scrubber bar to position your playhead.

iMovie gives you three ways to position the scrubber bar's playhead.

- **Click the scrubber bar** at the point where you want to be. The playhead will move there and the screen area will display that frame.
- **Drag the playhead** (this is called *scrubbing* and is where the scrubber bar gets its name). You'll actually see the frames flash by in the screen area.
- **Use the left and right arrow keys** on your keyboard. Each press moves you one frame backward (←) or one frame forward (→). Combining Shift with the arrow keys will move ten frames at a time in the corresponding direction and holding down the arrow keys keeps you moving continuously in the indicated direction.

You will likely find that scrubbing or clicking to approximately the position you want and then using the arrow keys to refine your position the most effective method.

Use the crop markers to select portions of your clip for copying, cutting, or cropping (see the "Cropping clips" section later in this chapter). To make the crop markers appear, click below the playhead while pressing the Shift key. Now, you can drag the crop markers to bound the desired clip segment. Even better, if the playhead is positioned at one end of the segment you want, you can Shift-click the scrubber bar at the other end of your segment and iMovie will select the segment and move the playhead to the point where you Shift-clicked.

You can use the left and right arrows (←, →) to position the crop markers just like the playhead. Click a crop marker and then use the arrow keys to move that marker one frame in the indicated direction (ten frames if you hold down the Shift key when pressing an arrow key).

To remove the crop markers, just click the clip in the shelf or the clip viewer and you're back to a clean slate.

Splitting clips

There are obvious uses for splitting clips, a couple of which are specific to working within iMovie. Among the obvious is when you want to interleave — that is, cut back and forth between — two scenes. Just split the clips and you can position the pieces in any order you please. The iMovie-specific reasons generally involve working with Transitions or other iMovie Effects and we'll get into that in the "Transitioning between clips," section later in this chapter.

Once again, iMovie makes your job easy, as follows:

1. Position the playhead where you want the split to occur.
2. Choose Edit ⇨ Split Video Clip at Playhead (⌘-T).

We told you it was easy. You now have two clips with similar names. The first retains the name of the original clip and the second is selected and has /1 appended to the name, as shown in Figure 14-11.

Figure 14-11: iMovie isn't exactly original when it names split clips.

Trimming or removing clip segments

You'll often want to trim a little from the start or end of a clip. Proceed as follows to trim from the end of a clip:

1. Position the playhead to the beginning of the extraneous footage.
2. Click past the end of the scrubber bar while pressing Shift. iMovie will select everything from the playhead to the end of the clip and move the playhead to the end of the clip.
3. Choose Edit ⇨ Clear or press the Delete key on your keyboard. Poof, that footage is gone.

You should notice that the clip's length (in the shelf or clip viewer) indicates the new length and the amount in the iMovie Trash has just increased.

To trim from the beginning of the clip, just reverse the process. Position to the end of the extraneous footage, Shift-click to the left of the scrubber bar, and choose Edit ⇨ Clear.

 Tip While you could trim from both the beginning and end, you'll find cropping (described shortly) to be easier than performing two trims.

The obvious corollary to trimming a clip is that you can also remove a chunk from the middle. Just select the segment you want to remove and choose Edit ⇨ Clear (or press Delete). The one major difference is that you'll now have two clips where you had one before. Notice that this is equivalent to splitting your clip and then trimming it.

Cropping clips

iMovie also gives you a convenient method to combine trimming from both ends at once, called *cropping*. Position the crop markers to bound the segment you wish to keep and then choose Edit ⇨ Crop (⌘-K). iMovie will remove the footage from either end, leaving just your selection.

 Note Cropping and clearing remove both the video and the associated audio. Sometimes you're going to want to retain the audio (maybe for narration over new video, like in a newscast). We'll show you how to do this in Chapter 15.

Of course, iMovie is a faithful Mac application, which means that you can also cut or copy then paste selected footage as well. When you copy (Edit ⇨ Copy or ⌘-C) a segment and then paste it (Edit ⇨ Paste or ⌘-V), a new clip appears on the shelf. What's cool about this is that you have now performed a crop without losing the original footage. Similarly, a cut (Edit ➪ Cut or ⌘-X) followed by a paste is the same as splitting and then splitting again.

Creating a still clip

We're sure you've all seen examples of still clips in movies and on television, even if you weren't aware that was what you were looking at. One common use for a still clip is when a scene transitions from what looks like a painting or daguerreotype into live action and full color. Another use is when you want to freeze a moment in your movie, such as a sign or a shocked expression.

Once again, iMovie makes creating a still clip simple:

1. Position the playhead to the frame from which you wish to create the still clip.
2. Choose Edit ➪ Create Still Clip (Shift-⌘-S) and you're done.

iMovie will name the first still clip Still 01 and number subsequent stills from there.

We're sure you recall that there was an Importing preference (see the "Setting Import Preferences" section in Chapter 13) establishing a still clip's duration as 5 seconds. The reason that option is an Importing preference is that you can also create still clips by Importing a graphic file.

Restoring a clip

Remember we told you that if you didn't empty iMovie's Trash, you could undo your way back to earlier states (up to 99 steps)? That method has some drawbacks, the greatest of which is that you end up undoing a whole lot of things that you might still want done to get a clip back to an earlier state. iMovie has a neat and easy solution to this quandary.

1. Select the clip. It doesn't matter whether it is in the shelf, in the clip viewer, or on the timeline viewer.
2. Choose Advanced ➪ Restore Clip Media. iMovie now alerts you, as shown in Figure 14-12, what it is going to do and how much data this will add to the beginning or end of the clip, and asks whether you want to proceed.

   You might also notice that it is one of the singularly least attractive alerts you're likely to see in iMovie or OS X.
3. Click OK if you wish to proceed.

Figure 14-12: iMovie will tell you how much material will be restored and ask whether to proceed.

Note If you split the clip or removed material from the middle, generating a second clip. That second clip will still exist, taking up disk space.

Reversing a clip

Here's an editing tool that falls into the category of special effects, and a pretty cool one at that when you use it appropriately. You can run a clip backwards as follows:

1. Select the clip from the shelf, clip viewer, or timeline viewer as appropriate.
2. Choose Advanced ➪ Reverse Clip Direction (⌘-R) and the clip is reversed.

Now, when you play the clip in the monitor everything in the clip runs backward, even the sound. If you don't want the sound to play backward, you'll need to extract it first, as we describe in the "Extracting the audio from a clip" section later in this chapter.

 Note If you look in the upper-right corner of a reversed clip icon's border, you will see a left-pointing triangle.

Working with the clip viewer

The shelf is a handy place to store clips, especially when you're working on them as described earlier in the "Editing clips" section. The clip viewer is where you assemble your movie, apply transitions and effects, and add titles and subtitles.

Moving your clips from the shelf to the clip viewer is, as usual, simplicity itself. Just select the clips in the shelf and drag them to the clip viewer. Being the obliging program that it is, when you select a clip (or group of clips) in the clip viewer, iMovie (again) presents you the opportunity to edit them in the monitor. But, far more than that, the clip viewer tells you a lot about your selected clip. Figure 14-13 shows the clip viewer with all its informational displays. If you have multiple clips selected, the clip name is replaced by "<multiple>" and the recording date/time isn't displayed.

Figure 14-13: The clip viewer tells you a lot about your selected clip(s).

> **Tip:** Deviating from our OS X coverage, there is one OS 9-specific problem that you might encounter in iMovie and which is particularly evident in the clip viewer. If the clip viewer's information display looks funny and truncated, you're running into a font-related bug. In OS 9, iMovie keeps a copy of the Lucida Grande font inside the application. However, Microsoft Office 2001 installs a font, Curlz MT, that has the same font id number and the wrong font gets used to display your information. The only way around this is to make sure that Curlz MT is not available when you run iMovie.

Now that you have your clips arranged in the clip viewer (hopefully, in the order you want them to play), it is time to start putting the polish on your movie: transitioning between clips, applying effect, and adding your titles, subtitles, and captions.

If you have some clips with which to work, you might want to follow along through the next few topics and get a real feel for how transitions, effects, and titles work. We can eloquently describe them, but there is no way in a static medium (such as this book) that you can actually experience the visual effect they produce.

Transitioning between clips

Every situation in filmmaking is different. You can apply rules until you're blue in the face and get serviceable results, but creating a movie still involves art and feel. One place where you'll find this very evident is when you are moving from one scene to another. Do you apply a transition or not? If you choose to apply a transition, which one do you use? By the way, if no transition is used between scenes, you're said to have *cut* from one scene to the next.

To cut or transition, that is the question

If you've got all your clips in the clip viewer, in the order you want them to occur, you're at a good starting point. One assumption we're going to make is that you already split your clips at scene breaks, if iMovie hadn't already done that for you.

iMovie provides a collection of common transitions: Cross Dissolve, Fade In, Fade Out, Overlap, Push, and Scale Down, as shown in Figure 14-14. Transitions exist between clips, becoming additional entities in the clip viewer and on the timeline viewer. As you can see in the figure, each transition has a little icon to its left. (It's green with gray arrowheads in real life.) If there are two arrowheads (e.g., Cross Dissolve), that means the transition affects the clips on either side of it. When there is just a right-pointing arrowhead at the left edge of the icon (e.g., Fade In), you have a transition that affects only the beginning of the clip that follows. Similarly, a left-pointing arrowhead on the right side of the green icon (e.g. Fade Out) indicates that the transition affects the ending of the clip preceding it.

Figure 14-14: Select and control your transition in the shelf's Transitions panel.

You might be tempted to put transitions between every scene. Don't succumb, but don't consider yourself unusual, either. Transitions are like a shiny new toy and the temptation to see how they look is almost unbearable. A transition's purpose is to segue your movie from one concept to the next, in other words, to indicate a change of focus. For example, you probably shouldn't put a transition between two clips during a battle scene where all you did was change the camera angle. But, if you are moving from viewing the battle to what's occurring on the home front, you probably want a transition.

Briefly, transitions are used to convey a change of focus or the passage of time. If you examine a movie closely, you'll find that cuts are used far more often than transitions and, with the addition of scoring or narration, the cuts are almost unnoticeable unless you're looking for them.

Checking out iMovie's transitions

As shown in Figure 14-14, iMovie comes with six transitions, but you can add more, either from the iMovie Plug-in Pack 2.1.1 for Mac OS X (http://docs.info.apple.com/article.html?artnum=120059) or from a commercial package. Apple includes a link to third-party plug-in collections on the main iMovie page, www.apple.com/imovie. Here are the six supplied transitions and their descriptions:

- **Cross Dissolve:** This transition works on two clips, making the first clip appear to gradually disappear, revealing the second clip running behind it. By setting the Speed, you can control how long the dissolve lasts. Cross Dissolves are especially effective for minor changes in time.

- **Fade In:** Use Fade In to cause a clip to gradually appear from a black background. Fade Ins are most useful when introducing the story or a significantly different scene, such as someone waking up the morning after.

- **Fade Out:** Fade Out will cause your clip's end to fade to black and is effective at the end of your movie or to signal the end of a significant scene.

- **Overlap:** Working on two clips, an Overlap is similar to a Cross Dissolve. The primary difference is that the second clip now appears in front of the first clip. Overlaps are used primarily to indicate a change of location.

- **Push:** Kind of a hokey transition, the second clip slides in and pushes the previous clip off screen. When you choose a Push, the Direction arrows become enabled and you can choose whether things slide from left-to-right, right-to-left, bottom-to-top, or top-to-bottom. The only really good uses for this transition are in a slide show presentation or when looking for a comedic touch.

- **Scale Down:** Another special-purpose, somewhat hokey transition, Scale Down causes the first clip to shrink down to a dot and disappear, revealing the second clip running behind it. Scale Down is also good for slide shows and might be useful if your film is science fiction.

Setting up and applying a transition

Unless you have selected clips in the clip viewer, iMovie will assume that you wish to operate on the first clip or pair of clips in the clip viewer and those are the clips it'll use in the Preview pane for demonstration purposes. That's not a big deal if all you're interested in is seeing how the effects work, but if you want to see how the transition looks on the clips for which you intend it, select them in the clip viewer (or timeline viewer).

By clicking on a transition name in the Transition list, you tell iMovie to preview what it will look like in the Preview pane. Most of the time, previewing is a really good idea, because you're probably going to want to customize the transition a bit. There are two customizations possible: Speed and Direction, but Direction is only available to some transitions. For example, of the six transitions that come with iMovie, Direction is active only for Push.

- **Speed** might also be called duration. By moving the slider, you control how long the transition takes to complete. When you release the slider, iMovie will display the new preview. Just to be perfectly clear, the times on the slider are in seconds and frames. In general, iMovie will not allow a transition of less than 10 frames nor one longer than 4 seconds. The time you've selected is displayed in the lower-right corner of the Preview pane, which is a lot easier than estimating just how far you've moved the slider.

- **Direction** lets you specify the direction for movement-related transitions like Push.

When you're pretty sure you have things the way you want them, you should probably click the Preview button and check it one more time, this time in the monitor window so you don't have to squint so hard.

Be aware that the preview will not be as smooth as a finished transition. iMovie has to perform lots of computations to smooth things out and the preview is just an approximation.

Drag one-clip transitions on top of the clip they are to affect and drag two-clip transitions between the clips of interest. iMovie doesn't actually *render* (apply) the transition until you drag it into place in the clip viewer (or timeline viewer). While iMovie is performing the myriad calculations necessary to make the transition as seamless as possible, a small progress indicator (shown in Figure 14-15) appears below the transition's icon. The black bar gradually turns red as the rendering takes place.

Figure 14-15: The rendering progress indicator turns red as the rendering takes place.

Progress indicator

With shorter or simpler transitions, the indicator often disappears before you even notice it is there. As Macs get faster, the progress indicator's lifespan also grows shorter.

You can still do other things, like edit or view other parts of your movie. About the only thing you can't do while the rendering takes place is view the transition. Be aware that rendering is a processor-intensive activity, so your Mac might be a little less responsive than usual while it concentrates on the rendering.

Now that you have your transition selected and rendered, you're obviously going to want to admire your handiwork. If it is a one-clip transition, you need only select it and the clip it affects in the clip viewer (or timeline viewer) and click the monitor's Play button. For two-clip transitions, select both clips (iMovie will also select the transition) and click the monitor's Play button. You could select just the transition in the timeline to play only the transition. If you do this, be aware that you won't see any context.

Tip
Transitions will show up to best effect if played back to your camera or an external monitor.

Modifying and deleting transitions

If, after you've gone to all that effort creating and rendering a transition, you see that it isn't quite what you want, iMovie empowers you to modify it. Just select the transition in the clip viewer with the Transitions panel showing and you can modify any of the settings, even the selected transition. When you're done (or think you are), click the Update button and iMovie will render the new transition choice.

Deleting transitions is Mac-simple. If adding it was the last thing you did, you can choose Edit ➪ Undo Add Transition (⌘-Z). Or, even if you've gone on and done other things, you can select the transition's icon and choose Edit ➪ Clear (or press Delete). Poof, the transition is gone and iMovie returns any affected clips to their unmodified states.

Understanding visual effects

We noted (briefly) in Chapter 13 that what you find on the iMovie Effects panel (Figure 14-16) are not what we normally consider "special effects" — like a sunburst or a man morphing into a dog. What you can do here is affect the brightness, contrast, even color in your clips. When used in conjunction with transitions, you can emulate some of the classier visual effects of professional moviemakers.

Figure 14-16: The Effects panel lets you choose, tweak, preview, and apply your effects.

iMovie comes with seven built-in effects, but you can add more. The iMovie Plug-in Pack 2.1.1 for OS X adds five more and various third-party sources sell larger collections. Bob is a big fan of the Gee Three Slick transitions and effects (www.geethree.com), which are inexpensive and give professional-looking results.

Exploring the Effects panel

The Effects panel in Figure 14-16 is chock-full of possibilities. Some of the effects offer additional sliders below the list that you use to customize that particular effect. Others, such as Black & White, don't — what you see is what you get. As with transitions, every time you select an effect or change a setting, iMovie will run a preview of your effect in the (small) Preview pane at the upper-right of the panel.

Two sliders are present above the Effects list for all effects though: Effect In and Effect Out. Use Effect In to specify when the effect is to start relative to the beginning of the clip (0:00 says to start it at the beginning of the clip). Similarly, you use Effect Out to specify when the effect terminates relative to the end of the clip. That's a critical point: 0:00 means that it ends when the clip does, 1:15 would indicate that it ends 1.5 seconds before the clip ends (30 frames to a second). So, if you know the timecode (from the time display next to the playhead) where you want the effect to end, you're going to have to do a little subtraction: length of clip minus the timecode.

Another behavioral oddity relating to effects is that if you specify that the effect is in effect (pun intended) for the clip's full length (Effect In = 0:00 and Effect Out = 0:00), then you will see a constant application of the effect, be it Sepia Tone, Soft Focus, or whatever. On the other hand, if either Effect In or Effect Out is not zero, you will get a gradual increase (kind of like a fade in) effect to the effect (okay, we promise to stop abusing this pun opportunity).

Tip

You can apply multiple effects to the same clip, with the same or different in and out times. While overuse of this capability can make your movie kind of tacky, judicious application, say sequential Color Shifts, could produce a stylish result.

Checking out iMovie's Effects

The seven effects supplied with iMovie fall (pretty much) into three categories:

✦ **Brightness and Contrast Adjustments:** There's just one here, named (appropriately) Brightness/Contrast.

This is very much like the Brightness and Contrast adjustments on your TV set. Adjusting brightness up makes everything closer to white whereas adjusting down makes everything darker, but at different rates. Dark pixels get darker faster than light pixels and light pixels get lighter faster than dark pixels. Increasing contrast makes dark pixels darker and light pixels lighter. Adjusting contrast can be helpful when you had too much light on your subject, washing out the image.

- **Color Adjustments:** Again, you just have one here with the original name, Adjust Colors. Three sliders, Hue Shift, Color, and Lightness appear beneath the list and provide this effect with great power to do good or evil.

  - **Hue Shift** changes the colors in your image from red/yellow on the slider's left end toward blue/green at the right. If you have too much red/yellow/orange in the picture, moving the slider right a bit can help.
  - **Color** adjusts individual pixels between pure (Vivid) and gray (B&W). Again, subtle changes are your best bet. A slight change toward black-and-white can give your movie an "aged" look, like some of the early color movies of the '30s and '40s.
  - **Lightness** also creates a pixel shift. Unlike brightness, the shift rate is linear, everything lightening or darkening at the same rate.

- **Specialty Effects:** The remaining five effects—Black and White, Sepia Tone, Sharpen, Soft Focus, and Water Ripple—modify the clarity or fidelity of your images.

  - **Black and White** is a simplified color adjustment all the way to black-and-white and has no additional controls.
  - **Sepia Tone** gives your image the look of daguerreotypes from the Old West, with a brownish tinge to everything. Color experts call this shade of brown, sepia, hence the name, but we're guys and aren't supposed to know that much about color. Again, this effect has no additional controls.
  - **Sharpen** adjusts each pixel (like Photoshop's Sharpen filter), making the image appear to have had a focus adjustment. You have one slider here, from low (less sharpened focus) to high (very sharp focus). We tend to use this one frequently when we're going to export our movie to QuickTime (especially to VideoCD using Toast 5 Titanium's VideoCD export plug-in, which we'll discuss in Chapter 17).
  - **Soft Focus** is the opposite of Sharpen. If you've used Photoshop's Blur filter, you've seen the effect. Adjust the slider to High if you want a really fuzzy picture, close to Low if you just want to soften some of the sharp edges that digital video sometimes produces.
  - **Water Ripple** is the closest thing on the Effects panel to a classic special effect, making your picture look like you filmed it under water and there was a current. No controls are available for this one.

When applied to a full clip, most of the above effects really don't appeal to us (or to experienced filmmakers of our acquaintance). Why, then, are they present in iMovie and why are we discussing them at such length? The answer is simple, when used as *transitional* effects (yeah, roll-your-own transitions) these effects can be very, well, effective as the image changes gradually. The trick to making them transitional is to master the use of Effect In and Effect Out. Here are a few examples using Effect In to transition into a clip:

- Employing Sepia Tone and a still clip of the final frame, you can transition from a full-color motion picture to a daguerreotype-like still image. Set your Effect In time to late in the clip. Similarly, apply Sepia Tone to the entire still clip.

- Using Soft Focus, you can show what a person who is getting woozy might be looking at, just before they pass out. Select the clip, select Soft Focus in the Effects panel, move the slider to High, and set Effect In time to the end of the clip. Of course, the clip needs to be 10 seconds or shorter, so prepare to split the clip if necessary.

- Selecting Brightness/Contrast and dragging both sliders all the way to the right, you can get the opposite of a fade-to-black — a total whiteout. Again, making sure that your clip is 10 seconds or less in length, set Effect In to the end of the clip and put on your polarized lenses.

Adjusting Effect Out lets you move from the effect to normal color and action. Here are a couple of examples that you might find useful:

- If you remember the TV series, *The Wild Wild West,* you'll remember scenes starting out as black-and-white stills, progressing to normal colors, and starting the action when full color was achieved. To emulate this effect, create a still clip of the opening frame and set it to Black & White. Then, in the real frame, set the Effect Out time to a few seconds after the start of the clip. (Yes, once again, you might need to split the clip so that the 10 second limit doesn't bite you.)

- You can achieve a gradual focus by setting Soft Focus to High and setting the Effect Out time to just a couple seconds into the clip. This effect is a cool way to emulate what someone who is just waking up might be seeing.

Finally, by tweaking both the Effect In and Effect Out on a clip, you can have the effect gradually take over at the beginning of a clip, be in place for a while, and then have the clip return to normal at the end. One possible use for this would be sliding into a hazy daydream perspective (Soft Focus) and then returning to full consciousness.

Tip

In the preceding discussion we frequently referenced the 10-second limitation on Effect In and Effect Out relative to a clip's beginning and end, respectively. This is one of the primary uses for splitting a clip. Since there is no perceptible difference between a clip that is one minute long or the same footage split into six ten-second clips when viewed, split the clip if it is at all advantageous. One use would be to have a visual effect, like Black and White or Water Ripple, be in complete sway for part of a clip (no gradual intro or exit). Just split out the segment you want, select it, pick your effect, and set the Effect In and Effect Out to 0:00.

Adding text

The old saying goes, "A picture is worth a thousand words." We don't know how true that is, but when it comes to movie credits, everybody involved in a movie wants their name to appear on the screen, whether their picture is there or not.

Similarly, we expect to see a title appear, identifying the movie and, sometimes, the scene. The teletype intros on *JAG* and *X-Files* scenes, as well as those in some action movies (e.g., *Clear and Present Danger*) really help set the scene.

In addition, we can't forget the subtitle. Subtitles don't have to be a language translation, either. You can use subtitles to identify characters in your movie when they first appear or use them to display the lyrics to a song as it plays. Is anyone else here old enough to remember "Sing Along with Mitch"?

Note You can't add a title to the portion of a clip containing a transition. If you *really* want a title inside the transition (it's usually an ugly idea, anyway), you have to add the title before applying the transition.

Exploring the Titles panel

As you can see in Figure 14-17, the Titles panel is the busiest we've seen yet. At the top is the ubiquitous preview area, with its miniature screen, the Preview button so that you can check your title out in the monitor before applying it, and the Update button for when you want to tweak an existing title. In the center, you see a list of title (and subtitle) types and a compass of directional arrows for controlling the motion of the animated title styles. iMovie comes with thirteen and the iMovie 2.1.1 Plug-in Pack for OS X provides four more. While it is possible that they exist, we haven't yet found third-party plug-in packs containing new title variations. So, if you hear of any, let us know.

Figure 14-17: The Titles panel gives you lots of options.

Other than the two basic areas we just mentioned, the Titles panel contains three more areas of interest: the duration sliders (Speed and Pause), the options area (Color, Over Black, QT Margins, font, and size), and the text area.

The Duration sliders are used as follows:

+ Set the **Speed slider** to how long the text should take to show up completely.
+ Set the **Pause slider** to how long the text should remain on-screen once it has appeared. The Pause slider will be enabled only when the title type involves some motion.

Tip

When the Preview pane reverts to black, you'll see the Speed and Pause times and their sum displayed in the bottom-right corner. By the way, if you find the slider names less than descriptive, don't feel like you're all alone. We feel the same way.

The Options area contains the following controls:

+ The **Color** button is not a check box, but rather a display of the currently selected text color. Click and hold on this square and you'll see a pop-up palette (see Figure 14-18) with the limited number of colors iMovie offers for text (there are 32 choices). Light text on a dark background and dark text on a light background look best. In fact, almost anything else approaches unreadable. Click a color to preview it (the palette will stay) or double-click a color to select it and dismiss the palette.

Figure 14-18: You have a small palette of text colors from which to choose.

If you look closely, you'll see that iMovie adds a slight black drop-shadow to the text. This can make dark (particularly, black) text look a little strange.

+ The **Over Black** check box is really handy. By opting for Over Black, you create a new clip displaying your title text against a solid black background.

Note

Adding an Over Black title increases the length of your movie.

+ The **QT Margins** check box is a safety net of sorts. If you leave QT Margins off (the default), iMovie protects the text from appearing too close to the edge of the image. The 720×480 NTSC resolution in iMovie doesn't protect against the overscan common in TV sets. (There's more of the picture than is displayed within the TV screen's borders.) If your video is not going to be displayed on a TV set, you can check QT Margins and iMovie will let your titles and subtitles sit a little closer to the screen's edges.

- What can we say about the **Font** pop-up list that hasn't been said in hundreds of books? Use the pop-up to select a typeface for your text. (Please try to be tasteful.)
- The **Size** slider (little A on one end, big A on the other) is pretty straightforward. Use it to decrease (slide left) or increase (slide right) the size of your title text.

The Text area is pretty straightforward as well. It will either display two lines of text, a scrolling list of two-line text groups, or a wrapping text input box, depending upon the Title type you select. (We'll discuss the supplied Title types next.)

Exploring iMovie's Title types

With the 13 title types iMovie provides, most common titling and captioning needs are met. The following is a brief rundown of what you get in the box as it were:

- **Bounce In To Center** works with two lines of text. The directional arrow controls the movement of the first line of text (the second line enters from the opposite edge of the screen). Set the Speed to determine how quickly the text moves and the Pause to set how long it stays on screen once it has reached its final position.
- **Centered Multiple** works with multiple two-line blocks. Each two-line group fades into view in the center of the screen as set by the Speed slider, sits there for as long as the Pause slider indicates, and then fades out to be replaced by the next two-line block until all your two-line blocks have been displayed.
- **Centered Title** is the same as Centered Multiple, but with just one two-line text group.
- **Drifting** also works with just one two-line text group. The second line slides in the direction indicated by the directional arrow, the first line in the opposite direction until the two lines are centered onscreen, then the title fades out. There is no Pause option for this title effect.
- **Flying Letters** also works with just one two-line text group. The letters fly into position one at a time from the top-right corner if the directional arrow is down or from the bottom right if the arrow is up. The left and right arrows are disabled. After all the text is in place, the title will stay onscreen for the Pause time.
- **Flying Words** is just like Flying Letters except that the text flies in a line at a time.
- **Music Video** is one of our favorites, just because it lets you put large blocks of text onscreen at one time. There is no Pause time for this effect, but the Speed slider sets the duration. (No fade-in or fade-out is involved.) The text displays in the left half of the screen, pinned to the bottom and growing upward the more text you enter, as shown in Figure 14-19.

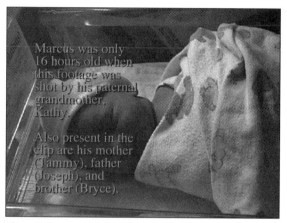

Figure 14-19: Music Video captions can span many lines of text.

+ **Rolling Centered Credits** uses multiple two-line groups, with a twist. The first line of each group is right-justified at the screen's center (minus a little margin) and the second line is left-justified at the center (plus a little margin). This gives you side-by-side credits and is useful when you want to give the character name followed by the performer's name. You can have the credits roll up from the bottom or down from the top using the direction arrows. No Pause setting is available; you can only control how quickly the lines scroll.

+ **Rolling Credits** are similar to Rolling Centered Credits. The difference is that instead of aligning to the center of the screen, the first line is left-aligned, the second line is right-aligned, and they are connected by a row of periods.

+ **Scroll with Pause** is a straightforward, means-what-it-says, effect. You get two lines of text that scroll in the direction you set, pause at center screen for the duration you specify, and then scroll out of view.

+ **Scrolling Block** is one of our favorites. You can create large blocks of text (like with Music Video) and they will scroll up or down the screen (centered horizontally). If we just had a perspective effect on this we could emulate the opening of a Star Wars movie.

+ **Stripe Subtitle** changes the way some things work. For example, the color selection now describes the base color for the gradient stripe (dark on the left and fading out on the right) that spans the bottom third of your monitor (unless you choose a white, in which case the stripe will be black to dark gray) with the two lines of text displayed in white against this background, as shown in Figure 14-20.

+ **Typewriter** is the effect we're all familiar with from *JAG* and *X-Files* where letters (and numbers) appear one-at-a-time in the lower-left portion of the screen as if they're being typed on the screen (although you'll have to provide your own sound effects).

Figure 14-20: Striped Subtitles give you white text against a colored gradient stripe.

Assuming that you're displaying your title against a fairly static background or using Over Black, you can create some interesting variations. You might notice that Scrolling Block has no Pause option to display the text centered on your screen. To work around that, create a Scrolling Block title, extract a still frame with the text centered on your screen, split the original placing the extracted frame in the middle, and adjust its duration as desired. Using a similar technique, you can get around the 2-second limitation on Pauses. Like we said before, art (imagination) is a big part of making the most of iMovie.

Adding and removing titles

Once you have the title the way you want it (that *is* what Preview is for), you're ready to add it to your movie. Drag the title type from the Title Type list to the left edge of the clip to which you want it applied. iMovie will start to render the title, displaying a progress bar as shown in Figure 14-21, right on the title clip, telling you how many frames are to be rendered and how many it has rendered so far.

Note If the title is shorter than the clip to which you're applying it, iMovie will automatically split the clip. If the title is longer than the clip, iMovie will run over into the next clip.

Figure 14-21: Title clips give frame-by-frame progress while rendering and sport a little T badge in the upper-right corner.

Title clips are marked with a T in the upper-right corner as you can see in Figure 14-21 and, if a new clip is created (as is usually the case), it gets the name of the title.

Removing a title is really easy — just select it and choose Edit ➪ Clear or press Delete. iMovie even does your housekeeping for you, adding the content from the title clip back into the clip from which it came (assuming that it did its usual split). In short, deleting a title clip only deletes the rendering.

> **Tip**
>
> When you want to insert a subtitle, you're frequently going to find that you want it somewhere in the middle of the clip, not at the beginning where iMovie wants to put it. This reiterates our earlier advice: When in doubt, split a clip.

You can even combine title sequences, creating some interesting effects. For example, you could create a Flying Letters title for your male lead that flies in from the top (use just the first line of the two available) and another Flying Letters title for your female lead (use just the second line of the two available) that flies in from the bottom. The only thing you have to remember is that you can't set the second title up until you've dragged the first one down and started it rendering if you're using Over Black. If you're not using Over Black, you have to wait for the rendering to finish before you can add the next title.

Working with the timeline viewer

There's a reason the timeline viewer shares screen real-estate with the clip viewer. Underneath the skin, they're the same thing. Virtually any action you can perform in the clip viewer can be performed in the timeline viewer as well: transitions, effects, and titling are all doable in either view. The big difference is that the timeline viewer has an awesome collection of editing tools available and gives you a more detailed view of how your movie is coming together. Where the clip viewer presents an outside view of your movie, the timeline viewer is like Superman's x-ray vision and shows you the different tracks and lets you make adjustments at a much finer level.

Additionally, some effects (those on the Audio panel) can only be applied in the timeline viewer since you need to have access to the two audio tracks. There are a few other tasks you can perform only in the timeline viewer and, while most of them have to do with audio, not all do so.

When we introduced the timeline viewer in Chapter 13, we pointed out that iMovie does give you one cool special effect in the timeline viewer: fast-mo and slo-mo. Just select your clip and move the slider. Clips that have had their speed altered appear in the clip viewer with a Fast Forward badge (double arrowhead) or Slow Down badge (vertical bar and arrowhead).

> **Caution**
>
> Make a speed change the last thing you do to a clip. Any other effect, transition, or title applied to a speed-changed clip will revert it to normal speed.

Also, in the timeline viewer you can select a still clip as shown in Figure 14-22 and change its duration by typing in a new length.

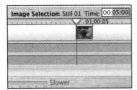

Figure 14-22: Type in a new length to change a still clip's duration.

With the volume slider at the bottom of the timeline viewer, you can change a clip's volume. Maybe it was too soft or too loud when you recorded it, relative to the rest of your clips. You can also select the Fade In or Fade Out check boxes, causing a clip's audio to start soft and build to normal volume at the start or soften from normal to silent at the end. You can even check both.

Tip

If you use the Fade In and Fade Out check boxes, you don't control how long the fade takes. Double-click the clip to display the Clip Info dialog if you want to control the duration as well.

Using the timeline viewer for transitions, effects, and titles

The only real differences between using the clip viewer and the timeline viewer for these features are in appearance. For example, clip miniatures are smaller and harder to recognize in the timeline viewer. The miniatures are also more spread out, so you'll probably need to change the timeline viewer's zoom factor to 1x to get everything in view.

The behavioral differences are very minor. To apply a transition to the beginning of a clip, drag it to the left of the icon or, if you want to apply it to the end of a clip, drag to the right of the icon. Applying a title is roughly the same, but you get feedback where the title will go when a blue vertical line appears (let go if that's where you want the title). Similarly, for effects, just drag the effect to the clip's strip in the timeline viewer.

Working with audio tracks

Now we're getting to the timeline viewer's raison d'etre. Working with and manipulating your movie's individual tracks is how you'll distinguish your efforts from those of your grandfather with his 8mm Bell & Howell.

A simple but incredibly powerful iMovie feature is that you can separate the video and audio you've imported from your camcorder. Why, you ask, would I want to do this?

Just as a "for instance," suppose that you have background noise interfering with your kid's dance recital tape. You can separate the audio and replace it with a clean recording of the music, minus the jackhammer sounds from the construction going on outside or the gossipfest by the two parents in front of you whose kids have yet to do their performance.

Another handy use is best exemplified by a TV news show, where the reporter's voice describes what you're seeing on their news footage.

Extracting audio

Editing your existing audio begins with a single step. Select your clip in the timeline viewer and choose Advanced ⇨ Extract Audio (⌘-J). iMovie will present a progress dialog (shown in Figure 14-23) telling you that it is extracting audio and naming the clip from which the extraction is taking place. When the extraction is complete, you'll see a new audio clip (a pale orange strip) in the #1 audio track, as shown in Figure 14-23.

This audio clip will, at least until you start doing other things to it or the source video clip, be the same length as the video clip from whence it came and coincide with it in your movie's timeline. Those cute little pushpin icons at the start of the separate video and audio clips are iMovie's way of telling you that the audio is pinned (iMovie calls it *locked*, but we guess OS X has overdone the padlock metaphor) to that point in the video. If you move the video, the audio will follow along.

Removing, copying, cutting, and pasting audio

As with any other clip, one of the simplest things you can do with an audio clip is delete it. To delete the clip, select it (the pale orange gets darker) and choose Edit ⇨ Clear (or press Delete). The only way to get it back is to use Edit ⇨ Undo (⌘-Z).

Being the good Mac application that it is, iMovie also lets you select a clip and use the standard Mac editing commands: Cut, Copy, and Paste. If you cut (Edit ⇨ Cut or ⌘-X), you remove the clip from the timeline viewer but leave a copy in the Mac clipboard. Copying (Edit ⇨ Copy or ⌘-C) leaves the clip in the timeline viewer and places a copy in the clipboard. Paste (Edit ⇨ Paste or ⌘-V) places a copy of the clipboard in the timeline viewer at the current playhead position (so be sure to move the playhead to where you want the audio to appear.

Figure 14-23: iMovie keeps you informed of the extraction progress (a); after extraction, you have separate, matched-up video and audio clips (b).

Tip

If you paste audio to a location where the video clip still has audio, you'll hear both audio tracks when you play the clip (or movie). This might (or might not) be what you want, but you should be aware of it. If you don't want the original video's audio track, extract and delete it before pasting the new audio clip.

Locking and unlocking audio clips

As we mentioned earlier in the "Extracting audio" section, iMovie locks the audio clip to the video clip from which it was extracted. You, too, can lock audio clips to video clips, actually to specific points within video clips. When audio is locked to a video clip, that means that no matter what else happens in the movie, this audio clip starts to play at the marked point in that video clip.

There are occasions (we'll cover some in the "Getting Advanced with iMovie" section in Chapter 15) where you will want to edit the video and have the audio associated with a new point on the timeline viewer. To achieve this, you'll need to unlock the audio from the video.

To unlock an audio clip:

1. Select the locked audio clip (it turns bright orange).
2. Choose Advanced ⇨ Unlock Audio Clip (⌘-L). The pushpin disappears, revealing the triangular marker it was hiding the whole time.

After you've accomplished your video editing, you're going to want to associate that audio clip with a new (video) point on the timeline viewer and lock them together 'til death or your next editing brainstorm does them part.

To lock an audio clip:

1. Select the audio clip. Okay, there's a gotcha hidden here, especially if you have multiple audio clips in the track: You want to make sure that iMovie synchronizes the audio clip's start with the video position to which you're going to lock it down. Click in the playhead's tick bar above the end of the audio clip you're going to lock down before you click on the audio clip. The playhead will snap to the start of the audio clip.
2. Move the playhead to the position where you want the audio to start using any or all of the standard playhead positioning gimmicks we've described.
3. Choose Advanced ⇨ Lock Audio Clip at Playhead (⌘-L) to lock the audio and video clips (and make the little pushpins appear).

Moving audio clips

iMovie only recognizes an audio clip's lock when a video edit would affect the audio. This means that you can move even locked audio around in the timeline viewer as you wish; however, if the audio was locked, iMovie will lock it to the point you place it.

iMovie lets you select audio clips and move them by dragging or using the arrow keys. You also have a (not well-documented) trick to position an audio clip to begin or end at a specific spot on the timeline viewer:

1. Position the timeline viewer's playhead to the exact point where you want your audio clip to begin (or end).

2. Select the audio clip by clicking in the front half if you want to align the beginning or in the back half if you want to align the ending. You'll now see a dimmed time reference on the timeline viewer (Figure 14-24) and a ghostly playhead afterimage line as the playhead moves along with the clip you're dragging. When the end you're aligning gets close, the clip will snap into position.

Figure 14-24: The clip will snap into place when the playhead gets close to its ghost.

We can barely see the ghostly line on our LCD screens, but you can still tell you're getting close by checking the playhead's time reference against the dimmed time reference.

Splitting and cropping audio clips

Further demonstrating that audio clips are really clips, you can split and crop them just as you can video clips. The only real difference is that the splitting and cropping occurs in the timeline viewer rather than the monitor.

To split an audio clip:

1. Select the audio clip in the timeline viewer

2. Position the playhead where (when?) you want the split to occur by clicking along the playhead's tickline or dragging the playhead, itself. You can make fine adjustments to the playhead location with the arrow keys, just as you did when working with video clips in the monitor.

3. Choose Edit ⇨ Split Selected Audio Clip at Playhead. If the clip is locked to the video, the left portion of the split clip will still be locked, but the right portion will be fancy-free, as shown in Figure 14-25.

Figure 14-25: Only the beginning of a locked clip stays locked after splitting.

To crop an audio clip:

1. Select the audio clip you want to crop. There are inward pointing triangles at each end called crop markers. If the clip is locked, the pushpin might be hiding the beginning crop marker.
2. Grab each crop marker in turn and move it toward the other one until you have the desired portion selected. Portions outside the crop markers turn almost white, indicating deselection as shown in Figure 14-26. You can use the arrow keys for fine positioning of the crop markers.
3. Choose Edit ⇨ Crop (⌘-K) to delete the material outside the crop markers.

Figure 14-26: Move the crop markers to bracket the material you wish to retain.

Strangely enough, even if you don't issue the Crop command, the material outside the crop markers is effectively deleted from your movie. Even though it is still present, it won't play in your movie. So, if you aren't sure yet that you really want to delete it, don't issue the Crop command — you can check it out to see how it plays before you make up your mind. Then, if you decide to keep it, you can drag the crop markers back and restore it to your magnum opus.

Check out Chapter 15 for discussion of J-cuts, L-cuts, and intercutting — some of the really cool things you can do with audio editing.

Unleashing iMovie Audio effects

We're (finally?) going to hit the last panel in the shelf: Audio. You discovered the panel in Chapter 13, but now you're going to learn how to use it. The Audio panel (shown in Figure 14-27) has three sections which we call, from top to bottom: Sound Effects, Narration (or Voice overs), and Music (alias "ripping").

Adding sound effects

iMovie starts you off with 18 sound effects, with durations varying from a cat meowing for 18 frames to 6 seconds and 24 frames of footsteps. Pay special attention to those lengths, because one thing you can't do with the sound effects is edit them for length — the closest you can come is to fade it out or fade it in if it's too long.

Click once on a sound effect to hear it through your Mac's speakers or, if you have headphones or external speakers attached, through them. The volume slider in the monitor can be used to adjust the playback volume.

Figure 14-27: The Audio panel lets you add sound effects, narrations, and background music.

As usual, adding a sound effect is Mac-simple. Just find the sound effect you want in the scrolling list and drag it to the timeline viewer, dropping it on either of the two audio tracks. A blue box will appear on the selected audio track, as shown in Figure 14-28.

Figure 14-28: Blue boxes in an audio track indicate a sound effect.

Tip

Although you can place a sound effect in either audio track, you're well-advised to keep them all in the same track for organizational purposes. We tend to reserve track one for soundtrack items and track two for background items like sound effects and background music. Obviously, you can do what you want, but as your movie grows, you'll benefit from a consistent approach.

Adding narration

Narrations, which iMovie refers to as *voice overs,* provide you with the tool to set the scene, documentary-style, or act as a master of ceremonies. That little Record Voice button in the middle of the Audio panel in Figure 14-27 looks simple, but conceals a great many headaches.

Dealing with the microphone

You might get lucky. Many Macs have a microphone built-in, but in some cases you're going to have to connect one, which raises a few issues of its own.

First, to find out if you have a built-in microphone, face your Mac with the Audio panel open and speak to it, (We promise not to tell the folks at Bellevue that you talk to your computer.) If your Mac has a functioning built-in microphone, you should see the little lights flicker in green and amber just above the Record Voice button. This probably also means that you're running iMovie in Mac OS 9 or OS 10.2, because we haven't been able to get iMovie to recognize the internal microphone in OS X versions earlier than 10.2.

As a practical matter, most OS X Macs (especially those manufactured since January 2001) don't provide a built-in microphone or even the traditional line-in port through which you could connect a PlainTalk microphone. This has undoubtedly saved a cubic centimeter or so inside your Mac, reduced the manufacturing costs by a couple of cents, and promoted the sale of such USB microphones as the iVoice (Macally Peripherals, www.macally.com), the Verse-704 (Labtec, www.labtec.com), or the iMic (Griffin Technologies, www.griffintechnology.com).

Note Griffin Technology's iMic isn't really a microphone. It is a USB device into which you can plug almost any type of consumer microphone or speaker. So, if you have a microphone from some other piece of electronics, you can just plug it in and go to work. (Dennis *knew* there was a reason keep all those various recorders he owned over the years.)

Whether or not you have a built-in microphone, you're almost surely going to be better off with an external USB microphone. The sound quality of Apple's built-in microphones is really not adequate for a work of art such as you're going to produce in iMovie.

Sometimes, though, even a USB microphone won't give you the quality you want or you might not have one available (or want to spend the extra money on one). You do have another solution—your digital camcorder. You can record yourself speaking directly to it, import the clip, extract the audio, throw away the video, and be done with all the headaches. That, however, doesn't involve using Record Voice, so we'll get back on-topic now.

By default, iMovie stores your voice over recording on audio track 1, which is also where extracted audio gets placed. You can overlap audio clips on the track and both will play, but you'll have a difficult time discerning what ends where.

If you don't have a lot of experience speaking into a microphone, here are a few tips to help you achieve better results:

- ✦ Position yourself close to, but not directly in contact with, the microphone.
- ✦ Make sure that your throat is clear and that you're ready to start speaking.
- ✦ Test your microphone to make sure that it's working.
- ✦ Time a run-through of what you're going to say to make sure that you can fill the planned clip. Adjust your presentation or pace accordingly.
- ✦ Practice your presentation enough that you're familiar with it and that your speaking voice is natural when you are reading (or reciting) it.

Now that the prep work is done, you're ready to narrate. Here's what you do:

1. Position the timeline viewer's playhead where you want your clip to start.
2. Click the Record Voice button and begin speaking. The Record Voice button changes to Stop.
3. When you're done narrating, click Stop.

Just as with imported video, iMovie limits an audio clip's length to just short of 10 minutes. But here, there's a difference. Instead of continuing the recording in a new clip, iMovie stops recording. Since you're aware of this, you should plan breaks in a narration exceeding this limit so that you can create multiple clips that flow smoothly from one to the next. (Paragraph breaks are a good place to stop a clip and start a new one.)

Adding background music

Successful movies (and videos) always, in our experience, have a great soundtrack. Whether it is a musical where a soundtrack is expected, science fiction (like *Star Wars*), or even a war story (like *Apocalypse Now*), there is background music setting the mood.

Getting your music from CD

Unless you're well-funded enough to hire musicians or musically gifted so that you can provide your own score, you're probably going to be looking for a music source. That generally equates into importing music from a CD or using MP3s (maybe from iTunes). There are some excellent scoring tools, such as SmartSound's MovieMaestro (www.smartsound.com), which we'll cover in Chapter 17, that provide access to professional-quality music without you risking a copyright violation lawsuit.

Whether or not you have copyright issues and regardless of their status, actually adding CD tracks for use in your movie is, as usual, quite simple. As you can see in Figure 14-29, the Audio CD interface offers a familiar look and familiar controls. You can select tracks in the scrolling list and use the Audio CD Player control buttons below the list to move to the beginning of a track, move to the next track, play (or stop playing) a track, pause play of a track, or eject the CD. Clicking the Record Music button starts the process of extracting the music from the CD and placing it in audio track 2.

Copyright and You

Even though iMovie (and iTunes) make it easy to use CD tracks for your own purposes, you should remember that repurposing the contents of a copyrighted commercial CD is likely to get you sued (and lawyers can be *very* expensive, even if you manage to win).

Fortunately, if your movie is going to be purely for the personal enjoyment of you and your family, the likelihood of any studio siccing their legal barracudas on you is pretty remote, even in the unlikely event that it ever comes to their attention. Although the music industry (and movies and TV) are pushing hard to eliminate its existence, the courts in the U.S. have long established a *fair use* clause slightly limiting the absolute power of copyright. Private, noncommercial usage of legally purchased recordings is generally considered as a fair use (as opposed to the legal principle called "fair use").

Note the "noncommercial" and "private" qualifiers. Using copyrighted material in a corporate video would not fall under any definition of fair use. In such a scenario, you should seek to obtain permission or acquire a license from the copyright holder to use their work. Unfortunately, artists rarely own the copyrights to their work, and dealing with the legal departments of Sony, Disney, or other media giants is not a pleasant, speedy, or inexpensive endeavor.

One prospect is to acquire royalty-free recordings. Now, royalty-free doesn't mean totally free — it just means that once you purchase them, they're yours to use. Collections of royalty-free music are available from many sources: Sonic Desktop (www.smartsound.com), Media Tracks (www.media-tracks.com), and Fresh Music (www.freshmusic.com) are just a few, and more pop up all the time. Do a search for *royalty-free music* on Google and find dozens of sources.

Since we're not lawyers, you should not take assume that what's in this sidebar constitutes legal advice. These are generally accepted guidelines at this time, but very little in copyright law is cut-and-dried, and new precedents are set and new laws written all the time. If you have any doubt, consult an attorney.

Figure 14-29: Select the track you want added to your movie from the scrolling list.

Note As strange as it may seem, even if iTunes knows the name of your album and what the tracks are, iMovie doesn't talk to that database or any other. All you're going to see for a CD name is Audio CD and the various songs are just going to be Track 01, Track 02, and so on. You might want to have iTunes running in the background so that you can easily find the number of the track you want.

The following step-by-step instructions tell you how to record music from a CD:

1. Position the timeline viewer's playhead at the point where you want the sound to start.

2. Select the track you want to record in the Audio panel's scrolling list. You can preview the song before recording by using the Play button. If, as is occasionally the case, you only want one part of the song, play it until you get to the desired starting point and click the Pause button.

Tip If you're bringing in only part of a song, allow for a little slop at both ends. That way, even if you mistimed your click by just a bit, you're going to get everything you need. You can crop the audio clip to remove the extraneous material after it's in track 2.

3. Click the Record Music button. It changes to a Stop button while recording. The song starts playing and you can watch the video it will be accompanying in the monitor.

4. When you're finished, click the Stop button.

Tip If you want the entire track, there's a shortcut. Just drag the track from the list onto the audio track where you want it. iMovie will show you with a yellow bar in the timeline viewer where the clip will begin and put up an Importing CD Audio Track progress dialog box when you release the mouse.

Importing audio files

CD audio isn't the only way to get your music into iMovie. Up until iMovie 2.1.1, any audio file you imported had to be an AIFF file, but now iMovie will also import MP3s directly. Since iTunes can convert WAV files to AIFF or MP3 (see Chapter 5, iTunes Advanced Operations), you're just one easy, and free, step away from using WAV files from the Wintel world in your movie.

Slightly more expensive, but an expense we strongly encourage, is to upgrade your QuickTime to QuickTime Pro. This is $30 well spent if you're going to do much with iMovie or iTunes. Now, you'll be able to translate from a myriad of audio formats into AIFF or MP3.

Tip We'll discuss this more in Chapter 17, but if you own Toast 5 Titanium, you also have access to a wonderful little utility called CD Spin Doctor which enables you to bring in audio from such analog sources as cassette tapes and vinyl LPs, assuming that you have either a line-in jack on your Mac or something like the Griffin iMic to which you can connect your legacy hardware. (That's a polite term for "old-fashioned stuff.")

Once you've managed to get the AIFF or MP3 file to show up in the Finder, you're just a few short steps from having it in your soundtrack:

1. Position the timeline viewer's playhead where you want the imported audio to begin.
2. Choose File ⇨ Import File (⌘-I). An Import File dialog box (gee, it looks like an Open dialog box except for the name) as shown in Figure 14-30 appears.

Figure 14-30: Select the AIFF or MP3 you want to import and click Import.

3. Select the file you want to import and click the Import button. iMovie will start to import the file and will display a progress dialog while it does so.

We told you it was just a few short steps.

Importing Images

Depending upon how old you are (or how technologically advanced your school was), you might remember traditional slide shows, where the teacher put a collection of slides in a circular tray atop a slide projector and let it project the pictures on the same roll-down movie screen where you watched 8mm and 16mm educational (read "boring") films. If your grandparents were anything like ours, they also had a slide projector and just looked for an excuse to embarrass you by showing candid shots of you to friends and family.

Apple seems obsessed with slideshows. You can make them in AppleWorks using the Presentation module. You can make them in QuickTime Player Pro. iPhoto makes slideshows as well (see Chapter 9, "Getting Started with iPhoto") and exports them as QuickTime movies (see Chapter 10, "iPhoto Advanced Operations"). iDVD also makes slide shows (see Chapter 19, "Getting Started with iDVD"). But, you can make even better slide shows using iMovie than with any of these other applications. (Okay, QuickTime Player Pro matches up pretty close in capabilities, but it is way more difficult to use.) With iMovie, you control the picture and you control the sound. Each image can have its own duration. You can vary the soundtrack and apply the transitions, captions, and effects you want. In short, you can do anything with the images in your slide show that you can do with any other movie.

Here are some other uses for still images in iMovie:

✦ Creating your own, customized title screens (maybe you want Over Blue instead of Over Black). You can create slides, shorten their duration, and then (using Transitions) get some very cool titles.

✦ Importing the slides from a presentation so that you don't have to shoot them with your camcorder when filming the boss's presentation to the Board of Directors.

✦ Creating your own video storybooks to entertain the kids.

Getting the image into iMovie

The ever-handy File ➪ Import File (⌘-I) command is the portal through which your images pass. As you can see from the Show pop-up menu in Figure 14-31, iMovie can import five different graphics formats: Macintosh PICT, Compuserve® GIF, JPEG, Adobe® Photoshop®, and BMP. (That last one is Windows bitmap format, for those of you who've never had to deal with the dark side of computing.)

Note   Here's something that strikes us as more than just a little odd. iMovie will not import TIFF files, even though MacOS X uses them extensively and QuickTime handles them quite well. Similarly, it won't bring in PDF files, even though PDF is the underlying graphics format in Quartz and OS X.

Figure 14-31: You can restrict the file types that iMovie will show as importable.

Realistically, though, you will probably encounter still images you want in other formats: TIFF (Tagged Image File Format), PNG (Portable Network Graphics), WMF (Windows Metafile), or QTIF (QuickTime Image File) to name just a few. Upgrading to QuickTime Pro will let you convert anything QuickTime can read, but that will still leave a whole bunch of formats you can't handle. One superb shareware program for converting files between formats (and not a bad little image editor, either) is Lemke Software's GraphicConverter (www.lemkesoft.de).

Even assuming that you can get the image in the right format, you still have one hurdle to leap: size and resolution. Images imported into iMovie should be 72dpi (dots per inch), sometimes referred to as 72ppi (pixels per inch), resolution. They should also be 640×480 pixels in size.

"But," you exclaim, "we read in Chapter 2 that NTSC TV resolution is 720×480 pixels! What's with this 640×480 stuff?" The answer to that question is that TV screens are not like your computer screen; pixels on a TV aren't squares, they're rectangles that are narrower than they are tall. iMovie makes the compensation automatically when dealing with video so that you don't see a distorted image on your computer and those 720 horizontal TV dots fit in 640 computer dots. Thus, if you feed iMovie a 640×480 still image, it will make the conversion to 720 horizontal TV dots when it generates your clip.

If your image is larger than 640×480, iMovie will scale it down in size so that it fits within the 640×480 space. So long as the width to height ratio is 4:3 (yeah, a little bit of your elementary school math is going to come in handy), you'll have a picture that looks like your image. If the ratio isn't 4:3, you're going to have some black bars either on the sides or on the top and bottom. For example, if your picture was 1800×1200 (like those produced by Dennis's Kodak digital camera), you'll get a picture that looks like the one in Figure 14-32. You'll get the same matting, except that it might be on all four sides, if you import an image that is less than 640×480 in size—iMovie won't scale up because that produces blotchiness (technical term for "it don't look good").

Caution We hope this gets fixed before the book goes to print, but just in case@@el At the time we're writing this, iMovie is version 2.1.2 and iPhoto is version 1.1.1. iMovie looks for a standard (old-fashioned) Macintosh type and creator pair (it doesn't actually care about the creator) to determine whether the file type is one it recognizes. iPhoto does not include a type and creator on, for example, the JPEG files it creates, either in your iPhoto Library or when it exports the file. Because of this, if you want to import a photo from iPhoto into iMovie, you're going to need to give it a Macintosh file type. You can do this by opening the file in most graphics applications (GraphicConverter, QuickTime Player Pro, Photoshop, etc.) and saving it.

You might recall (if you've read the chapters on iPhoto) that one of the options in iPhoto's export dialog box is to scale the image to be no larger than 640×480. If you use that option, iPhoto will do the scaling for you and save iMovie from doing so. This is especially handy if you're exporting multiple images from iPhoto for use with iMovie.

Figure 14-32: iMovie will pad your image to fit in a 640×480 rectangle, after scaling it down if necessary.

Tip

We're going to assume that you've read or are going to read the iPhoto chapters or that you're familiar with at least one graphics program for creating and editing your images. There is one more caveat about your images that is pretty specific to iMovie (or at least, to digital video). Just as there is a *Web-safe color palette* to use when creating Web pages if you want them to show up correctly in all browsers, there is a NTSC color-safe palette in some applications (Adobe's Photoshop is one). If you don't have such an application, just stick to colors where the red, green, and blue components are all 200 or lower. Playing through to a TV (see Chapter 13) is a good way to see what your colors look like. If they shimmer or seem to bleed, you've probably exceeded the threshold. You might also run into problems with small checked patterns or narrow striped patterns. Some cynics say that NTSC stands for "Never The Same Color."

Assuming that you have a conforming image that you want to include in your movie, importing it is really easy:

1. Choose File ⇨ Import File (⌘-I) to present the Import File dialog box as shown in Figure 14-31.
2. Locate and select your file, applying one of the Show filters seen in Figure 14-31, if you wish.
3. Click the Import button.

You now have a new still clip on the shelf. Everything that you learned earlier about working with still clips is in play.

Exporting Your Video

After you've sweated and slaved over your video, making it just so, you probably want to share it with the world (or at least your family and friends). You could export it back to your camcorder and, using the analog connections from it, either play it on the TV or record copies of your masterpiece on a VCR. Exporting back to your camcorder also lets you archive your movie on a tape, letting you delete the project from your hard disk and free up the gigabytes of hard disk space your movie consumes (so that you can start on your next magnum opus). If e-mail or a Web page is the distribution medium you choose, you can export it to QuickTime and let people view it on their computers. (Apple makes a version of QuickTime that runs on Windows computers, too.) Finally, you could pass it on to iDVD and burn DVDs to pass out to friends, family, customers, or whoever your intended audience might be.

As you'll see in Chapter 17, when we talk about Toast Titanium, there's also the world of VideoCDs, but that involves a QuickTime export as well and doesn't qualify as a fourth topic here.

Exporting back to a camera

The process of exporting back to your camera is really straightforward, but there are a few things to do first and a few decisions to make.

Probably the first thing to do is run through your movie two more times, making sure that everything is just the way you want it. Even if you make this check, you'll probably have some gaffes in the movie, even the Hollywood blockbusters do, with their legions of editors and professionals poring over the footage. That doesn't mean that you shouldn't try your best to eliminate the really silly errors.

The reason we say two more times is that one pass should be done with your Playback Preferences set to Smoother Motion and one pass with it set to Better Image Quality. When checking at Better Image Quality, you look for the obvious visual defects such as misspelled captions, video effects you tried and rejected but forgot to remove, or transitions that aren't quite right. Using Smoother Motion, check for audio problems: clicking, skipping, unexpected volume shifts, or sound effects that aren't quite right.

If you have Video Play Through to Camera turned on and a TV monitor hooked up to your camera, you can probably verify both audio and video with a single check pass set to Smoother Motion. Another advantage of previewing on a TV set is that you'll get a chance to catch any problems arising from using QT Margins for your titles and subtitles as well as any color problems.

We generally use a fresh tape to hold our finished product, keeping the raw footage tape in case we ever want to grab something from it that we didn't include in this movie. (Yes, that foresight has paid off more than once.)

Note The one lesson it did take us a while to learn was, Label the <expletive-deleted> tapes! Inserting, checking, and ejecting tapes gets really annoying really quickly when you're trying to find the footage you know you have *somewhere*.

At any rate, you have the movie just the way you want it, the camera is hooked up and powered on with a tape inserted and positioned to where you want to start recording — you're ready to start exporting.

When iMovie exports to your camera, it converts all your tracks back into a single DV Stream file sent via FireWire to your camcorder. If you're still using OS 9, this process is so demanding that it takes over your whole computer — go take a walk or drink a soda. The improved multitasking in OS X means that you can still use your Mac to do things, but unless you have a really fast Mac, response might be a bit sluggish.

Caution If you are using OS 9, turn off any background applications that might try to do things while the export is taking place. Typical culprits include file sharing, iTunes, e-mail programs that automatically check for and download mail, and calendar programs that put up notifications.

Here's how to export to your camera:

1. Choose File ⇨ Export Movie to present the Export Movie dialog box shown in Figure 14-33.

2. Check the message box in the middle of the dialog box. iMovie will tell you whether it is ready to start exporting (Figure 14-33a) or ask if you want it to render any speed-altered or direction-reversed clips (Figure 14-33b).

   Assuming that you are saving a "finished product," we can't conceive of a good reason not to do the rendering. If you don't render these clips, they'll really look bad. Click Render Now and iMovie will present a progress dialog with an estimate of how long the rendering process still has to go.

(a)   (b)

Figure 14-33: The Export Movie dialog box defaults to Camera as your destination (a). If there are unrendered transitions or effects, you'll see the variation (b).

3. Assuming that you're now ready to export (double-check your connections), make sure that the three text boxes reflect the settings you want:

- Wait *nn* seconds for camera to get ready.

    This tells iMovie how long to wait after you click Export and send the Record command to your camcorder before data should start flowing. The reason for this is that, as we're sure you've seen by now, the tape might take a few seconds to get up to speed and start recording.

- Add *nn* seconds of black before movie

    We always use this option. By placing the black on the tape, future exports to VHS (or Beta, if you're one of the very few stalwarts) will have a little bit of slack time to get past the tape leader and get the videotape up to speed.

- Add *nn* seconds of black to the end of the movie

    This is particularly useful if you're not using a new tape and are recording over something else. At least, you'll have a bit of black to signal the transition from your work to the old material and at best, you'll avoid messed-up timecodes on the tape resulting from overlapping recordings.

4. Ready, set, press the Export button. If you didn't Render Now in step 2, iMovie will check with you again.

    Once the movie starts exporting, you will see it playing in the monitor window while an Exporting to Camera progress dialog displays its sideways thermometer.

If anything interrupts the export, your export is pretty much guaranteed to be useless. Here are some things to do or not do which should improve the likelihood of a successful export:

- Plug your camera into an outlet instead of running off battery. Having the camera shut down for a lack of juice is easily avoided.

- Don't do anything else on the FireWire bus. Connecting and disconnecting FireWire devices will virtually guarantee a signal going through that will terminate your export.

- Don't touch the cables or connectors between your Mac and your camera. (Don't let the kids, cats, or dogs near them, either.) A simple jiggle could interrupt the connection for a moment.

We'll discuss the process of transferring your DV footage to your VCR in Chapter 15.

Exporting to QuickTime

One of Apple's greatest and least understood accomplishments is their QuickTime technology. Most people think of it as just the QuickTime Player, but that Player is just a single window into many QuickTime capabilities.

To use some geek terms, QuickTime defines some APIs (application programming interfaces), codecs (compressors-decompressors), and a flexible and extensible document format (QuickTime Movie format). We'll get into what QuickTime is and how it works in Chapter 17 when we talk about QuickTime Pro and why you should upgrade to it.

If you know a lot about how to use QuickTime, you'll be able to tweak the QuickTime export settings to be just what you want; however, 99 percent of the time, iMovie's canned settings for different purposes are going to be all you need.

As with exporting to camera, there are some preparations to be made in terms of previewing your movie before exporting to QuickTime. In fact, they're mostly the same ones. A couple things, though, should be remembered:

✦ Titles and captions should be in a fairly large and distinct font. It is unlikely that you're going to export to QuickTime at 640×480 resolution, so the text is going to shrink, possibly a lot. Eighth-inch (roughly 9 point) text at 640×480 is only going to be three sixty-fourths of an inch tall if you export at 240×180 (the Web Movie, Small setting) and even smaller if you export it at the small e-mail setting. Similarly, titles and captions are more distinct Over Black than against motion when you reduce the image's size.

✦ Make sure that you have enough free disk space for the QuickTime movie to be saved. The Free Space indicator will tell you how much space is available on the disk containing your project. You'll need to go outside iMovie to find out the free space on other volumes.

Figuring out how much space you need is where guesswork and experience are going to come into play. As a rough rule of thumb, the e-mail option takes about 1MB per minute, small Web movies take about 4MB per minute, the CD-ROM setting will chew up about 10MB per minute, and a full-quality movie will be essentially the same size as your DV Stream—about 200+MB per minute.

Let's take a look at the canned Export to QuickTime settings shown in the Formats pop-up menu displayed in Figure 14-34.

Figure 14-34: iMovie provides five common QuickTime export configurations (and an Expert option where you do all the work).

- **Web Movie, Small:** Running at 12 frames per second versus your video's 30fps, you should get motion reminiscent of some (non-realistic) cartoon animation with images at about 14 percent the resolution you started with. While the sound is still stereo, the sample rate has been cut in half to 22Khz (approximately that of FM radio).

- **Email Movie, Small:** Down to 10fps and only 6.25 percent the resolution of your original, the video is going to be hard to see and pretty ragged. Additionally, the audio is now mono at 22Khz, so you've got fair degradation there as well. The sole virtue of this format is that you can get a little over three minutes of video into a message that will fit in most 5MB mailboxes.

> **Note** Even though a .Mac mailbox, for example, can hold 15MB of messages, that doesn't mean the movie can be close to 15MB. Attachments like pictures, files, or video to e-mail messages have to be encoded for transmission and that will add between 30 and 40 percent to the size of the file.

- **Streaming Web Movie, Small:** With the exception of streaming hints (which we'll discuss in Chapter 15) being added, this is the same set of options that you see above in Web Movie, Small.

- **CD-ROM Movie, Medium:** At last, full CD-quality stereo sound. At 320×240 resolution, we're also getting back into the realm of watchable video where we can discern some detail. At 15fps, the motion should be fairly smooth, assuming you weren't filming a martial arts matchup.

- **Full Quality, Large:** You now have the same quality picture and sound as your original, because to all intents it is your original. This is only really useful if you're going to work on the movie with another DV application like iDVD, Final Cut Pro, or DVD Studio Pro.

You might have noticed that if any of the Small options were chosen, the QuickTime 3.0 compatible check box becomes available. Selecting this check box will result in even slightly lower-quality movies (less efficient codecs), but they will be playable by more people — those who haven't upgraded to QuickTime 4, 5, 6 or later. Our Bible editors love step-by-step instructions, so we'll now walk through the steps to QuickTime export:

1. Choose File ➪ Export Movie (⌘-E) to present the Export Movie dialog box.
2. Choose To QuickTime(tm) from the Export pop-up menu and watch the options change (compare Figure 14-33a and Figure 14-34).
3. Choose the type of movie from the Formats pop-up menu.
4. Click the Export button. An export progress dialog box will appear. Plan to wait a long time for this to complete. Times between five and twenty minutes per minute of video are not uncommon, even on relatively fast Macs, when QuickTime is performing significant compression.

Exporting for iDVD

We'll be covering this more in Part V, "iDVD," but the basics are the same as when exporting to QuickTime. Check to make sure everything is the way you want it in your movie, just as you did for the camera and QuickTime.

Make sure that you have enough disk space. An iDVD export will chew up over 200MB per minute of video, so be sure that you have as much space free as your project folder uses.

Now, for the final step-by-step in this chapter:

1. Choose File ➪ Export Movie (⌘-E) to present the Export Movie dialog box.
2. Choose For iDVD from the Export pop-up menu, if your version of iMovie includes it. (It disappeared in the 2.1.2 version that came with OS X 10.2.)

   OR

   Choose Full Quality, Large as described previously in the "Exporting to QuickTime" section.

   If you have any reversed clips or any fast- or slow-motion clips, you'll see the information box with a Render Now button shown in Figure 14-33b; otherwise, that information box will tell you how large your movie is and that you're ready to export. As with exporting to camera, you should deal with the rendering at this point unless you want a sloppy look to your video. (With the cost of DVD-R discs, you probably don't want to waste the money.)
3. Once the information box tells you that you're ready to export, click the Export button. An export progress dialog box will appear.

   Since iMovie isn't doing any compression, you might expect this to be a pretty quick process, but it isn't necessarily. Even doing a Finder copy of that much data takes a while (remember, over 200MB per minute of video).

Whew! Now we're ready to go on to more advanced things you can do with iMovie. We'll see you in Chapter 15.

Summary

In this chapter, you learned to connect your camcorder, import video from it, and export video back to it. You also saw how to work with the clip viewer, the timeline viewer, and the shelf in all its persona: adding titles, subtitles, transitions, effects, and audio. You learned to do basic clip editing in the monitor and to add and work with still clips. We also covered exporting to QuickTime and iDVD.

✦   ✦   ✦

Getting Advanced with iMovie

In This Chapter

The cutting room floor

Working with non-DV video

Plugging into iMovie

Becoming expert with QuickTime Export

Postproduction tricks with QuickTime Pro

Putting your movie on the Web

Using what you've learned in Chapters 13 and 14, you can already make better home movies than your parents or grandparents ever dreamed of making. But, we've barely touched the surface. Using iMovie, you can easily produce movies that could be mistaken for professional work, and we aren't talking about cheesy B-movies, either.

Now that you know how to use iMovie's tools, we're going to discuss how to achieve your artistic production goals. In other words, what to do and when to do it.

In addition, you'll learn how to use non-DV video clips, extend iMovie's capabilities with plug-ins, become an expert at QuickTime exports, use QuickTime Pro to add some cool special effects to your movie after you get done with it in iMovie, and how to make your movie available on the Internet.

If you didn't need your hands free to work the mouse, we'd tell you to sit down, buckle in, and hang on.

The Cutting Room Floor

The best footage in the world won't do you any good unless you can put it together and present it for people to enjoy. And the secret to making an average movie good or a good movie great is the editing.

The art of the intercut

Putting first things first, let's get a little terminology front-and-center. A *cut* is the break from one clip to the next, without transition. More than that, though, there are special cutting techniques where you use the video from one clip with the audio from another. This is usually called *intercutting*, a technique most often used with documentaries, presentations, and news broadcasts. We don't know about you, but most people (including us) get really bored if the camera stays trained on a speaker as he or she drones on about the new frammis their company is announcing. However, if the presentation continues, but the picture changes to one showing the frammis in operation, we get a little more interested. Steve Jobs and the folks at Apple have this down to a fine art. Just watch Steve when he announces Apple's latest and greatest products. The video footage cuts back and forth between him and the products, but his soundtrack is in play the whole time. Of course, they're doing this live, using multiple cameras and switching between them on signal. But you can do this too, with intercutting.

Tip You can also use this technique to create your own lip-synching effect or, more likely, to reshoot some video that didn't turn out too well and mate it with good audio.

The cuts used for a Steve Jobs–type presentation or when the video changes from the performer to the audience are called *cutaways*. The latter (when people are involved) are also called *reaction shots*.

Note To get a real reaction shot requires two or more cameras. Otherwise, you're not catching the actual reaction, you're staging a response and (other than in fiction) that is considered ethically dubious, which is a polite term for fraudulent.

Another really handy intercut is called a *cut-in*. In reality, all this means is that you cut to a close-up. For example, you are filming Tiger Woods teeing off on the 72nd hole of the U.S. Open and then cut-in to a close-up of the driver impacting the golf ball.

One of the intercut's beauties is that you don't have to use two video clips. In many cases, such as a presentation or a lecture, you can cut to a still image. When your boss is talking about the departmental budget, you can cut to a chart. When we prepare a presentation about a software program, we can cut to a clip of the screen doing what we're discussing.

Tip There are two convenient ways to get a movie of your screen. One is to hook your computer's video out to play to a TV. (Just stick a VCR in between to record the action.) Many Macs (like the iBooks) come with the circuitry to make this easy. The second method is a software solution: Snapz Pro X from Ambrosia Software (www.AmbrosiaSW.com) will take QuickTime movies of your screen that you can then convert and import into iMovie. If you have one of Apple's desktop G4 models or a PowerBook G4, you might have received a licensed copy with your computer.

Transitioning Between Intercuts

A really common use of intercuts with still images is inserting customized title and credit clips in your movie's opening sequence. This is one situation where you might consider transitioning between the still and live action.

One technique we particularly like is used in a lot of TV shows. You'll have an opening scene and there will be a short freeze of an actor and their name (maybe even the character name) and then the action will continue. Follow these steps and you'll be able to create this effect:

1. With your opening sequence displayed in the timeline viewer, extract the audio (Advanced ⇨ Extract Audio or ⌘-J).

2. Advance the playhead to where you want your first "freeze" and choose Edit ⇨ Create Still Clip (Shift-⌘-S). Write down the timestamp.

3. Select the still clip in the shelf and set its duration (at the top of the timeline viewer), as shown in the following figure.

With the still clip selected, set its "play time" in the timeline viewer.

Continued

Continued

4. With the clip still selected in the shelf, choose Edit ⇨ Copy (⌘-C). If you don't want to retain the clip on the shelf for later use, you may use Edit ⇨ Cut (⌘-X) instead.

5. Advance the playhead back to the time you wrote down in Step 2 and choose Advanced ⇨ Paste Over at Playhead (Shift-⌘-V).

6. Repeat Steps 2 through 5 for as many items as you wish.

There's one thing of which you should be careful, though. Don't let your last title freeze extend past the end of the clip. Doing so will cost you part of your next clip's video or, if this is the only clip in the timeline viewer, result in video sans audio.

Now it's a simple matter to go back to your various title clips and, using what you learned in Chapter 14, add the text and apply the title style. One side effect of this approach is that the still clip and the resumed action will often be similar enough that the image will appear jumpy. This is a time to smooth your intercut with a transition. A short fade-in transition (maybe 10 to 12 frames) at the start of each resumed action clip should do the job.

You might also want to use Photoshop or AppleWorks to create customized title slides employing styles not available in iMovie. (The Presentations module in AppleWorks 6 is great for this, because 640×480 is the default slide size.) Save your stills in an importable format and then import them, one at a time, into iMovie. Once they're on the shelf, follow Steps 3 through 5 for each of the clips, except that now you have to pick their insertion points.

Another cut technique that you'll see a lot in battle scenes and sporting events is the *jump cut*, where the perspective changes from one camera angle to another on the same action. It's also used in the opening credits of some movies.

There are a couple of obvious techniques resulting in a jump cut effect. The simplest is to just split the clip into multiple clips and remove one or two of them. The downside of this method is that you won't be synchronized with the audio (or the audio will also have gaping holes). This style works best when you aren't going to use the original clip's audio, replacing it with a soundtrack of your choice. The following steps explain this technique:

1. Place the original clip in the timeline viewer and extract its audio (Advanced ⇨ Extract Audio or ⌘-J).

2. Select the video clip and choose Edit ⇨ Copy (⌘-C) to place a copy on the clipboard.

3. Select a clip in the shelf and choose Edit ⇨ Paste (⌘-V) to put the copy in the shelf.

Note The reason you have to select something on the shelf is so that iMovie will know where to paste it. (Otherwise, it would end up back in the timeline viewer because that's where you were working.)

4. Select the shelf copy of your clip, so that it appears in the monitor screen.
5. Locate the desired split location and choose Edit ➪ Split Video Clip at Playhead (⌘-T).
6. Repeat Steps 4 and 5 until you have all the pieces you want. Name the clips you're going to use so that you can recognize them easily for the following steps.
7. Select the first clip you're going to use and choose Edit ➪ Cut (⌘-X) or Edit ➪ Copy (⌘-C).
8. Position the playhead on the timeline viewer and choose Advanced ➪ Paste Over at Playhead (Shift-⌘-V).
9. Repeat Steps 7 and 8, with the playhead positioning to be at the end of the previously pasted clip.
10. Either trim the existing audio to match the new sequence length or replace it with a soundtrack of the proper length.

You can shorten this process quite a bit if you know that you aren't going to use the clip's audio, as follows:

1. With the timeline viewer showing, select the clip (on the shelf) that you're going to use and turn its Volume off. (The Volume control is at the bottom of the timeline viewer.)
2. Drag the clip to the clip viewer and do your splitting, dragging the pieces you don't want to use to the iMovie Trash.
3. Switch back to the timeline viewer and add your soundtrack.

Note While writing this chapter, Dennis took a little break to watch *Windtalkers* (history buff with a strong interest in WW II) and, maybe because it was fresh in his mind, he noticed the movie credits were in a sequence of landscape jump cuts against a subtle audio background, each cut introduced with a short fade in. If you watch movies and are aware of these techniques, you'll start to notice them, too, without even trying.

The coolest cuts of all

Similar in many respects to an intercut, the *J-cut* (so named because its audio track begins before the video, reminiscent of the letter *J* shape) and the *L-cut* (yeah, because its audio continues after the video ends, looking like the letter *L*).

The J-cut is a common effect in movies and on TV. You're watching a scene and hear a phone ring just before the scene transitions to the person going to answer it. Now that you've seen how to perform intercuts, performing a J-cut is a breeze:

1. Place the two clips you're going to work on in the timeline viewer. Make sure that the zoom factor lets you see both clips without scrolling.
2. Extract the audio from the first clip if it has any.
3. Extract the audio from the second clip.

4. If you don't need any audio from this clip, choose Edit ⇨ Clear (Delete) and skip to step 12. If you do need the early audio from the clip, select the second audio clip and unlock it (Advanced ⇨ Unlock Audio Clip or ⌘-L) from its video clip. Your timeline viewer should now resemble Figure 15-1.

Figure 15-1: Unlock the audio track before proceeding.

5. You're going to need a third clip, at least temporarily. If you don't have one handy, choose Edit ⇨ Create Still Clip (Shift-⌘-S). Place your third clip in the timeline viewer after the second clip.

6. Position the playhead to the end of the second clip as pictured in Figure 15-2.

Figure 15-2: Move the playhead to the end of the second clip.

7. With the second audio clip selected, move the playhead exactly one frame forward (pressing → one time works best).

8. Choose Advanced ⇨ Lock Audio Clip at Playhead and the audio clip's end will now be locked to the temporary clip, as shown in Figure 15-3.

Figure 15-3: Attach the audio clip to the video clip that follows.

9. Select the second video clip and remove (using the monitor's crop markers) the requisite amount of video for your desired overlap. Notice that the two audio clips now overlap beneath the first video clip as shown in Figure 15-4.

10. Select the second audio clip and press ← one time. The audio clip unlocks from the third video clip, moves back one frame, and locks its ending to the second video clip's ending. If the third clip was a placeholder, you can get rid of it now.

Figure 15-4: You've made the audio clips overlap.

11. Select the first audio clip and drag its right crop marker left to the beginning of the second clip's audio. You're done. Remember that audio cropping of this type doesn't remove the audio, it merely tells iMovie not to play it.
12. Select the second video clip and, using the monitor's crop markers and Edit ⇨ Clear (Delete), remove the amount of video by which you want the audio to overlap.
13. Move the second audio clip so that its end is once again synchronized with the end of the video clip. You're done, too.

Obviously, for Step 13, it is helpful to know just how much you eliminated in Step 12. With that knowledge and a little time arithmetic, you can position the audio clip precisely where you want it.

Caution

Before you ask, "But why don't I just lock the ends of the second video and audio clip before I eliminate the early frames?" we'll just tell you that iMovie doesn't move the audio clip over. Bug or feature, we don't know (smells like a bug to us, though), but the obvious doesn't work here.

More common than a J-cut is the L-cut (and a lot easier). You see it in narrations and presentations all the time where the speaker keeps talking, but the picture changes to show what he's talking about. The place we see this most is on TV, when some sporting event or (un)important news bulletin has cut into one of the programs and then we're told, "Now rejoining our regularly scheduled programming. . ." with the program's picture on-screen just before the audio comes back. To perform an L-cut:

1. Place the two clips you're going to work on in the timeline viewer. Make sure that the zoom factor lets you see both clips without scrolling.
2. Extract the audio from the both clips.
3. Verify that each audio clip is locked to the beginning of its respective video, as shown in Figure 15-5.

Figure 15-5: Start with the audio and video clips separated, but locked.

4. Select the first video clip and, using the monitor's crop markers and Edit ⇨ Clear (Delete), remove the desired amount of video from the end. If you don't mind some audio overlap, you're finished; however, usually you'll want to clear out the overlapping audio from the second clip, so. . .

5. Select the second audio clip, making it the only selected item.

6. Position the playhead at the end of the overlapped portion, as shown in Figure 15-6.

Figure 15-6: The playhead should be at the very end of the overlapped audio.

7. Choose Edit ⇨ Split Selected Audio Clip at Playhead (⌘-T).

8. Select only the portion that overlaps the first clip and remove it by choosing Edit ⇨ Clear (Delete).

9. Select the second audio clip's remains and choose Advanced ⇨ Lock Audio Clip at Playhead (⌘-L). You're done!

If you find the audio cut from the first to the second clip a bit abrupt, you can select the second audio clip and use the timeline viewer's Fade In check box.

Working with Non-DV Video

iMovie is made to work with DV Streams, pure and simple. If you're going to feed it video, that video must be DV. So, what's this hoohah about working with non-DV video?

Sometimes we don't get a choice about our source material's format. We might get a QuickTime clip from a client that they want included in the movie. One example might be a PowerPoint presentation that was saved as a QuickTime movie. At other times we might find some video on the Web and (after getting all the requisite permissions, of course) wish to include it in our movie.

The quandary, of course, is that we need some way to make that footage available to iMovie. Put bluntly, we have to convert the material to a DV Stream. While there are a number of commercial products such as Media Cleaner (Discreet Systems, www.discreet.com) that will perform this task, they're pretty pricey and overkill if you're working with QuickTime files. Nevertheless, if you need to repurpose some MPEG files (either MPEG-1 or MPEG-2) or a multitude of other formats not included in QuickTime Pro's arsenal, Media Cleaner is something we would recommend. What we're going to discuss here is using QuickTime Pro to translate your source material into DV Stream format, making the assumption that you've already upgraded your QuickTime to QuickTime Pro.

Tip   If you have QuickTime Pro, you can also use Apple's "Convert to DV Stream" AppleScript, available from www.apple.com/applescript/quicktime.

What (and Why) Are All These Formats?

If you've ever been given a word-processing or spreadsheet document that your software doesn't understand, you've probably cursed either at the person who gave it to you, your software for not recognizing the format, the software developers for creating multiple formats that are not compatible, or some combination of the above. While each of these formats was developed for a reason, they are only trouble for you now. Think of formats as languages. If you're monolingual, you'll need to find a translator or interpreter to understand what was said in languages other than your own. Well, iMovie is monolingual when it comes to video and bilingual for audio. It only understands DV Stream when dealing with video and has fairly recently added MP3 fluency to its native AIFF audio tongue.

Apple developed QuickTime to deal with time-based data (video and audio, primarily). To facilitate dealing with time-based data, QuickTime also defines a container format, recognized by the .mov file extension. One of the things the MOV format does is tell which compressor was used to create the data and which decompressor is needed to extract it. On Windows, AVI files fall into the same general category — they hold data and information about the compressors-decompressors. In either case, unless you have the needed decompressor, the data won't do you much good.

Basically, though, all movies are a sequence of images (like flip-cards) with attached sound. The devil, as they say, is in the details. To make these movies consume less space on your disk and less time to transmit across a network, compression is used to compact repetitive data and eliminate superfluous data. Various compressors and compression algorithms have been developed, are being developed, and will be developed in the future to optimize the compression to meet specific goals.

For example, data you're going to stream over the Internet needs to be compressed not just for the number of bytes, but for how fast it can be decompressed at the receiving end so that it might be played as it is received. This will often create an emphasis on space savings. On the other hand, data stored on disk might strike a different balance, trading some of that space savings for more decompression speed — after all, the data is all present and we can read from a disk a lot faster than we can receive data across the Internet.

Continued

Continued

Most of the time, you will find a video track and an audio track in the container and you will need decompressors for both. The Motion Picture Experts Group (MPEG) adds yet another complication to our lives with their MPEG-1 and MPEG-2 formats: *multiplexed* (also known as *muxed*) tracks. This means that the video and sound are interwoven into a single track. That's why, if you try to use QuickTime Pro to convert a MPEG file to a DV Stream you'll lose the audio. The conversion process doesn't separate the two types of data and only passes on the one it deems more important.

Microsoft and Real Networks also complicate matters with proprietary formats (ASF, WMV, and the like from Microsoft and the various RM types from Real). If their player is out there (particularly, Microsoft's) on almost every computer sold, the broadcasters have an incentive to pay for the tools that can deliver content to those players.

Converting compatible formats

QuickTime Pro, at least according to Apple, recognizes and plays QuickTime movies, MPEG files, and AVI files. We qualified that statement for several reasons:

- ✦ QuickTime files, those with filenames ending in .mov, .qt, or .moov usually, are QuickTime container files. You will, sometimes, encounter QuickTime files that your perfectly up-to-date QuickTime Pro won't open and you'll be told that you might have difficulty with a track because the required compressor couldn't be found, as shown in Figure 15-7.

Figure 15-7: QuickTime sometimes can't find the compressor for a QuickTime file.

The simple reason behind this is that whoever created this QuickTime file did so using a compressor that isn't part of the standard distribution. One common source of this error is when you encounter QuickTime movies created with the freeware tool DivX Doctor II, which uses a freeware compressor called 3ivx Decoder for OS X (which will probably have a version number in the middle of its name).

- ✦ MPEG files are those whose names end in .mpg and cover a wide range of possibilities. QuickTime recognizes and plays most MPEG-1 files. Although we haven't encountered an uncorrupted MPEG-1 file that causes QuickTime to hiccup, we have seen reports in newsgroups and on mailing lists, so we can't discount the possibility that such exist. The real problem arises from the fact that MPEG-2 files, used for SVCD (Super VideoCD) and DVD discs also employ the .mpg extension. QuickTime 5.x doesn't understand MPEG-2. QuickTime 6 does, but it requires that you purchase a $20 add-on decoder. Also, new in QuickTime 6, is support for MPEG-4 files. MPEG-4 is mostly used for streaming video as it generates small files that retain impressive quality.

✦ AVI is the Windows equivalent of QuickTime (it stands for Audio-Video Interleaved) format. Apple claims that QuickTime understands AVI files and if there is a gross overstatement anywhere in the marketing materials for QuickTime, that's it! AVI is a catch-all file extension used for files encoded with the various Indeo compressors from Intel (some of which have never been ported to the Macintosh), various DivX formats comprising another half-dozen or so compressors, and some other minor variations. Only a few of the Indeo compressors are recognized by QuickTime Pro and the others will display a message similar to Figure 15-7 unless you find suitable compressors from other sources.

Now that we've looked at all the things that can go wrong, we'll tell you that most of the time things just work. Assuming that QuickTime 6 is available by the time you read this (and we really hope it is), there will be even fewer possible problems.

Knowing what to import

Any video file that QuickTime can play can be exported to DV Stream format in QuickTime Pro. That doesn't mean that you'll necessarily like the results. There are few situations where *GIGO* (Garbage In, Garbage Out) is more clearly demonstrated that with video. Files saved for distribution on CD, over the Web, or in e-mail typically have made some compromises in terms of resolution, frame rate, and compression. If the movie isn't smooth and clear when played at 640×480 resolution in QuickTime Player, it won't be any better when exported to DV Stream. (Use Movie ⇨ Double Size or ⌘-2 to get a 320×240 up to 640×480.) Similarly, most QuickTime movies are saved at a frame rate significantly lower than 30fps, resulting in jumpiness when exported to NTSC's 30fps DV frame rate. Finally, if the compression ratio used is more than 4:1, you're going to see blurry images when you export to DV Stream.

As a case in point, Microsoft added a Save as QuickTime feature in PowerPoint 2001 and improved it in PowerPoint for OS X that should have resulted in a lot more iMovie QuickTime imports. Saving a presentation as a QuickTime file means that you can tape the boss (or be taped, yourself) delivering a presentation and import the actual presentation. A little judicious intercutting as described earlier in this chapter ("The art of the intercut"), and you can create a great business video, one that just a few years ago would have required professionals and cost a small fortune to produce.

At least, that's the theory. In practice, you need to have quality input files before you can convert them to DV. The main problem with PowerPoint's QuickTime settings is that they overcompress. Using PowerPoint's Business Plan template as an example, we saved it as a 640×480 QuickTime movie. In Figure 15-8, you can see what it looks like in QuickTime and how blurry (it's called pixilation) the text appears after you export to a DV Stream.

(a)

(b)

Figure 15-8: A 640×480 QuickTime movie created by PowerPoint (a); the same movie after exporting to DV Stream format (b).

"Aha!" you cry, noticing that the DV Stream is wider (720×480) than the QuickTime movie, "Things got distorted in the translation." Well, that's not the case, we're forced to say. As you can see in Figure 15-9, we also saved the presentation at 720×480 resolution and then exported that, with similar sorry results.

(a)

(b)

Figure 15-9: A 720×480 QuickTime movie created by PowerPoint (a); the same movie after exporting to DV Stream format (b).

The lesson here is that you should still import the presentation as 640×480 still images and do your magic completely within iMovie. You'll lose PowerPoint's special effects, but you can't have everything (yet).

What then, does work well imported into iMovie? There are PCI and USB video capture cards and devices which you could bring into iMovie with good results, so long as they work at 640×480, 30fps, and use a lower than 4:1 compression ratio. You can also make some slideshows in QuickTime Pro employing masks and other special effects that aren't available in iMovie. We'll show you one of them later in this chapter under "Postproduction Tricks with QuickTime Pro." Since QuickTime Pro lets you set all the parameters necessary, getting DV-friendly files is pretty easy.

Translating to DV Stream in QuickTime Pro

Once you're viewing your movie in QuickTime Player Pro, you can save it as a DV Stream (although multiplexed MPEG files will lose their audio). Take the following steps:

1. Open the movie you want to translate in QuickTime Player.

2. Choose File ⇨ Export (⌘-E) to open the dialog box shown in Figure 15-10.

Figure 15-10: QuickTime's Export File dialog box.

3. Enter a name for the exported file and select a location to save it if you don't like QuickTime Player's default choice of your Documents folder. You might need to click the down-pointing triangle button next to the Where pop-up menu to reveal the file browser if your destination folder isn't in the Where pop-up menu.

4. Choose Movie to DV Stream (if it isn't already selected as in Figure 15-10) from the Export pop-up menu.

5. (Optional) Click the Options button to display the dialog box shown in Figure 15-11. You can specify whether the output should be PAL or NTSC and also specify the audio sampling rate.

6. Back in the Export File dialog box, specify Audio format and sampling rate in the Use pop-up menu. These options were also available in Step 5, if you did it.

7. Click Save and initiate the export.

Figure 15-11: Click the Options button to present this dialog box.

Exporting to DV Stream can be quite time-consuming. If you're running OS 9, your machine is essentially unavailable until the process completes. With OS X's improved multitasking, you can switch to another application and continue working. Using QuickTime Pro's Movie Info dialog you can chart the progress and see just how fast frames are being exported. On Dennis's iMac G4/800, it took just under ten minutes to export a two-minute movie (about 18 minutes on his G4/400 PowerMac).

Importing DV Streams into iMovie

At last, we've come to the culmination of this whole exercise: actually importing the DV Stream file into iMovie. Appropriately, it is also the easiest and shortest step in the entire process, as follows:

1. In iMovie, choose File ⇨ Import File (⌘-I)
2. Select the DV file you want to import in the Import File dialog box shown in Figure 15-12.

Figure 15-12: iMovie's Import File dialog box.

3. Click Import. iMovie will start the import, which can also take a while to accomplish depending upon how large the file is.

Now, as shown in Figure 15-13, you'll have a new clip on the shelf, ready to be edited in the monitor or used like any other clip.

Figure 15-13: At last, you have your imported clip, ready for use.

Quite frankly, we don't use the Import File command very often for DV files. In our experience, it is primarily for audio files and stills. Having said that, we do find it convenient in one instance: when we want to steal a clip from a different iMovie project. Just as one example, Dennis makes a lot of iMovies that involve friends, family, and (of course) Spenser. He found that he was creating very similar title and credit sequences for a lot of these movies, so he created a project of just title and credit sequences. Now, he just goes to that project's folder and uses File ⇨ Import File to bring in the ones he wants. The moral? Since iMovie doesn't provide a template facility, ya gotta roll your own.

Plugging into iMovie

Way back in 1986, when Apple and Bill Atkinson were preparing WildCard's birth as HyperCard, it was obvious that Mac users (particularly "power users") wanted to extend the capabilities of their software. HyperCard introduced XCMDs (external commands) to satisfy that lust and, as a result, created a cottage industry. Adobe and other developers saw this and put a plug-in architecture together for their products — there are, literally, hundreds of plug-ins for Photoshop. Much of the really cool stuff you do with your Web browser (watch movies on the Web, read PDF files, play music, view Flash animations, and so forth) results because your browser supports plug-ins. No fool, Apple realized that the Effects, Transitions, Titles, and such provided with iMovie were not going to quench your directorial thirst. Thus, iMovie also has a plug-in architecture.

In fact, just to get the ball rolling, Apple offers a free download from iMovie's Web page www.apple.com/imovie: iMovie Plug-in Pack 2.1.1 for Mac OS X. There's also a link to a plug-ins page, showcasing third-party plug-in collections for use with iMovie. Some of these even include free sampler packages that you can download and try out.

While we're writing this, there are collections from three companies: GeeThree, Virtix, and eZedia. All three have some really cool transitions and effects, but (at least for the moment), one of our favorites is eZeMatte from eZedia. Being able to overlay a still on top of our clips opens all sorts of possibilities: framing, fancy titles and credits, or applying a logo just touch the surface. Another favorite is GeeThree's picture-in-picture from "Slick Transitions & Effects – Volume 4."

Installing plug-ins

How and where you install iMovie plug-ins depends on whether the plug-ins come with an installer application, what version of iMovie you're running and what version of Mac OS. Just to get it out of the way, we'll deal with the OS issue first. If you're running Mac OS 9 or if you are running an iMovie version earlier than 2.1.1 in OS X:

1. Locate and open the iMovie folder (it's probably in Applications (OS 9).
2. Open the iMovie subfolder.
3. Open the Resources folder.
4. Drag the plug-in (or its folder) onto the folder named Plugins.
5. Clean up by closing folders (unless you want to leave a lot of window clutter).

If you're running OS X and iMovie 2.1.1 or later:

1. Locate the Library folder in your Home directory
2. Find and open the iMovie folder. If it doesn't exist, create it.
3. Drag the plug-ins to the Plugins folder. If the Plugins folder doesn't exist, create it.

Now, wasn't that easy? Launch iMovie and you'll see the new effects, transitions, titles, and sounds appear in the appropriate shelf panels.

Exploring iMovie Plug-in Pack 2.1.1 for Mac OS X

Just to whet your appetite for more plug-ins, Apple provides seven transitions, five visual effects, and four new title styles in this collection. Table 15-1 names the plug-in and gives a brief description. Sometimes we even include a personal opinion (but that shouldn't surprise you by this point in the book).

Table 15-1: iMovie Plug-in Pack 2.1.1 for OS X Plug-ins

Plug-in type	Plug-in name	Description (maybe including comment)
Transition	Circle Closing	This two-clip transition has the first clip shrink down to a circle in the center of your screen, revealing the second clip.
Transition	Circle Opening	You've probably already figured this one out. The second clip starts as a small circle in the center of your screen and grows to fill the screen, replacing the first clip.
Visual Effects	Flash	This effect is supposed to look like camera flashbulbs are going off. You can set how many times the flash will occur, how frequently they'll occur, and how bright they'll be.
Visual Effects	Ghost Trails	Kind of a gimmicky effect, it adds a blur to things that are moving in your clip. If you want to make your dog look like he's running at superspeed or your Hyundai is about to go to Warp 3, you could find it amusing.
Visual Effects	Mirror	Easier to show than describe (see Figure 15-14), you can reflect part of your picture onto the other half of the screen. Some folks really like it, but we don't see it as particularly useful.
Visual Effects	Mirror Advanced	Similar to mirror except that you can reflect vertically instead of or in addition to horizontally.
Visual Effects	N-Square	Turns your image into multiple (N × N) miniatures, as shown in Figure 15-15.
Transition	Radial	Another two-clip transition, radial sweeps away the first clip as a line (similar to that on a WW II radar screen) rotates around the monitor. This one is entertaining if used sparingly, and can give the impression of a time shift.

Plug-in type	Plug-in name	Description (maybe including comment)
Title	Subtitle	This is a handy addition. You now have a way to center text along the bottom of the screen, providing a nice way of captioning a presentation. If, however, you're going to use it for subtitles (as the name implies), you'll probably have to split the clip a few times to keep the subtitles in sync with the dialog.
Title	Subtitle Multiple	Like Subtitle, but it allows you to present multiple lines of text.
Transition	Warp In	Similar to Circle Closing, but with the first clip shrinking down and distorting into a bow-tie shape before disappearing.
Transition	Warp Out	Guess what? This is like Circle Opening, but with the first clip distorting as it gets pushed off-screen.
Transition	Wash In	Think of this as a Fade In where the clip starts as all white rather than all black.
Transition	Wash Out	A Fade Out variant where the clip goes from full-color to all white. We like the Wash effects a little better than Fades, especially if we're coming from or going to a still clip.
Title	Zoom	Creates a one-line title that starts small in the center screen and zooms up in size until it fills the screen. Not a bad effect, but you'll probably find more use for Zoom Multiple (next).
Title	Zoom Multiple	Like Zoom, but supporting multiple lines of text. Alfred Hitchcock used this title effect in some of his movies.

Adding other stuff to iMovie

In addition to the Plug-in Pack, Apple provides a number of sound effects and music clips for use with iMovie. Just click the Enhance button on the iMovie Web page and you can pick and choose the one(s) you want. You can even try them out to see how they sound. Installation and usage instructions are on the page. The ones available as we write this are all provided free, courtesy of Sound Dogs (sound effects) and Killersound (music clips). Additionally, Apple makes Freeplay Music's (www.freeplaymusic.com) collection of 2100 royalty-free songs available on your iDisk.

> **Tip** If you haven't sprung for a .Mac account yet, you really should consider it. Go to www.mac.com and create yours. In addition to the mac.com e-mail address, the iDisk is a phenomenal resource, even if you never use it for storage or as a Web site. Apple makes a lot of software, both their own and third-party, available in the Software folder on every iDisk.

Figure 15-14: The mirror effect reflects your image so that it appears on both sides of your chosen dividing line.

Figure 15-15: N-Square gives you a split screen with multiple, miniature copies.

Also, at the time we're writing this, Apple is providing seven collections of still images (they call them *background sets*) for your use. Apple's recommendation is to use them as backgrounds for titles and credits. You can find these through the Background Sets link on iMovie's Enhance page.

Becoming Expert with QuickTime Export

As we saw in Chapter 14, iMovie comes with canned settings for what Apple considers the most common QuickTime Export configurations: small e-mail attachments, small Web pages, medium-sized CD movies, and huge DV-quality movies to watch from your hard disk.

You're observant, though, and saw one other option at the bottom of that QuickTime Export pop-up menu: Expert. That name is not pure hyperbole, either. You need to understand what you're trading off and what you're trying to accomplish, because you'll be making all the decisions here.

With your movie in the clip viewer take the following steps:

1. Choose File ⇨ Export Movie (⌘-E).
2. From the Export pop-up menu, choose To QuickTime(tm).
3. From the Formats pop-up menu, choose Expert to open the Expert QuickTime Settings dialog box (Figure 15-16).

Figure 15-16: The Expert QuickTime Settings dialog box puts you in complete control of your movie's export.

The Expert QuickTime Settings dialog box is divided into three areas: Image Settings, where you decide what to do with the video; Audio Settings, where you specify compression, sampling, and channels for your sound; and "Prepare for internet" if you're setting your movie up to be accessed from a Web page.

Determining image settings

The first thing you see is where you set your image size. You can specify them independently or, if you click the 4:3 check box, iMovie will compute the second for you if you specify one.

Note The 4:3 setting is called the *aspect ratio*. Standard TV has a 4:3 aspect ratio and that's why iMovie makes it easy for you to get the math right and avoid distortion.

Clicking the Settings button presents the Compression Settings dialog shown in Figure 15-17. The topmost Compressor pop-up presents a long list of compressors you might use, similar to the one in Figure 15-17. (We have a couple of choices in the figure in addition to those offered by a basic QuickTime Pro installation.) We're not going to cover all of them, just the ones appropriate to video — some of them, like BMP and JPEG, are compressors that apply to still images rather than video. Here are the major video compressors:

- **Animation** is a lossy compression format and the more you compress your video, the more the quality suffers. At its High and Best quality settings, you don't achieve much compression. As its name implies, it is probably best suited to cartoon-like images and image sequences.

- **Cinepak** is one of the oldest compressors available and, if you use it, you can be pretty certain that any user with QuickTime installed, even really old versions, will be able to view your work. The downside to Cinepak is that it doesn't achieve a lot of compression and what it does achieve is lossy. You should have at least one, preferably two or three, key frames per second, at least 12 (preferably 15) frames per second, and a data rate of at least 150KB per second. A 320×240 video, at 150KB/sec, 15fps, and a key frame every 7 frames will consume about 12MB per minute.

- **DV-NTSC/DV-PAL** generate files about the same size and quality as they are in iMovie. Reducing the frame size to 320×240 and the frame rate to 15fps will only reduce your space consumption by about 50 percent (to about 100MB/min). These formats are best suited as an intermediate format to feed to third-party video postprocessing tools. (We'll discuss some of those in Chapter 17.)

- **H.261** was developed over ten years ago (1990) by the ITU (International Telecomm Union). It's optimized for streaming data, particularly those with data rates that are a multiple of 64Kbits/sec and is particularly well-suited for ISDN connections.

- **H.263** is one of your better trade-off choices. You can get about the same (or slightly better) quality in half the space used by Cinepak and don't require as many key frames for good results.

- **Motion JPEG A/Motion JPEG B** are extensions to video of JPEG image compression. Using Motion JPEG, each frame is a JPEG-compressed image. The difference between the A and B variants is that Motion JPEG-B doesn't support markers to denote start-of-image. This format is common in many PCI- and USB-based capture cards.

- **Sorenson** has, since its inclusion with QuickTime 4, been the quality champion, at least until Sorenson 3 showed up with QuickTime 5.0.2. Sorenson (more accurately, Sorenson 2) comes with a performance price tag, though. Compressing can take a long time and playback requires QuickTime 4.0 or later and, if you want decent performance, a G3 or better processor. While this isn't a problem for you, using Mac OS X, not all of your audience is guaranteed to be so well prepared.

- **Sorenson 3** significantly improves on Sorenson 2's performance, delivering equivalent quality in about half the time. The software bar has been raised, though, requiring QuickTime 5.0.2 or later to view Sorenson 3-compressed movies. Both Sorenson and Sorenson 3 offer another advantage, they play back well when scaled up to double their size. This means that a 320×240 movie will still look good at 640×480.

- **Video** is another of the older compressors and can be a good choice when compatibility with older versions of QuickTime and older, slower Macs is a consideration. Video's main failing is that it doesn't achieve significant compression. At 12fps and 320×240 resolution, 25MB/minute is not uncommon.

Note Now that QuickTime 6 is shipping, it adds more compressors, in particular MPEG-4, to the list. MPEG-4 delivers superior quality at high rates of compression and promises to be heavily used in streaming Internet video. DivX and 3ivx are both offshoots of preliminary MPEG-4 proposals.

Actually establishing your video compression options follows pretty easily:

(a) (b)

Figure 15-17: The (video) Compression Settings dialog box (a); Lots of choices in the Compressor pop-up menu (b).

1. Choose the compressor (as described in the previous sequence) from the upper Compressor pop-up menu.

2. Choose the number of colors, sometimes expressed as the Bit Depth, from the lower Compressor pop-up menu.

3. Use the Quality slider to set the desired quality. The higher the quality you set, the larger the resultant file.

4. Specify the speed of play in the Frames per second text field (or select from the adjacent pop-up menu).

   A rate between 12 and 24fps is usually a good choice for CD-based movies. 24fps is the frame rate associated with film and generally results in a very high-quality playback, if the computer is fast enough to support that speed. If there is a lot of action (a hockey game, for example), you might want to use higher frame rates as well.

5. Set the key frame rate in the Key frame every *nn* frames text box. Make sure the check box is selected. Most video compression is achieved by computing differences from a reference image (called the key frame). The more variation there is, the less advantage this technique achieves. You can actually get to the point where the differences record comprises more data than a complete image. We tend to use at least one key frame per second (generally two or three if the image isn't relatively static).

6. If available (for example, Animation disables it), you can select the Limit data rate check box and specify an upper limit on how fast data should be moved. This is where the "×" in CD drives designated 2×, 8×, and so on comes into play. Many older drives are 1× (by definition) and, if compatibility with those drives is an issue, the data rate should be kept under 300KB/sec (probably far under).

Specifying audio compression

If QuickTime's default audio settings are not to your liking, click the Audio section's Settings button to display the Sound Settings dialog box shown in Figure 15-18. As you can see, this dialog box doesn't have quite so many variations for you to consider.

(a)   (b)

Figure 15-18: The Sound Settings dialog box (a); choose one from the Compressor pop-up menu (b).

You can save space by lowering the quality of your audio (but video compression has a much higher impact on size). How you're going to distribute your movie should have a major impact on the audio settings you choose.

1. Choose an audio compressor from the Compressor pop-up menu.

    - **24-bit Integer/32-bit Floating Point/32-bit Integer/64-bit Floating Point** are primarily intended for use with processor-specific hardware and software storage. They aren't generally useful for video editing.
    - **ALaw 2:1** is similar to >Law 2:1 (see last in list), but is based on European digital telephone standards.
    - **IMA 4:1** is highly recommended for CD-based movies. It compresses rapidly at about a 4:1 ratio and works well with both the Mac's AIFF format and the WAV format common on Windows.
    - **MACE 3:1/MACE 6:1** are the Macintosh Audio Compression and Expansion codecs that have been part of the Macintosh Sound Manager seemingly forever (a long time, anyway). Included with QuickTime 3.0 or later, they are good general-purpose, cross-platform choices and work well when older hardware might be in play.
    - **QDesign Music 2** is, as the name implies, optimized to compress music. Choosing this compressor enables the Sound Settings Options button, which you can click to set a target data rate between 8Kbps and 48Kbps. This compressor works well for streaming music as it can deliver CD-quality sound over a 28.8Kbps modem connection (though not with video included).
    - **Qualcomm PureVoice(tm)**, in contrast to QDesign Music 2, is optimized for the spoken voice. Supporting only mono settings, it can greatly compress spoken audio. It's based on the same CDMA (Code Division Multiple Access) technology used in cellular telephones. When you choose this compressor, you have access to the Options button, which will let you specify 9:1 or 19:1 compression and whether to optimize for streaming.
    - **>Law 2:1** is purely 16-bit audio, with the low (2:1) compression rate used in the United States and Japan for digital telephony. It is generally a poor choice for video due to its low compression, but does have the advantage of being fast and not very lossy.

2. Choose your sample rate, either from the pop-up button or by typing it into the Rate textbox.
3. If applicable, specify whether to use 8-bit or 16-bit sound on the Size line.
4. Specify Mono or Stereo sound as appropriate (if the choice is available)
5. Click OK and return to the Expert QuickTime Settings dialog box, which will now reflect the choices you've made.
6. Assuming you're done, click OK to dismiss the dialog box.

We'll discuss the "Prepare for internet" option later, under "Putting Your Movie on the Web."

Postproduction Tricks with QuickTime Pro

Now that you have a movie exported to QuickTime, you might think that you're done. You could be right as the movie is now ready to be viewed by anyone with a compatible QuickTime version installed on their computer.

QuickTime Pro, though, offers some additional editing features, including a few rather interesting special effects that aren't available in iMovie. (Although eZedia and others are producing some stunning third-party plug-ins — see the "Plugging into iMovie" section earlier in this chapter — that bring QuickTime Pro-like effects to iMovie.)

The control center for QuickTime effects is the Properties dialog box (Movie ⇨ Get Movie Properties, or ⌘-J), shown in Figure 15-19.

Figure 15-19: QuickTime Player Pro's Properties dialog box.

The key to the Properties dialog box is the pair of pop-up menus at the top. Although they appear to be peers, the pop-up on the right changes depending upon what you select from the left-hand pop-up. By default, you open to the Movie selection in the left pop-up menu. At this point, your choices in the right pop-up will be:

✦ **Annotations** is where you can add textual information such as a copyright notice, a date stamp, or a myriad of other possibilities. If you wish to annotate your movie, click the Add button shown in Figure 15-20, to display the Add Annotation dialog box. Select the category in the scrolling list at the top and enter your text in the textbox at the bottom of the dialog box. When ready, click Add.

When annotations are selected in the Properties list, you can choose to Edit or Delete them as well.

Figure 15-20: Click the Add button to include annotations, such as copyright information.

✦ **Auto Play** is really straightforward. It presents you with one check box, labeled Auto Play Enabled. If this check box is selected, opening the movie will start it playing automatically (at least on Macs where that feature is available and enabled).

✦ **Colors** is only useful if your movie is going to be played on computers that don't support thousands or millions of colors (i.e., 256, or 8-bit, video). You can attach a color palette to your movie by clicking the Set button and navigating to the color palette file. In today's computing world, this selection is an anachronism.

✦ **Controller**, shown in Figure 15-19 is where you specify which type of QuickTime Player window the user should see when opening your movie. For movies created with iMovie, the only two of interest are Movie Controller (the default) and None (which just eliminates the scrubber bar and the VCR-like controls from the window).

✦ **Files** tells which files are used for the movie. On a movie resulting from an iMovie export to QuickTime, it will just be the file you double-clicked to launch QuickTime.

+ **General** just informs you how many tracks are in your movie, their speed, and their size.

+ **Preview** lets you specify the portion of your movie to display in an Open dialog's Preview pane or the Mac OS X Finder's column view.

+ **Size** refers to dimensions, such as 640×480 or 320×240. You will be informed of both the default (Normal) size and the current size, in case you've chosen to resize the Player window.

+ **Time** tells you where the playhead is (Current Time), how long the movie is (Duration), the timestamp of a current selection's beginning (Selection Start), and how long the selection is (Selection Duration).

While much of this is very interesting (and useful) information, it really doesn't get you any closer to using QuickTime Pro's special effects. They work on individual movie tracks, not on the movie as a whole. Select a video track (as shown in Figure 15-21) and the right-hand pop-up menu changes a bit. Two of these, Graphics Mode and Size, allow for some interesting effects.

Figure 15-21: With Video Track selected in the left-hand pop-up menu, you have many options available in the right-hand pop-up menu.

Masking out part of the screen

Somewhat of a contradiction, you use transparency to black out part of your video image. Actually, block out is more accurate than black out, since you specify the single color to ignore in an image.

There is no fudge factor or tolerance on the color chosen. The color must be specified exactly. An RGB color specification of 0, 0, 128 is not going to affect any other shade of blue, no matter how close they appear to the male eye. (We've given up on underestimating the female ability to distinguish between two colors that most men would find identical.)

What we're going to describe here is a fairly simple example: putting a speech balloon, like the ones in comic books, on a section of our video. Starting with the image in Figure 15-22, we're going to add a balloon of text saying, "But I don't wanna get up!" above and to the right (partially hiding the fan base).

1. Using your graphics program of choice, create the thought balloon and make everything other than the text and the balloon's outline the color that you want to have disappear. To make things easy, we're going to have black be our transparency color and we'll put the text and balloon in any other color or combination, as shown in Figure 15-22b (okay, we'll choose white). The image file should be 640×480 (or whatever size your video track is) at a 72dpi resolution.

   We used GraphicConverter, but you could accomplish this equally well with AppleWorks, Photoshop, Corel, or many other programs.

(a)

(b)

Figure 15-22: Our movie (a); our mask, as created in GraphicConverter (b).

2. Save the file as a PICT image.

3. Open your movie in QuickTime Player and find out how long it is.

4. Choose File ⇨ Import, locate the PICT file you created in the Open dialog box (or sheet) and click the Open button.

5. Choose File ⇨ Save (⌘-S), name the movie you've just created, and click Save.

6. Select the entire movie (Edit ⇨ Select All or ⌘-A) and choose Edit ⇨ Copy (⌘-C).

7. Switch to the QuickTime Player window with your real movie.

8. Place the playhead where you want the overlay to take effect.

9. Holding down the Shift key, drag the playhead to the end of the sequence you want overlaid. Your window should resemble that in Figure 15-23. (The very light gray in the scrubber bar might not show up well in the figure, so look for the crop markers.)

10. While pressing the Option and Shift keys, choose Edit ⇨ Add Scaled (or, for the suitably dexterous, just press Option-Shift-⌘-V). Add Scaled only appears in the Edit menu if both Option and Shift are pressed. With just the Option key down, Add appears in the menu, but that adds for just one second.

11. Now, since the mask is hiding your movie, it's time to make it (at least partially) transparent. Choose Movie ⇨ Get Movie Properties (⌘-J).

Figure 15-23: Use the crop markers to select the frame sequence you want masked.

12. In the left pop-up, choose Video Track 2 (the track you just added).

13. In the right pop-up, choose Graphics Mode, and select transparent from the list.

14. Click the Color button and, using your color picker of choice (we chose RGB) specify the color you want to make transparent. In our case, it was black (0, 0, 0).

15. Click OK and see the result, as shown in Figure 15-24.

Figure 15-24: But Spenser doesn't wanna get up!

We're sure that you can come up with many variations on this theme if you unleash your imaginations. Remember, any colors other than your mask color remain.

 Tip

If you want a black-and-white mask to apply to the whole track, there is a shortcut. Choose your video track in the left pop-up, choose Mask from the right pop-up, click the Set button, and select the image you want to use for a mask.

Making better subtitles with Text Tracks

Subtitles and captions can really augment a movie. While iMovie gives you some pretty nice styles for the subtitles, they aren't exactly flexible about mixing fonts, text styles, and sizes within a single subtitle (to put it mildly). QuickTime's Text Tracks are a lot more freewheeling in this regard, but you're stuck with the text appearing on a black bar at the bottom of your screen, reminiscent of closed caption TV.

1. Create your text, using all the formatting you deem appropriate in a text editor. (TextEdit is a pretty good choice for OS X, as is SimpleText in OS 9.)
2. Select the text and choose Edit ➪ Copy to put it on the system clipboard.
3. Switch to your QuickTime movie and position the playhead where you want the text to first appear.
4. While pressing Shift, drag the playhead to the point where you want the text to disappear. Adjust the crop markers as necessary if you missed your spots by a bit.
5. While pressing Shift and Option, choose Edit ➪ Add Scaled (Option-Shift-⌘-V).

Now, wasn't that easy? When you play your movie back, the text will appear as shown in Figure 15-25.

Figure 15-25: Closed captioning, with style.

You can even do some resizing and skewing of the text track, just go to the Properties menu to tweak it.

1. Choose Movie ➪ Get Movie Properties (⌘-J).
2. Choose the text track from the left pop-up menu and then choose Size from the right-hand pop-up.
3. Click the Adjust button and some red handles appear around the caption. These handles are a little strange but, if you drag the corner handles, you can resize the caption horizontally or vertically. If you drag the circled X handles, you skew or rotate the caption.

If you have multiple lines of text (kind of like the flashing billboard signs you see on the highway) where you want one line to show up and, when it disappears, have the next line appear, and so forth. That, too, is made to order for QuickTime text tracks. Here, though, you start by making your story a QuickTime movie.

1. Create your text file and save it. Each paragraph will be considered a text frame and have a two-second duration.
2. In QuickTime Player, choose File ⇨ Import and select your text file in the Open dialog box.
3. Select the entire movie (Edit ⇨ Select All or ⌘-A) and choose Edit ⇨ Copy (⌘-C).
4. Switch back to your original QuickTime movie.
5. While pressing Option, choose Edit ⇨ Add (Option-⌘-V).

You have just added a multiframe text track to your movie.

Putting Your Movie on the Web

There is a human compulsion to chronicle our lives for future generations. Prehistoric man did it with drawings on cave walls, the early Egyptians used hieroglyphics in and on their tombs, Renaissance man kept diaries and journals, and people of the mid- to late-20th century took photographs and made home movies. One thing all those methods have in common is that only a small number of copies exist (sometimes only one) and distribution is extremely limited. Now, with digital movies and photographs, in conjunction with e-mail and personal Web sites, distribution is almost unlimited. In the past few years, we've received digital photo and movie substitutes via e-mail and Web links for the ubiquitous Christmas letters, birth and wedding announcements (not necessarily in that order), and vacation summaries that used to arrive in the mailbox.

We're going to ignore e-mail here, assuming that you know enough about your individual e-mail client to attach a file for transmission. Besides, there are just too many possible e-mail clients for us to try to cover them all.

Ah, but the Web is a different story. Just as you saw how to create Web pages for your iPhotos in Chapter 10, you're now going to see how to create Web pages to let people watch your movies.

You have two restraints on unfettered Web movie hosting: space and bandwidth. Unless you have your own Web-hosting server, with lots of hard disk space, your ISP is going to constrain you to somewhere between 2MB and 20MB. Usually. AOL is at the low end, with 2MB per member name. Apple's .Mac far exceeds the upper end with 100MB. Most ISPs offer between 5MB and 10MB. You can, however, opt to pay your ISP a greater monthly fee for expanded service, including more Web hosting space. Likewise, unless you know that the folks visiting your page have broadband access (DSL and cable-modem, for example), large, high-quality movies are going to take a long time to download for viewing. Even with broadband, though, there are limits. Dennis has a rather fast (150KB/sec) cable modem connection, for example, and he still sometimes runs into bottlenecks with some larger (say 640×480) movies. So, a variation of computing's golden rule, using the same acronym, is in order: KISS (keep it small, sonny/sister).

There are (essentially) three ways to make your movie accessible through a Web page:

+ It can be downloadable via a hyperlink. People download it and view it with QuickTime Player on their Mac.
+ It can be downloadable via an embedding command. Here, it looks like part of your Web page and people view it using their browser's QuickTime plug-in.
+ It could be streamed. This means that your visitor views your movie while it is downloading.

We already saw in Chapter 14 how to export our movie to QuickTime. For convenience sake, let's choose Web Movie, Small or Streaming Web Movie, Small as our Export format.

Tip

When exporting a movie for the Web, you should avoid using spaces or special characters (ones other than letters, numbers, hyphens, and underscores) in the filename. In fact, since many Web servers are hosted on Unix systems (which are case-sensitive in nature), you might want to use only lower-case characters in the filename. Also, be sure to include the .mov filename extension so that Windows computers will recognize that the file is a QuickTime movie. If you want to include spaces, your HTML is going to have a whole bunch of "%20" entries in the middle of the name to make sure that browsers and servers can find your file.

Creating the HTML for a downloadable movie

You're going to need to know something about coding HTML to follow along here, but it isn't that difficult. If you just want to make the movie downloadable from your Web page, your task is a piece of cake. All you have to do is add a hyperlink similar to this one:

    <a href="my_movie.mov">Click here to download my movie.</a>

Note

For quite a while, it was considered common to use all uppercase characters for tags and attributes. With the computing world migrating from HTML to XML, we're doing a 180. Tags and attributes must be lowercase, now. In our code snippets, we're going to follow modern convention. In the expository text, we use uppercase references on occasion, where we want to make sure the reference stands out from the surrounding text. (Sometimes the simple font change just isn't enough.)

Of course, as a courteous Web page designer, you would probably include a little more information such as the size and, maybe, an icon (like a filmstrip picture) to make the fact that it is a movie absolutely clear. The following code would do that job (assuming you had an image file named filmstrip.gif present in the directory with your Web page):

```
<a href="my_movie.mov"><img src="filmstrip.gif" alt="filmstrip
icon" width="18" height="16"></a>
<a href="my_movie.mov">Click here to download my movie
(2.1MB)</a>
```

Figure 15-26 shows what a simple Web page with this code in it might look like when seen in Microsoft Internet Explorer 5.1.4.

Figure 15-26: Click either the text link or the QuickTime filmstrip icon to download the movie.

Embedding a movie in your Web page

If you know that visitors to your page have the QuickTime plug-in installed for their Web browser, you can use the `EMBED` tag. The `EMBED` tag has lots of options, covered in exquisite detail on Apple's Web site. Check out www.apple.com/quicktime/authoring/embed.html if you want to know everything about this tag. For our purposes, we're going to use a subset covering common usage.

For example, we're going to demonstrate using the `SRC` attribute for a still image with the `HREF` attribute accessing the real movie, just like the big guys (Apple's Web pages) do. You use the `EMBED` tag's `CONTROLLER` attribute to specify the presence (=`"TRUE"`) or absence (=`"FALSE"`) of the QuickTime control strip along the movie's bottom.

 Note   If you want the control strip to be present, increase the height by 16 pixels so that everything fits.

Figure 15-27 shows a simple variation of our example page with the movie embedded on the page (including a controller) and no click-on-me still image.

Figure 15-27: Embedding the movie on your Web page is a straightforward exercise.

The HTML for this page follows:

```
<!DOCTYPE HTML PUBLIC "-//W3C//DTD HTML 4.01 Transitional//EN"
        "http://www.w3.org/TR/1999/REC-
html401-19991224/loose.dtd">
<html lang="en">
<head>
   <meta http-equiv="content-type" content="text/html;
charset=iso-8859-1">
   <title>Chapter 16 Embedded Movie Example</title>
   <meta name="generator" content="BBEdit 6.5.2">
</head>
<body>
<h1 align="center">Embed My Movie Page</h1>
<p>
This page shows you a simple example of an embedded QuickTime
movie.
</p>
<embed controller="true" width="320" height="256"
src="spenserwontplay.mov">
</body>
</html>
```

As you can see, Dennis uses BBEdit as his HTML editor of choice; however, you can use anything that will save your HTML as plain text. Be sure, if you use TextEdit that you save as text rather than RTF. The code isn't fancy, but it gets the job done.

One of the things you'll notice is that this movie starts playing while it is loading. If you don't want it to start playing until your page's visitor clicks the Play button, add the `autoplay="false"` attribute to your `embed` tag.

Figure 15-28 shows an almost identical page, but with a one-frame "poster" movie, awaiting your visitor's click to load the real movie. You'll want to turn off the controller here so that your visitor doesn't click it to make the poster frame play. Another thing you need to include is a `TARGET` attribute, so that the browser knows to load the `HREF` into the same space as the `SRC` when clicked.

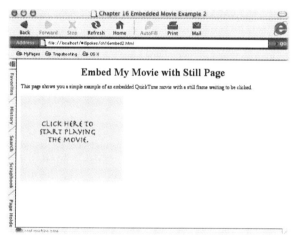

Figure 15-28: Click on the still to load your movie and start it playing.

The HTML source for this page follows:

```
<!DOCTYPE HTML PUBLIC "-//W3C//DTD HTML 4.01 Transitional//EN"
        "http://www.w3.org/TR/1999/REC-
html401-19991224/loose.dtd">
<html lang="en">
<head>
    <meta http-equiv="content-type" content="text/html;
charset=iso-8859-1">
    <title>Chapter 16 Embedded Movie Example 2</title>
    <meta name="generator" content="BBEdit 6.5.2">
</head>
<body>
```

```
<h1 align="center">Embed My Movie with Still Page</h1>
<p>
This page shows you a simple example of an embedded QuickTime
movie with a still frame waiting to be clicked.
</p>
<embed controller="false" autoplay="false" width="240"
height="180" src="ch16embed2.mov" target="myself"
href="spenserwontplay.mov">
</body>
</html>
```

Streaming your movie

You can stream your movie from a standard Web server (called an http server) or you can, if you're lucky or are willing to pay for it, stream your movie from a QuickTime Streaming Server, also known as an RTP/RTSP server (Real-time Transport Protocol/Real-Time Streaming Protocol).

Tip

Streaming media, particularly from a QuickTime server, is a complex and somewhat arcane, subject. If you're really interested in setting up a streaming server, we recommend that you start by checking out the QuickTime for the Web FAQ (Frequently Asked Questions) page at `www.apple.com/quicktime/products/qtss/qtssfaq.html`.

Going back to our download example, change the http to rtp and you're just about done. We say "just about" because on an RTP server, you have designated directories in which you place your movies, so you'll have to specify a full path to the movie. For example, if your stream (mymovie.mov) is stored at `www.mystreamingserver.com`, in the streams directory, you would make your anchor tag read as follows:

```
<a href="rtp://www.mystreamingserver.com/streams/mymovie.mov">
```

When the Web browser encounters this directive, it will launch QuickTime Player and show the user all the progress information in the little progress pane between the movie and the controls, as depicted in Figure 15-29.

Figure 15-29: QuickTime Player keeps you informed when preparing to play a streaming video.

When you aren't using a streaming server, the hints QuickTime places in your movie to help a streaming server put things together in the right order are ignored. You end up with what is, in essence, a *fast start* movie. That just means that QuickTime will begin to play the movie as soon as 50 percent or more has been downloaded. On a slow connection the playback could still catch up with the continuing download, which means that playback will pause while more data gets buffered.

Putting your iMovies on your iDisk

If you've signed up for a .Mac account, the .Mac focus points squarely at your iDisk. One of the folders Apple places on every iDisk is the Movies folder, another is Public, and a third is Sites. Any one of these folders is a suitable repository for iMovies you want to share — it just depends upon *how* you want to share them.

> **Note** We're not going to provide screen shots of the .Mac Web pages for two reasons: 1) They change appearance frequently as .Mac evolves, and 2) the permissions forms to use the screen shots take a lot of time away from preparing the book. (Besides, dealing with lawyers isn't good for our blood pressure.)

The simplest method is to place your movie in the Public folder. Then, anyone who knows your .Mac username (not your password) can access your movie by mounting your iDisk Public folder on their desktop. They can either play it from there, although that can result in stuttering playback if the connection isn't fast enough to download the movie before it finishes playing, or (more likely) they can copy it down to their disk to enjoy over and over.

If your friends or family are .Mac-deprived, they can still see what's in your Public Folder if you create a FileSharing Web page, a quick and easy task. On the main iDisk page click the link for Sharing Your Public Folder (which used to be called Publish Personal Folder, and might change names again — in any event, the link should be obvious). This will take you to the HomePage page with the FileSharing tab already selected. Pick a theme. (At present there are two themes, identical except for color: graphite and magenta.) In the page that appears, click the Edit button and customize the text in those areas where text boxes appear. Click the Publish button and anyone with a Web browser can access the contents of your Public folder at `http://homepage.mac.com/yourname/FileSharing.html`. Figure 15-30 shows Spenser's (Dennis's Boston Terrier) file sharing page.

If you want to make your movie available via the .Mac HomePage Web page mechanism, copy the movie to your Movies folder (the one on your iDisk, not the one in your Home directory). .Mac will make it easy to create a Web page to present your movie without you having to learn any HTML at all:

Figure 15-30: .Mac makes it easy to get files from a member's Public folder.

1. Fire up your Web browser, log into .Mac, and click on the HomePage button or icon, to present the HomePage page. (Even though it sounds like it, we're not stuttering.)
2. Click the iMovies button under the Create a Page heading to present the various Themes (templates). At the time we're writing this, Apple offers seven themes.
3. Click on a theme to present the page customization screen.
4. Click Change Text and enter a title and short description for your movie page.
5. Click the QuickTime area's Choose button. If you don't see the movie(s) you've uploaded to your Movies folder in the list, click the Update button. If you need to add the movies to your Movies folder and you don't have your iDisk open, click the Open My iDisk button.
6. Select your movie from the list and click the Preview button. Your Web browser will show you the page in its current state and start to download your movie. This should give you a good idea what visitors with connections similar to yours will experience.
7. If you like what you've created, click the Apply button to return to the Themes page.

8. If you want to see how the whole page will look, click Preview.

9. When you're satisfied with your creation, click Publish. .Mac will congratulate you on your fine work and tell you the URL for the page you just created.

The pages (HTML files) for sites you create are stored, surprise, in your iDisk's Sites folder. You can open those files in a text editor if you wish to modify them, or if you're new to HTML, to learn from them.

Summary

In this chapter you learned some advanced audio and video editing techniques. You also saw how to work with and convert non-DV video, and how to enhance iMovie with plug-ins. We also presented you with a crash course in using QuickTime Export's Expert settings and how to do postproduction editing of your movie with QuickTime Pro. Finally, you learned how to publish your movies on the World Wide Web.

✦ ✦ ✦

More iMovie Tips, Tricks, and Techniques

CHAPTER 16

In This Chapter

Sharing clips between projects

Making menu-driven VideoCDs

Plan your shoot and shoot your plan

Taping tips for better footage

We've covered iMovie's editing capabilities to a fare-thee-well in Chapters 13–15, and in Chapter 17, "Enhancing Your iMovie Experience," we'll show you all sorts of things you can acquire, either free or by using a little plastic, to make your movie-making more productive.

This chapter provides you with tips about shooting better footage in the first place, reusing clips from one movie in another, and (even though it involves a couple of add-on software products) how to create a "poor-man's DVD" — a menu-driven VideoCD that will play in many set top DVD players and can be navigated by the player's remote control.

Sharing Clips between Projects

TV and movie studios keep large libraries of what they call *stock footage*. These are clips and scenes that they reuse in multiple productions (crowd scenes, car crashes, and explosions, for example). You can do the same thing with iMovie if you know a little bit about how iMovie stores its clips, and that's what we're going to tell you here.

There are two ways you can add clips to your iMovie project:

- ✦ Use File ⇨ Import, the recommended (and slow) method to import DV Stream files into iMovie.
- ✦ Copy or move the clip into project's Media folder.

If you choose the second method, the next time iMovie opens your project you'll see an alert similar to the one shown in Figure 16-1, although the number of clips will vary depending upon how many you moved into the Media folder. Click the

OK button and your footage appears on the shelf, as shown in Figure 16-2. A really nice feature of this method is that iMovie picks up the names you've given the clips.

Figure 16-1: iMovie offers to add clips you move into the Media folder to your shelf.

Figure 16-2: iMovie even displays them with the names you gave them.

Unfortunately, iMovie doesn't rename the clip files in the Media folder when you rename them on the shelf or in the clip viewer, so you'll have to know which clips you want to rename in the Finder, because you probably don't want your collection of stock material to all be named Clip 01, Clip 02, and so on. A fast way to do this is to open each clip in QuickTime Player to determine which one it is and then name it accordingly. An even faster way is to switch to Column view in the Finder and check out the live previews appearing when you select a file. (This doesn't work if you have multiple files selected.)

Caution Rename the clip's file in the Finder. Doing a Save or Save As in QuickTime Player won't retain it as a clip file that iMovie will "adopt."

Making Menu-driven VideoCDs

VideoCDs are an inexpensive and handy format in which to distribute your iMovie work. You can write up to 80 minutes of VHS-quality video to a standard 700MB CD-R (or CD-RW) blank. Best of all, you can write VideoCDs on any CD burner with the help of added software that can write VideoCD format or Multitrack CD-ROM XA format (of which VideoCD is a special case). We strongly recommend Toast Titanium (www.roxio.com) and will assume its presence in the following discussion.

Like the DVD-R media used by iDVD, CD-R-based VideoCDs works in *most* DVD players, though not always the same machines. For example, one of Dennis's DVD players will play VideoCDs (and SVCDs) written to CD-R media, but won't play the DVDs written to DVD-R media by iDVD or DVD Studio Pro. On the other hand, his neighbor's DVD player plays the DVD-Rs, but doesn't recognize the CD-R or CD-RW media on which he writes VideoCDs. Check www.vcdhelp.com for a breakdown of which players support which formats and disk types.

You could just put multiple movies on the VideoCD and, when you stick it in your DVD player, they'll play one after another. That's effective, but it isn't particularly interesting. As you'll see in Part V of this book, iDVD can create menu-driven DVDs, but they aren't really comparable to the menu structures on commercial DVDs — chaptering (scene selection) being one of the most obvious missing features. With the help of a wonderful freeware utility, VCD Builder by Johan Lindström (homepage.mac.com/johan), you can create VideoCDs that do support chapters. And, if you're a programmer-type, Lindström even makes the source code available on his Web page. We'll be mentioning VCD Builder again in Chapter 17, "Enhancing Your iMovie Experience."

Note Actually, VCD Builder is donation-ware. Johan doesn't charge for it and there are no annoying reminders, limitations, or registration dialog boxes, but he is set up to accept donations through PayPal if you consider it worthwhile. We did.

Planning for chapters

DVD players will just play one movie after another from a VideoCD. This is a continuous stream, with no pause between movies. By taking advantage of this behavior and the fact that we can override the default behavior with a VCD menu structure we're well on the way to creating VideoCDs that behave like commercial DVDs.

The first thing we do is break our movie into scenes in iMovie and export each of those scenes as a self-contained VideoCD-compatible MPEG file using Toast's VideoCD Export plug-in as described in the "Have a Little Toast with Your iMovie" section in Chapter 17. After you have your entire movie exported as separate mini-movies, you're ready to start constructing your VideoCD.

Building a menu-driven VideoCD

VCD Builder lets you designate a movie or picture as a menu, something that you can have playing until you interrupt it with a command via the remote control or until you have it automatically advance to the "next" movie. For our purposes, we're going to assume a picture will be used for the menu. We tend to use Photoshop or Photoshop Elements to create our menu pictures (640×480 resolution at 72 dpi), but you can use any program that creates QuickTime-readable image files of the appropriate size.

> **Note** For those of you wondering about the 640×480 resolution rather than the 720×480 resolution for DV Stream video, it is because the video stream pixels aren't square like those on a computer monitor; iMovie, QuickTime, and VCD Builder interpolate them into the 640 horizontal, square pixels that are displayed. If you supply a 640×480 digital photo, it will be converted to the rectangular pixels required for DV when output.

You create *sequences* in VCD Builder, specifying a picture, a movie, or group of pictures and movies that exist as a unit and play in order. You can then connect the sequences to move from one to another (called the *target sequence*), as follows:

- ✦ **Play:** Jump to the target sequence when the remote control's Play button is pressed.

- ✦ **Stop:** Jump to the target sequence when the remote control's Stop button is pressed. On some DVD players, this will be invoked by the Menu button rather than the Stop button.

- ✦ **Previous:** Jump to the target sequence when the remote control's Previous button is pressed.

- ✦ **Next:** Jump to the target sequence when the remote control's Next button is pressed.

- ✦ **1 . . . 9:** Jump to the target sequence when the remote control's corresponding numeric button is pressed.

✦ **Timeout:** Jump to the target sequence when the source sequence finishes playing. If there is no Timeout connection, the Next connection takes control, and if the Next connection isn't present, the Stop action takes over.

Figure 16-3 shows a simple VideoCD with a menu and three additional sequences, the third of which is being connected back to the menu using a Timeout connection. Creating the connection is simple: Just hold down the Control key, click and drag from the source sequence to the target sequence. When you release the mouse button, the circular menu shown in Figure 16-3 appears. Move the mouse to the icon for the desired connection (its name appears in the center) and click.

Now that you have your structure, you can start filling the sequences with content. In the simplest case, the one we're describing here, drag your menu picture to the box with the number one badge on it and drag each scene, in order, to the corresponding sequence boxes.

For more involved sequences, such as a menu that cycles through four images or one that will automatically advance to the next item after a specified length of time, double-click a sequence box to display the window shown in Figure 16-4. Drag your pictures and/or movies into this window to populate the sequence. If you don't like the order, you can drag the thumbnails around as shown in Figure 16-5 to reorder them.

Using the pop-up menu, you can choose whether your images are scaled or cropped to fit in the display area and you can check the Use TV-safe Borders box for any image that you think might have important information falling outside the viewable area on a TV set.

Figure 16-3: Connecting your sequences is a simple control-click and drag.

Figure 16-4: This window is where you build the sequences that give the boxes their name.

Figure 16-5: Drag your images and clips around to get them in the order you want.

Burning a VideoCD

After you have all your sequences populated, save and name your project file. (This way the VideoCD you create will have the name you want rather than "Untitled.") Then click the Burn VCD button in the window's toolbar (see Figure 16-3). VCD Builder will start converting your still images to VideoCD-compatible form (your movies must already be in VideoCD-compatible MPEG-1 format) and creating the various tracks for your VideoCD. Once those image files are created, VCD Builder will launch Toast Titanium with the format set to Multitrack CD-ROM XA and the image files loaded into Toast. Click Toast's Burn button when you're ready, sit back, and wait for your masterpiece to emerge.

Note VCD Builder creates the image files regardless of whether you click the Make Images or Burn VCD toolbar button. If you don't want Toast launched, click Make Images instead. This is handy if you're using some burner software other than Toast or if your CD burner drive is busy doing something else. (Dennis sometimes watches a DVD while he has VCD Builder creating his VideoCD images.)

With a little imagination, you can see that one menu can point to another menu, which gives you the flexibility to create really complex projects, just like commercial DVDs.

Plan Your Shoot and Shoot Your Plan

If you follow the Boy Scout motto, "Be Prepared," you're well on your way to shooting better video. Make sure that you have extra tape, a well-charged battery (and a spare), a microphone or two are often beneficial, as well as lenses or filters for the expected (or unexpected) lighting conditions. (See Chapter 17, "Enhancing Your iMovie Experience," for some lens and filter suggestions.) Additionally, have a tripod handy or some other tool to provide a steady base for your camera.

Tip If your camera's battery can be recharged when detached from the camera, take a spare battery or two and the charger. There is little more aggravating than to run out of juice while taping. If you see your battery power running down quickly, close the LCD and use the viewfinder. That might be a little harder on you, but it will extend your battery life significantly.

As an example, let's assume that you're planning to shoot footage of your kid's school play or recital. Get there early and stake out a good camera location or two — ones where you won't have audience member heads popping into the frame. Arrange to place a microphone or to tap into the auditorium's sound system so that you can pick up the sound.

If you're actually creating a movie rather than taping a staged or extemporaneous event, storyboard the project. Determine what shots will be needed for the different scenes and set up camera locations and lighting to make them work. If you need an external microphone, find a place to position it so that it will pick up the sound without intruding on the scene. Finally, whenever possible, shoot multiple takes of scenes, possibly from different angles, or, if you're fortunate enough to have two video cameras available, tape from two positions. In either situation, you'll have a fallback position if something doesn't come out the way you had hoped and, in the latter case, you can cut from one camera angle to the other for a better cinematic effect when you edit your footage in iMovie.

Tip With more and more people running around with camcorders, you might be able to borrow someone else's tape to mix with your own when you're both recording the same event. This worked out really well when Dennis and two friends were taping a Little League playoff game — they pooled their tapes and were able to cut to different angles and distances on plays without missing any of the action.

You've all seen those scenes from movies about making movies where the assistant holds up a clapboard with the act, scene, and take information on it while the director calls out "Roll 'em!" Having that clapboard on film accomplishes two things: It labels the footage and it makes sure that the camera is rolling before the action starts. The introductory footage can be cut out later — editing is really easy in iMovie, as you've seen — but if you miss the start of the scene, you can't get it back. Get the camera running early and let it run past the end of the scene. Having the extra footage on either end means that you always have the footage you need.

Taping Tips for Better Footage

The three best tips we can give you to improve the quality of your footage are to use a tripod, optimize your lighting, and get the best sound capture you can. Regardless of how good iMovie might be for movie editing, it can't make a silk purse out of a sow's ear (the acronym for this is GIGO — garbage in, garbage out).

Bouncing is bad

There is little that looks more amateurish than footage where the picture is jiggling up and down or weaving when you pan the action. A tripod is your best friend when you want a solid base from which to shoot. And, with a good panhead on it, you can smoothly follow the action.

If your budget can handle it and you need to move with the action, invest in a Steadicam (www.steadicam.com), about $900, or some other gyro-stabilized attachment so that you can simultaneously walk and shoot footage that won't make your audience seasick when they watch it.

If you don't have a tripod or some other (expensive) stabilizing device, try to improvise using a wall, table, bench, automobile hood, or some other solid, stationary object. When moving the camera to follow the action, rotate as slowly and smoothly as possible.

Just as excessive bouncing can make your audience nauseous, so can frequent or rapid zooming. Avoid unnecessary zooming while taping by framing your shot with the zoom before you start shooting whenever possible. If you must use the zoom while taping, zoom as slowly as possible.

Tip   When given a choice between optical and digital zooming, there really isn't a choice. Ignore the fact that digital zoom even exists. As discussed in Chapter 12, "Enhancing Your iPhoto Experience," digital zoom is just a magnification and interpolation by your camera — you lose resolution and the end result is usually fuzzy and blurry. Turn it off if your camera will allow you to do so, so you aren't tempted by the Dark Side.

Getting good lighting

Never forget that your camera, an electronic device, doesn't see light the same way your human eye sees it. Just because your eye dilates enough to make you think there's enough light for a night (or indoor) scene, doesn't mean that your camera will agree.

First, whenever possible get extra lighting on a scene. Use reflectors or fill lights to eliminate shadows.

Learn which adjustments your camera allows. Many camcorders have settings for low-light conditions, low-contrast settings, and what is called *white balance* (filtering out color casts).

> **Note** The human eye filters out color casts associated with individual lighting sources. Sunlight usually has a blue cast, incandescent lights tend toward yellow, and fluorescent lights gravitate toward green. While our eyes filter these before we notice them, the camera's optical sensors don't and you're likely to get some strange tints in your footage if you don't white balance your camera when taping under different lighting conditions.

Most (good) digital camcorders provide a menu of preprogrammed settings for common lighting conditions. They might be called Programmed Auto-Exposure (AE) Settings (Sony), Presets (Canon), or something similar. Dennis's Sony provides the following AE settings:

- **Spotlight** mode prevents objects (like people's faces) from washing out to white when shot under a strong light.
- **Soft portrait** brings out the subject while softening the background.
- **Sports lesson** minimizes jitter on fast-moving objects like a baseball pitch or a tennis serve.
- **Beach & ski** prevents faces from appearing dark when under bright light and before a reflective background (like a ski slope or a sunny summer beach).
- **Sunset & moon** maintains atmosphere when recording bright objects (for example, fireworks) against a dark background.
- **Landscape** lets you focus on distant objects, even if nearby objects are present, such as the glass in a window through which you might be taping.
- **Low lux** brightens subjects in low light conditions.

What this boils down to is that you should read your camcorder's manual, no matter how poor the English, and learn what capabilities your camera offers. Every make and model has some variation in the features available and there is no way we would even attempt to go through them all here. Check the manual out, learn what your camera offers, and try out the various settings to become familiar with them.

Tip Your camera might also have some special effects, such as Sepia or Solarize. Avoid them! You can do a much better job with iMovie's Effects panel, especially if you acquire some of the add-on effects you'll see covered in Chapter 17.

Huh? What'd they say?

Your digital camcorder comes with a built-in (probably stereo) microphone and you might think that takes care of obtaining your audio. For simple jobs, it very well might — assuming that you are relatively close to the verbal action, that there isn't a lot of ambient noise (cars, trains, and peripheral conversations, for example), and that your subjects speak loudly (and clearly) enough that the microphone picks them up.

Note Camera-integrated microphones occasionally pick up some camera sounds that you might not even hear. For example, if you're using a zoom lens, the motor makes a whirring sound and is next to the microphone input.

There's only so much you can do to fix bad sound without spending tens of thousands of dollars on high-tech audio editing gear like you see in various police and spy shows (*CSI: Crime Scene Investigation* and *The Agency* come to mind), where they isolate the perfect pieces of an audio mish-mash. Even with that equipment, it's still easier to work with good audio in the first place.

The question before us is, "How do we get great audio?" The answer, at least the first step, is to get the microphone as close to our sound source as possible without generating feedback.

Tip Most camcorders have a headphone jack and its purpose is to let you hear the sound the way the camera hears it. When taping, have your headphones on and plugged into this jack. Now, you'll be able to hear what the camera is capturing and you can make adjustments before you get to postproduction with damaged audio.

Second, don't rely on your camera's built-in microphone if you don't have to — even an inexpensive clip-on mic will do a better job in many cases. Microphones fall into various categories, as follows:

+ **Cardioid** microphones have a heart-shaped (hence the name) pickup pattern and, though directed forward, will pick up ambient sounds from the sides and rear. Camcorders with built-in cardioid mics are more susceptible to camera sounds such as the tape transport mechanism and zoom lens operation.

+ **Directional** microphones, such as the shotgun mic, have a very focused field.

+ **Super-cardioid** microphones, the type present on most camcorders, is a compromise between the cardioid and directional mics, eliminating the sound from behind the mic.

+ **Omnidirectional** microphones pick up sounds from all directions equally well. Many clip-on and lavaliere mics fall into this category.

Bob created Figure 16-6 to illustrate these types.

Figure 16-6: Two-dimensional cross sections of microphone pickup patterns.

Remember that the patterns in Figure 16-6 are cross sections and that the pattern is equally true whether you think of it as a vertical slice, horizontal slice, or anything in between.

If you know your subjects are going to be (relatively) stationary, you might consider a boom mic, even if it is a roll-your-own boom made by dangling a super-cardioid mic from a hook, just out of the picture.

Lots of microphones come with foam covers. Use them, don't lose them. The covers aren't (just) to protect the mic from getting dinged, they're really wind-guards used to filter out the sound of wind and some speech side effects, like the popping sound of *p* and *b* or the sibilance of *ss*.

Summary

In this chapter you saw how to share clips between projects, You also learned how to use VCD Builder together with Toast Titanium to create professional-quality, menu-driven VideoCDs. We also gave you some tips and techniques for creating better footage to use in iMovie.

✦ ✦ ✦

Enhancing Your iMovie Experience

CHAPTER 17

✦ ✦ ✦ ✦

In This Chapter

Hardware enhancements

Software enhancements

✦ ✦ ✦ ✦

Adding certain accessories, hardware and software, that enhance your iMovie usage are no-brainers: A digital camcorder with a FireWire connector and Apple's free iMovie 2.1.1 Plug-in Pack fall into that category.

What else can you do, though, to enrich your iMovie-making? In this chapter, we'll list items we think should head anyone's list (and a few that we just think are cool).

Hardware Enhancements

There was a time when hardware was expensive, especially hardware for video editing. You're lucky, though, you already have the two big-ticket items: your FireWire-equipped Mac and your digital camcorder.

That doesn't mean you can't find good ways to use your credit cards (and maybe earn some frequent-flyer miles or cash rebates along the way) in your quest for great iMovies.

Adding RAM

We both believe that most Macs ship with just enough memory to let you use them. iMovie can run on a 128MB iMac with OS 9 or OS X, but it will operate noticeably better on that same Mac with 256MB, better yet with 384MB, and even better with 512MB or 640MB — well, you get the idea.

You probably won't see much difference when importing video, but more memory will speed even that process up a bit. You'll see the biggest performance gains when you render transitions and special effects or export your video using one of the QuickTime codecs. Processor-intensive operations such as these thrive on large amounts of RAM.

Boosting mass storage

iMovie gobbles disk space. We know we've told you this before, but it's something we feel cannot be overemphasized.

It's almost comical to remember the first iMovie-equipped iMac DVs with their 6GB or 10GB drives. Unless you stripped all the preinstalled software except iMovie and what it needed to run, you only had room for between 15 and 45 minutes of video before your disk was full. Today's 20GB, 40GB, and 60GB internal drives are a big improvement, practically guaranteeing you'll have room for at least one or two iMovie projects. But it still won't take long to fill a hard disk if you don't monitor and manage its contents carefully.

Furthermore, if you're going to use iDVD to burn a DVD-R disc, you're going to need even more free disk space for the special files that iDVD requires you to save (in iMovie). All of a sudden, a one-hour video requires (at least temporarily) at least 25GB of disk space. So a 20GB drive won't come close to having enough space for the job, and a 40GB drive may be too small if you already have a lot of stuff on it. (See Chapter 18: "Introducing iDVD.")

Another problem with using your main drive for digital video work is *disk fragmentation*. As files are written, rewritten, removed, and replaced, you get to the point that pieces of your files are scattered all over the disk, resulting in much slower read and write operations as the Mac has to bounce the disk's read head around from place to place on the disk.

Note   You can purchase software, such as Norton Utilities or Alsoft's PlusOptimizer, to defragment your drives. In fact, these are good programs to have even if you aren't dealing with huge digital video files. However, defragmenting takes a lot of time, especially when you have to reboot to run the optimization software.

Dennis has these three drives in his old G4/400 (which has 896MB of RAM):

✦ An 8.5GB SCSI drive that holds OS X, his applications, and other basics

✦ A 20GB ATA drive used for accumulated data (like the files for this book)

✦ A 30GB ATA drive dedicated (almost exclusively) to iMovie work

Now that Dennis has a new flat-panel iMac G4/800 with a 60GB drive, the G4/400 isn't getting as much use for digital video. (It doesn't have a SuperDrive and it's a lot slower than his new iMac.) Still, that configuration worked great for over a year-and-a-half. Even with the 60GB drive (and 768MB of RAM), the iMac also has a 30GB FireWire drive connected — it makes a great place to export the movies for iDVD. When Dennis is done creating and burning a DVD, he can erase the files, leaving an unfragmented drive from which to work the next time.

Bob, on the other hand, thinks it's a waste of time and energy to defragment. He has an external 60GB FireWire dedicated to video. When a project ends, he burns or backs up what he needs, then erases the hard disk. That defragments it quite nicely for the next project, thank you very much.

Burning drives

Apple currently includes CD-R/RW burners in most Mac models, but if you don't have one in yours, we strongly encourage you to get one. The SuperDrive is both a CD-R/RW burner and a DVD-R burner and this is a great combination. Distributing your movies on CD or DVD is a cost-efficient way to send out high-quality copies to family and friends. It's also a great way to distribute business and promotional materials you create in iMovie to coworkers and clients. Purchased in quantity, CD-R media, even including jewel cases and labels, can be had for under $1 per unit.

Unlike videotapes, you can duplicate digital video CDs without *generational loss* (the signal degradation that occurs when copying analog data). This means that you can keep making copies as the need arises and not worry about deteriorating quality. You can also write CDs faster than you can write videotape.

CDs and DVDs are also an excellent archival medium, taking up very little space while holding large amounts of data. Because they are random-access media, it's also much quicker to retrieve something from a CD or DVD than it is from a (sequential access) taped backup.

Getting out of the shadows

Dark indoor shots or heavy shadowing in outdoor clips can ruin a scene. This is where lighting kits, fill lights, and reflectors come in handy.

For those troublesome indoor scenes, consider a portable lighting kit, especially one where the key light fits on your camera's *accessory shoe*, that little slotted mount on the top of most digital camcorders. Some very nice kits, ranging up in price from a few hundred dollars, are available from Lowel (www.lowel.com), Cool-Lux (www.cool-lux.com), and NRG Research (www.nrgresearch.com).

Almost any photography store will stock fill reflectors, as described in Chapter 12, "Enhancing Your iPhoto Experience." Two popular manufacturers are Photoflex (www.photoflex.com) and Bogen Photo Corporation (www.bogenphoto.com).

Keeping a steady hand

Even more than with still photography (Chapter 12 again), keeping the camera steady while taping is critical. Most digital camcorders have some built-in stabilization control, minimizing motion caused by trembling hands, but using a tripod beats the built-in adjustments all to heck.

If you need to move around while taping, though, a tripod won't help. This is where a stabilizer should enter your picture. Ranging from about $250 for entry-level models to thousands of dollars for professional units like those shoulder-mounted mounts you see TV news cameramen using in popular films, stabilizers use gyroscopes and gimbals to eliminate undesirable motion.

Manufacturers of popular models include SteadyTracker (www.steadytracker.com), GlideCam (www.glidecam.com), and Kenyon Labs (www.ken-lab.com).

Filtering and focusing

Unlike better still cameras (both film and digital), most digital camcorders don't have interchangeable lenses. Many camcorder manufacturers offer a partial solution with attachable lens *adapters* and *filters*.

Adapters let you attach different lens types, such as wide-angle or telephoto lenses, to your camcorder.

Filters help you deal with varied lighting conditions and come in multiple flavors. Here are some of the more useful:

- **UV** (Ultraviolet) filters reduce haze by reducing the UV rays that get through to the camera's CCD.
- **ND** (Neutral Density) filters are best described as "sunglasses for your camera." They improve contrast and detail in bright to very bright sunlight.
- **Polarization** filters change the angle at which light enters the lens, reducing reflected glare and allowing you to tape through windows or a watery surface.
- **Diffusion** filters soften a scene. Romantic scenes and reminiscences are often shot through a diffusion filter, providing that slightly hazy effect.
- **Center Spot** filters are a special kind of diffusion filter. They diffuse the periphery while leaving the scene's center in sharp focus.

Check with your camcorder's manufacturer to see what, if any, adapters, lenses, and filters are available from them. Another good source to check is Tiffen (www.tiffen.com), probably the largest manufacturer and supplier of filters in the business.

Software Enhancements

The wonderful world of software provides numerous opportunities to do more with your iMovies. Best of all, many of the programs are free or quite inexpensive (although a few can put a serious dent in your plastic).

Going Pro with QuickTime

QuickTime Pro is a $30 (okay, $29.95 + tax) upgrade to the QuickTime that came with your Mac or that you downloaded for free. You don't get a disk, manual, or anything you can touch physically for that money; what you do get is a multicharacter unlock code, tied to your name, which unlocks extra features in QuickTime. We discussed many of them in Chapters 14 and 15. For the record, the features that put the Pro in QuickTimePro are worth paying for:

✦ Exporting to multiple formats

✦ A cornucopia of editing tools

✦ The ability to present your movie full-screen

If you're serious about making cool iMovies, QuickTime Pro's $30 price tag is money extremely well-spent. Figure 17-1 shows Bob entering his QuickTime Pro registration information, just to show how easy it is. (We smudged out his serial number, so you'll have to obtain your own.)

Figure 17-1: A QuickTime Pro upgrade requires just your name, company, and serial number.

The new MPEG-4 compressor, available through the Expert settings as described in Chapter 15, produces very high-quality streaming video relatively quickly. The downside of this compressor is that all your viewers need to have QuickTime 6 or another MPEG-4 decompressor, and there just aren't that many of them available yet.

Figure 17-2 shows a menu's eye glimpse of the extra commands available after you upgrade to QuickTime Pro.

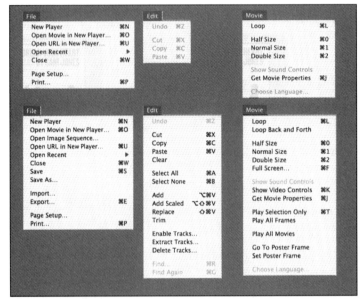

Figure 17-2: Comparing the File, Edit, and Movie menus from regular (free) QuickTime (top row) and QuickTime Pro (bottom row).

Have a little toast with your iMovie

As we've said repeatedly in this book, Roxio's Toast 5 Titanium is "must have" software if you burn more than an occasional CD. For use with iMovie, Toast 5 Titanium includes the VideoCD plug-in, which adds two more choices to the QuickTime Export pop-up menu, as shown in Figure 17-3.

Figure 17-3: Export a movie directly to VideoCD-compatible MPEG-1 format (either NTSC or PAL) with Roxio's VideoCD iMovie plug-in.

Also in the package are useful utilities, such as a Roxio-specific version of the Discus disk-labeling software, the Audion MP3 player application, CD Spin Doctor for extracting songs from cassette tapes and LPs, and iView Media for managing collections of digital media. While iView Media doesn't do everything that iPhoto does, iView Media is a more powerful and flexible photo database that also manages movies, sounds, and fonts.

Tip

If your iMovie usage is anything like Dennis's, you'll accumulate various clips that you'll want to use in more than one movie. Since keeping track of which clip does what is not exactly one of iMovie's strengths, you can use iView to store thumbnails of your clips and retrieve the one you want when you want it.

Because Toast can write so many different CD formats, some of the tools we'll tell you about a little later in this chapter in the "Free software" section create files for Toast to let you write Super VideoCDs (SVCDs), a very high-quality format playable on many set top DVD players.

Check it out at `www.roxio.com`. At the time we're writing this, it's $79, but they're running a $69 promotion at most stores.

Adding effects, transitions, and scoring

There's something about visual effects (including transitions) and soundtracks that appeals to people. Just as early Mac users went overboard with fonts, something new at the time to the general computer user, new iMovie users strive to try out all the effects and transitions they can get their hands on. We tried them all, eventually settling on the ones that work for our purposes, but that hasn't stopped us from looking for new effects and transitions.

If the ones that come with iMovie 2.1.1, combined with those in the iMovie Plug-in Pack 2.1.1 (`www.apple.com/imovie`) don't satisfy your cravings, check out these cool offerings:

- **eZedia (www.ezedia.com):** Their first effect is called eZeMatte ($29) and it is one of Dennis's favorites. You can use eZeMatte to overlay any image over an iMovie clip. If you want to make it seem like you're looking through a window, overlay a window frame. Add customized logos, if you wish, just like the networks do. The second eZedia plug-in is a variation on eZeMatte called eZeScreen ($39). The difference is that instead of overlaying a graphic, you can overlay a QuickTime movie. If the fixed logo capability of eZeMatte isn't enough for you, something like the animated Cartoon Network logo might be more to your taste. Better yet, you can do picture-in-picture by overlaying a small QuickTime movie in the corner. These aren't special effects in the car-exploding category, but they're getting a lot closer to special effects than the standard iMovie visual effects.

- **GeeThree (www.geethree.com):** We both really like Slick Transitions and Effects for iMovie (Volumes 1 through 4). In fact, Bob likes them so much that the folks at GeeThree quote him on their Web page: "An essential, no iMovie user should be without it!" They're $29.95 each for Volumes 1 and 2 and $49.95 each for Volumes 3 and 4, with discount pricing for multiple volume combinations. Each pack contains over 50 transitions and effects. Although you don't get to supply your own frames and overlays as you do with eZeMatte, some of the effects in Slick Collection 2 are frames. Volumes 3 and 4 were released just before this book went to press. Bob's seen them and he says, "Wow!" and Dennis thinks Bob is understating the case (especially for Volume 4).

- **Virtix (www.virtix.com):** Showcasing their Bravo collection of iMovie effects ($24.99) and Echo collection of iMovie transitions ($24.99), Virtix also offers a Zoom effects package and a Pan & Scan effects package at $19.99 each. Having discovered Virtix's offerings after the GeeThree packages, we were a little jaded and didn't get as excited by them as you might. The Bravo and Echo collections are quite well-done, with a bundle price of $39.99.

Each of these companies also offers a "sampler pack" of free effects, hoping that you'll like what you see so much that you'll purchase the whole package. It is quite likely that many of you will make their hope a reality.

For those more inclined to background music than visual effects, SmartSound (www.smartsound.com) offers Movie Maestro ($49.95) to help you create perfectly synchronized, custom movie soundtracks for your movies. In a simple three-step process, you can do the following:

1. Export a reference file (Web Movie, Small is what SmartSound recommends).
2. Open and score it in Movie Maestro, which does almost all the work for you.
3. Click Movie Maestro's Save Sound button and choose SoundTrack to iMovie from the Save Soundtrack dialog's Save popup menu.

Voila! You have the score, properly positioned on Track 2 in the timeline viewer, all set for you to export your movie in any available format. Dennis has been having a lot of fun with Movie Maestro. SmartSound includes a little over two dozen audio tracks for use with Movie Maestro and offers additional CD collections at $29.95

each. (There were six CD collections available when we wrote this, but more are surely on their way.) Bob's used it more than once to create an appropriate soundtrack for something he was whipping up in iMovie (or Final Cut Pro).

Putting a dent in your plastic

When you want to go in and tweak individual frames or sequences, add animated effects, or add special effects like transparency to your finished film, Adobe Systems (www.adobe.com) offers Adobe After Effects for about $650. Wiley already has a book larger than this one, just to cover all the things this high-end program can do — check out the *After Effects 5 Bible* by J. J. Marshall and Zed Saeed for the complete scoop. (It even includes a DVD-ROM rather than a CD.)

Final Cut Pro offers some of the same tweaks as After Effects along with a suite of video and audio editing tools. Both are great if you want to step beyond the simple effects possible with iMovie.

Free software

Because OS X's underpinnings are Unix, we have access to the work of a large software development community. An even greater benefit is that much of this software is free. Unfortunately, most Unix software is written for the command-line interface and doesn't provide the user experience Mac users expect. Many considerate developers are putting nice front-ends on these tools, though, and our software horn of plenty is starting to brim over with the fruit of those labors.

Of particular interest to iMovie users are encoders, particularly ones that will generate formats unavailable from QuickTime Pro. MediaPipe (http://mediapipe.sourceforge.net) is a framework to handle media under OS X, and it comes with a few encoders:

- ✦ MPEG-2 is the encoding method used for DVDs. But, MPEG-2 is also used for SVCDs, which in addition to playing in many set top DVD players, are burned on standard CD-R media, making them much less expensive. (And they don't require a SuperDrive, just a CD burner and Toast.)

- ✦ MP3 is a format with which we should all be familiar by now.

- ✦ MP2 is MPEG-1 Layer II, the standard for VCD and SVCD audio streams.

Note Due to licensing restrictions imposed by the Motion Picture Experts Group on MPEG-2 encoders, the MPEG-2 encoder is distributed in source code form and not as an executable binary. Those licensing restrictions (and accompanying fees) are the reason the MPEG-2 decoder for QuickTime is a separate $20 option. You need to have the Apple Developer Tools installed to compile the encoder. If you purchased Mac OS X, the Developer Tools are one of the CDs in the box. If OS X came installed on your Mac and you haven't already done so, you'll need to download the tools from www.apple.com/developer. Create a free Apple Developer Connection account to download the tools.

You can create VCDs containing multiple MPEG-1 files using Toast 5 Titanium's VideoCD setting. Similarly, you can create multiple SVCD image files from MPEG-2 files using GNU VCDToolsX and burn those with Toast's Multitrack CD-ROM XA setting. These tools, as the name implies, are ports of GNU (Gnu's Not Unix) programs. Jesper Nilson, the fellow who's brought them to OS X, updates them regularly and you can find the most recent version and documentation at `www.sbpr.a.se/systemjammers/vcdtoolsx`. The documentation and documentation links are thorough, but it is quickly obvious that English is not the author's native tongue, so some sentence construction will seem a bit awkward. As with anything GNU-based, the source code is also available for the intrepid among you who wish to tweak things.

Another handy tool is VCD Builder by Johan Linström (`homepage.mac.com/johan`). Using VCD Builder, you can create menu-driven VCDs and SVCDs by building *sequences* (boxes) and connecting them with lines showing the control flow. You can even use still pictures for some of the sequences — VCD Builder will convert those to an appropriate format for you; however, you'll need to have compatible MPEG-1 and MPEG-2 files for your movies as VCD Builder won't convert those for you. When you have the disk structure you want, you can generate image files to be burned later or you can click VCD Builder's Burn VCD button to have it create the images and pass the data to Toast. Then, all you'll have to do is click Toast's Record button and tell it at what speed to burn.

Summary

In this chapter you learned about some of the hardware you can purchase to help you make better movies and some other hardware to improve iMovie's performance. You also learned about software you can purchase, or just download, to help you create even better iMovies and make even better use of the iMovies after you've exported them.

✦ ✦ ✦

iDVD

PART

V

In This Part

Chapter 18
Introducing iDVD

Chapter 19
Getting Started with iDVD

Chapter 20
Getting Advanced with iDVD

Chapter 21
More iDVD Tips, Tricks, and Techniques

Chapter 22
Enhancing your iDVD Experience

iDVD

Introducing iDVD

CHAPTER 18

✦ ✦ ✦ ✦

In This Chapter

Understanding DVDs

Exploring the iDVD window

Setting iDVD preferences

✦ ✦ ✦ ✦

Just a few years ago, if you went into your neighborhood Blockbuster or Wherehouse, the unit of currency in video entertainment, from wall-to-wall, was the videotape. Today it's the ubiquitous DVD (Digital Video Disc or Digital Versatile Disc, depending on who you ask). They're everywhere, and most frequent renters (and buyers) will only *settle* for videotape if they can't get their hands on the movie's DVD version. With a DVD, you get *random access,* which means you can jump to any scene you want nearly instantly. With DVDs you don't get yelled at or penalized for being unkind because there's no need to rewind. And, best of all, most DVDs are somewhat interactive: You use the DVD player's remote control to navigate and activate (point and click) buttons on the screen.

Note DVD's predecessor in the consumer digital video market, LaserDiscs, are the size of LPs and much heavier. In fact, comparing LaserDiscs to DVDs is very much like comparing LPs to CDs. DVDs hold more and can display a higher-quality picture, just as CDs hold more than an LP and produce better audio. Besides, DVDs and CDs have the same physical dimensions, just like LaserDiscs and LPs.

In January 2001, Apple introduced the first affordable personal computer that could burn a DVD that could be viewed on most major DVD players — the $3,499 PowerMac G4/733. This was a major price breakthrough and not just in the Macintosh world. Before the G4/733 with SuperDrive, the cheapest DVD burner alone cost two or three times that much and software for making DVDs was expensive and rare.

The SuperDrive was actually Pioneer's new (at the time) A103, and for the first few months, the only way to get one was inside one of these G4/733s—Apple bought every A103 drive Pioneer could build. Once production caught up with demand, the retail price of an A103 fell to around $1,000. Soon other companies were competing in the DVD-R market, driving the street price of a SuperDrive (a second-generation Pioneer A-104 at this writing) even lower to around $400.

Caution As of this writing, external DVD-R drives *do not work with iDVD*. If you want to burn DVDs with video that can be played on a set top DVD player, you need to buy a Mac with a built-in SuperDrive. Third-party external FireWire SuperDrives won't be recognized by iDVD—you'll need the $999 DVD Studio Pro or some other solution to burn DVDs.

Blank DVD-R media started out costing $10 per disc or more, but as DVD-R became more popular, the price quickly fell to today's more reasonable $4 to $5 a disc (in 5-packs).

The SuperDrive alone wasn't enough to popularize the DVD burning technology. It would have been far less useful had Apple not included a neat little piece of software called iDVD.

iDVD is a remarkable program that lets you make your own menu-driven DVDs, with up to 90 minutes of video content, just like the big studios—almost. We say "almost" because iDVD maxes out at 90 minutes of video per DVD-R. Also, you have little or no control over compression levels, are limited to six buttons per screen, and can't easily have chapter stops.

Of course, such things are trivial with iDVD's $999 big brother, DVD Studio Pro, which lets you do anything and everything you see on studio release DVDs. Still, you can make amazing DVDs with nothing more than a Mac, a copy of iDVD, and some still or moving digital images.

Understanding DVDs

Most people think that DVDs are simply just another media with higher-quality video and audio than videotape. The better quality *is* a big thing, but DVDs are much more than that.

DVDs also specify a disc layout that allows for alternative audio tracks. For example, one DVD can contain a movie with English, French, Spanish, German, Japanese, and other soundtracks. You can also have subtitles available in multiple languages.

We already mentioned interactivity, and that's key. DVDs are the first consumer media choice with the interactivity that used to be tied exclusively to computers or a Web connection like WebTV.

And all that is just for video DVDs. DVDs can also be used like a giant CD-ROM to hold data — 4.7GB of data on a single DVD-R is the equivalent of about seven CDs (a little more than seven 650MB CDs, a little less than seven 700MB CDs). They're even called DVD-ROMs. In iDVD 2.1, Apple added the feature of being able to create *hybrid* DVDs, which are DVDs that have a DVD-ROM section where you can place data files.

Just to make things a little easier, when we write "DVD," we are referring to the video DVD format that you watch on a DVD player. When we want to talk about a data DVD that you access via your Mac (or a suitably equipped PC), we'll call it a "data DVD" or "DVD-ROM." (Boy, isn't that original?)

Also, DVDs aren't just about movies. You can also include slideshows on the DVD. Apple even has AppleScripts available for download at www.apple.com/applescript/idvd that take photos from iPhoto and create a slideshow on the DVD for you. You can even add your own background music to iDVD menu screens and slideshows.

Assuming that you have your content — the movies you want to burn to a DVD — you still need software that does three things:

✦ Creates the menu buttons and other interactive features for the DVD

✦ Encodes your video to meet the specifications required for DVD players

✦ Burns the DVD on your DVD burner (in the case of iDVD, that's a built-in SuperDrive)

iDVD provides all these features, and more, through a simple, straightforward user interface.

Authoring a DVD

The process of creating a DVD is called *authoring*. You aren't creating or editing the content that will be watched; it's assumed that you already did that in another program, such as iMovie 2. When you use iDVD, you're building a framework for your content.

Here are some of the authoring tasks you'll know quite well:

✦ Importing content

✦ Creating on-screen menu buttons

✦ Choosing background images

✦ Selecting music or audio for menus

✦ Choosing a frame or sequence to represent each button

✦ Choosing a shape and label for each button

Those are just a few of the things we mean when we talk about authoring in iDVD.

> ### Most of What You Need to Know About MPEG
>
> This part gets a little acronym-crazy and more than a little geeky. It's all background material you don't really need to know before you roll up your sleeves. We put it here in this sidebar in case you're interested.
>
> Uncompressed digital video gobbles up hard disk storage at better than 200MB per minute. Without compression, you could fit roughly only 23 minutes of video on a DVD, and that wouldn't leave room for interactive menus or anything else.
>
> The Motion Picture Experts Group (MPEG) has developed and standardized a number of compression formats for video and audio. The best known of these are MPEG-1 (used on VideoCDs), MPEG-1 Layer 3 audio (more commonly known as MP3), MPEG-4 (the new standard for streaming media), and MPEG-2 (the format used for DVDs and Super VideoCDs).
>
> Not just any MPEG-2 file can be used for a DVD, though. The frame rate and frame size have to be right, and both the audio and video bit-rates must fall within specified ranges.
>
> If you want all the gruesome details concerning what is required for a DVD's MPEG-2 and just about anything else related to MPEG-2, we recommend these three Web sites:
>
> + **VCDHelp.com** (www.vcdhelp.com): This site's a little or a lot biased towards Windows solutions, but the specification and link information is comprehensive and it has a great database of DVD players, citing features and compatiblity with different formats and media.
>
> + **MPEG Home Page** (mpeg.telecomitalialab.com): The home of MPEG.
>
> + **Berkeley Multimedia Research Center** (http://bmrc.berkeley.edu/frame/research/mpeg/mpeg2faq.html): A great frequently asked questions (FAQ) collection at UC Berkeley.
>
> iDVD will adjust all the parameters to make the movie you give it match the DVD specifications and then it will encode it. No fuss, no mess, and no fiddling with settings.
>
> Best of all, iDVD will do the encoding in the background while you continue working, either in iDVD or in another application. Frequently, by the time we're done creating our menu structure and annotating things, the encoding is done.

DVD-R burning application

Once you have your authoring completed and the material encoded (well, iDVD has encoded it for you — there's nothing you need to do), all that's left is to burn it to a DVD-R.

iDVD only works if there is an internal SuperDrive present. As long as you've got one, you're ready to start cookin'. Just insert a blank DVD-R disc, click iDVD's Burn button, click it again when it changes to the radioactive icon, and then sit back and wait for the burn to complete.

Unfortunately, unlike burning a CD-R or CD-RW, burning a DVD can't be accelerated so that you can burn 64 minutes in 8 minutes using 8× speed. Burning a DVD happens at 1× or 2× speed, so burning 60 minutes of DVD video will take at least 30 minutes, plus a little bit of time to dot i's and cross t's (write the menus and the other support files that the DVD specification requires, plus close out the burn). And that time estimate assumes that the encoding is complete before you tell iDVD to burn the disc.

Exploring the iDVD Window

Each of the applications in this book has a different feel. iTunes has a window where buttons appear, change, and disappear based upon what's selected in the source list. iMovie has one window that fills the entire screen, but controls change based upon whether you're in camera or clip-editing mode. iPhoto has one window and an always-present tools panel whose contents change based upon your mode. iDVD has a static, nonresizable window, but has a drawer (the Help files call it a panel) that slides out the left side when you click one of the buttons, similar to the drawer in OS X's Mail program.

Apple's Human Interface documentation for OS X refers to this OS X feature as a *drawer* and that's the terminology with which we're comfortable. Why Apple calls it a panel in iDVD is a mystery to us.

The Main Window

When you first launch iDVD, you see the window shown in Figure 18-1. This simple window, with its project pane and six buttons, is really approachable, but those six buttons conceal a lot of functionality.

The parts of the window are as follows:

✦ **Project pane:** This is where you build your DVD project. It displays the menus (screens) that will be on your finished DVD.

✦ **Theme:** This button slides out the Theme drawer if it's closed or shuts it if it's open. We introduce the Theme drawer separately, in the next section, and cover its use in Chapter 19, "Getting Started with iDVD."

✦ **Folder:** Create a new folder button. iDVD allows up to six buttons on a single menu. Clicking on a folder button moves you to a new menu which can also have up to six buttons on it.

✦ **Slideshow:** As we mentioned earlier in this chapter, you can create slideshows as part of your DVD. We introduce slideshow creation a little later in this chapter (see "The Slideshow pane") and cover the process in detail in Chapter 19, "Getting Started with iDVD."

✦ **Motion:** Turns Motion menus on and off. One of the coolest features added in iDVD 2.0 was motion menus. Not only can your menus now be animated, but your menu buttons can play segments from the movies they represent. Check out Chapter 19 for full coverage of motion menus.

✦ **Preview:** Click this button and iDVD displays a floating window resembling a DVD remote control, as shown in Figure 18-2. Using this control, you can preview your project just as if it were burned and playing in OS X's DVD Player application.

✦ **Burn:** If you remember the Burn CD button in iTunes, this button will be very familiar. It looks the same and it works the same. Click it once and the shutter opens, displaying a pulsing orange and black button reminiscent of the radiation warning symbol. Click it again, and the burn will commence.

Figure 18-1: iDVD's window, ready for you to start creating your project.

Figure 18-2: Preview your DVD before burning with this remote control window.

The Themes drawer

Clicking that little Theme button in iDVD's lower-left corner opens the Themes drawer shown in Figure 18-3. The Theme drawer has three tabs: Themes, Customize, and Status. What is a *theme?* In iDVD, themes are templates that define the look and feel of your project.

Figure 18-3: The Themes drawer, showing the Themes tab.

Choosing a theme

Near the top of the Themes tab is a popup menu where you can filter the themes displayed in the scrolling list. iDVD comes with 14 themes, divided into three categories:

- **Motion** themes are, not surprisingly, themes with motion menus.
- **Picture-only** themes provide a static background for your menus, although the buttons can still have motion.
- **Picture with audio** (Claim Check is the only supplied example) is a picture theme with an associated soundtrack.

Customizing a theme

Apple's categories can be changed — you can add or delete audio, change from image to video or vice versa, in the Customize tab as shown in Figure 18-4.

Figure 18-4: Modify a theme to your heart's content in the Customize tab.

The Customize tab is divided into four parts, the main tab and three sections:

- **Background:** This section contains two *wells:* Image/Movie and Audio. Simply drag a media file and drop it onto the appropriate well.
    - Drag the graphic or video you want to appear behind your menu buttons and drop it on the Image/Movie well.
    - Drag the sound file (AIFF, MP3, or WAV) you want as background music when your menu buttons are on screen and drop it onto the Audio well.
- **Title:** This section contains a pop-up menus to specify the menu title's position, font, and text color, plus a font size slider .
- **Button:** The section has a variety of controls:
    - The pop-up button in the upper-left lets you select a shape for your buttons.
    - The **Snap to Grid** and **Free Position** radio buttons specify whether iDVD positions your buttons in a nice neat two-row, three-column grid, or whether you get to position them where you want them.
    - The **Position, Font,** and **Color** pop-ups and the Size slider do for button labels what the corresponding controls do for titles in the Title section.

+ The main tab has two controls on it:
  - **Motion Duration:** Drag this slider to set a playtime for the menu background's video and accompanying audio from 0 to 30 seconds.
  - **Save in Favorites:** This is a handy button. When you have customized a theme that you might want to reuse, you can save it as a Favorite and be able to recall it at a later time.

We'll be covering these in glorious detail in Chapter 19, "Getting Started with iDVD" and Chapter 20, "Getting Advanced with iDVD."

Checking Project Status

The Project Status tab probably doesn't belong in the Theme drawer, since it doesn't have any impact on the themes chosen. In iDVD 2.0, this tab displayed the Project size and Encoder Status. iDVD 2.1 added a popup menu with Encoder Status and DVD-ROM Contents, as shown in Figure 18-5.

Figure 18-5: iDVD 2.1 added putting data files on your DVD-ROMs.

Project size displays, both graphically and textually, how much space you've used on the DVD image. The text display shows both time used and gigabytes consumed out of the total available time/space.

DVD-ROM Contents enables you to utilize extra space on your DVD for data storage. For example, you could put the JPEG files used in a slide show on the disc as data so that friends with a computer (and a DVD drive) could copy the images to their onboard disk.

The last item, Encoder Status, displays encoding progress for each of the movies on your DVD.

The Slideshow pane

Clicking the Slideshow button creates a Slideshow button in the Project pane. Double-clicking the slideshow's button replaces the Project pane with the Slideshow pane, as shown in Figure 18-6. Click the Return button to go dismiss the Slideshow pane.

Figure 18-6: This is where you build your iDVD slideshows.

Each slideshow is limited to a maximum of 99 images and we'll give the lowdown on all the Slideshow pane's controls in Chapter 19,"Getting Started with iDVD."

Setting iDVD Preferences

iDVD has few preferences for you to set, but some of them are quite important. Choose iDVD ⇨ Preferences to display the dialog shown in Figure 18-7.

Figure 18-7: iDVD's Preferences dialog.

The iDVD Preferences dialog is divided into three sections:

+ **Project Settings** has two check box items:

    • **Delete rendered files after closing a project:** Selecting this option tells iDVD to eliminate the encoded files it created when you close the project.

    Selecting this option can also free up a great deal of disk space, because the MPEG-2 files are generally about 25 to 50 percent the size of the DV files from which they were encoded (between 50MB and 100MB per minute of video). The downside of selecting this check box is that the next time you open the project, iDVD will have to encode the files again.

 iDVD encoded files are hidden (invisible), so you can't easily find and delete them in the Finder.

    • **Show Watermark:** This option determines whether the white Apple logo will appear on the DVDs you create. Apple turns it on by default. Leave it there if you want folks to know that your DVD was made on a Mac or uncheck the box if you don't feel like advertising. Bob usually leaves it on, but he also ends most of his movies with a huge credit proclaiming, "Made with Mac OS X!"

+ **Video Standard**'s two radio buttons determine whether new projects will be created as NTSC (American/Japanese television standard) or PAL (most of the rest of the world's TV standard).

+ **Slideshow Settings** is a new section, added in iDVD 2.1, with two options:

    • **Add Slideshows to DVD-ROM:** Selecting this option tells iDVD to automatically include a copy of all the slides in any slideshows you create in the DVD-ROM (data) portion of your DVD.

    • **Always scale slides to TV-Safe area:** Selecting this option tells iDVD to make sure that your slides fit in the portion of the screen which will be visible on a properly adjusted TV set.

Note As we discussed in Chapter 14, "Getting Started with iMovie," when we covered QT Margins, the video frame is wider than will fit on a TV screen, and parts of the image will be cropped when you show your movie on TV. The TV Safe area is that portion that will be within your TV screen's borders.

Summary

In this chapter, you learned what a DVD is and what is involved in creating one. You also were introduced to the high points of the iDVD window, the Themes drawer, and the Slideshow panel. Finally, you saw what iDVD Preference settings are available and what they do.

✦ ✦ ✦

Getting Started with iDVD

CHAPTER 19

✦ ✦ ✦ ✦

In This Chapter

Creating DVD menus

Creating a slideshow

Previewing your DVD

Burning a DVD

✦ ✦ ✦ ✦

Whether you have a bunch of family movies you want to share, product demonstration films to distribute, or a set of presentations to deliver, DVDs are a superb medium and iDVD will help you package your content in an attractive, easy-to-use form.

You could just make QuickTime movies, stick them on CD or DVD, and send them out for use on a computer. You know, open in the Finder (or Windows Explorer), find the file the user wants, and play it — *if* they have the correct player(s) and codec(s) installed. You could, but it would be wrong. Not only do you have to worry about whether your audience is computer-savvy enough to deal with what you send them, but a Finder/Windows Explorer interface isn't very attractive packaging.

One of our favorite introductions to DVD sites is Apple's own Seminars Online (www.seminars.apple.com/seminarsonline). One of their free seminars is *DVD Authoring Made Simple,* and the advice they give on the DVD creation process is great, breaking things up into five steps:

1. Plan what you want to present and how you want to present it.
2. Create your content. This includes not just the raw video, but your menu backgrounds, audio, and other graphics.
3. Encode your video and audio content.
4. Author your DVD. This means creating an easily navigable, interactive layout and structure.
5. Record the DVD (burn to disc).

iDVD does Step 3 for you while you're working on Step 4. We give you a few tips on planning in Chapter 21, "iDVD Tips and Techniques." For creating content, think back or refer to the 15 iTunes, iPhoto, and iMovie chapters that have led you to this point in the book.

Creating DVD Menus

One huge DVD advantage over videotape is that DVDs are *random-access* and tape is *sequential-access*. You can instantaneously jump from one point to another on the disc, unlike videotape, which requires you to wait while fast-forwarding and rewinding tape. Taking advantage of DVD's quick access, you create menus containing buttons that take your audience from one item to another with a click or two on the remote control, just like clicking the links on a Web page to navigate a Web site. In fact, authoring a DVD is very much like designing a Web site.

Just as a Web page will have a background color or graphic, a DVD menu screen will have a background image or movie, possibly with a soundtrack. A menu's content consists of text and buttons that are very much like links on a Web page.

> **Note** Before you get too excited, iDVD doesn't support *chaptering*, which is where buttons take you to a specific point within a larger movie. For that, you'll need DVD Studio Pro or some similar high-end authoring tool. This missing feature is kind of frustrating, too, because we can use free tools to author menus for VCDs and SVCDs that support chaptering. Granted, they aren't as easy to use as iDVD, but even the addition of a "Play from here to end of disc" command could let us fake it by creating separate movies for each scene and putting in buttons that played from that point on.

Before you get started with anything else, choose File ➪ Save Project As (Shift-⌘-S) or File ➪ New Project so that you'll have your own project and won't be monkeying around with the Tutorial project. Either you or someone else in your home or office may actually want to use the tutorial in the future.

What's your theme?

To help get you started, iDVD 2.1 includes 14 templates, called *themes*, for your interactive menu structure. Maybe we're unusual in this respect (we don't think so, though, after talking to other people), but we seldom like any of the designs supplied in templates accompanying software products; however, iDVD actually does quite well in this respect. Of the 14 templates, there are at least a half-dozen we might actually use, at least as a starting point. (We'd probably change the font or music, for example.) The presupplied themes are shown in Figure 19-1.

Figure 19-1: Thirteen of the presupplied iDVD themes.

Note There are more than a dozen other themes present in the iDVD application, but they aren't immediately available to you. We'll tell you about them in Chapter 21: "iDVD Tips and Secrets."

Just so you know, that little "running man" icon in the lower-right of some themes isn't part of the theme; it indicates that the theme either has a motion menu, an audio track, or both. From iDVD's perspective, there are three kinds of themes:

- **Motion themes** are short videos (up to 30 seconds in length), that loop in the background. They might have associated audio or they might be silent.

- **Picture only** themes sport a static background picture with no motion or sound.

- **Picture with audio** themes are Picture themes with a sound track that loops in the background.

Note Introduced in iDVD 2.0, menu screens with video (rather than still images) as the background are called *motion menus*.

You select your theme from the Theme drawer's Themes tab, and you open the Theme drawer by clicking the Theme button or choosing Project ⇨ Show Theme Panel (Shift-⌘-B).

Caution Unlike some other drawer-savvy applications, such as OS X's Mail program, the Theme drawer *always* opens out of the iDVD window's left side, even if it would be completely off-screen. If you're going to use the Theme drawer (and we really think you will), be sure to leave room on the left for it to appear. Fortunately, every OS X machine that supports iDVD also supports at least 1024×768 resolution, so there will be room.

Menus are composed of backgrounds, text, and buttons. The background can be a still picture or a video clip, and it can have an audio track associated. The text is just a title for your menu; you can't place text annotations on the menu.

Tip

If you want text, such as instructions or descriptive prose, like those sported by professionally produced DVDs, you'll need to make it part of your background image or clip. This isn't quite as dynamic as the moving menu text on *X-Men* or the like, but it's as close as you're going to come with iDVD 2.1. (You need DVD Studio Pro or some other high-end — read expensive and complicated — DVD-authoring tool to create menus containing text frames.)

Buttons can be still pictures, video clips, text, folders (links to subsidiary menu screens), or navigation aids. Buttons also have (optional) associated text, called labels. Even if they include a sound track, the sound doesn't play in the menu — just think of the cacophony that would result from six movie sound clips playing at once!

Note

Navigation buttons are created and maintained by iDVD. You don't have any control over them other than setting their appearance by your theme choice.

Don't worry if you don't like the themes iDVD offers. You can modify the themes to your heart's content. You can even change them to the point that you create your own, and we show you how in "Customizing your theme," a little later in this chapter.

Adding movie content

There's little simpler than adding a movie to your DVD. You can drag its icon into iDVD's Project pane or choose File ⇨ Import ⇨ Video and then navigate a file selection sheet to locate and select your movie.

Tip

We think that dragging and dropping is by far the easier method, and faster too. But if your monitor is space-constrained or you really like using the Open sheet, by all means use the Import Video method.

After you've dropped a movie onto the Project pane or selected a movie file after choosing to import video, iDVD creates a button in the Project pane. Depending upon the theme, the button could be just text, an outlined object displaying one frame of your movie, or an outlined object that plays up to 30 seconds of your movie in miniature, as shown in Figure 19-2.

Note

Because the figures in a book such as this just capture an instant in time, you'll have to take our word for it that the still image button and the movie button are different.

Figure 19-2: A still image button (left), a text button (middle), and a movie button (right).

If you're anything like us, a lot of your DVDs are going to contain numerous short movies. After all, at $5 a pop you don't want to waste 90 percent of the disc by including only one 6-minute movie.

iDVD allows a maximum of only six buttons per menu. To work around this constraint, you create folders which, when clicked, take you to a subordinate menu screen that can, again, have up to six buttons, and so on. As with almost each of its actions, iDVD provides two ways to add a folder:

+ Click the Folder button in the iDVD window.
+ Choose Project ⇨ Add Folder (⌘-K).

Tip As we stated in the beginning of this chapter, the first step in creating a DVD is to plan. One of the things you should plan is your DVD's menu structure — that is, which buttons go on which menu and how you want your menus organized. It's really annoying to have to remove a button that you've set up the way you want it to make room for a folder button, and then find a new home for the removed button and recreate it.

Using either method, the result is the same. iDVD adds a button with the standard OS X folder icon on it (My Folder in Figure 19-3).

Neither of us is fond of the default folder icon's appearance even when used in the Finder. We think it looks really tacky on a beautiful DVD menu, so here's how simple it is to put your own graphic in its place: Just drag a graphic file's icon from the Finder into the button and you've got a custom folder button.

A movie button is automatically given the movie's name, minus any file extension such as .mov. You might want to leave those names in place, but you're surely going to want to change the menu's title from "Click to edit text" and any folders' names from My Folder. To change any of these names, just click them and edit the text in standard Mac fashion.

Figure 19-3: Folders let you create a hierarchical structure and work around iDVD's six-buttons-per-menu limitation.

Customizing your theme

If all you could do is use the themes the way Apple supplied them, iDVD would be really boring and our job would almost be done, but you can customize themes so much that Apple wouldn't even recognize them and save them under new names for future use. You can even save these modified or new themes so that other people using your Mac can use them.

You're probably a little ahead of us and have already figured out that you use the Theme drawer's Customize tab to perform this magic. Before you jump to the Customize tab, though, pick an existing theme as your starting point — one that has at least a vague resemblance to what you have in mind, even if it's only a motion menu or a font you want to use. Anything you can use from a theme will mean a little less to change.

Changing the background

Although several iDVD themes have attractive backgrounds, they probably aren't quite right for your DVD. For example, none of them fit a sports theme like your kids' soccer season highlights or an event theme like a graduation ceremony. iDVD makes it easy for you to replace the background:

+ Drag a picture or clip to the Image/Movie well, as shown in Figure 19-4.
+ Choose File ⇨ Import ⇨ Background Video and navigate the file selection sheet that appears over the Project pane to locate and select your new background movie or image.

Figure 19-4: Change your theme's background by dragging a movie or image file to the well.

The old image is replaced and, if the movie has a soundtrack, the audio will be used, as shown in Figure 19-5. We were somewhat chagrined to see that a generic icon is displayed without the surrounding image thumbnail — oh well, maybe next version. If you don't want the audio portion to play while your background is in use, just drag the icon out of the Audio well, let go, and watch it disappear in a puff of smoke.

Tip — Use QuickTime Player or some other program with a timeline to determine just how much of the clip should play. You are allowed up to 30 seconds, in 1-second increments. Use QuickTime Pro or iMovie to create a small clip that looks good when looping, because abrupt scene changes can be jarring in the background.

Figure 19-5: iDVD replaces the background with the clip you chose and uses the clip's soundtrack, if present.

Understanding the TV safe area

Most TVs don't display the full width and height of the picture received. Depending upon the TV set and the signal, the portion of "lost" picture will vary. Just as iMovie uses QT Margins (see Chapter 14, "Getting Started with iMovie") to help you stay within the portion you can count on seeing displayed, iDVD defines a TV safe area for your assistance, as shown in Figure 19-6. To have iDVD place a thin red border around the TV safe area for you, choose Advanced ➪ Show TV Safe Area (⌘-T).

To hide it, choose Advanced ➪ Hide TV Safe Area (⌘-T).

Tip Bob says he never hides it. Ever. Dennis doesn't say "never" (but it's close to never).

Adjusting menu titles

A menu screen has only one line of text, called the *title*. That's not one paragraph or even one sentence, it is one line! Nevertheless, iDVD gives you a lot of control over how that line appears. Using the controls in Figure 19-7, you can control the following title elements:

- ✦ Font
- ✦ Font size
- ✦ Font color
- ✦ Location on the menu

Figure 19-6: Stay within the borders to make sure that your content shows up on screen

Figure 19-7: Position and control your title's appearance with these controls.

Taking the last item first, the Title section's Position pop-up menu gives you five choices, as shown in Figure 19-8:

- ✦ **No Title** is pretty self-explanatory. If you don't want a title line on your menu, choose this.
- ✦ **Top Left** left-justifies the title about one line below the top of the TV safe area.
- ✦ **Top Center** centers the title horizontally about one line below the top of the TV safe area.
- ✦ **Top Right** right-justifies the title about one line below the top of the TV safe area.
- ✦ **Custom** lets you drag the title wherever you want on the menu, even outside the TV safe area.

Choose the font you want for your title from the Font pop-up menu, and adjust its size using the Size slider. You really only have five choices for size (the tick marks on the slider). Choose the font color from the Color pop-up, as shown in Figure 19-9. You have 18 color choices: Black, White, and two shades (light and dark) of eight more colors.

Figure 19-8: The Title section's Position pop-up menu.

Figure 19-9: You have a limited, but useful selection of title text colors.

Configuring your buttons

Your menu's buttons are links to your content and any other menus. iDVD enforces a consistent appearance between buttons on a single menu, but lets you define that appearance with the controls shown in Figure 19-10.

Figure 19-10: You get the same text controls for buttons as you do for menu titles, as well as a couple of extras.

At first glance, the Button section's controls look just like the Title section's, with a couple of additions. For Font, Color, and Size, that's an accurate impression. The Position pop-up menu's contents, though, have changed, as shown in Figure 19-11.

Figure 19-11: The Button section's Position pop-up menu.

Your button position choices reflect the relationship between the button and its caption, as follows:

+ **Text Only** means that the caption is the button, just like a textual hyperlink on a Web page.
+ **Top, Bottom, Left,** and **Right** indicate that the caption will be centered adjacent to that button edge.
+ **Middle** tells iDVD to center the caption across the middle of the button. We haven't found a good use for this choice yet, but we imagine that someone will.
+ **No Text** means that the button shouldn't have a caption.

The two radio buttons control placement of the buttons within the menu, as follows:

+ **Snap to Grid** tells iDVD to place the buttons within the TV safe Area aligned according to the grid the underlying theme defines.
+ Selecting **Free Position** lets you arrange the buttons wherever your artistic sense dictates within the menu, even outside the TV safe area.

The unlabeled pop-up button in the Button section's upper-left specifies the frame used for the button, as shown in Figure 19-12.

Figure 19-12: Choose a frame style for your menu's buttons from this pop-up menu.

Caution If you choose From Theme in this pop-up menu, any changes you made to the buttons' position, font, color, size, or placement will be changed back to those defined by the theme, so you might think of this choice as a revert option. Also, because it behaves this way, you may want to choose your button shape before you do any further customizing.

When you add one of your movies to a menu, iDVD creates a button and that button displays your movie clip unless your theme uses a Text Only button style. iDVD provides one more button customization (or two, depending on how you look at it).

Click the button and a small controller appears, as shown in Figure 19-13. Clear the Movie check box and your button no longer plays. Move the slider to the frame you want for your still image (if Movie is cleared) or the frame where you want the button to start playing. You can also drag a still image or a short clip into the button's frame to replace the default display without affecting the movie that plays when the button is selected.

Figure 19-13: Control what your buttons display.

Saving your favorite themes

When you have set up your theme the way you want it, you should consider saving it for use in other iDVD projects. That's where the Save in Favorites button comes into play. Click Save in Favorites and iDVD will drop a sheet, as shown in Figure 19-14, where you can name your theme and, optionally, make it available to other iDVD users.

If you don't select the "Shared for all users" check box, iDVD will grind away, saving a copy of the Theme in the Library/iDVD/Favorites folder in your home directory. Select this option and iDVD saves the theme in the Library/iDVD/Favorites folder at the root level of your hard disk so that any account on your Mac can access it.

Now, if you select the Theme drawer's Themes tab and scroll down, you'll find your theme with a small "favorites" badge, seen here next to this paragraph, in its lower-left corner.

Figure 19-14: Save your theme for later use.

Note   You can't remove a favorite from within iDVD. To eliminate favorites you no longer want, delete them in the Finder. Remember: Personal favorites are in your home directory's Library/iDVD/Favorites folder and shared favorites are in the hard disk's Library/iDVD/Favorites folder.

Just in case you have your artistic breakthrough partway through the project, iDVD gives you a way to apply your new theme to all your project's menu screens after the fact and in one fell swoop. Simply choose Advanced ➪ Apply Theme to Project. Right below that helpful menu choice is Apply Theme to Folders, which (as the name implies) converts all your folder menu screens to the new theme while leaving the main menu as is. Of course, if you're the do-it-yourself type, you can go from menu to menu, applying the theme by selecting it in the Theme drawer.

Creating a Slideshow

It's not clear whether the folks at Apple are convinced that slideshows are integral to everyone's digital life or they simply have a slideshow fetish. QuickTime Player Pro, AppleWorks 6, iMovie, iPhoto, and now iDVD all prominently promote slideshow creation. If you want to create slideshows, you now have a wealth of tools at your disposal.

Dennis still makes most of his slideshows in iMovie (see Chapter 14, "Getting Started with iMovie") for the flexibility it provides; Bob likes to use Final Cut Pro for his slide shows, but he knows it's overkill. That said, iDVD makes slideshow creation really simple if you don't need the kinds of slide-to-slide customization and precision timing offered by iMovie or Final Cut Pro.

As usual, you have two methods available to create a slideshow: Click the Slideshow button shown here or choose Project ➪ Add Slideshow (⌘-L). Either route creates a button named My Slideshow, as shown in Figure 19-15. Click the button once and watch the button sprout a frame, a slider, and a name-editing box.

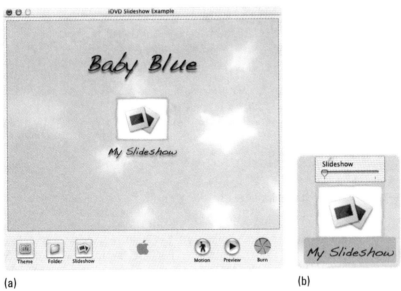

Figure 19-15: A slideshow button on your menu (a) and what a single click displays (b).

Double-clicking the slideshow button replaces the Project pane with the Slideshow Editor shown in Figure 19-16. Once again, you have two ways to add photos or other image files to your slideshow. You can drag them from the Finder (or another drag-enabled application, like iPhoto), or you can choose File ➪ Import ➪ Image. As usual, we prefer dragging, but feel free to use the menu if that's your preferred method.

> **Note** AppleScript support was added in iDVD 2.1. To show off its scriptability, one of the free scripts Apple made available (www.apple.com/applescript/idvd) is the iPhoto to iDVD Slideshow script. Just drag items from iPhoto to the script's icon and, using the script's preferences, iDVD will add the photos as an iDVD slideshow with a number of the options preset.

Should you choose to use the File ➪ Import ➪ Image command, don't let the singular name Image fool you. You can select multiple items in the Open dialog box, as shown in Figure 19-17. To select multiple contiguous items, click the first item in the range and then Shift-click the last item. To select noncontiguous items, ⌘-click them. When you have your photos selected, click the Open button or press Return or Enter.

Figure 19-16: The Slideshow Editor.

Figure 19-17: You can select multiple items when importing images.

The Slideshow Editor has six controls at the bottom:

✦ **Audio:** Drop an AIFF, WAV, or MP3 file in this well to use it as your slideshow's audio track. In fact, you can drag pretty much any QuickTime-compatible file to the well and iDVD will use the first audio track it finds in the file.

+ **Thumbnail:** Choose whether to show Small or Large thumbnails in the Slideshow Editor using the Thumbnail pop-up menu.
+ **Slide Duration:** This pop-up menu enables you to choose how long each slide should play. If there is an audio track, you have an extra choice: Fit To Audio. This is a handy choice because it tells iDVD to divide the length of the audio track by the number of slides so that the last slide finishes at the same time as your song. When you choose Manual from this pop-up, viewers must advance from slide to slide manually, using their DVD player's remote control; this is iDVD's default behavior.

Note After you have images in your slideshow, dragging a song to the Audio well will switch the menu choice from Manual to Fit To Audio.

+ **Add to DVD-ROM:** This check box was added in iDVD 2.1. Selecting this option tells iDVD to include copies of each image in the data portion (DVD-ROM) of your DVD when you burn the disc.
+ **Display ◀ ▶ during slideshow:** This option puts arrowheads on the screen for previous and next slide. These arrowheads are not clickable, just a reminder to your viewer to use the previous and next buttons on their remote control to move from slide to slide.

Note We don't know about you, but we don't much care for the buttons on top of our photos. As they say in automobile mileage disclaimers, "Your mileage may vary."

+ **Return:** Click this button when you want to exit the Slideshow Editor.

Caution You should be aware of the following information when importing images for an iDVD slideshow.

iDVD has certain behaviors and limitations that affect how imported images appear in slideshows. Keep the following things in mind when importing images:

+ **iDVD scales the image to fit the screen.** Images that don't have a 4:3 aspect ratio are going to display a letterbox effect. You should consider matting portrait images against an attractive background to avoid large black stripes on the sides, for example. Similarly, images smaller than 640×480 will exhibit jaggies and other artifacts as they're enlarged. The upside is that larger images, such as 1280×960 or 2048×1536, scale down beautifully, so you don't need to scale larger images before importing them and, if you tell iDVD to save them to DVD-ROM, the full-resolution image will be stored.
+ **You can reorder the images in your slideshow at any time before burning.** Just drag them in the Slideshow Editor, as shown in Figure 19-18.

Figure 19-18: Reorder your slides by dragging them in the Slideshow Editor's list.

+ **If you choose Fit To Audio, manually advancing the slide (or moving back) moves the audio playhead.** This happens because each slide is linked to a specific portion of the audio track. iDVD is trying to synchronize the video and audio to end together.

+ **You're limited to 99 slides in a slideshow.** If you have more than that, you're going to have to break them up into multiple slideshows or cull the list down to 99 (or fewer).

+ **Changing your Preferences setting to Add Slideshows to DVD-ROM will not affect existing slideshows.** It will automatically select the Add to DVD-ROM check box for new slideshows.

+ **For proper viewing on a TV screen, you should choose iDVD ⇨ Preferences and ensure that the "Always scale slides to TV-safe area" check box is selected.** This results in a letterbox effect when you Preview your slideshow. (See "Previewing Your DVD" later in this chapter.)

Video is great, but some subjects display better in a slideshow. For example, infants don't really move enough to make video truly entertaining, but a slide show with a musical background works great when showing off the newborn. Similarly, a slideshow is a wonderful way to commemorate a prom night. Of course, there are also the more pedestrian business slideshow uses, like presentations and catalogs. Maybe Apple isn't obsessed, just observant.

Previewing Your DVD

One frequent complaint about iDVD 1.0 was that you had to burn your DVD to see what it would look like, and at $10 a burn (the price hadn't dropped to $5 yet), creating DVDs could quickly get expensive. iDVD 2.0 responded to this criticism with the Preview button, shown in the margin to the left of this paragraph. When you click the Preview button, it turns blue, and a remote control appears, as shown in Figure 19-19.

Figure 19-19: Preview your DVD before burning using the on-screen remote control.

iDVD's on-screen remote control has three groups of buttons:

- **Four arrow buttons:** The four buttons surrounding the Enter button are used to navigate to and select buttons on your menu. Your keyboard arrow keys and the Return and Enter keys are synonymous with these remote control buttons.

- **Pause/Play, Stop, Previous Slide, and Next Slide:** You can find these buttons in a row just above the navigation buttons. The Pause button toggles to Play when clicked.

- **menu**, **title**, and **exit:** Clicking menu takes you to the menu for the currently playing movie; otherwise it does nothing. Clicking title takes you to your main DVD menu (if you have multiple menus). Clicking exit terminates Preview mode.

    Clicking either menu or title while watching a movie or slideshow and then clicking menu again will return you to your movie or slideshow at the point you interrupted play.

At the bottom of the remote control is a volume slider.

If you're like us, you find the motion menus distracting while you're creating your DVD structure (besides the fact that they slow things down), so you probably turn them off while authoring. Remember to turn them back on by either clicking the Motion button or choosing Advanced ⇨ Motion (⌘-J) before entering Preview mode or you won't see the DVD the way you intend; instead, it plays without motion menus, motion buttons, or menu audio.

Burning Your DVD

You've created your DVD, previewed, edited, and previewed it again until you're certain that everything is just the way you want it, and now the moment of truth has arrived. It's finally time to burn your DVD.

The interface to burning a DVD should be really familiar to you — it's the same interface you see for burning CDs in iTunes. (See Chapter 4, "Getting Started with iTunes.")

Wait — there's one more thing you might want to do before you burn your DVD. On the Theme drawer's Status tab, you can check to see how much progress iDVD has made toward encoding your content, as shown in Figure 19-20. You can also see how much of your DVD this opus uses. When you see a lot of the disc going to waste, you might decide to include some items in the DVD-ROM portion and let the disc do double-duty — movie *and* storage. We'll cover the DVD-ROM capabilities in Chapter 20, "Getting Advanced with iDVD," even though there isn't a whole lot to the subject.

Figure 19-20: Check to see how much of your disc is being used and how much progress has been made encoding your content.

When you click the camera-shutter-like Burn button (shown left), it opens in an iris effect to reveal a pulsing button, reminiscent of a radioactive materials label. Click the pulsing button and you'll see one of the two alerts shown in Figure 19-21.

(a) (b)

Figure 19-21: If you have Motion turned off, iDVD gives you a gentle reminder when you click Burn (a); otherwise, you'll be prompted to insert a DVD-R (b).

Assuming that you have Motion turned on and that you inserted a blank disc, iDVD starts the burning process either immediately or as soon as it's done encoding your DVD's content. We wish that we could tell you the process is fast, but it depends on how much content is being burned, how fast your Mac is, and which model of SuperDrive you have in your Mac. The original SuperDrive used the Pioneer A103 mechanism and it burned at 1x. In other words, burning 30 minutes of video took 30 minutes plus some overhead time. The newer SuperDrives use the Pioneer A104 and can burn at 2× speed, so that same 30-minute disc now only takes 15 minutes plus the overhead.

Tip Here's our standard recommendation: Add more memory if your encoding takes a long time. You can, as Apple says, run iDVD on a 256MB Mac, but we found that upgrading from 256MB to 768MB in Dennis's flat-panel iMac cut the encoding time by almost 50 percent. Encoding to MPEG-2 is a time-consuming, processor-intensive, memory-gobbling operation and anything you can do to give the encoder more memory or a faster processor will help.

Summary

In this chapter you've learned the basics of authoring, previewing, and burning your DVD. You've seen how to select and customize themes, add video content, create a hierarchical menu structure, create slideshows, operate iDVD's remote control when previewing, and burn your DVD.

✦ ✦ ✦

Getting Advanced with iDVD

In This Chapter

Storing data on your DVD

Monitoring your DVD's status

Using iDVD Companion

AppleScripting iDVD

iDVD 2.0 is a marketer's dream and a Bible author's nightmare. It's simple, elegant, useful, and easy-to-use. And you get great results even if you barely know what you're doing. Finally, there are no complicated features included.

If you want chapter stops in your video, get DVD Studio Pro.

Although this makes iDVD easy to sell to users (and, we suspect, reduces Apple's support costs), it makes it tough for us authors. How do we cover the advanced functionality when the program offers exactly zero advanced features?

In fact, for quite a while we thought this was going to be the shortest chapter either of us had ever written. Rescuing us from this dilemma, Apple released iDVD 2.1 in July 2002 and finally gave us some advanced features to cover, including DVD-ROM data storage on your DVD, using AppleScript to automate iDVD and communicate with other programs, and a handy utility program, iDVD Companion (written in AppleScript Studio and with source code available), to help you construct and rearrange your iDVD menus.

Storing Data on Your DVD

Just as you can create multitrack CDs where part of the disc is an audio CD and part is a data CD, you can create multitrack DVDs. iDVD 2.1 adds this capability to iDVD's feature set. Chapter 19, "Creating a Slideshow," shows you how to have iDVD automatically add a slideshow's images to your disc's DVD-ROM portion. But you aren't limited to just the slideshow images. You can add any files you want to the DVD-ROM portion, so long as there is available space.

To add data to your DVD, follow these steps:

1. In the Theme drawer's Status tab, click the pop-up menu just below the disc usage image and statistics.
2. Choose DVD-ROM Contents, as shown in Figure 20-1. Don't ask us to explain why a data collection and management function is in the Theme drawer. The best answer we can come up with is a guess: There wasn't anyplace better to put it. Actually, that guess applies to the Status tab in general, which we finish covering a little later in this chapter.

   iDVD creates a Slideshows folder in the DVD-ROM portion as the resting place for the images added when you have iDVD automatically add a slideshow's image files, either in the Slideshow pane or in your iDVD preferences.

Figure 20-1: You manage your disc's DVD-ROM portion in the Theme drawer.

3. In the Finder, locate the files you want included and drag them into the Theme drawer's Status tab, as shown in Figure 20-2. These files can be anything: MPEG-1 versions of your movies, Microsoft Office documents, AppleWorks documents, MP3 files, and so on.

You need to have the original files available when you choose to burn the DVD so that iDVD can verify that they haven't changed since they were encoded. This means that files on removable media or network servers must be present when you burn a DVD referencing them.

In an unusual move for iDVD, there is no menu item or button available for adding other items to the DVD-ROM portion. All you have available is the method we usually find the easiest, drag and drop.

Note Depending upon how long it takes, a progress sheet might appear briefly over the Project pane.

Although you can't tell in the black-and-white image, iDVD even color-codes the relative amount of disc space used in the little disc icon (upper-left of the Status tab) — the DVD content is green and the DVD-ROM content is blue, which will only be a problem for people who are color-blind (or, at least, blue-green color-blind).

4. If you change your mind about including some file(s) on the DVD-ROM, just select the ones you don't want and press the Delete key.

(a) (b)

Figure 20-2: Drag your files into the DVD-ROM Contents area (a); iDVD adds them to your project (b).

You can even use the New Folder button (at the bottom of the Status tab) to create folders in the DVD-ROM and reorganize the files by dragging files into or out of folders, just like a Finder list view.

Monitoring Your DVD's Status

When it comes to monitoring what's on your DVD, iDVD suffers from a multiple-personality disorder. As mentioned in the previous section, you find out what's on the DVD-ROM portion by choosing DVD-ROM Contents from the Theme drawer's Status tab pop-up menu (say that three times, quickly). You switch the Status tab back to Encoder Status to see how far along the background MPEG-2 encoding has gotten. Finally, you choose Project ⇨ Project Info (⌘-I) to display the Project Info dialog box shown in Figure 20-3 when you want to know what files are being used in your project and where they reside on your Mac.

Figure 20-3: The Project Info dialog box displays a list of all your project's files.

Note   We find it strange that Status is in the Theme drawer rather than part of the Project Info dialog. Apple's gotten really good at creating tabbed dialog boxes, keeping related information and functionality together and their reasons for not doing so here escape us.

Using iDVD Companion

The iDVD themes do a good job arranging buttons against the provided backgrounds, but we don't think that many people are going to use the themes out of the box very often. Users are going to provide their own backgrounds and, at that point, arranging the buttons to best effect is going to involve using the Free Position setting in the Customize tab's Button section.

Unfortunately, free position means just that — drag the button into place and let go. There are no rulers, no grid, and none of the other alignment aids we've come to expect in a design layout environment. Everything is done by eyeballing the result and hoping that what we've done is close enough.

iDVD 2.1's AppleScript support (see "AppleScripting iDVD" later in this chapter) opened the door for a wonderful little accessory program called iDVD Companion, a free download from www.apple.com/applescript/idvd. A collection of AppleScripts, packaged together by AppleScript Studio into a normal OS X application (Cocoa, if that matters to you), iDVD Companion gives you several nice enhancements:

✦ A variety of alignment and placement controls for your buttons

✦ Access to the Back button on subordinate menus

✦ AppleScripts to import

- Songs from iTunes to use as background music
- Photos from iPhoto to use as backgrounds or button images
- Albums from iPhoto to create a slideshow

Figure 20-4 shows iDVD Companion running with iDVD in the background.

Figure 20-4: iDVD Companion provides a palette to adjust iDVD menu buttons and titles.

Employing the iDVD Companion palette

iDVD Companion's tabbed palette (Figure 20-5) enables you to move selected buttons, optionally including the menu title, up, down, left, or right in 1-, 6-, 36-, or 72-pixel increments using the Nudge tab.

Figure 20-5: Nudge selected items by set increments.

Tip

You can choose Edit ⇨ Select Back Button (⌘-B) to reposition the Back button, something not allowed in the iDVD application's interface.

The Align tab (see Figure 20-6) enables you to align the edges of two or more selected buttons. If you have only one button selected, nothing happens except that you hear whatever alert sound you set in your OS X sound preferences.

Figure 20-6: Align the left, right, top, or bottom edges of multiple selected buttons.

Use the Title tab to specify an absolute position for your menu's title (Figure 20-7). When you first display the Title tab, iDVD Companion fills in the current title position. The position is measured in pixels from the top-left corner of the Project pane.

Figure 20-7: Precisely position the menu title using the Title tab.

Using the iDVD Companion menu bar

In addition to providing a palette full of positioning tools, iDVD Companion adds even more features in its menus.

The File menu has only one choice: Generate Projects. This choice sprouts a submenu, which (as of the initial release) has only two templates. The first generates a template of slideshows, as shown in Figure 20-8. The second is a template for a single movie where the button is the screen in a flat-panel iMac, as shown in Figure 20-9.

Figure 20-8: Create an alphabetic arrangement of your slideshows.

Figure 20-9: Kind of simple, but attractive.

The iDVD Companion's Edit menu doesn't sport any of the traditional Undo, Cut, Copy, or Paste commands; those are left to iDVD's Edit menu. What you get are the handy Select Back Button (⌘-B) command, unavailable in iDVD. Additionally, you find a few time- and click-saving commands, including Delete Every Button, Select All Buttons (⌘-A), and Deselect All Buttons (⌘-D).

The Go menu relieves you of having to navigate your project's menu structure to find a specific menu or slideshow. Choosing Go ⇨ Go To Menu (⌘-G) displays a list of all your project's menus, assuming that you have named them as described in the Menu menu discussion later in this section. Just select the one you want, and Companion tells iDVD to display that menu. Similarly, choosing Go ⇨ Go To Slideshow (Option-⌘-G) displays a list of your slideshows so that you can select the one you want to have appear in the Project pane, as shown in Figure 20-10.

> **Tip** As you can see in Figure 20-10, Unnamed slideshow isn't a very helpful designation. Use the Button ⇨ Name Selected Button command described a little later in this section so that you can tell your slideshows apart.

(a)   (b)

Figure 20-10: Choose your slideshow (a); iDVD Companion directs iDVD to position it in the Project pane (b).

The Theme menu's first two choices, Choose Theme (⌘-T) and Toggle Motion (Option-⌘-M) aren't very interesting as their equivalents are readily available in iDVD's interface. The Layouts submenu, though, provides you with four scripts to arrange the current menu's buttons (assuming that there are four buttons):

+ **4 Corners** places your buttons at the four corners of the TV safe area.
+ **4 Center Diamond** places your buttons in a diamond (rhombus) arrangement, with one on the top row, two in the middle row, and one on the bottom row.
+ **4 Across Top** places your buttons along the top row within the TV safe area.
+ **4 Across Bottom** is analogous to 4 Across Top, except that the buttons are now at the bottom of the TV safe area.

If you have fewer than four buttons, you'll get an AppleScript error message that the variable `button_list` is not defined. This is not a fatal error and your existing buttons will be positioned according to the chosen layout.

The Menu menu offers eight choices:

+ **Name Current Menu** (⌘-N) is where you name your menus to make them accessible via the Go menu's Go To Menu command.
+ **Snap To Grid • On** (⌘--) is equivalent to clicking the Snap to Grid radio button in the Theme drawer's Customize tab.
+ **Snap To Grid • Off** (⌘-=) is equivalent to clicking the Free Position radio button in the Theme drawer's Customize tab.

- **Import Audio From iTunes** (Option-⌘-I) brings iTunes to the front, while displaying a floating window, and enables you to select a track from your iTunes Library. Click Transfer in the floating window and iDVD comes to the front with that audio track playing as your current menu's background audio.
- **Import Image From iPhoto** (Option-Shift-⌘-I) enables you to select an image from your iPhoto Library to use as the current menu's background.
- **Import Album From iPhoto** enables you to select an iPhoto album to use as a slideshow in iDVD.
- **Delete Background Image** (Option-⌘-D) removes any background image, reverting to the theme's original background.
- **Delete Background Audio** (Option-Shift-⌘-D) removes any background audio file you've added to the current menu.

The Button menu offers three choices:

- **Name Selected Button** (Option-⌘-N) does as the name implies. As noted previously, this is really handy when you have a lot of slideshows.
- **Set Button Position** (Option-⌘-P) enables you to precisely position a button on the menu. The position is relative to the menu's upper-left corner and a menu is 640×480 pixels.
- **Swap Button Positions** (Option-⌘-S) requires that you have two buttons selected. If so, it will swap their positions within the menu.

AppleScripting iDVD

First things first. We're not going to attempt to teach you AppleScript here. If you want to learn AppleScript, we direct you to www.apple.com/applescript, where you'll find an abundance of tutorial references as well as online and downloadable documentation. This discussion assumes that you have at least a passing acquaintance with AppleScript, what a script is, and how Script Editor works.

iDVD 2.1 introduced the first scriptable version of iDVD. iDVD Companion, described earlier in this chapter, provides a wealth of example scripts, most of which are available as separate downloads from www.apple.com/applescript/idvd, where you'll also find several additional sample scripts.

 If you get error messages when attempting to open iDVD's AppleScript Dictionary in Script Editor, check www.apple.com/applescript/idvd for the Scripting Terminology updater. Early releases of the iDVD 2.1 updater did not include this critical resource.

We don't know about you, but we find modifying existing scripts the easiest way to start scripting a new application. We encourage you to peruse the sample scripts to find snippets that do something similar to what you want and tweak to your heart's content. Before you know it, you'll be creating useful (and original) scripts.

One of our biggest quibbles with iDVD is the lack of fine control over button placement and alignment. iDVD Companion provides some useful tools to ease our pain, but it is sometimes a bit cumbersome. What we're going to do is write a little script that distributes three buttons horizontally, spaced about the horizontal center, and one-third of the way up from the bottom.

This boils down to aligning the center of each button with specific grid points. Vertically, the center should be two-thirds of the way down from the top of the screen. Because a screen is 480 pixels tall, the button centers should be 320 pixels from the top. Buttons are 128 pixels wide by 96 pixels tall, so the top of the button should be 320, that is, 48 pixels (272) from the top of the screen. Similarly, we are placing buttons one-fourth, one-half, and three-fourths of the way across the screen, which is 640 pixels wide. Doing that arithmetic, we find that the left edges of the buttons should be 96, 256, and 416 pixels, respectively, from the screen's left edge.

As you can see in Figure 20-11, we perform these computations at the top of the script. After that, we make sure that iDVD won't override our computations with its preset grid coordinates. Next, it's just error-checking to make sure that exactly three buttons are selected and telling the buttons where to position their upper-left corners.

Figure 20-11: Our little AppleScript distributes three buttons evenly.

If the user has selected more or fewer than three buttons, the alert dialog shown in Figure 20-12 appears.

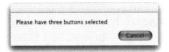

Figure 20-12: We have to let them know that they must select exactly three buttons.

Figure 20-13 shows before and after images of what happens when the script runs with three buttons selected.

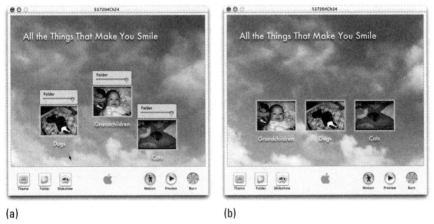

(a)   (b)

Figure 20-13: Our menu with three buttons selected (a); our menu after iMovie has positioned the buttons (b).

As you peruse the example scripts and let your imagination soar, you'll come up with ideas to make your iDVD use even easier. Give it a shot, programming AppleScript isn't as hard as you might think. Just remember that computers, even Macs, are just incredibly literal and obedient idiots. If you forget to tell them to do something, they don't do it; they do *exactly* what you tell them, without understanding nuance or assuming anything.

Summary

In this chapter you learned how to use the DVD-ROM portion of your DVD and how to monitor your DVD's status as iDVD does its work. You saw how to take advantage of the AppleScript capabilities Apple added in iDVD 2.1 and to use the very handy little utility, iDVD Companion (built with AppleScript Studio), to access some iDVD capabilities not present in its menus.

✦ ✦ ✦

iDVD Tips, Tricks, and Techniques

CHAPTER 21

In This Chapter

Inside projects

Inside themes

Planning your iDVD project

Inside encoding and compression

We have to tell you up front: This is going to be a relatively short chapter and you may even find it a bit geeky. iDVD is a great entry-level program for authoring, encoding, and burning your DVDs, but it's pretty much "what you see is what you get" and Chapters 19 and 20 pretty much exhausted iDVD's repertoire. Even the Advanced menu isn't very advanced.

There are currently no tools to create themes from scratch. All you can do is customize the ones included with iDVD. And you can't control the encoding process other than to force a lower bit rate by putting more than 60 minutes of content on your DVD.

What we do in this chapter is tell you how DVD projects and themes are constructed. Next, we give you a few tips on planning your projects. Finally, we finish up by covering a couple of esoteric points about MPEG-2 encoding and Photo-JPEG.

Inside Projects

When you create an iDVD project you get a document icon just as you do when you create an AppleWorks document or a FileMaker Pro database, right? Well, almost right. Unlike most documents, an iDVD project is really a folder that the OS X Finder treats like a single file, just as it does with most applications. You can see this by Control-clicking the project file, as shown in Figure 21-1, and noticing the contextual menu's Show Package Contents item.

Figure 21-1: iDVD projects are really special folders, called *packages*.

Choosing Show Package Contents opens a new Finder window in icon view. We've switched to list view and ⌘-Option-clicked the Contents folder's disclosure triangle to display all the Completed Tutorial project's levels in Figure 21-2. The project's main menu screen is shown in Figure 21-3.

Figure 21-2: Even a small project is made up of lots of files and folders.

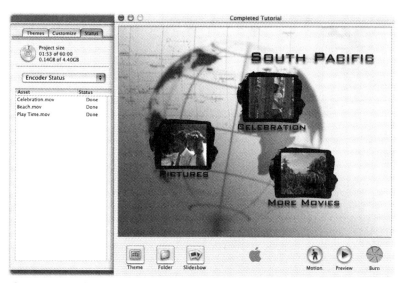

Figure 21-3: The Completed Tutorial project's main menu.

The main thing to notice is that the Thumbnails and MPEG folders hold most of your data. Encoded movie files go, as the name suggests, in the MPEG folder. The Thumbnails folder is the repository for all your buttons and the scaled-down, soundless clips that play in them.

However, the really important file is the one called ProjectData. It doesn't include a filename extension nor does it sport a traditional file type (like "TEXT"), but it is an XML file and it describes the entire project's structure, as illustrated in Figure 21-4.

Caution

If this book were in color, we'd put this warning in big red letters: Don't modify the ProjectData file or anything else you find in the project's package. From your perspective, this is read-only data and the best you can hope for is to not break things if you fiddle with it. The only time we recommend even looking in the ProjectData file is when iDVD can't find some of your content. You might be able to get a clue what you misplaced that iDVD needs.

Figure 21-4: ProjectData's top two levels are displayed in Property List Editor.

Inside Themes

Themes, like projects and the iDVD application, are packages. In fact, if you look inside the iDVD application package's Resources folder, you'll see the 14 themes stored in iDVD's Themes drawer, and you'll find another 18 themes that don't appear, as shown in Figure 21-5. The inaccessible themes are numbered 901 through 919, with no 904. These themes were created for the iDVD 1.0 application.

Borrowing a background

It's really a shame that some of these themes aren't available in the Themes drawer. For example, the Happy Days theme would be great for commemorating a birthday party, and Surfs Up has a beautiful background. We have to assume Apple had some reason for leaving them, consuming as they do a little over a megabyte each of disk space, in the application package. At the moment, the only use (other than a hack we'll tell you about in a bit) we have is borrowing some of the backgrounds to use in our own customizations, as follows:

Figure 21-5: iDVD stores its themes in the application package.

1. With iDVD not running, Control-click the iDVD icon and choose Show Package Contents.
2. Navigate down through the Contents folder to the Resources folder.
3. Control-click the theme whose background you want to borrow and choose Show Package Contents.
4. Navigate down through the Contents folder into the theme's Resources folder.
5. Select the Background.tif file and, holding down the Option key, drag it to the Desktop or some other conveniently accessible location.
6. Close all the theme's folders and all the iDVD package folders you've opened.
7. Launch iDVD and open the Theme drawer if it isn't already open.
8. Select the Customize tab.
9. Drag the Background.tif file into the Image/Movie well, as shown in Figure 21-6.

Figure 21-6: You now have the background from Surfs Up, perfectly proportioned and sized, in your menu.

Creating custom themes seems like a solid niche product for an enterprising developer with XML skills. We hope to see a small cottage industry developing before long.

Resurrecting an iDVD 1 theme

You can, with just a little effort and care, make one or more of the iDVD 1 themes available. Proceed as follows:

1. While pressing the Option key, drag the themes you want to your home directory. This will make a copy of the theme for you to work on.
2. Control-click on the theme copy and choose Show Package Contents.
3. Navigate down into the Resources folder within the Contents folder.
4. Open the language folder for your version of iDVD and find the Description.plist file. We open the English.lproj folder.
5. Open Description.plist with Property List Editor (if you have the OS X Developer tools installed) or a plain text editor like BBEdit. Almost at the end of the file, you'll find an entry that says the version is 1.

Note You can edit the Description.plist file with TextEdit, but you have to be extra careful to make sure that you save it as plain text. TextEdit likes to convert things to RTF and that would make the file unusable by iDVD.

6. Change the 1 to a 2 (as shown in Figure 21-7) and save the file.

7. Close the theme's window(s) and move it to your home directory's Library/iDVD/Favorites folder (creating the folder, if necessary).

8. Change the filename extension from .theme to .favorite.

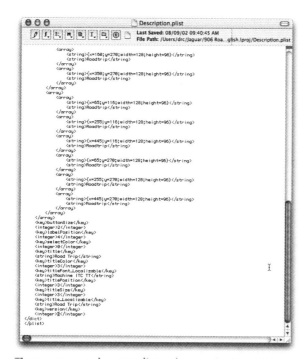

Figure 21-7: Using BBEdit to change the Road Trip theme's version to 2.

Now if you launch iDVD and open the Theme drawer, you'll find Road Trip, or whichever themes you edited, available after the built-in themes as shown in Figure 21-8.

Figure 21-8: The resurrected theme is now available to you.

Planning Your iDVD Project

We can appreciate how easy and tempting it is to just throw a few buttons onto a menu screen, click Burn, insert the blank DVD-R, and sit back awaiting the finished DVD. In fact, we've even done it ourselves when we needed something (anything) quickly.

But, if you want your DVDs to be something special, you'll have to put a little work into planning your DVD. Bob likes to use an outliner to organize the whole project. Because he does his writing in Microsoft Word, he tends to use Word's outliner; you, on the other hand, might also consider OmniOutliner, a really Aqua-beautiful OS X-only outliner from the Omni Group (www.omnigroup.com) or even the outliner included in AppleWorks. Meanwhile, Dennis is rapidly switching from pads of quadrille paper filled with barely recognizable sketches to OmniGraffle (also from the Omni Group) to diagram what he wants on his DVDs.

We'll get more into Bob's approach in the "Movie- and DVD-Making Like the Pros" section in Chapter 24, because he starts with planning the movie creation process as well as the DVD authoring. Dennis's use of iDVD is more geared to combining iMovie footage and photos he already has on hand into DVDs for friends and family.

Assuming that you already have your content, you need to plan your presentation. Just as high-priced restaurants receive critical acclaim for average food, mediocre service, and minuscule portions when the meal is properly presented, you can receive kudos for everyday footage and slideshows if you package and present them properly.

The first thing you need to do is collect your content into one place. You could navigate your hard disk to find all the pieces as you build your DVD, but you'll be making your job harder than it needs to be. Additionally, if your content is all in one folder and you keep your iDVD project file in that folder, backing up your work becomes easy. (You do back up, don't you?)

Find music to complement or enhance your menus and slideshows. For example, Rocky Balboa running up the steps wasn't a great scene until it was driven by the music. If you have a .Mac account, Apple and FreePlay Music make 1.3GB of music available in varying clip lengths, providing a wealth of choices at the right price — free (or, almost free, as .Mac does have a price). Alternatively, you can search the Web for other free or inexpensive music sources or use a commercial product like Sonic Desktop's Movie Maestro or SonicFire Pro (www.smartsound.com) to create a soundtrack.

Organize your menus and buttons so that your audience can easily find what they're looking for. Keeping movies with movies and slideshows with slideshows is a good start, but you can do more. Figure out the sequence in which your content is best viewed and arrange the buttons to match. Your audience can still select randomly, but at least you'll be giving them a starting point if they don't know ahead of time which movie they want to view.

Inside Encoding and Compression

Encoding and compression are two separate concepts even though most people use them interchangeably, and incorrectly. *Encoding* converts the form of the data on which it acts and may result in a data set that is larger or smaller (or even the same size) than the original. For example, when you convert the analog signal from a VCR to digital form using a digital camcorder as a pass-through device, you are digitally encoding the signal. When you attach a file (like a picture) to an e-mail message, your mail software encodes the attached file into a form compatible with Internet mail protocols. *Compression,* however, makes things smaller and falls into two categories:

✦ **Lossless compression** means that the original data can be completely reconstructed from the compressed copy. Compression and archival software like StuffIt and Zip use lossless compression.

✦ **Lossy compression** means that unnecessary data is discarded as part of the compression process. (Well, you hope the data is unnecessary.) MP3, JPEG, and MPEG are examples of lossy compression schemes. The more data (quality) you're willing to discard, the smaller the resulting file, possibly to the point where the data loss is easily visible, as shown in Figure 21-9.

Figure 21-9: You can see the artifacts and blurring around the auto antenna when heavy JPEG compression is used in this Photoshop 7 before and after screen shot.

The Motion Pictures Experts Group (MPEG) is an industry coalition responsible for defining such standards as MP3 (MPEG-1 Layer 3 audio), MPEG-1 (used on VideoCDs), MPEG-4 (used for streaming media), and MPEG-2 (used for DVDs and Super VideoCDs).

We're not going to delve into all the mathematics and mind-numbing specifications describing MPEG-2. If you want that level of detail, check out `http://mpeg.telecomitaliab.com` or `http://bmrc.berkeley/frame/research/mpeg/mpeg2faq.html`.

Just because a file is compressed and encoded as an MPEG-2 file doesn't mean that you can burn it to a DVD. The frame size has to be right for either NTSC or PAL, as does the frame rate (frames per second, or fps). More than that, though, the data bit rate has to fall within a specified range. Table 21-1 gives a requirements and features breakdown for both NTSC and PAL DVDs.

Note Both AIFF and WAV are examples of PCM (Pulse Coded Modulation) audio.

Table 21-1
DVD Specifications

	NTSC	PAL
Bit Rate	Up to 9.8 Mbit/sec MPEG-2. May be CBR or VBR.	Up to 9.8 Mbit/sec MPEG-2. May be CBR or VBR.
Frame Size	72×480	72×576
Frame Rate	29.97 fps	25 fps
Audio	Up to 8 audio tracks containing Dolby Digital, DTS, PCM (uncompressed audio), MPEG-1 Layer2; but one track must either have DD or PCM Audio (48 kHz).	Up to 8 audio tracks containing Dolby Digital, DTS, PCM (uncompressed audio), MPEG-1 Layer2; but one track must either have DD or PCM Audio (48 kHz).

Even after attending to all these technical details, we're still not ready to burn a DVD. The DVD disc format requires that certain files need to be in specific places and that a naming convention is enforced. Fortunately for all of us, iDVD takes care of that bookkeeping as well.

iDVD 2 uses constant bit-rate encoding at one of two preset speeds. The higher speed fits 60 minutes of video on a DVD-R, the lower is set to record 90 minutes per disc.

Basic MPEG Compression

We're going to get more than a little nerdy in this discussion. Unless you're prepared to follow along, bail out now.

Movies are filmed at 24 fps and, as an analog medium, that means that there are 24 distinct images recorded every second. When you view television (we'll assume NTSC for this discussion, only the numbers change for PAL), you see almost 30 fps (29.97 is the "book" answer). That 30 fps is misleading, though, because 60 frames (okay, 59.94, but we're going to just round off) are actually transmitted each second, with alternating frames containing the even and odd scan lines, which your TV then *interlaces* (reassembles in order) back into an image.

Encoders, in our case MPEG-2 encoders, perform a mathematical analysis of each frame, determining how to encode the data for optimum results. Much of the analysis is similar to that in JPEG compression, where the encoding software decides which data can be eliminated without visually degrading the image quality.

Continued

Continued

But, no frame is an island. The encoder also compares each frame with the frames around it, analyzing the differences and deciding in which of three ways to encode the frame:

- **Intraframes** contain the frame's complete image data which, obviously, means that compression is minimal. Think of it as a reference frame.
- **Predicted frames** contain just enough data to tell the DVD player's decoder how to reconstruct the image based upon the most recently displayed intraframe or predicted frame.
- **Bidirectional frames** tell the decoder to use the surrounding intraframes and predicted frames to interpolate (approximate or average out) the frame contents.

The more variation from frame to frame, the more intraframes required and, as a result, less compression achieved. All of this analysis, which requires more than one pass through the data, takes time. That's why encoding is so slow. There is an upside to this time expenditure, though. Almost no analysis needs to be done at decoding time, and your DVD player can easily reconstruct the images and display them without having the picture stutter.

If you want to delve even deeper into this process, we recommend www.howstuffworks.com/video-format.htm. Actually, we recommend the How Stuff Works site in general. It's a great reference and answers most of our questions about how things work (probably how it got its name).

Summary

In this chapter you learned about how iDVD projects are constructed and that both projects and themes are implemented as packages. You also saw how to obtain access to the iDVD 1 themes that still reside within the iDVD 2 application package. Then, we gave you some tips on planning your iDVD project. Finally, you saw, briefly, how compression works and how DVDs come to be.

✦ ✦ ✦

Enhancing Your iDVD Experience

In This Chapter

Hardware enhancements

Software enhancements

If any of the iApps in this book could be considered "high-end," it would be iDVD, which seems odd because iDVD is pretty much a one-trick pony. In fact, if Apple hadn't added the capability to write data DVDs in version 2.1, we would have called it just that.

Because of that, and the fact that iDVD is only available on Macs with *internal* SuperDrives, you'll understand why there are fewer hardware and software add-ons for iDVD than other iApps.

Most of what you need to get the most out of iDVD with the least effort is covered in Part IV, "iMovie," and, to a lesser extent, Part III, "iPhoto." We touch on a few items here that aren't covered elsewhere (and a couple that were, but bear repeating) and then get on to Part VI, "Putting It All Together."

Hardware Enhancements

iDVD works only with internal SuperDrives, the Pioneer A103 and A104 model DVD-R/CD-RW burners. For a very short time there was a third-party enhancement from Other World Computing that enabled iDVD to work with external drives, but Apple's lawyers had that software withdrawn from the market. That is not, however, the same thing as saying that iDVD requires that your SuperDrive be one that came with your computer from Apple.

Pioneer A104 (SuperDrive)

If your Mac didn't come with a SuperDrive, you're not necessarily out in the cold, forced to pay $1,000 for DVD Studio Pro if you want to create and burn DVDs. You can replace your Mac's original internal CD or DVD drive with a Pioneer A104, if you're comfortable working with hardware or know someone who is and who can do so without voiding your Apple warranty.

Bob did just that to one of his Macs, a G4/500 that came out before the SuperDrive became available and was equipped instead with a DVD-RAM drive. He removed that drive (and sold it on eBay) and installed a Pioneer A104 in its place. iDVD couldn't tell the SuperDrive (er, A104) didn't ship with the computer and worked flawlessly.

> **Note** It still does. He sold it to a friend who uses it daily in his recording studio. The friend reports that the Pioneer drive is still going strong.

You can find internal A104 drives for approximately $400-$500 at the time we're writing this. For an additional $70 or so, you can get a FireWire enclosure into which you might place your original drive and continue to use it as an external — a particularly attractive option if you ever desired to have two optical discs mounted simultaneously. Both of us have external drives in addition to our built-in drives — we frequently find the need (or have the desire) to access one CD (or a DVD) while another is burning in the background.

DVD players

If you're using iDVD, then you're burning DVDs to play in what Apple refers to as "most standalone DVD players." We're not going to argue with the use of "most" in this context, because it is almost certainly accurate; however, it is a bit misleading if you think it means "almost all" rather than "a majority of."

> **Note** Dennis's experience with DVD-R compatibility has been mixed. His Konka plays VCDs, SVCDs, CD-R, and CD-RW, but doesn't recognized DVD-R discs. His neighbor's GE doesn't recognize any of the above, just commercially pressed DVDs and VCDs. But his Philips and the neighbor's Apex play just about everything. Price and brand name also don't tell the story. There are some expensive Sony models, for example, that don't recognize various media and others (both expensive and not) that do. Bob's Samsung set top DVD player will play everything he burns on a DVD-R disc, but not a VCD. His neighbor's older Panasonic DVD player doesn't play most DVD-Rs but does play VCDs just fine. And his father's DVD player (who knows what kind *that* was) wouldn't play anything Bob burned — neither DVD-R nor VCD.

Before purchasing a DVD player, check out www.vcdhelp.com. Although the site is mostly geared to VideoCD variants and Windows users of digital video software, it has the most extensive compatibility database concerning standalone DVD players we've seen or heard of. You can check out whether they support DVD-R, DVD-RW, CD-R, CD-RW, VideoCD, SVCD, and a raft of other features. Additionally, the user commentary that gives tips on street price for the models as well as any other quirks that have been encountered is very valuable. It's not as formal as *Consumer Reports*, but we love the depth of detail and the honesty (bluntness?) of some reviews. We really love useful information that also entertains.

Media

While no longer the price leader, Apple-labeled DVD-R blanks were the first (relatively) inexpensive media available for DVD recording. Some other brands, including TDK and General, are now selling for less. We've actually seen them advertised for under $2 each, in quantity purchases (spindles of 25 or 50). Our experience with Apple DVD-R discs has been uniformly excellent, but we've experienced a few "coasters" when using other brands.

Want details? Dennis had two out of ten TDKs fail, and Bob had half of the generic pink DVD-R disks someone gave him fail. And don't even ask about DVD-RW (rewritable) discs. Bob's tried most of the brands and had more failures than successes. Not to mention how DVD-RW discs burn slowly and erase even more slowly. He gave all of his away and sticks to DVD-R for now.

At this point, we would advise you to stick with Apple-labeled discs for anything important. If you wish to experiment with less costly brands, try small quantities first to see how they work for you before purchasing a spindle or other large lot.

It's even more critical with DVDs than with CDs to protect the shiny surface from scratching, fingerprints, and the like. Keep them in their protective sleeves or cases when you're not playing them and, for goodness sake, purchase sleeves or cases to use when you buy spindles. A ruined DVD is not just five times the cost of a ruined CD, but it's also a loss of almost seven times as much data.

Software Enhancements

Because you already have iMovie and iPhoto (they come with OS X, and iDVD requires OS X), we're not going to include them in our recommended software acquisitions, but they're tools you'll find very useful when creating your DVD's content. Some of the items we'll mention have been recommended or discussed elsewhere in the book, but we hope that we'll be providing a new context here.

QuickTime Pro

One of iDVD's best features is motion menus and, using QuickTime Pro, you can create nice movie files to use as a motion menu. As we've belabored, iDVD puts rather restrictive controls on what text elements may appear in a menu and restricts those to one line each; however, with QuickTime Pro, you can create multiline or animated text for a more professional-looking menu.

Check out the "Post Production Tricks with QuickTime Pro" section in Chapter 15 for a basic sampler of things you can do with QuickTime Pro and a movie file, the exact kind of file that you drag into iDVD for use as a motion menu.

Photoshop or Photoshop Elements

If you want a still menu rather than a motion menu, you can obviously use iPhoto when you want to select an already-existing graphic. To customize one of these photos in any way, however, such as by adding text or creating a composite of multiple photos, you need a good graphics editing tool. Adobe Photoshop and Adobe Photoshop Elements are considered by most to be about the best of breed; if they're not the best, they're definitely the industry standard.

Photoshop has a few more bells and whistles and, if you need those features for other tasks, by all means spend the $600+ that Photoshop costs. Although we both own Photoshop 7 and think very highly of it, Photoshop Elements (at $99) does everything we need for iDVD and photo retouching with iPhoto, as well as a lot more.

In fact, the combination of Photoshop Elements and QuickTime Pro is a decent little menu-creation toolbox.

iDVD Companion

We cover iDVD Companion in Chapter 20, but we really feel that it bears repeating here. iDVD Companion will unlock, through the wonders of AppleScript, features that iDVD just doesn't make available in its standard interface. This is a free download from Apple at www.apple.com/applescript/idvd.

Actually, iDVD Companion just touches the surface of what you can do with iDVD when you bring AppleScript into the arena. If you don't already know how to write AppleScripts, work through Apple's online and downloadable tutorials at www.apple.com/applescript and check out the example AppleScripts available alongside iDVD Companion.

Summary

This chapter was short and sweet. We reminded you how iDVD Companion and AppleScript can increase your control and options within iDVD. We also showed you what to look for and where to look when purchasing a DVD player or blank media. Finally, you learned that QuickTime Pro and Photoshop (or Photoshop Elements) can help you make better still or motion menus for your DVDs.

✦ ✦ ✦

Putting it All Together

PART VI

In This Part

Chapter 23
Using the Four "i"s Together

Chapter 24
Movie- and DVD-Making Like the Pros

Chapter 25
Taking Slideshows Beyond iPhoto

Chapter 26
When you Outgrow the "iStuff"

Using the Four "i"s Together

CHAPTER 23

✦ ✦ ✦ ✦

What's the score?

Slip, slideshowing away

Feeding iDVD

✦ ✦ ✦ ✦

Although each of our four featured applications are useful all by themselves, there's a reason Apple refers to this constellation (and a couple of other applications) as "spokes on your digital hub."

All by themselves, spokes are just sticks (or rods), useful for a variety of purposes. Attached and working together they let you do even more. For example, you can use songs from iTunes or images from iPhoto in your iMovie and iDVD productions. You can even, with a little help from QuickTime Pro, take your iMovie's soundtrack and create a soundtrack CD in iTunes, just like the studios do with their movies.

In this chapter, we'll explore the above and other ways to leverage the capabilities of one iApplication to enhance another.

What's the Score?

Simultaneous with (or, often, before) a movie's theatrical release, motion picture studios release a CD containing the movie's musical score. (We both remember, vividly, when these were LPs, not CDs — not that long ago.)

While your productions are not on the same scale or scope as those of Universal, MGM, or Warner Bros., you can emulate them in this respect. Just as one example, assume that one or more of your family is part of a play or recital and you decide to make a movie of the event.

Because you're making a movie, it seems likely that you'll distribute it on DVD, VideoCD, and/or videotape to reach the widest audience. However, you might also consider distributing just the audio portion, all packaged up as a commemorative CD, or just an album to carry around on your iPod.

In the case of a musical recital or a live performance, we're going to assume that you positioned your microphones or audio pickup, as we advised in the "Huh, What'd They Say?" section of Chapter 16, and have a clean audio feed. The old adage of "garbage in, garbage out" is especially true in audiovisual work. Barring extraordinarily expensive equipment, a lot of time, and the assistance of an audio specialist, there isn't too much you can do to make a bad audio track sound decent and, if you missed recording the audio, you're probably out of luck.

Tip

If you know you're going to get only one take, try to have a backup recording going. Maybe you have a friend or family member who also has a digital camcorder. Sometimes redundancy is a virtue.

What we're going to show you isn't really snazzy or state-of-the-art, but it works. Follow the steps and have QuickTime Pro handy — you'll have a sound track that you can turn into a CD with multiple tracks:

1. In iMovie, with your movie in the Clip Viewer or Timeline, choose File ⇨ Export Movie (⌘-E).

2. Choose To QuickTime in the Export Movie dialog's Export pop-up menu.

3. Choose Expert from the Formats pop-up menu. The Expert QuickTime Settings dialog box appears.

4. In the Expert QuickTime Settings dialog, click the Settings button in the Audio Settings area, as shown in Figure 23-1. The Sound Settings dialog box makes an appearance.

Figure 23-1: Make sure that the audio settings are appropriate for your high-quality soundtrack.

5. Either by typing or choosing from the pop-up menu, set the Rate to 44.100 kHz, as shown in Figure 23-2, making sure that 16 bit and Stereo are selected for the Size and Use.

Figure 23-2: Set the audio to 44.1 kHz, 16 bit, Stereo for CD-quality sound.

6. Click OK to dismiss the Sound Settings dialog box and OK to dismiss the Expert QuickTime Settings dialog.

7. Click Export in the Export Movie dialog box and, in the Export QuickTime Movie dialog box, name your movie and select a location. If your desired location isn't available in the Where pop-up menu, click the disclosure button we point out in Figure 23-3 to display the usual Save dialog box's column view.

Figure 23-3: Click the indicated button to display the Finder-like column view.

Note We *really* wish that there were a preference setting so that Save dialog boxes could be forced to open with the column view displayed. We frequently want to save files someplace other than the directories in the pop-up list.

8. Sit back and wait for QuickTime to export your movie. When it's done, quit from iMovie and open the movie you just saved in QuickTime Player.

9. (optional) Choose Edit ⇨ Enable Tracks and turn off the Video Track, as shown in Figure 23-4, and click OK.

Figure 23-4: If you don't need the video to cue you into where you're going to make your selections, you can save some screen space by turning off the Video Track.

10. Using the techniques described in the "Post-Production Tricks with QuickTime Pro" section in Chapter 15, select the section of your movie with the audio you want to use for your first track.
11. Choose Edit ➪ Copy (⌘-C).
12. Choose File ➪ New Player (⌘-N).
13. Choose Edit ➪ Paste (⌘-V). Your new movie's audio track is now the same as the selection made in Step 10.
14. Choose File ➪ Export (⌘-E). The Save exported file as dialog box appears.
15. Choose Sound to AIFF from the Export pop-up menu as shown in Figure 23-5, and name the file you're creating. Click Save to store the file on disk. To make things easier later on, you should save this file and subsequent files to a folder created for this project.

Figure 23-5: Save the movie's audio track as an AIFF file by choosing Sound to AIFF from the Export pop-up menu.

16. Repeat Steps 10 through 15 for as many songs or audio selections you want to create.

17. Quit from QuickTime Pro and start iTunes.

18. Drag the folder containing your songs to the iTunes Source pane, creating a new playlist, as shown in Figure 23-6.

Figure 23-6: Create a playlist containing the AIFF files you've created.

19. Select your new playlist in the Source pane and proceed as described in the "Making Your Own CDs" section in Chapter 4.

Congratulations! You've just created your soundtrack album—look out, AOL/Time-Warner!

Slip, Slideshowing Away

Slideshows are everywhere—screensavers, travelogues, business presentations, family reminiscences, you name it. And, if Apple has their way, they'll be even more common. In AppleWorks 6, Apple eliminated the communications module, replacing it with a Presentations feature. Microsoft includes PowerPoint as a major part of their Office for the Mac product. QuickTime 6 creates slideshows from folders of images. iPhoto creates slideshows from your photo collection. iMovie creates slideshows out of still images you import. iDVD also has a very nice slideshow feature. In fact, you have so many slideshow tools available that you could be whirling around trying to figure which door (application) to choose.

Here, we give you the definitive answer as to which slideshow tool to use. That answer is, "It depends."

Many factors weigh into the determination of which tool is the right one to use. There are three critical questions to ask:

- What is the subject?
- Where is it going to be viewed?
- How much flexibility do you need to build into your slideshow?

If your slides are mostly text and business-related graphics (charts and the like), your best bet is a presentation tool: PowerPoint or the AppleWorks Presentation module are great choices. We won't get into them here as they are not germane to this book. Check out *Macworld Microsoft Office 2001 Bible* by Bob LeVitus and Dennis R. Cohen or *Macworld AppleWorks 6 Bible* by Steve Schwartz and Dennis R. Cohen (both published by John Wiley & Sons) for coverage of PowerPoint and AppleWorks presentations, respectively.

We categorize slideshows as basic or complex depending upon whether they are viewing-oriented (basic) or message-oriented (complex). Screensavers and kiosk-oriented travelogues are basic slideshows. Each image is displayed for the same amount of time and everything is automated to go from one slide to the next and, possibly loop back to the beginning after displaying the final slide. Product presentations, where individual slides might have different on-screen durations, and other information-purveying slideshows fall into the complex category.

Basic slideshows

A simple, themed slideshow like "Our Day in Mazatlan" with a musical accompaniment is made to order for iPhoto. Just organize the pictures you want in an album, as described in the "Creating a Slideshow" section of Chapter 9, and pick your music.

You can watch these shows in iPhoto or you can export them as you learned in "Sharing a Slideshow" in Chapter 10. They also make great screensavers, if you've updated to Mac OS X 10.2 (Jaguar).

Using iPhoto is probably your best choice if a single, simple slideshow is sufficient for your needs.

The preceding example, "Our Day in Mazatlan," could also be part of a set of vacation slideshows: Mazatlan, Acapulco, On Ship, and so on. Using the Import iPhoto Album or the iPhoto to iDVD Slideshow AppleScripts from `www.apple.com/applescript/idvd`, you can import each of these albums to its own iDVD slideshow and then burn them to a DVD.

If you don't have iDVD and a DVD burner, though, you're not left out in the cold, so long as you have Toast Titanium and a CD burner. Using the wonderful freeware utility, VCD Builder, which we describe in the "Making Menu-Driven VCDs" section of Chapter 16, you can create inexpensive menued VideoCDs that will compare favorably with the iDVD productions. Just proceed as follows:

1. Create your slideshow in iPhoto. See Chapter 9 for the details.
2. Export the slideshow using the Toast-supplied QuickTime component to create a VideoCD-compatible MPEG-1 file. See Chapter 10 for the details.
3. Repeat Steps 1 and 2 until you've created all the slideshows you want.
4. Create your menu screen in AppleWorks, GraphicConverter, Photoshop Elements, or any other handy graphics editor. We tend to like captioned miniatures of each show's title slide, but your mileage may vary.
5. Launch VCD Builder and create your sequences (or use one of the templates). Chapter 16 covers using VCD Builder.

Dennis used this method to create a collected slideshows VideoCD featuring his friends' first baby, Marcus. (You've seen pictures of Marcus several times in this book.) He also created a nice label and CD jewel case cover, and Marcus's family really loved the result. In other words, VideoCDs and DVDs of this sort make great gifts.

Complex slideshows

When you want variable intervals for on-screen images, multiple soundtracks, or varied transitions and effects (such as captioning), be prepared to do a little more work and use iMovie.

The additional work arises mostly because each image has to be separately imported. We can only hope that the next version of iMovie has useful AppleScript support. The "Importing Images" section in Chapter 14 covers getting your pictures into iMovie and setting durations for each slide.

Employing iMovie's voice recording capability and taking advantage of the two audio tracks, you can easily have a background music track while narrating your presentation, travelogue, or photo essay. Add iMovie's transitions, titling, and other special effects (including those available via plug-ins) and you have a presentation tool for digital images that fills a gaping hole between PowerPoint and the iPhoto slideshow.

On those occasions where you want complete control while giving the presentation, go with iDVD and set the slideshow to be manually advanced. You now have all the flexibility of the rotary slide projector and remote control. This method is great for classroom or lecture hall presentations, where the slideshow's purpose is to illustrate your presentation but the timing is variable and backtracking might be desired.

Tip If you want that extra special effect in your slide show, you might want to check out Slick Motion from GeeThree (www.geethree.com). It's part of their Slick Transitions and Effects Volume IV.

Feeding iDVD

Although iDVD can leverage all three of our other applications, it's a one-way street. iPhoto, iTunes, and iMovie are both providers and consumers, but iDVD consumes, period. But, when all is said and done, iMovie is iDVD's favorite source.

iTunes can provide music for your iDVD menus and slideshows. iPhoto can provide photos for slideshows and images for still menus.

When you say "DVD" to most people, they think "Movie." For this reason, it's obvious that iMovie is iDVD's supplier of choice. Okay, Bob uses Final Cut Pro for a lot of his movies, but that's an expensive alternative that doesn't really gain you too much if iDVD is your next step in the creation process. DVD Studio Pro offers a lot though, like chaptering capability (more about that in Chapter 26). What isn't so obvious is that iMovie's also a great place to create the up-to-30-second clips you'll want for your motion menus.

You don't even have to have video footage to create these motion menus. You can use iMovie-created (or iPhoto-created and exported) slideshows for the menus (Slick Motion can be useful here as well).

Summary

In this chapter you learned at least one way to create a soundtrack recording from your movies. You also discovered how to decide which of your army of slideshow tools to employ for different tasks. Finally, you saw some ways to provide fodder to iDVD, such as using iMovie to create short (up to 30 second) movies to use as buttons and motion menus.

✦ ✦ ✦

Movie- and DVD-Making Like the Pros

✦ ✦ ✦ ✦

In This Chapter

Storyboarding the movie

Shooting extra footage

Setting the stage in iMovie

Choosing transitions

Planning the DVD

✦ ✦ ✦ ✦

Granting the fact that the vast majority of iMovie and iDVD use is casual, we still see serious use made of these basic, but functional, applications. Aspiring performers create music videos, students develop documentaries and original dramas as film projects, and businesspeople assemble presentations for clients or stockholders. Visiting Apple's iMovie Web pages at www.apple.com/imovie will link you to all sorts of more-than-merely-casual projects.

The one thing that all these projects have in common is that they were planned and executed, using all (or almost all) the production techniques employed by professional moviemakers.

You don't need to do all the things we're going to talk about on every project, but you do need to know what they are so that you make an informed decision when you skip something.

Storyboarding the Movie

Before you remove your camcorder's lens cap, plan your project. We know that planning can be really boring and that you might begrudge the time you would rather spend doing the fun stuff.

There are two kinds of lazy: *smart lazy* and *just plain lazy*. We like to be smart lazy, and that means spending a little time up-front so that we don't have to spend a whole lot more time down the road trying to do the things we forgot, redoing things we messed up due to inadequate preparation or understanding, and trying to fit all the parts together.

Collecting your notes

Bob is a habitual note-taker. He has little notepads filled with ideas, many of which come when he isn't in front of the computer. Dennis tends more toward self-stick notes as a recording device for his ideas. We both transcribe our notes onto our Macs, though, when we return to our digital comfort zone.

We strongly recommend that you do something similar. It doesn't have to be fancy, but if you have the notes in front of you, you have a reminder of the things you still have to accomplish and there's less likelihood that something will fall through the cracks.

In journalism, they teach that the five *W*s are the backbone of any news story: who, what, when, where, and why. Creating a movie isn't that different. Your project's *what, why,* and *who* are generally referred to as your goals and objectives. (What's your subject? Why are you doing this? Who is your target audience?) If you keep these points in mind, you'll be able to tailor your movie for maximum benefit. We cover the *when* and *where* next.

Outlining or charting your project

Bob keeps folders for each project and a project checklist is in each of those folders, used for tracking all his ideas as well as keeping a status list. Dennis doesn't keep a checklist or status list; he keeps a chart full of boxes and arrows.

Bob started using ThinkTank 512 back in the Mac's early days and became addicted to outlining. His books, presentations, videos, you name it, all have outlines stored somewhere on his Mac (or on an archive disk). Figure 24-1 shows part of one of Bob's video project outlines.

Note You can see the short film that resulted from this outline at `http://homepage.mac.com/boblevitus/iMovieTheater1.html` if you're interested.

Because our publishers insist on Microsoft Word documents, we both spend a goodly portion of our digital lives in Microsoft Word. And, because Bob spends so much time in Word, he tends to use Word's outline mode to maintain his lists. Now, Word's outliner, like most of Word, is very powerful but not really too intuitive. If you choose outlining, but either don't use Word or don't feel comfortable using it, you might consider the AppleWorks outliner or OmniOutliner, a beautiful product of the Omni Group designed specifically for OS X. (It's $21.12, but there's a free demo available at `www.omnigroup.com/applications/omnioutliner`.) Bob agrees, and though he's proficient at outlining in Word, often uses this simple but powerful application instead.

Figure 24-1: Bob plans and tracks projects using a Microsoft Word outline.

Dennis comes from the old programmer's school and started his career when flowcharting a software project was de rigueur. He still charts his projects, but has changed tools a number of times. Currently, his tool of choice is OmniGraffle, also from the fine folks at Omni Group. Figure 24-2 shows part of a project chart in OmniGraffle.

Professionals might use a *PMS* (no, that stands for Project Management System) to track the costs, activities, and schedule for their project and, if you're so inclined, you can do the same. Neither of us has gone that far because we're satisfied with the tools we have, but Intellisys Project Desktop (shareware, $59, from Intellisys, Inc. www.webintellisys.com) has gotten good reviews and looks quite capable at first glance.

> **Note** Dennis developed and maintained PMS software during part of his software development career. He warns you that if you choose to use such a tool, the reports you get are only as accurate as the data you supply. Unless you are really fastidious in planning the project and entering all the data accurately, you can draw some really erroneous conclusions from the output. Until you become comfortable with their use and have tracked the history of a few completed projects to make sure you've got the hang of organizing your data, don't rely too heavily on the schedule projections.

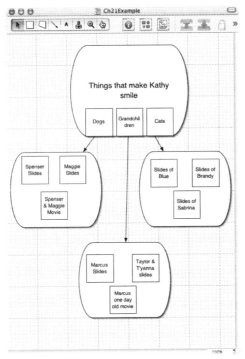

Figure 24-2: If you like a visual overview, consider OmniGraffle.

It's really of no consequence what method or tool you use to keep track of your project, but it is very important that you track it somehow. If not, we can guarantee that it won't be as good as it might be and it will almost surely take longer to complete.

Does your movie need a script and, if so, do you and your cast have it? Have you established a *shot list* (list of locations and scenes to remind you what you're shooting, where, and when)?

Note   The shot list should also have your camera positions and angles charted out. Getting the right angle on a scene and taking maximum advantage of lighting helps a lot.

Scripts

This is unusual in the world of computers, but these scripts don't involve writing code. If your movie has planned dialog, you need a script. Even narration should have a written script — extemporaneous narrative does not flow as well.

Besides, scripts aren't just about the spoken word. Scripts also provide direction to the performers and the camera person/people.

Shot lists

Sometimes, though, you won't have any dialog or scripted action. In those rare cases, you should consider a script subset — the shot list. Figure out the scenes you're going to require and the best angles from which to shoot and write them down.

If you do this, you won't miss any shots you need. You might shoot additional footage and even use that in addition to or in place of something you planned, but at least you'll get what you know you want.

For example, if you know you're going to be shooting footage of a horse race, decide whether you want footage of the horses' heads, full body shots, and/or shots focused on pounding hooves.

Storyboards

In a full-fledged, professional production, there will be a series of artist conception drawings, sometimes referred to as mockups, laying out precisely the look being sought. In a very casual movie, the storyboard might just be written descriptions of the various elements.

Because the desired end-result is a DVD, you'll actually need two storyboards: one for the movie and one for the DVD's menus. Figure 24-3 shows the mockup Dennis created for a gift DVD and the DVD menu implementing it.

Budgets

Sometimes you're going to need to purchase or lease equipment, license music, hire actors or writers, purchase tapes and media, or rent a location. Even the simplest and cheapest DVD production requires at least a tape (even a recycled one) and blank media.

If you stop to really think about it, you're going to be spending something on the project and, the larger the project, the more money you're apt to spend and the more different things you'll find to spend it on.

Plan for these expenses. If your budget can't handle what you come up with, at least you'll know it before you blow the dough on a project you can't afford to finish and you can revise your plan.

(a)

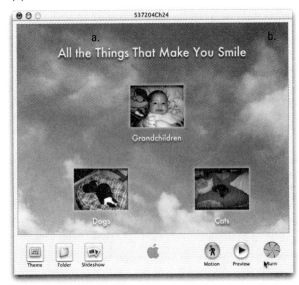

(b)

Figure 24-3: The concept (a); the implementation (b).

Schedules

The old adage says, "Time is money." We don't know if that's literally true, but there are a lot of similarities when it comes to creating and delivering a video project.

After you've figured out what shots you need to take, when you need to take them, and so forth, chart this all out. If there's a deadline on this project, you might find that you don't have time to do everything you want to do. In that case, you should refine your goals, revise your script and shot list, and redo the schedule.

Do you have enough tape? Have you got all the cables, microphones, batteries, and lights you'll need for the shots you plan to take? How about a tripod or gyro-stabilizer? Keeping abreast of what you'll need to shoot your footage is also an important part of your planning process.

We both tend to keep kits containing these sorts of things ready, just so we'll have them when they're needed. It's really frustrating to go on location and have to stop shooting because our battery went dead and we didn't have a spare. Also, when we're shooting stationary indoor scenes and there are convenient electrical outlets, we keep the camera plugged in. Why run down the battery and have to recharge or replace it later?

Shooting Extra Footage

Whenever possible, shoot more than you think you need. Not only will starting a little early and stopping a little late guarantee that you don't miss the beginning or ending of your scene, it might also provide you with some useful framing shots. And don't forget, when you use transitions like the dissolve, you need extra frames on the beginnings and ends of shots to accommodate them.

Similarly, when shooting background and transitional scenes, shoot them from different angles and, maybe, with different filters or lenses. You can often stumble across a good alternative effect for your movie.

Finally, whenever you have the opportunity to film extra footage of interesting scenes as *file shots*—scenes that can be used generically in future projects—do so. Random people walking down the street, cars in traffic, cable car riders in San Francisco, subway riders in New York—all of these can be used over and over again to set a context.

Setting the Stage in iMovie

Now that you've got something resembling a plan of attack and you've shot some footage, you're ready to start editing, right? Well, maybe.

Assuming that you've dotted all the i's and have your tape ready to feed into iMovie, there's still at least one thing to do. Clear all the disk space you're going to need for your project before you get started. While it probably isn't practical for everyone, we recommend having a dedicated hard disk that you can erase or reformat before you start a project. As noted elsewhere, that's what we both do.

Plan for iDVD's limitations

Remembering some of iDVD's limitations while creating your movie can pay large dividends. To that end, the greatest limitation is that iDVD burns movies as indivisible entities that play only from start to finish. If you're going to want to show specific segments of your movie in addition to the whole movie (maybe your day in Rome, which is just one part of your Mediterranean vacation), you'll need to save that segment as a separate, standalone movie, as well as part of your magnum opus.

Preparing more than just the movie

Whether you're going to use still or motion menus in iDVD, you can use iMovie to extract the relevant audio, video, and still images from your movie. Additionally, you can use tools like Movie Maestro (see Chapter 17, "Enhancing Your iMovie Experience") to score the menu's video. You should remember that motion menus only play the first 30 seconds of video and audio (repeating it ad nauseam), so you should plan accordingly and avoid jarring breaks in either the video or audio portions.

Similarly, you can create motion buttons (but without audio) that cycle through a scene of up to 30 seconds.

Another somewhat obvious use for extracted still images is the making of CD jewel case covers, inserts, and even posters.

Choosing Transitions

Less is more. iMovie provides a buffet table of transition choices and, with the addition of the iMovie plug-in pack (www.apple.com/imovie) and various available third-party collections, you can turn the selection into a menu of unmanageable dimension. Most of these transitions look cool when viewed in isolation, but they rarely do anything to enhance your movie and often detract from the continuity.

We covered transitions and the philosophy behind them pretty thoroughly in the "Working with Clips" section of Chapter 14; you should review that material before selecting and applying transitions.

Professional cinematographers use transitions sparingly and, when they do choose a transition, they tend to be very subtle (usually a fade or dissolve). We try to emulate the masters and use the more noticeable transitions only in special circumstances — slideshow presentations are good venues for radial and push transitions, for example.

Tip Radial is also a good transition when you're going for a sci-fi effect, like Clark Kent staring at a wall and then the scene shifting to what's on the other side of the wall.

Because adding transitions alters your movie's length, you should apply your transitions before scoring your movie. You don't want the audio to be mangled in the transition.

Planning the DVD

The storyboard layout we discussed earlier in this chapter (and embodied in Figure 24-3) is only one part, even if it's the biggest part, of planning your DVD. Creating useful storyboards will tell you how many menus you will need and how they're organized. What it won't tell you is what movies and still images you'll be using for your menus, nor what background music your menus will play.

iDVD isn't too fussy concerning which QuickTime-compatible format your video is in, but you'll get much better results with a video frame rate of 29.97 and using uncompressed 48-kHz audio for NTSC discs. PAL movies should have a 25-fps frame rate. iMovie makes this easy for you with the For iDVD choice in its Export Movie dialog's Export pop-up menu, shown in Figure 24-4.

Figure 24-4: iMovie makes preparing a movie for iDVD a simple menu choice.

When creating menus from still images, or when creating slideshows, remember that resolution is critical to good results. Images should be 640×480 to fill the screen. Once again, iMovie can make this easy for you if you extract your still images from the movie—they'll always be the right dimensions. If, however, you use a different source for your stills, you should use a graphics editing program to make sure that the pictures are 640×480 and 72 ppi. Of course, iPhoto will do this for you easily. Just select the image in iPhoto, click Share, click Export, select the File Export tab in the Export Images dialog box, and then select the "Scale images no larger than" radio button, as shown in Figure 24-5.

Figure 24-5: You can use iPhoto to scale your images to 640×480.

We also recommend that you have a single folder serving as the repository for all your DVD's parts: stills, audio, and video for use in your menus, folders for any slideshows, and a folder for any material you intend to include on your DVD-ROM portion. Having all this material collocated will reduce the likelihood that you'll misplace or, accidentally of course, delete something you're going to need.

Summary

In this chapter you learned the things you need to know about planning and organizing a DVD project. You're the only one who can decide which steps you're going to omit, but at least you'll know what it is that you aren't doing and what the repercussions might be.

✦ ✦ ✦

Taking Slideshows Beyond iPhoto

In This Chapter

Adding a little control over iPhoto slideshows

Taking slideshows to VideoCD

Slideshows are such a pervasive topic throughout this book that our publishers felt that they deserved a chapter of their own, tying the threads together and showing you some of the other ways to create, use, and share your slideshows. We happen to agree.

The digital slideshows you can create with iPhoto, iMovie, iDVD, and QuickTime Pro Player (as well as numerous applications dedicated solely to creating slideshows and presentations) have come a long way from the overhead projectors, slide viewers, slide trays, and rotary attachments of our youth. Organizing digital photos takes far less time, and we don't have to worry about losing or scratching the originals. Nor do we have the slightest concern about the risk of dropping them and getting them out of order. Additionally, we can now add precisely timed musical backgrounds or narrations to complement the slides. Finally, we have all sorts of visual special effects at hand, a mixed blessing that can either enhance a presentation or make our audience question our aesthetic judgment.

Getting More Control over iPhoto Slideshows

We think that iPhoto provides the easiest venue we've ever seen for creating attractive slideshows. Just stick the photos in an album, rearrange them in the order you want, add background music if you like, and click the Slideshow button. Until computers can read your mind, what could be simpler?

There are two limitations, though, to an iPhoto slideshow that become apparent as soon as you start wanting to use them for anything other than a kiosk-style presentation.

The first, and most glaring, limitation is that every slide appears on-screen for the same predetermined duration; and, second, a user's manual control over the slideshow's presentation is limited to clicking the mouse to terminate it. Fortunately, a few undocumented keystrokes provide you a modicum of manual slideshow control:

- **spacebar:** Pause/resume the slideshow.
- ↑: Make the slideshow faster by decreasing slide duration in 1-second increments.
- ↓: Make the slideshow slower by increasing slide duration in 1-second increments.
- ←: Pause the slideshow and go to previous slide.
- →: Pause the slideshow and go to next slide.

Tip

After you pause (spacebar) use ← and → to move back and forth from slide to slide, just like you would with a hot-bulb slide projector and remote control clicker. If you look closely, you can see the dimmed pause, forward, and back buttons in the lower-right portion of Figure 25-1.

Figure 25-1: They're not really obvious, but control buttons appear when you have a paused slideshow.

Note Any soundtrack you have playing continues uninterrupted while the slideshow is paused.

The third limitation is that you can assign only one soundtrack to a slideshow. If, for example, your slideshow were composed of Mediterranean vacation slides, you might want Spanish music for the photos taken in Barcelona, Italian for Rome and Venice, and Greek for Athens. iPhoto prevents you from doing this, but you can get around this limitation by using an audio-editing program to put together the music you want. QuickTime Player Pro lets you edit AIFF and MP3 files, creating composites. You'll just need to compute how long each segment will be and in what order you want them to appear. For example, if you have 15 slides from Barcelona, 20 from Rome, 18 from Venice, and 18 from Athens, and each is going to be on-screen for three seconds, you'll require 45 seconds of Spanish music, 1:54 of Italian, and 54 seconds of Greek.

Proceed as follows:

1. Open your three song files in QuickTime Player Pro.
2. Select segments of the appropriate length in each song's window. Figure 25-2 shows QuickTime Player Pro with the three song windows open and durations selected.

Figure 25-2: Select a portion of each song of the appropriate length.

3. Create a new song window by choosing File ➪ New Player (⌘-N), as shown in Figure 25-3.
4. For each song window in turn:
    a. Choose Edit ➪ Copy (⌘-C).
    b. Select your new window and choose Edit ➪ Paste (⌘-V). The playhead advances to the end of the selection just pasted, as shown in Figure 25-4.
5. Save (File ➪ Save) your new song window and name it.

Figure 25-3: Create a new player window to hold your composition.

Figure 25-4: The playhead moves to the end, ready to accept your next paste.

Alternatively, if you've purchased Movie Maestro or a similar product, you can create your own musical soundtracks from the clips they provide. (See Chapter 17, "Enhancing Your iMovie Experience.")

When you have the soundtrack you desire, just choose it in iPhoto's Slideshow dialog box, as follows:

1. With your slideshow album selected, click iPhoto's Share button.
2. Click Slide Show. The Slide Show Settings dialog box appears.
3. Choose Other from the Music pop-up menu, as shown in Figure 25-5.

Figure 25-5: Choose Other from the Music pop-up to add your song to the available music list.

4. In the Open dialog box that appears, locate and select your song, as shown in Figure 25-6.
5. Click Open
6. Click OK in the Slide Show Settings dialog box.

The slideshow starts playing with your soundtrack, and that music will be associated with this slideshow until you change it.

Figure 25-6: Select the audio file you created.

Taking Slideshows to VideoCD

Not having a SuperDrive and, thus, access to the iDVD application doesn't mean that you can't create slideshow CD collections for your friends and family to view on TV using their DVD player. Besides a CD burner, all you need is Roxio's Toast Titanium, which includes a handy little QuickTime component that will turn QuickTime movies into VideoCD-compatible MPEG-1 files, and the freeware application VCD Builder (described in Chapters 16 and 17).

Follow the directions in the "Sharing Your Slideshows" section in Chapter 10 to export your slideshows to QuickTime. VideoCDs expect image resolutions of 320×240, so you should export at a resolution that is an even multiple of 320×240. We tend to prefer 640×480 as that's a good size to preview on the Mac's screen.

Note   VideoCDs actually expect 352×240 images, but that resolution applies to rectangular pixels instead of square. QuickTime does the conversion for you.

Converting QuickTime to VideoCD

After you have exported your slideshows, the first step is to convert the QuickTime movie to VideoCD. This process is very simple and straightforward:

1. Launch Toast Titanium.
2. Choose VideoCD from Toast's Other button popup menu as shown in Figure 25-7.

Figure 25-7: The Other button hides a pop-up menu where you can choose Video CD as the destination format.

3. Drag your movie into Toast's window (the white area) as shown in Figure 25-8. The Toast Video CD Options dialog box appears.

Figure 25-8: Drag the movie to be converted.

4. If you are in the United States or Japan, use the settings shown in Figure 25-9. If you're in a PAL country, choose PAL (25 fps) from the Format pop-up menu.

Figure 25-9: These are the settings you'll want for a good-looking VideoCD.

5. Click OK. A Save Video CD Stream As dialog box now appears.

6. Select a location for your VideoCD file (it will have a .mpg filename extension) and, if you don't like the name suggested by Toast, rename it. Then click Save. Toast displays a progress bar, as shown in Figure 25-10 as it creates your VideoCD file. When the encoding is complete, the progress bar disappears.

7. Repeat Steps 3 through 6 for as many slideshows as you wish to encode.

Figure 25-10: Toast encodes your movie into a VideoCD-compatible MPEG-1 file.

You could, at this point, just burn the VideoCD and when you put it in a DVD player, the slideshows will play, one after the other, with no user intervention, as if they were one long movie. But, we want to make a VideoCD that behaves more like a DVD (navigated via menus), so you need to exit Toast and do a little more work.

Note You could also use QuickTime Player Pro's Export command and choose Movie to Toast Video CD from the "Save exported file as" dialog box's Export pop-up menu for each slideshow, but we think dragging into the Toast window is easier.

Creating menus

The first thing to do is to select a representative image from each slideshow's collection of photos to use in your menu and decide whether you want your menu to be a rotating sequence of pictures or a collage. We tend toward the collage view, because it is the way almost all DVDs offer their scene selections. This means you're going to need to use a graphics program (Photoshop or Photoshop Elements, GraphicConverter, or AppleWorks are all reasonable choices) to create your (preferably, 640×480) menu picture. VCD Builder can scale other sizes to fit, but most graphics programs have optimized scaling routines that might be preferable. Because the editing and saving methods differ from program to program, we'll leave you to use whatever method makes you most comfortable and just illustrate, in Figure 25-11, what a sample menu might look like. (We used Photoshop Elements.)

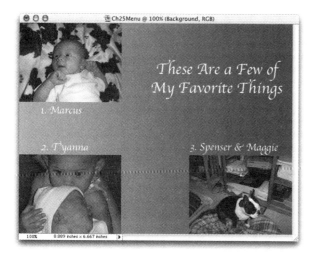

Figure 25-11: Create a menu screen that will help your viewers find the slideshow they want.

Building the VideoCD

Now that you have your menu screen and the various MPEG slideshow movies, you're ready to create your VideoCDs as follows (using the three slideshow example matching the menu in Figure 25-11):

1. Launch VCD Builder.
2. Click New Sequence. A rectangle with a 1 in the upper-left corner appears, as shown in Figure 25-12.

Figure 25-12: Create the first sequence to hold your menu.

3. Drag your menu's icon to the rectangle.
4. Click New Sequence and drag the rectangle to a nonoverlapping position.
5. Drag your first MPEG file's icon to that rectangle.
6. Holding down the Control key, click in the menu rectangle and drag into the new rectangle, and let go. A circular selection menu appears, as shown in Figure 25-13. Click on the number section.

Note: The bottom of the window keeps you informed as to how large your VideoCD is at each step.

7. Holding down the Control key, click in the slideshow's rectangle and drag into the menu's rectangle, and let go.
8. From the circular menu, select the Timeout section (looks like a clock dial).

The Timeout action is taken when the sequence finishes playing.

Figure 25-13: Choose the number button for your DVD player's remote control that corresponds to the selected slideshow.

9. Repeat Steps 4 through 8 for each of your slideshows.

Note

The movie rectangles show the first frame of your movie. This will often be pure black. You can double-click it to get its name and size if you forget which is which.

You should now have a window that resembles that shown in Figure 25-14.

Figure 25-14: Each of your slideshows is now connected to the menu and will return to the menu when completed.

10. (optional) Create Next and Previous connections between the slideshow rectangles, if desired, to respond to clicking the DVD player's remote control's next and previous buttons.
11. Choose Project ⇨ Save (⌘-S) or Save As (⌘-Shift-S) to give your project and the VideoCD a name.
12. Click Save to store the vcd project file on disk.
13. Click Burn VCD to burn the VCD files in Toast. VCD Builder presents a Save sheet where you must specify a name and location for the temporary image files. Once you have done so, click Save.
14. Sit back and wait for VCD Builder to finish creating the images.
15. When VCD Builder launches Toast, it sets Toast to Multitrack CD-ROM XA format, and load the image files. The Toast window comes to the front.
16. Click the Burn button.
17. Feed your CD burner a blank disc.
18. Click Burn Disc in the dialog box that appears to tell Toast to proceed and wait for your VideoCD to be burned.

Note The "temporary" files aren't really temporary. They remain on your hard disk until you throw them away, which is handy if you later decide to burn more copies; just be aware that these large files can consume disk space pretty quickly.

You now have a VideoCD that behaves almost identically to a DVD created in iDVD. Some differences include that you have more control over the sequence and flow of control on the VideoCD, but that you don't have the manual slideshow operation via the remote control that you get from an iDVD-created slideshow.

Just as with an iDVD creation, you can mix and match slideshows and movies on the same VideoCD. Because VideoCD takes up significantly less space than DVD, the 80 minutes that you can put on a VideoCD comes very close to the 90 minutes available to iDVD, at a fraction of the cost.

Summary

In this chapter, you learned a few undocumented iPhoto slideshow keystrokes. You also saw a way to create customized audio tracks for your slideshow. Finally, you saw how to create a menu-driven VideoCD slideshow disc that looks very similar to (and operates similarly to) an iDVD-created DVD.

✦ ✦ ✦

When You Outgrow the "iStuff"

In This Chapter

When iTunes isn't enough

Moving beyond iPhoto

Moving beyond iMovie

Authoring beyond iDVD

Apple designed and positioned the iApps really well. They provide a 100 percent solution for 90 percent of all users and a 90 percent solution for the other 10 percent.

But what happens when you or a particular project falls in those 10 percent areas? That's what we cover in this chapter.

In our opinion, not one of the applications to which you might need to migrate approaches any of the iApps in design elegance or ease-of-use, but that's one price you'll have to pay for increased power and flexibility. The other is measured in dollars, or whatever your national currency might be. Make no mistake about it; some of the steps up can result in some very real sticker shock.

When iTunes Isn't Enough

We're going to be really blunt here: iTunes is the application you're least likely to outgrow. Now in its third major version release, it's lost none of its ease of use and has added numerous power-user features. At least in our opinions, no other application we've seen or heard of matches iTunes' feature set.

That's not to say that you won't (possibly) find a need to augment iTunes. There are some gaps in its feature set. For example, it has no tools to import music from LPs or cassette tape, just CDs. Similarly, it has no tools for actually editing your audio files.

However, as a ripping, mixing, playing application, it is without peer. Throw in its integration with MP3 players (in particular the iPod), and you have the king of the MP3-playing hill.

What happens though, on those occasions that your MP3 or even your original source material contains hisses, pops, or clicks? At that point, you need an audio-editing tool. There are a number of such tools available, but we're going to focus on two: one shareware (Sound Studio) and one commercial (Roxio's Jam).

Sound Studio

Written by Lucius Kwok and distributed by his small company, Felt Tip Software (www.felttip.com), Sound Studio is a small, but feature-packed audio recording and editing utility. You can download it from Version Tracker and other fine shareware outlets and try it out for up to two weeks (yes, 14 days) to determine whether it is worth the $49 price to you.

Figure 26-1 shows you what Sound Studio looks like with a song loaded. We aren't going to even attempt telling you how to use Sound Studio. It comes with a 30+-page PDF user's manual as well as other useful documentation on the Sound Studio Web pages, including how-to descriptions for many common tasks.

Figure 26-1: Felt Tip Software's Sound Studio is an affordable, yet powerful audio-editing utility.

Roxio's Jam

No longer available as a standalone product, Jam is part of Roxio's Toast with Jam product ($189). Also included is BIAS Peak LE VST, a collection of highly optimized waveform editing tools. Using Peak, you can enhance your audio with various special effects, such as concert reverb (the pulsing echo you experience when listening to a live concert) and noise reduction.

Note: Roxio offers licensed Toast owners an upgrade path to Toast with Jam for $100. (They call it $99.95.)

We all know that we can use iTunes or Toast to burn audio CD-Rs that play in most CD players, but those CDs don't necessarily conform to all the Red Book standards for a CD-DA master disc — one that a CD duplicator can use to mass-produce "real" CDs. This is where Jam steps up to the plate. It has all the tools required to construct masterable discs. Figure 26-2 shows Jam with a playlist ready to master.

Figure 26-2: Create Red Book-compliant CD-DA master discs with Jam.

Moving Beyond iPhoto

Don't get us wrong, we both love iPhoto and use it regularly; however, it's still young and has some serious limitations for heavy users. iPhoto gets really slow with large photo libraries and has no built-in archival tools. This wouldn't be a serious limitation if iPhoto were scriptable, but it isn't. So, removing old photos from the Library and archiving them on some other medium (like CD-R) is a tedious, manual process. Not only that, but you lose your album information.

Various freeware and shareware authors have provided *kludges* (technospeak for nonwarranted workarounds) to handle multiple libraries, and we describe some of them in Chapter 12, "Enhancing Your iPhoto Experience."

In our opinion, however, the power-user solution to this problem is iView Media or iView Media Pro, which we also cover in Chapter 12. If you're having problems with iPhoto's performance as your Library grows, take a look at iView Media or iView Media Pro. (Remember, iView Media is bundled with Toast Titanium.) It could solve all your archival problems.

If that's the only way you're outgrowing iPhoto, we would encourage you to use one of the iView Media applications as an adjunct to iPhoto. iPhoto's sharing and organizational tools are just too nice to forego.

On the other hand, if you need to consolidate your photos with other supporting files, such as Word documents, audio files, movie projects, or presentations, then you'll probably have to make iView Media Pro your command center and use iPhoto as the occasional adjunct (for example, when you want a coffee table book, a feature not available in iView Media Pro).

iPhoto's other glaring weakness is its editing tools. Although they're useful for basic photo manipulation, they're not what you want for fine control or more sophisticated touchup jobs. Apple recognized this limitation, so iPhoto now lets you specify another application to employ as your photo editor. Just choose iPhoto ⇨ Preferences and then click the Other radio button under "Double-clicking photos opens them in." Click the Set button and nominate your photo-editing application of choice.

Obviously, the top dog in the photo-editing pack is Adobe's Photoshop 7. If you're a professional graphics person, you probably have and use Photoshop on a daily basis. For the rest of us, though, Photoshop Elements 2 provides just about any Photoshop feature you might want, often in a more accessible form, and at one-sixth the cost. Although Dennis owns both Photoshop and Photoshop Elements, he does almost all his photo retouching in Elements. Photoshop only gets brought into play when he's dealing with scans of photos that were in bad shape — times when tools like the new healing brush to repair imperfections are invaluable.

If you have a G4 "Pro" unit produced in 2002 or later, it is quite likely that Apple provided you a licensed copy of the wonderful shareware graphics tool, GraphicConverter. While GraphicConverter isn't Photoshop, it has a number of very nice features. One of Dennis's favorites is that you can tell exactly where you are in the photo (very handy when trying to make a selection of a specific size), as shown in Figure 26-3, where he's cropping a 1024×768 selection out of an 1800×1200 photo.

Figure 26-3: Know where you are and your selection sizes at all times by choosing Picture ⇨ Show Position.

Tip

Thorsten Lemke, GraphicConverter's author frequently updates the program, adding new features and additional supported formats in addition to fixing the rare bug that gets reported. Check at www.lemkesoft.de to determine the current version. You'll probably want to upgrade.

Assuming that you were not blessed with a copy on your Mac, we would encourage you to consider purchasing a copy. Not only is it one of the best shareware applications available, the support Thorsten provides his customers is top-notch. For $35, it is one of the best software deals out there.

Moving Beyond iMovie

Video is where moving to a more feature-rich program can get really expensive. The two major contenders in this arena are Adobe Premiere ($599) and Apple's Final Cut Pro ($999). We're both big fans of Adobe's products, but just don't see getting Premiere without also purchasing After Effects for the special effects and compositing functions. Even with the reduced bundle price of $999 when you buy them together, you're still paying as much as you would for Final Cut Pro, probably the finest personal computer video-editing software available on any platform.

Dennis hasn't outgrown iMovie yet (especially augmented by the wonderful plug-ins available from GeeThree, Virtix, and eZedia and described in Chapter 17), but Bob uses Final Cut Pro a lot. Figure 26-4 shows a screen shot of the Final Cut Pro editing table metaphor.

Figure 26-4: Final Cut Pro simulates a professional film editor's worktable.

Some of the features Final Cut Pro brings to the table include chapter markers and support for multiple formats including OfflineRT, a way of storing over 40 minutes of video in 1GB of hard disk for offline editing while still being able to reconnect it to the original DV source.

Authoring Beyond iDVD

If your DVD-authoring goals include making movie DVDs like the big shots in Hollywood, you'll outgrow iDVD fairly quickly. Once again, outgrowing a video product can quickly get expensive. DVD Studio Pro, at $999, is the professional-quality authoring solution. There's a hidden catch to this, making it even more expensive. You'll almost certainly have to upgrade to Final Cut Pro as well, so your movies will have the multiple tracks, marker (chapter) points, and so forth not provided by iMovie. Figure 26-5 shows a typical DVD Studio Pro project in progress.

Figure 26-5: Professional DVD authoring features are at hand when using DVD Studio Pro.

DVD Studio Pro includes a few bonus items as well. You get a QuickTime Pro license, in case you didn't already upgrade. (Final Cut Pro also includes a QuickTime license.) Here are a few other programs and a music library that you might find useful:

- **A.Pack** is a wonderful audio-encoding utility, enabling you to encode many different formats into Dolby Digital, ready for use on your DVD.
- **Subtitle Editor** is a sweet tool for creating multiple subtitle tracks for your movies, depending upon which language the viewer selects.
- **Peak DV,** a full version of the audio-editing application included with Roxio Jam (described earlier in this chapter), provides every software feature you might need to edit your projects' audio.
- **Corel PHOTO-PAINT 10** lets you build layered menus or even use it to touch up your photos and slides.
- The **FreePlay Music Library** (also available to paid-up .Mac account holders via their iDisks) is a huge collection of license-free music.

Note Although not nearly so popular nor, in our opinion, quite as powerful as Adobe Photoshop 7, PHOTO-PAINT 10 provides a huge feature set and is the closest thing to a competitor Photoshop has.

Summary

In this chapter, you saw some of the software available to handle the growing pains when one or more of the iApps just doesn't provide the power you crave. You've also seen that the next step up can be very expensive.

✦ ✦ ✦

System Requirements

A program's hardware and OS requirements lists are nebulous blends of facts. In some cases, they list the minimum configuration on which you can even hope to launch the program. Other times, they'll merely describe the minimum configurations on which the publisher has tested or certified the software as usable—the reality might be lower, but if it is, you're on your own with respect to support because the publisher won't acknowledge your configuration. And, once in a while, there will be parenthetical "recommendations" for more memory or a newer OS release than the minimum. As a rule of thumb, we treat these recommendations as the *real* minimum requirement for use where we won't be drumming our fingers on the table and muttering.

What we're going to do in this appendix is list Apple's requirements for these four wonderful applications and add our own editorial comments as to what we consider reality.

What Do I Need for iTunes?

Apple's listed requirements for iTunes 3.0.1 (current at the time we're writing this) are

- ✦ Mac OS X version 10.1.4 or later
- ✦ Mac with built-in USB ports
- ✦ 400MHz G3 or better
- ✦ 256MB RAM recommended
- ✦ Supported CD-RW drive if you wish to create your own CDs

These requirements come pretty close to reflecting our view, too, with one exception. We don't think that 256MB of RAM is enough to avoid frustration, especially if you want to have anything but the Finder and iTunes running. In fact, the slower your processor (and for OS X, 400MHz G3s are pretty darned slow), the more RAM we recommend. On a 400MHz G3 PowerBook, like Dennis's, 256MB wasn't enough to keep him from muttering imprecations — upgrading to 640MB made iTunes and everything else very pleasant, but 384MB seemed okay. Also, most everything runs a little better in Mac OS X 10.2 (Jaguar) than in earlier OS releases, so we also recommend stepping up to Jaguar, though it isn't as critical if you have enough RAM.

While Apple says you need a "built-in USB port," many users have reported success using iTunes with a third-party USB card in their earlier-model Macs. So while Apple may not support it officially, you may very well be able to run iTunes on a Mac that doesn't offer a built-in USB port.

What Do I Need for iPhoto?

iPhoto 1.1.1 is the current version as we're typing this material and Apple's requirements list is short:

- Mac OS X version 10.1.2 or later
- Macintosh with built-in USB ports
- Compatible camera, printer, or other device
- 400MHz G3 or better recommended
- 256MB RAM recommended

Technically speaking, you don't need a camera, a printer, a SmartCard reader, and so on to make use of iPhoto. iPhoto will work with almost any graphics you provide it (at least those in standard, QuickTime-compatible formats), so you could get them off the Web, via e-mail, or off of CD. With the on-demand printing and the book features, you don't need a printer, either. Having said that, the suggested items are good accessories to have for iPhoto.

Again, iPhoto will work with OS X, 10.1.2, but you'll be happier with 10.2 or later. Similarly, the more RAM you can feed it the better on any system, especially those with slower processors. Dennis found 640MB on the 400MHz G3 Powerbook to be tolerable, so long as the Library didn't grow too large. 256MB on an 800MHz flat-panel iMac G4 was agonizingly slow with just about 100 photos in the Library.

Upgrading to 768MB alleviated that frustration—even with 1,500 photos in the Library, in over 30 albums, response is quite zippy.

 Again, while Apple says you need a "built-in USB port," many users have reported success using iPhoto with a third-party USB card in their earlier-model Macs. So while Apple may not support it officially, you may very well be able to run iPhoto on a Mac that doesn't offer a built-in USB port.

What Do I Need for iMovie?

While we're writing this material, iMovie 2.1.2 is the current version. Apple's listed requirements for iMovie are

- 300MHz G3 or better with built-in FireWire port(s)
- CD or DVD drive
- Mac OS 9.0.4 or later (9.1 or later recommended) with 64MB of RAM or more (128MB recommended)

    OR

    Mac OS X 10.1.2 or later with 128MB of RAM or more (256MB recommended)
- 200MB or more of available disk space
- QuickTime 4.1 or later (OS 9) or QuickTime 5 or later (OS X)

iMovie is a program where we think that Apple's giving you a list of the bare minimums. We've used iMovie in Mac OS 9 and it's workable, with enough memory and disk space, but 200MB of disk doesn't come close to being a realistic number. That's only enough room for about one minute of video and it would leave your Mac groaning and moaning with the disk full very shortly. We think that you should have as much (fast) hard disk space available as possible, but a realistic minimum would be 200MB *more* than the space needed for the video itself (at 200MB/minute). Thus, for a 10-minute movie, you should try to have at least 2.2GB of available disk space, and that doesn't include the space you'll need if you choose to export the finished product to QuickTime or VideoCD. We also think that doubling the recommended memory gives a more realistic starting point if you want decent performance. Again, we've both gotten our best iMovie experiences in OS X, version 10.2.

What Do I Need for iDVD?

iDVD is currently at version 2.1, with the following requirements list:

- Mac OS X, version 10.1.3 or later
- Any Power Macintosh G4, G4 iMac, or eMac containing a built-in Apple SuperDrive
- 256MB RAM (384 MB recommended)

We consider the OS requirement accurate, but have experienced noticeable performance improvements under Jaguar (10.2). The hardware requirement is accurate, although (as we've noted elsewhere) replacing a built-in CD or DVD drive with a Pioneer A104 unit seems to work. The recommendation for 384MB RAM is, in our opinions, a workable minimum, but (as always) the more RAM the better. This is especially true if you want to run iDVD Companion (or any other software) simultaneously.

✦ ✦ ✦

Index

Symbols & Numbers
< > (brackets) HTML tag delimiters, 203
" " (quotation marks, double) HTML attribute value delimiters, 203
/ (slash) HTML end tag prefix, 203
3ivx compression, 318, 331
3ivx Decoder compressor, 318

A
.aa files, 92
access, random versus sequential, 388
ADC (Analog-to-Digital Converter), 240, 241
Add Annotation dialog box (QuickTime), 335
Adobe software. *See also* Photoshop
    After Effects, 371, 473
    Final Cut Pro, 371, 399, 473–474
    Premiere, 473
Adobe Web site, 229
Advanced ⇨ Apply Theme to Project (iDVD), 399
Advanced ⇨ Convert Selection to MP3 (iTunes), 48
Advanced ⇨ Convert to (iTunes), 89
Advanced ⇨ Extract Audio (iMovie), 289
Advanced ⇨ Get CD Track Names (iTunes), 58
Advanced ⇨ Hide TV Safe Area (iDVD), 394
Advanced ⇨ Lock Audio Clip at Playhead (iMovie), 290
Advanced ⇨ Lock Audio Clip (iMovie), 290
Advanced ⇨ Motion (iDVD), 405
Advanced ⇨ Paste Over at Playhead (iMovie), 312
Advanced ⇨ Remove Audible Account (iTunes), 92
Advanced ⇨ Restore Clip Media (iMovie), 272
Advanced ⇨ Reverse Clip Direction (iMovie), 273
Advanced ⇨ Show TV Safe Area (iDVD), 394
Advanced ⇨ Submit CD Track Names (iTunes), 58
Advanced ⇨ Unlock Audio Clip (iMovie), 290
After Effects 5 Bible (Marshall and Saeed), 371
AIFF (Audio Interchange File Format) files
    bit rate, reencoding to higher, 90
    iMovie audio track, saving as, 442–443
    iMovie, importing into, 297–298
    introduced, 15
    iTunes Library, adding to, 46
    iTunes, ripping from audio CD using, 41, 42, 57, 61
    PCM, 430
    size, 57
ALaw 2:1 compression, 333
album, iPhoto
    book, relation to, 158–159
    creating, 127, 147–148
    exporting, 201, 206
    folder structure, 141, 213
    iDVD slideshow, importing into, 418
    information about, displaying, 127
    List, 127, 147
    naming, 147
    photo, adding to, 148
    photo, removing from, 149, 152
    Web page, 183, 185, 193, 206
album, .Mac homepage, 183, 185
Alsoft PlusOptimizer, 364
Amadeus II, 111–113
Ambrosia Software Snapz Pro X, 310
analog audio, importing into iTunes, 109
analog video, 237–239, 240, 241, 256
Analog-to-Digital Converter. *See* ADC
A104 drive, 376, 406, 433–434
A103 drive, 376, 406
A.Pack software, 475
"Apple CD-RW Drive: Cannot Write to High Speed CD-RW Discs" (Knowledge Base article), 25
Apple ID, creating, 178–179
Apple Pro Speakers, 104–105
Apple Web site
    AppleScript documentation, 100, 418
    AppleScript tutorials, 100, 418, 436
    camcorder compatibility list, 264
    camera compatibility list, 135
    CD burner compatibility list, 61
    Convert to DV Stream AppleScript, 317
    Developer Tools, 371
    DVD Authoring Made Simple seminar, 387
    EMBED HTML tag resources, 343
    feedback page, 149
    iDVD AppleScripts, 400, 418
    iDVD Companion, 436
    iMovie page, 325, 447
    iMovie plug-in resources, 275
    iPod contact database script download, 78
    MP3 player compatibility list, 75
    QuickTime resources, 346
    Seminars Online, 387
    software development kits, 88
AppleDesign Powered Speakers, 106
AppleScript
    application, attachable, 100
    Convert to DV Stream script, 317

Continued

AppleScript *(continued)*
  documentation on Apple Web site, 100, 418
  GraphicConverter dictionary, 230
  iDVD Companion example scripts, 418
  iDVD, using with, 400, 413, 418–420
  iPhoto scriptability, 180, 472
  iTunes, using with, 100–102, 109–110
  slideshow script, 377, 400, 444
  tutorials on Apple Web site, 100, 418, 436
AppleScript Central Web site, 100
AppleScript Studio, 413
AppleWorks
  jewel case templates, 8, 102, 109–110
  slideshow, creating using Presentation module, 298–299, 312, 444
ASF files, 318
aspect ratio
  computer monitor, 154
  iMovie, 330
  introduced, 15
  iPhoto expectation, 159
  photo, digital versus print, 120, 154–155
  television, 154, 330
Audible.com, 92
audio CD
  capacity, MP3 disc compared, 22
  copy protection, 23
  copyright, 23–24, 296
  Finder, burning using, 13
  iMovie background music, importing from, 295, 296–297
  iMovie soundtrack, saving to, 440–443
  Internet database, getting track information from, 58, 59
  Internet database, submitting track information to, 58
  iTunes, burning using, 13, 43, 61–64
  iTunes, playing using, 39–40
  iTunes, ripping track from using, 40, 41, 42, 57–60, 61
  Mac computer, playing on, 23
  Red Book standard, 23
  Toast 5 Titanium Jam, creating using, 109, 471
audio, iDVD, 381, 389, 413, 418
audio, iMovie
  AIFF file, saving as, 442–443
  background music, 295, 296–298, 327, 370–371
  background noise, removing, 288–289
  camcorder, importing from, 256
  CD, importing from, 295, 296–297
  CD of soundtrack, creating, 440–443
  copying/pasting, 289–290, 442
  cropping, 292

cutting, 289
deleting, 289
effects, 292–293, 327
fading, 269, 288
filtering camcorder input, 256
format support, 317
importing, 256, 297–298
intercutting, 310, 311–314
locking/unlocking, 255, 289, 290, 314, 315
moving, 290–291
narration, 293–295
overlapping clips, 314–315
pinning, 289
QuickTime, audio settings when exporting to, 332–334, 440–441
recording, 251, 294–295
soundtrack, extracting from using iTunes, 48
splitting, 291
timeline viewer, working with in, 288–292
transition effect, 269, 288
video clip, extracting from, 256, 271, 289, 314–315
volume control, 245, 288
Audio Interchange File Format files. *See* AIFF files
audio, iTunes
  analog source, importing using Audion, 109
  audiobook download, 92
  CD, ripping from, 40, 41, 42, 57–60, 61
  format support, 64, 82
  formats, converting between, 48, 49, 89–90
audio, NTSC standard, 431
audio, PAL standard, 431
audio, QuickTime, 332–334, 440–441, 459
audio, recording, 251, 294–295, 440. *See also* microphone
audio, slideshow
  iDVD soundtrack, 401, 403
  iPhoto soundtrack, 132, 185–186, 198, 231–233, 459–461
audiobook download into iTunes, 92
Audion software, 109, 369
authoring, 16
AVI (Audio-Video Interleaved) files, 319

B

Background.tif file, 425. *See also* iDVD
backup
  CD, using for, 222
  iDVD, 429
  iPhoto, 136, 140, 152
  iView Backup, using, 227
  MP3, 98
battery
  camcorder, 261, 357

camera, 119, 120
MP3 player, 107
BBEdit utility, 345
Berkeley Multimedia Research Center MPEG resources, 378
BetaMax decision, 24
BetaMax video format, 237, 238–239
BetterHTMLExport iPhoto plug-in, 204, 205–206, 209
BIAS Peak LE VST waveform editing tools, 471
bit depth, 16, 332
bit rate
  CBR, 16
  iTunes, 41, 42, 89
  reencoding to higher, 90
  VBR, 18, 41, 42
Black & White iMovie effect, 280, 281
blackstriping, 267
BMP files
  iMovie, importing into, 299
  iPhoto, importing into, 138
<body> HTML tag, 203
book, iPhoto
  album, relation to, 158–159
  aspect ratio expectation, 159
  comment, assigning to photo, 130, 166–167
  cover color, 179
  cover photo, 159, 163–164
  end page, 165
  guideline display, 129, 170
  introduction page, 164
  organizing photos for, 160, 163
  orientation of photo in, 160, 165, 171
  page, locking when layout completed, 165–166
  page numbering, 130, 166
  page, specifying number of photos per, 159, 165
  paper quality, 179
  PDF file, saving as, 170
  previewing, 170–171
  printing, 129, 158, 170, 178 179
  resolution required for, 159, 178
  size, largest possible, 166
  size, smallest possible, 166, 178
  sizing photo for, 159
  spellchecking, 167–169, 170
  text areas, 161, 164, 166–170, 170
  theme, 159, 160–163, 179
  title, assigning to photo, 166–167
  title, main, 130, 164
BOSE QuietComfort Acoustic Noise Canceling Headset, 106
Bounce In To Center iMovie effect, 284

 HTML tag, 203

< > (brackets) HTML tag delimiters, 203
bridge analog-to-digital converter. See ADC (Analog-to-Digital Converter)
budget, video production, 451
bug alerts
  iMovie, 274, 315
  iPhoto, 170, 186
burning. See CD, burning
Button ⇨ Name Selected Button (iDVD Companion), 416
button_list variable, 417

C

cabling, 240–241, 259–261
Caffeine Software
  PixelNhance, 132, 204
  TIFFany3, 204
CAM files, 136
camcorder, digital. See also camera, digital; video production
  accessory shoe, 365
  ADC converter, using as, 241
  AE (Auto-Exposure), 359
  battery, 261, 357
  cabling, 240–241, 259–261
  color cast, filtering, 359
  compatibility list, 264
  cost, 238
  digital to analog converter, using as, 256
  filter, 366–367
  FireWire connection, 238, 240–241, 259–261
  focus, 366
  headphone jack, 360
  iMovie compatibility list, 264
  iMovie connection, 259–261, 264
  iMovie, controlling from, 265–266
  iMovie import, audio, 256
  iMovie import, disk space requirement, 253
  iMovie import, FireWire requirement, 240
  iMovie import, pausing, 247
  iMovie import, scene break option, 254, 265, 266
  iMovie import, starting, 247, 265–266
  iMovie import, still clip option, 254
  iMovie import, stopping, 247
  iMovie import to clip viewer, 254
  iMovie import to shelf, 254
  iMovie, importing video from, 302–304
  iMovie playback through, 245, 302
  input, analog, 241
  LCD, 261
  lens, 366–367

Continued

camcorder, digital *(continued)*
  microphone, built-in, 360
  pass-through device, using as, 256
  positioning, 357
  reflector, lighting, 366
  special effects, 360
  stabilizing, 357, 358, 366
  S-Video connector, 256
  tripod, 357, 358, 366
  VTR (Videotape Recorder) setting, 264
  white balance, 359
  zooming, 358, 360
camera, digital. *See also* camcorder, digital;
    photography, digital; *specific cameras*
  aperture control, 123, 217, 220
  attachment readiness, 123
  backup medium, using as temporary, 140
  barrel distortion, 223–224
  battery, 119, 120
  burst mode, 123, 221
  CCD, 118
  color balance, 123
  compatibility list, 135
  cost, 221
  erasing, automatic, 123–124, 128, 136
  EXIF support, 144
  film speed, simulating, 123, 220
  filter, 221, 223–224
  focal length, 223
  iPhoto, displaying camera information in, 127
  iPhoto, ejecting camera mounted as drive by, 137
  iPhoto, erasing memory using, 123–124, 128, 136
  iPhoto, importing to, 127–128, 136–138, 148
  iPhoto support, 135, 136
  LCD, 119, 122, 220
  lens, 221, 223–224
  lens cover, sliding, 221
  manual mode, 123, 220
  megapixel, 120
  memory, 121–122, 221
  memory, erasing using iPhoto, 123–124, 128, 136
  previewing photo, 220
  resolution, 118–121
  shutter speed, 123, 217, 220, 223
  size, 220
  specifications, reading, 120
  telephoto lens, 223–224
  tripod, 123, 223
  weight, 220
  wide angle lens, 223–224
  zoom, digital, 220
  zoom, optical, 123, 217, 220

Canon EF Lens 101 Web site, 234
capping, 16
CBR (constant bit rate), 16
CCD (Charged Coupled Device), 118
CD, audio
  capacity, MP3 disc compared, 22
  copy protection, 23
  copyright, 23–24, 296
  Finder, burning using, 13
  iMovie background music, importing from, 295, 296–297
  iMovie soundtrack, creating, 440–443
  Internet database, getting track information from, 58, 59
  Internet database, submitting track information to, 58
  iTunes, burning using, 13, 43, 61–64
  iTunes, playing using, 39–40
  iTunes, ripping track from using, 40, 41, 42, 57–60
  Mac computer, playing on, 23
  Red Book standard, 23
  Toast 5 Titanium Jam, creating using, 109, 471
CD, burning
  audio CD, 13, 43, 61–64, 109, 471
  burner, 16, 25, 108, 222
  DVD, 375–376, 378–379, 380, 405–407, 410
  Finder, using, 13
  iDVD, from, 375–376, 378–379, 380, 405–407, 410
  iMovie video, for, 9, 243, 353, 356–357, 365
  iPhoto, from, 9, 206
  iTunes, from, 13, 43, 61–64, 88, 108
  MP3 CD, 43, 88
  sleep mode, avoiding when, 63
  slideshow, 444–445
  VideoCD using Toast 5 Titanium, 353, 356–357, 372, 445, 468
CD Mark pen, 8
CD Spin Doctor, 297, 369
CD Stomper, 8
CD-DA (compact disc-digital audio), 16, 61
CD-R (CD-recordable), 16, 25–26
CD-ROM
  label, physical, 8, 369
  QuickTime movie, exporting for, 306
  size, CD-DA disc compared, 61
  VideoCD format, 353
  XA format, 353
CD-RW (CD-rewritable), 16, 25
Centered Multiple iMovie effect, 284
Centered Title iMovie effect, 284
Chambers, Mark (*Digital Photography Handbook*), 221
Chaotic Software MP3 Rage, 110–111

chaptering
    iDVD, 388, 410, 454
    VideoCD, 354
Charged Coupled Device. *See* CCD
Choose File ➪ Get Clip Info (iMovie), 269
Cinepak compression, 330
Circle Closing iMovie effect, 326
Circle Opening iMovie effect, 326
clapboard, 265, 358
Clip Info dialog box (iMovie), 269
clip viewer (iMovie), 244, 250–251, 254, 273–274
codec (compressor-decompressor) software, 239
Cohen, Dennis R.
    Macworld AppleWorks 6 Bible, 444
    Macworld Microsoft Office 2001 Bible, 444
color
    bit depth, 16, 332
    camcorder color cast, filtering, 359
    camera, color balance, 123
    iMovie, adjusting in, 279, 280, 281
    iMovie considerations when producing for
        television, 301
    iMovie, specifying bit depth when exporting to
        QuickTime, 332
    iMovie text, 283
    iPhoto book cover, 179
    iPhoto color correction, 205, 227, 228
    iPhoto color printing, 157–158, 175, 224–225
    iPhoto, converting color photo to black and white
        in, 129, 157–158, 227
    iView Media ColorSync profile, 226
    NTSC color-safe palette, 301
    QuickTime movie, applying transparency to part of
        screen, 336–339
    QuickTime movie, attaching color palette to, 335
    Web page background color, 200
    Web-safe palette, 301
Colors dialog box (iPhoto), 197–198
compact disc digital audio. *See* CD DA
CompactFlash memory, 121
compression
    ALaw 2:1, 333
    animation, 330
    Cinepak, 330
    codec software, 239
    decoding, 16
    DivX, 318, 319, 331
    DVD, 376, 378
    DV-NTSC, 330
    DV-PAL, 330
    Floating Point, 333
    H.261, 330
    H.263, 330
    iDVD, 376, 378, 429–432
    IMA 4:1, 333
    iMovie options when exporting to QuickTime,
        330–334
    Indeo compressors, 319
    Integer (24-bit/32-bit), 333
    iTunes, 42
    JPEG, 121, 172, 330, 430
    Law 2:1, 333
    lossless, 17, 429
    lossy, 17, 429
    MACE codecs, 333
    Motion JPEG, 330
    MPEG, overview of, 432
    MPEG-4, 331, 368, 378, 430
    MPEG-1, 239, 371, 378, 430
    MPEG-2, 371, 378, 430
    MP3, 21, 24, 57, 371
    MP2, 371
    multiplexed track, 318
    muxed track, 318
    QDesign Music 2, 333
    Qualcomm PureVoice, 333
    QuickTime, 305, 318, 319, 330–334, 368
    Sorenson, 331
    telephony, 333
    3ivx, 318, 331
    TIFF, 194
    Video, 331
Compression Settings dialog box (iMovie), 331
compressor-decompressor software. *See* codec
    software
computer screen activity, recording, 310
constant bit rate. *See* CBR
Convert to DV Stream AppleScript, 317
Cool-Lux lighting kits, 365
copyright
    fair use, 290
    music, 7, 23–24, 296
    permission, seeking, 296
    royalty-free music sources, 296, 327, 429, 475
Corel PHOTO-PAINT, 475
Create New Project dialog box (iMovie), 262, 263
Creative Technologies MP3 players, 75
Cross Dissolve iMovie effect, 274, 276
cutaway video footage, 310
cut-in video footage, 310

D

danz Retrospect, 98
Dazzle Hollywood DV Bridge, 241, 242
decoding, 16
Description.plist file, 426–427. *See also* iDVD
DeskPict software, 188
Desktop image, setting using iPhoto, 131, 187–191
Desktop System Preferences panel (Mac OS X), 188
Developer Tools (Mac OS X), 371
DHG-FlowerPowerX iTunes plug-in, 88
Diamond Rio MP3 player, 81
digital camcorder. *See* camcorder, digital
digital camera. *See* camera, digital
digital hub concept, 4–9
Digital Photography Handbook (Chambers), 221
Digital Photography Review Web site, 234
Digital Versatile Disc. *See* DVD
Digital Video Disc. *See* DVD
Dir.data file, 213. *See also* iPhoto
Discreet Systems Media Cleaner, 316–317
Discus software, 109, 369
DivX compression, 318, 319, 331
DivX Doctor II utility, 318
DMCA (Digital Millennium Copyright Act), 7
dpi (dots per inch), 16. *See also* resolution
Dr. Bott MP3 player auto adapter, 104
drawer (Mac OS X), 379, 389
Drifting iMovie effect, 284
droolingcat.com BetterHTMLExport iPhoto plug-in, 204, 205–206, 209
DV (Digital Video) Stream
    iMovie, importing into, 323–324
    QuickTime, exporting from, 316–317, 318–323
    resolution, 319
DVD Authoring Made Simple online seminar, 387
DVD (Digital Video Disc or Digital Versatile Disc). *See also* iDVD
    AppleScripting, 377
    archival medium, as, 365
    authoring, 377
    burning, 375–376, 378–379, 380, 405–407, 410
    compression, 376, 378
    data DVD, 377, 384, 385, 402, 409–411
    described, 376–377
    DVD-ROM, 377, 384, 385, 402, 409–411
    handling, 435
    hybrid, 377
    interactivity, 375, 376
    introduced, 16
    LaserDisc compared, 375
    length, 376, 377
    MPEG-2 file on, 318
    prevalence of, 239
    protecting, 435
    quality, 239
    random access, 375, 389
    resolution, 389, 455
    Seminars Online, 387
    slideshow, using for, 377, 379, 384, 385
DVD player
    iDVD compatibility, 434
    SVCD, playing in, 353
    VideoCD, playing in, 5, 353
DVD Studio Pro, 376, 409, 433, 446, 474–475
DVD-R (DVD-recordable), 16, 435
DVDRHelp.com, 434
DVD-ROM, 377, 384, 385, 402, 409–411
DVD-RW (DVD-rewritable), 435
DVMC-DA2 ADC converter, 241
DV-NTSC compression, 330
DV-PAL compression, 330

E

Edit ⇨ Add (QuickTime), 341
Edit ⇨ Add Scaled (QuickTime), 338
Edit ⇨ Arrange Photos ⇨ by Date (iPhoto), 141
Edit ⇨ Arrange Photos ⇨ by Film Roll (iPhoto), 141
Edit ⇨ Clear
    iMovie, 271
    iPhoto, 152
    iTunes, 55
Edit ⇨ Copy
    iMovie, 289
    QuickTime, 340
Edit ⇨ Create Still Clip (iMovie), 272
Edit ⇨ Crop (iMovie), 271
Edit ⇨ Cut (iMovie), 289
Edit ⇨ Done Editing Keywords (iPhoto), 145
Edit ⇨ Edit Keywords (iPhoto), 144
Edit ⇨ Enable Tracks (iMovie), 441
Edit ⇨ Font ⇨ Show Fonts (iPhoto), 168
Edit ⇨ Paste (iMovie), 289
Edit ⇨ Select Back Button (iDVD Companion), 414
Edit ⇨ Spelling ⇨ Spelling (iPhoto), 168
Edit ⇨ Split Selected Audio Clip at Playhead (iMovie), 291
Edit ⇨ Split Video Clip at Playhead (iMovie), 270
Edit ⇨ Undo Add Transition (iMovie), 278
Edit ⇨ Undo (iMovie), 252
Edit ⇨ Undo Remove Photo From Album (iPhoto), 152
Edit ⇨ View Options (iTunes), 33, 51
EF Lens 101 Web site, 234
EL GATO software Toast Export iPhoto plug-in, 9, 206

e-mail
    encoding, 180, 181
    iMovie video, exporting for, 7, 305, 306
    iPhoto photo, sending, 8, 125, 130, 180–181
    iPod contact database, exporting to e-mail client, 78
    QuickTime movie, sending, 306
EMBED HTML tag, 343
encoding
    A.Pack, 475
    described, 16, 429
    e-mail attachment, 180, 181
    iDVD, 378, 385, 405–406, 407, 429
    iMovie, 371
    iTunes, 41–42
    MediaPipe encoder, 371
    MPEG, 371, 378, 431–432
    MP3, 41–42, 73, 90
    Toast 5 Titanium, 464
Epson
    Perfection 1250U scanner, 222
    Stylus Photo 780 printer, 172, 173
    Stylus 777 printer, 173
equalizer (iTunes), 32, 35, 36, 74–75, 83–85
EXIF (EXchangeable Image Format), 144
Expert QuickTime Settings dialog box (iMovie), 329, 440
Export File dialog box (QuickTime), 322
Export Images dialog box (iPhoto), 195, 196, 199–200, 201
Export Movie dialog box (iMovie), 303
eZedia plug-ins
    eZeMatte, 325, 370
    eZeScreen, 370

F

Fade In iMovie effect, 274, 276
Fade Out iMovie effect, 274, 276
Favorites, saving iDVD theme in, 398–399
Felt Tip Software Sound Studio, 470
File ⇨Add to Library (iTunes), 29
File ⇨Eject (iPhoto), 137
File ⇨Export
    iPhoto, 193
    QuickTime, 322
File ⇨Export Movie (iMovie), 303
File ⇨Get Info (iTunes), 50, 67
File ⇨Import
    iPhoto, 139
    QuickTime, 338
File ⇨Import ⇨Background Video (iDVD), 393
File ⇨Import File (iMovie), 298

File ⇨Import ⇨Image (iDVD), 400
File ⇨Import ⇨Video (iDVD), 390
File ⇨New Album (iPhoto), 148
File ⇨New Player (QuickTime), 442
File ⇨New Playlist (iTunes), 54
File ⇨New Project (iDVD), 388
File ⇨New Smart Playlist (iTunes), 68
File ⇨Print (iPhoto), 172
File ⇨Save As PDF (iPhoto), 170
File ⇨Save Project As (iDVD), 388
File Transfer Protocol client. *See* FTP client
FileSharing Web page, 347. *See also* .Mac homepage
filter, lens, 221, 223–224, 366–367
Final Cut Pro, 371, 399, 473–474
Finder
    audio CD, burning using, 13
    iDVD-encoded file display, 385
    iPhoto Library Finder list view, 211–212
FireLite drive, 108
FireWire
    Apple computer, standard on, 238
    cabling, 240–241, 259–261
    camcorder connection, 238, 240–241, 259–261
    CD burner, 108
    connector, 260, 261
    drive dismounting problem when connecting device, 260
    IEEE standard, 238, 241
    iMovie requirement, 240
    introduced, 16
    iPod, 77
    logo, 260
    MP3 player, 76, 80
    storage, external, 107–108
    USB compared, 25
    video technology, effect on, 238
Floating Point compression, 333
FlowerPowerX iTunes plug-in, 88
Flying Letters iMovie effect, 284, 287
Flying Words iMovie effect, 284
Formac Studio DV/TV ADC converter, 241
fps (frames per second), 17
frame, movie, 243
frame rate
    NTSC standard, 243, 431
    PAL standard, 243, 431
    QuickTime, 319, 332, 455
frame size
    iDVD, 431
    NTSC standard, 431
    PAL standard, 431
FreePlay Music Library, 327, 429, 475

Freeway software, 202
Fresh Music Web site, 296
FTP (File Transfer Protocol) client, 204

G

Gallery feature (iMovie), 6
GeeThree Slick Transitions and Effects for iMovie plug-ins, 279, 325, 370, 446
generational signal loss, 257
GIF files
    iMovie, importing into, 299
    iPhoto, importing into, 138
GlideCam camcorder stabilizers, 366
GNU VCDToolsX, 372
Go ⇨ Go To Menu (iDVD Companion), 416
Go ⇨ Go To Slideshow (iDVD Companion), 416
Go ⇨ iDisk (iTools), 183
Grado SR-60 headphones, 107
GraphicConverter
    AppleScript dictionary, 230
    cost, 229
    editing tool, using as, 132, 204, 229, 231, 472–473
    file format, converting using, 229, 300
    iPhoto, dragging file from, 139, 229–230, 231
    Mac computer, bundled with, 229, 472
    position display, 472–473
    upgrading, 473
    Web site, 473
Griffin Technologies iMic, 294

H

HairerSoft Amadeus II, 111–113
Harman-Kardon speakers, 105–106
headphones, 26, 106–107
HomePage Web page builder, 6
"How Video Formatting Works" (Howstuffworks article), 432
HTML (Hypertext Markup Language)
    attributes, 202, 342
    `<body>` tag, 203
    `<br>` tag, 203
    case convention, 342
    commenting, 203
    editors, 202, 345
    `EMBED` tag, 343
    `<head>` tag, 203
    `<hr>` tag, 203
    `<html>` tag, 203
    `<img>` tag, 203
    metainformation, 203
    movie publishing on Web, for, 342–346
    photo page, 202–203, 205–206
    table, creating, 203
    tags, 202, 203, 342
    `<td>` tag, 203
    `<tr>` tag, 203
H.261 compression, 330
H.263 compression, 330
hub, digital, 4–9
HyperCard, 205, 324
Hypertext Markup Language. *See* HTML

I

iApps, 11
iCal, 78
iCard, 185
iDisk, 6, 183, 327, 347–349
ID3 tag, 72, 112
ID3v2 made easy Web site, 72
iDVD
    Apple logo option, 385
    AppleScripting, 400, 413, 418–420
    audio, 381, 389, 413, 418
    background image, 382, 393, 413, 418, 425–426
    background music, 382, 403, 413, 418, 429
    background sound, working with in iDVD Companion, 413, 418
    background theme, 382, 393, 424–426
    background video, 393
    Background.tif file, 425
    backup, 429
    bit rate, 431
    burning DVD, 375–376, 378–379, 380, 405–407, 410
    button consistency, 396
    button, folder, 390
    button frame style, specifying, 397
    button, image, 390, 391, 398
    button, motion, 380, 405, 454
    button, movie clip, 390–391, 397–398
    button, naming, 418
    button, navigation, 390
    button, positioning, 396–397, 419–420
    button, positioning using iDVD Companion, 412–413, 414, 417, 418
    button size, 397, 419
    button, slideshow, 400
    button, text, 390, 391, 397
    button theme, 382–383, 390, 397
    button thumbnail folder, 423
    button types, 390–391
    buttons, maximum number of, 391
    chaptering support, 388, 410, 454
    compression, 376, 378, 429–432
    content, centralizing, 429

described, 4, 13–14
Description.plist file, 426–427
disk space information, displaying, 383
disk space requirement, 364
DVD player, 434
DVD status, monitoring, 383–384, 405, 412
DVD-R brand, choosing, 435
DVD-R drive, using with external, 376
DVD-ROM, working with, 385, 402, 409–411
DVD-RW reliability concerns, 435
encoding, 378, 385, 405–406, 407, 429
files related to, 421–424, 429, 431
Finder display of iDVD-encoded files, 385
folder, adding, 391, 411
Folder button, 379
folder icon, changing, 391
frame size, 431
grid, working with, 397
iDVD Companion, using with, 413–418, 436
iMovie video, exporting for, 307, 446
import operations, 390, 400, 402–403, 413, 418
iPhoto, importing image from, 413, 418
iTunes, importing audio from, 413, 418
limitations, 454, 474
memory, 363–364, 407, 480
menu background, 382, 383, 390, 393
menu structure, planning, 391
menu title, changing, 382, 390, 391, 394–396, 414–415
motion button, 380, 405, 454
motion menu, 389, 454
movie, importing, 390
MovieMaestro, using with, 429
MPEG folder, 423
music, 382, 403, 413, 418, 429
navigation arrowhead slideshow option, 402
navigation button, 390
NTSC standard, conforming to, 385, 430–431
package, 422, 424–425
PAL standard, conforming to, 385, 430–431
Photoshop, using with, 436
planning, 387, 391, 428–429, 455–456
Position pop-up menu, 396
preferences, setting, 384–386
presentation, importance of, 428–429
previewing, 380, 404–405
project, adding movie to, 390
project, adding slideshow to, 400
project content, viewing, 422
project, creating, 388
project files, 421–424, 429
project folder, 421–422

project information, displaying, 383–384, 412
Project pane, 379
project, planning, 428–429
project preferences, setting, 385
project, saving, 388
project status, displaying, 383–384
project, theme application to, 399
ProjectData file, 423–424
QuickTime, using with, 393, 435
RAM (Random Access Memory), adding for, 407
rendering, deleting rendered files after closing project, 385
resolution, 389, 455
Resources folder, 425
running man icon, 389
slideshow, adding image to, 400
slideshow, adding to DVD-ROM, 385, 402
slideshow, adding to project, 400
slideshow, creating using AppleScript, 377, 400, 444
slideshow, creating using Slideshow Editor, 400–402
slideshow, importing from iPhoto album, 418
slideshow, importing image to, 400–401
slideshow, maximum size, 384, 403
slideshow menu button, 400
slideshow, navigation arrowhead display option, 402
Slideshow pane, 384
slideshow, reordering, 402–403
slideshow, scaling image, 402, 403
slideshow, slide duration specification, 402
slideshow soundtrack, 401, 403
slideshow, thumbnail display option, 402
slideshow, working with in iDVD Companion, 415–417
Slideshows folder, 410
SonicFire Pro, using with, 429
SuperDrive requirement, 376, 433–434
system requirements, 364, 376, 407, 433–434, 480
television standards, conforming to, 394, 430–431
text, working with, 382, 390, 394–396, 397
theme, application package storage of, 424–425
theme, applying from iDVD Companion, 417
theme, applying to project, 399
theme, background, 382, 393, 424–426
theme, button, 379, 382–383, 390, 397
theme, creating, 421, 426
theme, customizing, 381–383, 392–398, 424–426
Theme drawer, 381–384, 389, 410
theme from version 1, using, 426–428

Continued

iDVD *(continued)*
    theme, motion, 381, 389
    theme, picture with audio, 381, 389
    theme, picture-only, 381, 389
    theme, saving in Favorites, 398–399
    theme, title, 382
    themes, built-in, 388–389
    Thumbnails folder, 423
    tutorial, 13
    version covered in this book, 11
    watermark option, 385
iDVD Companion, 413–418, 436
iDVD ⇨Preferences, 384
IEEE (Institute of Electrical and Electronics Engineers) FireWire standard, 238, 241
i.Link, 16, 238, 241. *See also* FireWire
IMA 4:1 compression, 333
image editing using external program, 204–205, 227, 228–230
<img> HTML tag, 203
iMic, 294
iMovie
    ADC input, 240, 241
    Adobe After Effects, using with, 371
    AIFF file, importing, 297–298
    Apple Web page, 325, 447
    aspect ratio, 330
    audio, background music, 295, 296–298, 327, 370–371
    audio, background noise removal from, 288–289
    Audio button, 248
    audio clips, overlapping, 314–315
    audio, copying/pasting, 289–290, 442
    audio, cropping, 292
    audio, cutting, 289
    audio, deleting, 289
    audio effects, 292–293, 327
    audio, extracting from video clip, 256, 271, 289, 314–315
    audio, fading, 269, 288
    audio file, importing, 297–298
    audio format support, 317
    audio input from camcorder, filtering, 256
    audio, intercutting, 310, 311–314
    audio, locking/unlocking, 255, 289, 290, 314, 315
    audio, moving, 290–291
    audio narration, 293–295
    Audio panel, 292, 293
    audio, pinning, 289
    audio, recording, 251, 294–295
    audio, saving as AIFF file, 442–443

audio settings when exporting to QuickTime, 332–334, 440–441
audio soundtrack CD, creating, 440–443
audio, splitting, 291
audio transition effect, 269, 288
audio, volume control, 245, 288
audio, working with in timeline viewer, 288–292
Better Image option, 254–255, 302
Black & White effect, 280, 281
BMP file, importing, 299
Bounce In To Center effect, 284
brightness adjustment, 279, 281
bug alerts, 274, 315
cabling, 240–241, 259–261
camcorder compatibility list, 264
camcorder, controlling from, 265–266
camcorder, exporting video to, 302–304
Camera mode, 245, 246
CD, burning, 9, 243, 353, 356–357, 365
Centered Multiple effect, 284
Centered Title effect, 284
Circle Closing effect, 326
Circle Opening effect, 326
clip, adding to project, 351–352
clip, adding to timeline, 267
clip, audio extraction from, 256, 271, 289, 314–315
clip, copying/pasting, 271–272
clip, cropping, 271–272
clip, cutting, 270
clip, deleting, 252, 267
clip, deleting portion of, 271
clip display on timeline, 252, 255
clip duration, displaying, 250, 255
clip duration, slide, 254, 299
clip duration, still clip, 254, 288
clip, framing, 325, 370
Clip Info dialog box, 269
clip information, displaying, 250, 255, 273, 287
clip management, 369
clip miniature, 288
clip, moving from shelf, 273
clip, naming, 267–268, 352–353
clip, overlaying QuickTime movie, 370
clip, overlaying still, 325, 370
clip, positioning playhead in, 269–270
clip, restoring to previous edit state, 272–273
clip, reusing in another project, 351–353
clip, reversing, 273
clip, selecting, 247, 267, 312–313
clip, selecting portion of, 270
clip size, maximum, 265
clip, speed change effects, 251, 287

Index ✦ I

clip, splitting, 270–271, 312–313
clip, starting at scene break, 254, 265, 266
clip, still, 254, 272, 288, 299, 311–312
clip, trimming, 271
clip viewer, 244, 250–251, 254, 273–274
Clip Viewing mode, 245, 246–247
Clips button, 247–248
color adjustment, 279, 280, 281
color bit depth, specifying when exporting to QuickTime, 332
color considerations when producing movie for television, 301
color, text, 283
compression options when exporting to QuickTime, 330–334
Compression Settings dialog box, 331
computer screen activity, recording, 310
contrast adjustment, 279, 281
Create New Project dialog box, 262, 263
crop markers, 270, 292
Cross Dissolve effect, 274, 276
described, 4, 12
disk, dedicating to, 253, 263, 453
disk, defragmenting for, 364, 365
disk space needed, 240, 253, 305, 364–365, 453
Dock, accessing from, 261
Drifting effect, 284
Duration sliders, 283
Edit mode, 267
Effects button, 248
Effects panel, 278–279
encoder software, using with, 371
encoding, 371
Enhance button, 327
Expert QuickTime Settings dialog box, 329, 440
Export Movie dialog box, 303
Export pop-up menu, 306, 329, 442
exporting audio track to AIFF file, 442–443
exporting scene to MPEG file, 354
exporting video for iDVD, 307, 446
exporting video to camcorder, 302–304
exporting video to QuickTime, 304–306, 329–334, 440–441
exporting video to VideoCD, 353–357
Fade In effect, 274, 276
Fade Out effect, 274, 276
fast forward, 245
fast-motion effect, 251, 287
file format support, 317–318
file type recognition, 300
Final Cut Pro, using with, 371
FireWire, 240

Flying Letters effect, 284, 287
Flying Words effect, 284
format of movie, displaying, 250
Formats pop-up menu, 305–306, 329
frame, 243
Free Space status bar, 252, 253, 305
freezing motion, 272
full screen display, 247
Gallery feature, 6
GIF file, importing, 299
Home button, 247
HomePage, integrating with, 6
iDisk, publishing to, 347–349
iDVD, exporting video for, 307, 446
iDVD limitation, planning for, 454
Import File dialog box, 298
import from audio CD, 295, 296–297
import from camcorder, audio, 256
import from camcorder, disk space requirement, 253
import from camcorder, FireWire requirement, 240
import from camcorder, pausing, 247
import from camcorder, scene break option, 254, 265, 266
import from camcorder, starting, 247, 265–266
import from camcorder, still clip option, 254
import from camcorder, stopping, 247
import from camcorder to clip viewer, 254
import from camcorder to shelf, 254
Imported Clips Go To buttons, 254
importing analog video, 240
importing audio file, 297–298
importing DV Stream file, 323–324
importing image file, 298–301
importing video file, 264
intercutting, 256, 310–316
iPhoto, integrating with, 300–301
iTunes, integrating with, 297
iView Media, using with, 369
jewel case cover, using still image on, 454
JPEG file, importing, 299
launching, 261–264
.Mac homepage, publishing to, 347–349
Mac OS version compatibility, 12
memory, adding for, 363–364
memory requirement, 240, 363–364, 479
Mirror effect, 326, 328
Monitor area, 244, 245–247, 264
motion smoothness/sharpness setting, 254–255, 302
MovieMaestro, using with, 295, 370

Continued

iMovie *(continued)*
    MPEG file, exporting, 354
    MP3 file, importing, 297–298
    music, background, 295, 296–298, 327, 370–371
    Music Video effect, 284–285
    narration, 293–295
    N-Square effect, 326, 328
    Overlap effect, 276
    paste over operations, 256
    Pause slider, 283
    PDF file, importing, 299
    Photoshop file, importing, 299
    PICT file, importing, 299
    playback, starting, 245
    playback through camcorder screen, 245, 302
    playback through television, 256, 300, 302
    playhead, 247, 269–270
    plug-ins, 275, 279, 282, 324–329, 370
    preferences, setting, 253–257
    previewing footage, 245, 254, 276–277, 282, 302
    project, adding clip to, 351–352
    project, creating, 262–263
    project, naming, 262
    project, remembering, 244
    Push effect, 276, 454
    Quality slider, 332
    QuickTime, exporting to, 304–306, 329–334, 440–441
    Radial effect, 326, 454–455
    RAM (Random Access Memory), adding for, 363–364
    Record Music button, 297
    Record Voice button, 293, 295
    recording audio, 251, 294–295
    rendering, 277, 303, 307
    resolution, 264, 300, 305, 306
    Reveal Browser button, 262
    rewinding, 245
    Rolling Centered Credits effect, 285
    Rolling Credits effect, 285
    Scale Down effect, 276
    scene break, starting new clip at, 254, 265, 266
    scene, exporting as MPEG file, 354
    scenes, cutting between, 274
    scoring, 295, 296–298, 327, 370–371
    screen area, 245
    Scroll with Pause effect, 285
    Scrolling Block effect, 285, 286
    scrubber bar, 247, 268–270
    Sepia Tone effect, 280, 281
    Sharpen effect, 280

sharpness/motion smoothness setting, 254–255, 302
shelf, 244, 247–250, 254, 273
Size slider, 284
slideshow, 298–299, 445
slow-motion effect, 251, 287
Soft Focus effect, 280, 281
sound effects, 292–293, 327
Sound Settings dialog box, 440–441
soundtrack CD, creating, 440–443
soundtrack, extracting using iTunes, 48
Speed slider, 283
starting, 261–264
Status area, 245, 252–253
stock footage, 351
Stripe Subeffect, 285, 286
system requirements, 240, 253, 363–365, 479
television, playing movie on, 256, 300, 302
text, working with, 248, 249, 281–287, 288, 305
TIFF file, importing, 299
timecode, working with, 255, 266–267, 279
timeline, adding clip to, 252, 267
timeline, clip display on, 252, 255
timeline, thumbnail display in, 255
timeline, timecode display option, 255
timeline viewer, 244, 251–252, 255, 287–292
timeline zoom pop-up menu, 252
Title clip, 286–287
title, creating template for, 324
title, creating using plug-in, 327
title, creating using timeline viewer, 288
title, creating using Titles panel, 282–287
Titles button, 248
Toast 5 Titanium, using with, 9, 109, 243, 368–369
Toggle Switch, 245, 264
track, 243
transition, applying, 248, 249, 274–275, 276–277, 288
transition, audio, 269, 288
transition between intercuts, 311
transition, choosing, 454–455
transition, combining with visual effect, 280–281
transition, cutting versus, 274–275
transition, deleting, 278
transition direction, specifying, 276
transition, modifying, 278
transition, one-clip, 277
transition plug-ins, 275, 279, 326–327, 370
transition, previewing, 276–277
transition, rendering, 277, 303
transition speed, specifying, 276
transition, still clip, 254, 272, 311–312
transition, two-clip, 277

Trash, 252–253, 267
tutorial, 12
Typewriter effect, 285
Undo operations, 252, 272
VCR, recording to, 256, 302–304
version covered in this book, 11
video format support, 317–318
Video Track, turning off, 441–442
VideoCD, exporting to, 353–357
visual effect, adding from Effects panel, 278–279
visual effect, adding from shelf view, 248, 250
visual effect, adding from timeline viewer, 251, 288
visual effect, adding using plug-in, 279, 326, 370
visual effect, Effect In/Effect Out points, 279, 281
visual effect, transitional, 280–281
visual effects, built-in, 279–280
voice over, 293
volume control, 245, 288
Warp In effect, 327
Warp Out effect, 327
Wash In effect, 327
Wash Out effect, 327
Water Ripple effect, 280
Web, publishing movie to, 6, 306, 341–349
iMovie Plug-in Pack, 275, 279, 282, 326–327
Import File dialog box (iMovie), 298
Import Files dialog box (iPhoto), 139
Import from Camera dialog box (iView Media), 226
Indeo compressors, 319
index.html file, 183, 201
Info dialog box (QuickTime), 323
Institute of Electrical and Electronics Engineers FireWire standard. *See* IEEE FireWire standard
Intellisys Project Desktop, 449
intercutting video footage, 256, 310–316
interlacing, 431
International Press and Telecommunications Council tag. *See* IPTC tag
Internet radio, listening to using iTunes
    buffer setting, 44
    format support, 64
    newsgroups related to, 68
    station, adding to Library, 66–67
    station, finding, 66–68
    station information display, 32
    station list display, 33
    stations, prepackaged, 64–66
    Tuner, 32
interpolation, pixel, 118, 222
iPhoto
    Add button, 127
    album, adding photo to, 148

album, book relation to, 158–159
album, creating, 127, 147–148
album, exporting, 201, 206
album folders, 141, 213
album, importing into iDVD slideshow, 418
album information, displaying, 127
Album List, 126, 127, 147
album, naming, 147
album, removing photo from, 149, 152
album, Web page, 183, 185, 193, 206
AppleScripting, 180, 472
application, dragging photo from external, 139, 140
application, dragging photo to external, 194, 205
backup, 136, 140, 152
black and white, converting color photo to, 129, 157–158
BMP file, importing, 138
book, album relation to, 158–159
book, aspect ratio expectation, 159
book, commenting, 130, 166–167
book, cover color, 179
book, cover photo, 159, 163–164
book, end page, 165
book, guideline display, 129, 170
book, introduction page, 164
Book mode, 129–130
book, organizing photos for, 160, 163
book, orientation of photo in, 160, 165, 171
book page, locking when layout completed, 165–166
book, page numbering, 130, 166
book page, specifying number of photos per, 159, 165
book, paper quality, 179
book, previewing, 170–171
book, printing, 129, 158, 170, 178–179
book, resolution required for, 159, 178
book, saving as PDF file, 170
book size, largest possible, 166
book size, smallest possible, 166, 178
book, sizing photo for, 159
book, spellchecking, 167–169, 170
book, text areas, 161, 164, 166–170, 170
book theme, 159, 160–163, 179
book, title assignment to photo in, 166–167
book title, main, 130, 164
border, adding to image, 131, 155
brightness, changing, 129, 156
bug alerts, 170, 186
camera, importing from, 127–128, 136–138, 148
camera information, displaying, 127
camera memory, erasing, 123–124, 128, 136

Continued

iPhoto *(continued)*
    camera mounted as drive, ejecting, 137
    camera support, 135, 136
    CD, burning, 9, 206
    clip art gallery, using as, 138
    Collections pop-up menu, 189
    Colors dialog box, 197–198
    comment, assigning to photo, 130, 145–146, 166–167, 213
    comments, searching, 149, 151–152
    Constrain pop-up menu, 129, 155
    contact sheet, printing, 125, 173
    contrast, 129, 156–157
    cropping photo, 129, 154–155
    Data folder, 141, 213
    date information of photo/roll, changing, 143
    date, organizing photos by, 140–141, 142
    day-of-month folder, 212
    described, 4, 14–15
    Desktop image, setting from, 131, 187–191
    Dir.data file, 213
    disk space used in photo storage, 139–140
    Dock, accessing from, 125
    drop-shadow tool, 131
    editing tool, specifying external in Preferences, 132
    editing tools overview, 124, 128–129
    e-mailing photo, 8, 125, 130, 180–181
    Export button, 131, 194
    Export Images dialog box, 195, 196, 199–200, 201
    export operations, 131, 194–198, 201, 205–206
    features overview, 123–131
    File Export tab, 194
    file, importing, 138–139
    file, opening, 132
    file size, 222
    Film Roll, organizing photos by, 140–141, 142, 143–144
    FlashPIX file, importing, 138
    folder structure, 141, 206, 211–213
    font options, 168
    format support, 136, 138, 194
    GIF file, importing, 138
    GraphicConverter, dragging file to, 139
    greeting card, printing, 174
    grid, aligning objects to, 131
    HomePage button, 131
    iDisk, integrating with, 6, 183
    iDVD, importing image into, 413, 418
    iMovie, integrating with, 300–301
    Import Files dialog box, 139
    import operations, 127–128, 135–139
    Info display, 126, 127
    Information button, 127
    iPhoto Librarian software, using with, 230
    iPhoto Library Manager software, using with, 230
    iTools homepage, creating, 181–185
    iView Media, using with, 139, 226–228, 472
    JPEG file, exporting, 181, 194
    JPEG file, importing, 138
    keyword, assigning to photo, 128, 144–145, 213
    keyword display, 145
    keyword, removing from photo, 145
    keyword searching, 132, 148–149, 150, 213
    Kodak, ordering print from, 130, 172, 175–177
    Kodak PhotoCD, importing from, 137
    Last Import album, 126
    letterboxing, 155, 195, 197
    Library, accessing, 126
    Library, adding photo to, 139–140, 148
    Library as database, 148, 211
    Library, central store concept, 211
    Library, Date presentation, 140–141, 142, 212
    Library, exporting from, 131
    Library file structure, avoiding changing, 212
    Library, Film Roll presentation, 140–141, 142, 143–144
    Library, Finder list view, 211–212
    Library folder structure, 141, 211–213
    Library, removing photo from, 149, 152–153
    Library, searching, 132, 148–149
    Library, size considerations, 139–140, 143, 213
    Library storage structure, 211
    Library.cache file, 213
    Library.data file, 213
    limitations, 457–459, 471–472
    .Mac homepage, publishing to, 131, 181–185
    MacPaint file, importing, 138
    Mail Photo dialog box, 180
    memory card mounted as drive, ejecting, 137
    memory card reader, importing from, 136
    Mode buttons, 127
    modes, 125
    MovieMaestro, using with, 231–233
    naming album, 147
    naming photo, 143–144, 212
    New Album dialog box, 127, 147
    Order Book button, 130, 178
    order of photos, changing, 131, 160, 163
    Order Prints button, 130
    Order Prints dialog box, 176
    Organize mode, 124
    orientation of photo, 127, 132, 160, 165, 171
    Originals folder, 141, 213
    Page Design pop-up list, 130

Index ✦ I 495

Page Setup dialog box, 175
pane resizing, 147
PDF file, importing, 138
PDF file, saving book as, 170
Photoshop, using with, 472
PICT file, importing, 138
Play button, 127
plug-ins, 9, 193, 204, 205–209
PlugIns folder, 206
PNG file, exporting, 195
PNG file, importing, 138
preferences, setting, 131–133
Preview button, 130, 170
print, ordering from Kodak, 130, 172, 175–177
print preview, 175
Printer pop-up menu, 173
printer, specifying, 173
printer, using inkjet, 171–172, 225
printing, black-and-white, 157–158
printing book, 129, 158, 170, 178–179
printing, color, 157–158, 175, 224–225
printing contact sheet, 125, 173
printing, cropping photo for, 155
printing draft copy, 172
printing 4×6 print on 4×6 paper, 175
printing, full page, 173–174
printing greeting card, 174
printing in Share mode, 130, 172
printing, page setup, 175
printing, paper considerations, 121, 171–172, 225
printing, sizing photo for, 173–175
printing, wide-format, 225
PSD file, exporting, 181, 194
PSD file, importing, 138
Publish HomePage dialog box, 182
red-eye reduction, 129, 157
rotating photo, 127, 132, 154
scanning photo for, 136, 221–222
scrapbook, using as, 138
screen saver, setting from, 131, 188–191
searching, 132, 148–149, 150–151, 213
SGI file, importing, 138
Share mode, 130–131, 172, 180, 194
Show Package Contents feature, 206
sizing photo, 155, 159, 173–175, 181, 195
Slide Show Settings dialog box, 186–187
slideshow automatic advance timing, disabling, 187
slideshow, burning to VideoCD, 445
slideshow, controlling manually, 458
slideshow, duration of slide, 132, 458
slideshow, ending, 187
slideshow, exporting, 195–198
slideshow limitations, 457–459
slideshow, looping, 132
slideshow, manual control, 187
slideshow, music, 132, 185, 186, 198, 231–233
slideshow order, 186
slideshow, pausing, 187, 458
slideshow, photo size considerations, 187
slideshow, playing, 127, 186–187
slideshow, soundtrack, 132, 185–186, 198, 231–233, 459–461
slideshow, title screen, 195
slideshow, transition effect, 186, 187
speech interface, 169, 170
speed of performance, 213
system requirements, 478–479
Targa file, importing, 138
Theme pop-up list, 129
thumbnail, comment display, 205
thumbnail creation, automatic, 139
thumbnail, dragging to external application, 205
thumbnail file name, 212
thumbnail, Import mode display, 127
thumbnail lock icon, 165
thumbnail row/column preference, setting, 199
thumbnail, sizing, 127, 201
thumbnail storage in day-of-month folder, 212
thumbnail storage in Thumbnails folder, 201
thumbnail storage in Thumbs folder, 141, 212
thumbnail, title display beneath, 201, 205
thumbnail, Web page display of, 183, 184, 203, 206
thumbnails, aligning, 131
Thumbnails folder, 201
thumbnails per page preference, setting, 200
thumbnails, Web page, 183, 199–200, 201
Thumbs folder, 141, 212
TIFF file, exporting, 181, 194
TIFF file, importing, 138
Toast 5 Titanium, using with, 226
toolbar, customizing, 153
USB card, using with third-party, 479
version covered in this book, 11
Viewing pane, 126, 160–161
Web Page tab, 199
Web, publishing to, 6, 124–125, 131, 181–185, 199–204
Zoom buttons, 154, 170
iPhoto Librarian software, 230
iPhoto Library Manager software, 230
iPhoto Mailer Patcher software, 180
iPhoto ⇨Preferences, 131
iPhoto to OmniGraffle Album Export plug-in, 206
iPod, 21, 26, 76–80, 98, 104

iPod2iTunes software, 76
IPTC (International Press and Telecommunications Council) tag, 226
iRock
    530 MP3 player, 107
    300W MP3 player auto adapter, 104
iTools, 6, 181–185
iTunes. *See also* MP3 files
    accessories, 103–108
    AIFF file, ripping from audio CD, 41, 42, 57, 61
    Amadeus II, using with, 111–113
    analog source, importing using Audion, 109
    AppleScripting, 100–102, 109–110
    audio format support, 64, 82
    audio formats, converting between, 48, 49, 89–90
    audiobook download, 92
    Back button, 34
    backup, 98
    bit rate, 41, 42, 89
    Browse/Burn button, 35, 52
    Burn CD button, 62
    CD burner compatibility, 25, 61
    CD, burning, 13, 43, 61–64, 88, 108
    CD, playing, 39–40
    Change button, 43, 97
    channels options, 42
    Close button, 31
    compression, 42
    Configuration pop-up menu, 41, 42
    crossfade effect, 40–41, 109
    described, 4, 13
    Detail List, 33, 50, 52
    Dock, accessing from, 27
    Effects display, 40–41
    Eject CD button, 35
    encoding, 41–42
    equalizer, 32, 35, 36, 74–75, 83–85
    fader, 84
    filtering frequency below 10Hz, 42
    Forward button, 34
    gap between tracks, changing, 40, 43, 62, 109
    headphones, 26, 106–107
    Help files, 37–38
    iDisk, integrating with, 6
    iDVD, importing audio into, 413, 418
    iMovie, integrating with, 297
    iMovie soundtrack, extracting, 48
    import operations, 40, 41–43, 57–60, 109, 469
    Info text area, 36
    Internet connection, 28, 29, 40, 58, 96
    Internet database, exchanging track information with, 58, 59

iPod, using with, 79–80, 104
launching, 27
Library, 45
Library, accessing, 136
Library, adding file to, 28–30, 46–48, 58
Library, adding radio station to, 66–67
Library, archive, 97
Library as database, 46
Library, browsing, 39, 52–53
Library, displaying, 32
Library, iPod synchronization with, 79–80
Library, organizing, 44, 98
Library, relocating, 96–97
Library, removing file from, 48–49, 79
Library, searching, 49–52
license agreement, 27–28
limitations, 469
memory requirement, 477
Minimize button, 31
mono mode options, 42, 89
MP3 Encoder dialog box, 41, 42
MP3 file, ripping from audio CD, 40, 57–60
MP3 player, interfacing with, 75–82, 79–80, 104
MP3 Rage, using with, 110–111
Multiple Song Information dialog box, 51
Music Folder options, 43–44, 45, 97
On CD Insert pop-up menu, 39
playback options, presetting, 74–75
playhead, 32
playlist, 32, 53–54
playlist, adding entry to, 55–56
playlist, constructing using AppleScript, 100–102
playlist, creating, 35, 47, 54
playlist, deleting, 55
playlist, deleting entry from, 56
playlist, iPod synchronization with, 79–80
playlist, naming, 35, 54–55
playlist, opening in new window, 55
playlist order, changing, 56
Playlist, Smart, 32–33, 68–70, 90–92, 95–96
Play/Pause button, 34
plug-ins, 82, 87–88, 113–114
preferences, setting, 38–44
Quality pop-up menu, 41–42
QuickTime-readable movie file, extracting soundtrack from, 48
radio buffer setting, 44
radio format support, 64
radio station, adding to Library, 66–67
radio station information display, 32
radio station list display, 33
radio stations, prepackaged, 64–66

Index ✦ I–L

Radio Tuner, 32
Repeat button, 35
Resize box, 36
rewinding, 34
Search button, 35
Setup Assistant, 28
Shuffle feature, 34, 35, 44, 57
sleep mode, avoiding when burning CD, 63
Smart Playlist feature, 32–33, 68–70, 90–92, 95–96
Song Information dialog box, 67, 71–75
Song/Detail List, 33, 50, 52
Sound Enhancer feature, 41
SoundJam, relation to, 22
Source List, 32–33, 76–77, 82
speakers, 26, 104–106
Status Display, 32
stereo mode options, 42–43, 89
storage, external, 107–108
system requirements, 24–26, 96–97, 477–478
Toast 5 Titanium, using with, 98, 108–109
USB card, using with third-party, 478
version covered in this book, 11
View Options dialog box, 33–34
Visual Effects feature, 35–36, 85–88, 99, 113–114
Visualizer feature, 85–88, 99, 113–114
volume slider, 34, 41
WAV file, ripping from audio CD, 41, 42
Web, publishing to, 6–7
Zoom button, 31
iTunes ⇨ Preferences, 38
iView Media
    catalog, 226, 227
    ColorSync profile embedding, 226
    iMovie, using with, 369
    Import from Camera dialog box, 226
    introduced, 98
    iPhoto, using with, 139, 226–228, 472
    IPTC tag support, 226
    organizational tool, as, 139, 226
    Pro version, 226, 472
    slideshow, 227
    Toast 5 Titanium, included with, 109
iVoice microphone, 294

J

Jam version of Toast 5 Titanium, 108–109, 471
JBL Sonnet Power Satellite Speakers, 105
J-cutting video footage, 313–315
jewel case
    AppleWorks templates, 8, 102, 109–110
    iMovie image, using on, 454
JPEG (Joint Photographic Experts Group) files
    compression, 121, 172, 330, 430

iMovie, importing into, 299
introduced, 17
iPhoto, exporting from, 181, 194
iPhoto, importing into, 138
jump cut video footage, 312

K

Kenyon Labs camcorder stabilizers, 366
Killersound music clips, 327
Kodak DX-3500 camera, 120, 177
Kodak Ofoto Web site, 177
Kodak, ordering print from, 130, 172, 175–177

L

Labtec Verse-704 microphone, 294
LaserDiscs, 375
Law 2:1 compression, 333
LCD (Liquid Crystal Display)
    camcorder, digital, 261
    camera, digital, 119, 122, 220
L-cutting video footage, 313, 315–316
Lemke Software GraphicConverter. *See*
    GraphicConverter
lens
    cover, sliding, 221
    filter, 221, 223–224, 366–367
    telephoto, 223–224
    wide angle, 223–224
    zoom, camcorder, 358, 360
    zoom, camera, 123, 217, 220
letterboxing, 155, 195, 197
LeVitus, Bob
    Apple HomePage, 6
    Macworld Microsoft Office 2001 Bible, 444
Library, iPhoto
    accessing, 126
    central store concept, 211
    database, as, 148, 211
    Date presentation, 140–141, 142, 212
    exporting from, 131
    file structure, avoiding changing, 212
    Film Roll presentation, 140–141, 142, 143–144
    Finder list view, 211–212
    folder structure, 141, 211–213
    photo, adding to, 139–140, 148
    photo, removing from, 149, 152–153
    searching, 132, 148–149
    size considerations, 139–140, 143, 213
    storage structure, 211
Library, iTunes
    accessing, 136
    archive, 97

Continued

Library, iTunes *(continued)*
    browsing, 39, 52–53
    database, as, 46
    displaying, 32
    file, adding to, 28–30, 46–48, 58
    file, removing from, 48–49, 79
    introduced, 45
    iPod, synchronizing with, 79–80
    organizing, 44, 98
    radio station, adding to, 66–67
    relocating, 96–97
    searching, 49–52
Library.cache file, 213. *See also* iPhoto
Library.data file, 213. *See also* iPhoto
lighting, 217, 359–360, 365–366
Liquid Crystal Display. *See* LCD
Live365.com, 66
Lowel lighting kits, 365

M

.Mac homepage
    album, creating, 183, 185
    cost, 182
    disk space, 341
    FileSharing Web page, 347
    HomePage button, 184
    iDisk, 6, 183, 327, 347–349
    iMovie, publishing to using, 347–349
    iPhoto, publishing to using, 131, 181–185
    music source, as, 429
    Public folder, 347, 348
    Publish button, 185
    slideshow, 184
    themes, 348
Mac OS X For Dummies, 182
Macally Peripherals iVoice microphone, 294
MACE (Macintosh Audio Compression and Expansion)
    codecs, 333
MacPaint file, importing into iPhoto, 138
MacScripter Web site, 100
Macworld AppleWorks 6 Bible (Schwartz and
    Cohen), 444
Macworld Mac OS X Bible, 182
Macworld Microsoft Office 2001 Bible (LeVitus and
    Cohen), 444
Mail Photo dialog box (iPhoto), 180
Marshall, J. J. (*After Effects 5 Bible*), 371
McClelland, Deke (*Photoshop 7 Bible*), 229
Media Cleaner, 316–317
Media Tracks Web site, 296
MediaPipe, 371
megapixel camera, 120

memory
    camera, digital, 121–122, 123–124, 128, 136, 221
    CompactFlash, 121
    iDVD, 363–364, 407, 480
    iMovie, 240, 363–364, 479
    iPhoto, 478
    iTunes, 477
    MP3 player, 80, 107
    Secure Digital, 122
    Smart Media, 121
    Sony Memory Stick, 121, 122
microphone, 294–295, 357, 360–362
Microsoft Word X, using as HTML editor, 202
Mirror iMovie effect, 326, 328
.moov files, 318
Motion JPEG compression, 330
.mov files, 317, 318, 342
Movie ⇨ Double Size (QuickTime), 319
movie frame, 243
Movie ⇨ Get Movie Properties (QuickTime), 338
MovieMaestro, 231–233, 295, 370, 429
MPEG compression
    MPEG-4, 331, 368, 378, 430
    MPEG-1, 239, 371, 378, 430
    MPEG-2, 371, 378, 430
    overview, 430–431
MPEG Home Page, 378
MPEG (Motion Picture Experts Group) files
    DV Stream, converting to using QuickTime,
        317, 322
    DVD disc, on, 318
    encoding, 371, 378, 431–432
    frame, bidirectional, 432
    frame, predicted, 432
    iDVD MPEG folder, 423
    iMovie scene, exporting as, 354
    intraframe, 432
    introduced, 17
    multiplexing, 318, 322
    QuickTime support, 318–319, 371
    SVCD, on, 318, 372
    VideoCD, writing to, 372
    Web resources, 378
.mpg files. *See* MPEG (Motion Picture Experts Group)
    files
MP3 Encoder dialog box (iTunes), 41, 42
MP3 files. *See also* iTunes; MP3 player
    audio CD format compared, 22
    backup, 98
    bit rate, reencoding to higher, 90
    compression, 21, 24, 57, 371

Index ✦ M–P

converting to/from other audio format, 48, 49, 89–90
encoding, 41–42, 73, 90
ID3 tag, 72, 112
iMovie, importing into, 297–298
introduced, 17
iTunes, burning MP3 CD using, 43, 88
iTunes Library, adding to, 28–30, 46
iTunes, ripping from audio CD using, 40, 57–60
QuickTime-readable movie file, extracting from, 48
size, 57
utilities for working with, 108–113
MP3 player. *See also* MP3 files
    auto adapter, 104
    battery, 107
    compatibility list, 75
    cost, 81
    Creative Technologies, 75
    Dr. Bott auto adapter, 104
    FireWire, 76, 80
    introduced, 26
    iPod, 21, 26, 76–80, 98, 104
    iRock 530, 107
    iRock 300W auto adapter, 104
    iTunes, interfacing with, 75–82, 79–80, 104
    memory, 80, 107
    playlist support, 82
    plug-ins, 82
    Rio, 80–82, 107
    RioVolt, 22
    SonicBlue, 81
    USB, 80, 107
    wearable, 21
    WMA support, 81
MP3 Rage, 110–111
MP2 files, 371
Multiple Song Information dialog box (iTunes), 51
multiplexing, 318, 322
music
    concatenating files using QuickTime Player Pro, 459–460
    copyright, 23–24, 296
    iDVD, 382, 403, 413, 418, 429
    iMovie, 295, 296–298, 327, 370–371
    iPhoto slideshow, 132, 185–186, 198, 231–233, 459–461
    iTunes Music Folder, 43–44, 45, 97
    Killersound music clips, 327
    .Mac homepage resources, 429
    royalty-free sources, 296, 327, 429, 475
Music Video iMovie effect, 284–285

muxed track, 318
MyPublisher.com, 179

N

netcast, 64
New Album dialog box (iPhoto), 127, 147
Norton Utilities, 364
NRG Research lighting kits, 365
N-Square iMovie effect, 326, 328
NTSC (National Television System Committee) standard
    audio, 431
    color palette, 301
    DV-NTSC compression, 330
    frame rate, 243, 431
    frame size, 431
    iDVD output conformance, 385, 430–431
    introduced, 17

O

OfflineRT format, 474
Ofoto Web site, 177
OmniGraffle, 206, 428, 449–450
OmniOutliner, 428, 448
OpenGL Screen Saver, 131
Order Prints dialog box (iPhoto), 176
Other World Computing and FireWire Direct, 108
Overlap iMovie effect, 276

P

Page Setup dialog box (iPhoto), 175
PAL (phase alternating line) television standard. *See also* television
    audio, 431
    DV-PAL compression, 330
    frame rate, 243, 431
    frame size, 431
    iDVD output conformance, 385, 430–431
    introduced, 17
Panic Audion software, 109, 369
pass-through device, using camcorder as, 256
PCM (Pulse Coded Modulation), 430, 431
PDF (Portable Document Format)
    iMovie, importing into, 299
    iPhoto book, saving as, 170
    iPhoto, importing into, 138
Peak DV software, 475
Perfection 1250U scanner, 222
phase alternating line television standard. *See* PAL television standard
Photoflex reflectors, 366

photography, digital. *See also* camcorder, digital; camera, digital; iPhoto; resolution
    angle of view, 216
    aperture control, 123, 217, 220
    Apple innovation in, 117
    aspect ratio, 15, 120, 154–155, 159
    background, 215, 217
    barrel distortion, 223–224
    black and white, converting color photo to, 129, 157–158, 227
    brightness, changing, 129, 156
    close-up photo, 216
    color balance, 123
    color, correcting, 205, 227, 228
    composition, 214–216
    contrast, 129, 156–157, 228
    cropping, 129, 154–155
    distortion, adding, 205
    editing using external program, 204–205, 227, 228–230
    filter, 221, 223–224, 366–367
    flash, 129, 157, 217
    freeze photo, 217
    jaggiiness, 120, 121
    lighting, 217, 359–360, 365–366
    lighting, adjusting via software edit, 228
    perspective, 216
    pixel interpolation, 118, 222
    pixelization, 119, 120
    printing, black-and-white, 157–158
    printing, color, 157–158, 175, 224–225
    printing, full-bleed, 162
    printing, paper considerations, 121, 171–172, 225
    printing, paper size specification, 175
    printing, resolution required, 118–121, 155, 159, 172
    printing, sizing image for, 120
    printing using inkjet printer, 171–172, 225
    printing, wide-format, 225
    red-eye reduction, 129, 157, 228
    resolution required for printing, 118–121, 155, 159, 172
    scratch, removing, 205
    shadow, removing, 205
    sharpening image, 205, 227
    shutter speed, 123, 217, 220, 223
    stop-action, 217
    subject, accentuating, 217
    subject, positioning, 214–215
    telephoto, 223–224
    thirds, composing image based on, 214
    tripod, 123, 223
    Web sites, recommended, 234
    wide angle, 223–224

PHOTO-PAINT, 475
Photoshop
    cost, 436, 472
    Elements version, 204, 224, 228–229, 472
    iDVD, using with, 436
    iPhoto, using with, 472
    VideoCD menu, creating using, 354
Photoshop 7 Bible (McClelland), 229
PICT files
    iMovie, importing into, 299
    iPhoto, importing into, 138
    QuickTime, importing into, 338
Picture ⇨Show Position (GraphicConverter), 473
PIMA Web site, 144
Pioneer drives
    A104, 376, 406, 433–434
    A103, 376, 406
pixel interpolation, 118, 222
pixelization, 119, 120
PixelNhance, 132, 204
pixels per inch. *See* ppi
PlainTalk microphone, 294
planning
    iDVD, 387, 391, 428–429, 455–456
    slideshow, 443–444
    video production, 357–358, 447–453
playlist, iTunes
    AppleScripting, 100–102
    creating, 35, 47, 54
    deleting, 55
    described, 32, 53–54
    entry, adding to, 55–56
    entry, deleting from, 56
    iPod, synchronizing with, 79–80
    naming, 35, 54–55
    opening in new window, 55
    order of music in, changing, 56
    Smart Playlist feature, 32–33, 68–70, 90–92, 95–96
plug-ins. *See also specific plug-ins*
    iMovie, 275, 279, 282, 324–329, 370
    iPhoto, 9, 193, 204, 205–209
    iTunes, 82, 87–88, 113–114
    MP3 player, 82
    removing, 209
PlusOptimizer, 364
PNG (Portable Network Graphics) files
    iPhoto, exporting from, 195
    iPhoto, importing into, 138
Podestal software, 76
PodMaster 1000, 76
Portable Document Format. *See* PDF

PowerPoint presentation
    QuickTime, working with in, 319–321
    slideshow, creating using, 444
ppi (pixels per inch), 16. *See also* resolution
printing from iPhoto
    black and white, 157–158
    book, 129, 158, 170, 178–179
    color, 157–158, 175, 224–225
    contact sheet, 125, 173
    cropping photo for, 155
    draft copy, 172
    4×6 print on 4×6 paper, 175
    full page, 173–174
    greeting card, 174
    page setup, 175
    paper considerations, 121, 171–172, 225
    preview, 175
    Printer pop-up menu, 173
    printer, specifying, 173
    printer, using inkjet, 171–172, 225
    Share mode, in, 130, 172
    sizing photo for, 173–175
    wide-format, 225
printing from iView, 227
printing from Photoshop, 229
Project ⇨ Add Folder (iDVD), 391
Project ⇨ Add Slideshow (iDVD), 400
Project Desktop, 449
Project ⇨ Project Info (iDVD), 412
Project ⇨ Save (VCD Builder), 468
Project ⇨ Show Theme Panel (iDVD), 389
ProjectData file, 423–424. *See also* iDVD
Properties dialog box (QuickTime), 334
PSD files
    iPhoto, exporting from, 181, 194
    iPhoto, importing into, 138
Publish HomePage dialog box (iPhoto), 182
Pulse Coded Modulation. *See* PCM
Push iMovie effect, 276, 454

Q

QDesign Music 2 compression, 333
.qt files, 318
Qualcomm PureVoice compression, 333
QuickTake 100 digital camera, 117
QuickTime
    Add Annotation dialog box, 335
    APIs (application programming interfaces), 305
    Apple Web site resources, 346
    audio file, editing using, 459
    audio settings when exporting from iMovie, 332–334, 440–441
    Auto Play option, 335
    AVI support, 319
    captioning, 340
    CD-ROM, exporting for, 306
    color palette, attaching to movie, 335
    color transparency, applying to part of screen, 336–339
    compression, 305, 318, 319, 330–334, 368
    computer screen activity, recording, 310
    container files, 318
    crop markers, 338
    disk space considerations, 305
    DivX Doctor II compressor problem, 318
    document format, 305
    DV Stream, exporting, 316–317, 318–323
    editing video using Pro version, 242, 334–341
    e-mailing movie, 306
    embedding Web-published movie, 343–346
    Export File dialog box, 322
    exporting DV Stream, 316–317, 318–323
    fast start movie, 347
    frame rate, 319, 332, 455
    Graphics Mode effect, 336
    iDVD, using with, 393, 435
    iMovie clip, overlaying QuickTime movie, 370
    iMovie video, exporting into, 304–306, 329–334, 440–441
    importing non-DV Stream video, 319–322
    importing PICT file, 338
    Info dialog box, 323
    information about movie, displaying, 335–336
    masking part of screen, 336–339
    Movie Controller window, 335
    MPEG file, converting to DV Stream, 317
    MPEG support, 318–319, 371
    PICT file, importing, 338
    Player window type, specifying, 335
    playhead position display, 336
    PowerPoint presentation, working with, 319–321
    previewing portion of movie, 336
    Pro version, 242, 317, 334–341, 367–368, 435
    Properties dialog box, 334
    registering, 367
    resolution considerations in import/export operation, 319–320
    scoring using MovieMaestro, 231–233
    scrubber bar, hiding, 335
    Size effect, 336
    sizing movie, 336
    slideshow, using for, 193, 195–198, 322, 462
    special effects, 242, 336

Continued

QuickTime *(continued)*
    speech balloon, adding to movie, 336–339
    streaming, 346–347
    Text Tracks feature, 339–341
    text, working with, 335, 339–341
    track information, displaying, 336
    track support, 243
    VCD format, converting QuickTime movie to, 109
    video formats supported, 318
    VideoCD, converting to using Toast 5 Titanium, 109, 462–465
    Web, publishing movie to, 196, 306, 341–349
QuickTime Streaming Server, 346
QuietComfort Acoustic Noise Canceling Headset, 106
" " (quotation marks, double) HTML attribute value delimiters, 203

R
Radial iMovie effect, 326, 454–455
radio, listening to using iTunes
    buffer setting, 44
    format support, 64
    newsgroups related to, 68
    station, adding to Library, 66–67
    station, finding, 66–68
    station information display, 32
    station list display, 33
    stations, prepackaged, 64–66
    Tuner, 32
Rage software WebDesign, 202
Real Networks format, 318
Recording Industry Association of America. *See* RIAA
Red Book audio CD standard, 23
reflector, lighting, 366
resolution
    camera, 118–121
    cropping, considerations when, 155
    dpi value, 16
    DV Stream, 319
    DVD, 389, 455
    iDVD, 389, 455
    iMovie, 264, 300, 305, 306
    inkjet printer, appropriate to, 172
    interpolated, 222
    introduced, 17
    iPhoto book, 159, 178
    jagginess caused by insufficient, 120, 121
    low-resolution warning, 159, 177, 178
    optical, 222
    ppi value, 16
    QuickTime import/export operations, considerations in, 319–320

reference table, 177
scanner, 221–222
screen saver photo, 191
VideoCD, 354
Retrospect software, 98
RIAA (Recording Industry Association of America), 6
Rio MP3 player, 80–82, 107
RioVolt MP3 player, 22
ripping, 17
RM files, 318
Rolling Centered Credits iMovie effect, 285
Rolling Credits iMovie effect, 285
Roxio Toast 5 Titanium. *See* Toast 5 Titanium

S
Saeed, Zed *(After Effects 5 Bible)*, 371
Save As Web Page dialog box (Word X), 202
Save Video CD Stream As dialog box (Toast 5 Titanium), 464
Scale Down iMovie effect, 276
scanners, 136, 221–222
scheduling video production, 452–453
Schwartz, Steve *(Macworld AppleWorks 6 Bible)*, 444
screen activity, recording, 310
screen saver
    iPhoto, setting from, 131, 188–191
    slideshow, 444
scripting video, 450–451
Scroll with Pause iMovie effect, 285
Scrolling Block iMovie effect, 285, 286
Scruffy Software iPhoto Librarian, 230
SCSI (small computer systems interface), 17, 25
Secure Digital memory, 122
Seminars Online, 387
Sepia Tone iMovie effect, 280, 281
Sharing Preferences (Mac OS X), 204
Sharpen iMovie effect, 280
shelf (iMovie), 244, 247–250, 254, 273
ShortCourses Web site, 123
signal loss, generational, 257
/ (slash) HTML end tag prefix, 203
Slick Transitions and Effects for iMovie plug-ins, 279, 325, 370, 446
slide scanning, 222
Slide Show Settings dialog box (iPhoto), 186–187
slideshow, AppleWorks Presentation module, 298–299, 312, 444
slideshow, burning to CD, 444–445
slideshow, burning to VideoCD, 445, 462–468
slideshow, Final Cut Pro, 399
slideshow, iDVD
    AppleScript, creating using, 377, 400, 444
    duration of slide, specifying, 402

DVD-ROM, adding to, 385, 402
iDVD Companion, working with in, 415–417
image, adding, 400–401
image, importing, 400–401
image, scaling, 402, 403
iPhoto album, importing from, 418
menu slideshow button, 400
navigation arrowhead display option, 402
project, adding to, 400
reordering, 402–403
size, maximum, 384, 403
Slideshow Editor, creating using, 400–402
Slideshow pane, 384
soundtrack, 401, 403
thumbnail display option, 402
slideshow, iMovie, 298–299, 445
slideshow, iPhoto
  advance timing, disabling automatic, 187
  controlling manually, 458
  duration of slide, 132, 458
  ending, 187
  exporting, 195–198
  iTunes visual effect, adding, 113–114
  limitations, 457–459
  looping, 132
  .Mac homepage, on, 184
  manual control, 187
  menu, creating on VideoCD version, 465
  message-oriented, 444
  MovieMaestro, scoring using, 231–233
  music, 132, 185–186, 198, 231–233, 459–461
  order of slides shown, 186
  pausing, 187, 458
  photo size considerations, 187
  planning, 443–444
  playing, 127, 186–187
  PowerPoint, 444
  production tools overview, 443–446
  screen saver, 444
  soundtrack, 132, 185–186, 198, 231–233, 459–461
  title screen, 195
  transition effect, 186, 187
  VideoCD, burning to, 445, 462–468
  viewing-oriented, 444–445
  Zoomify iTunes plug-in, 113–114
slideshow, iView, 227
slideshow .Mac homepage, 184
slideshow, QuickTime, 193, 195–198, 322, 462
slideshow special effects using GeeThree Slick Transitions and Effects, 446
small computer systems interface. *See* SCSI

Smart Media memory, 121
Smart Playlist (iTunes), 32–33, 68–70, 90–92, 95–96
SmartDisk FireLite drive, 108
SmartMedia memory card, 107
SmartSound
  MovieMaestro software, 231–233, 295, 370, 429
  SonicFire Pro, 429
Snapz Pro X, 310
Soft Focus iMovie effect, 280, 281
softpress Freeway, 202
Song Information dialog box (iTunes), 67, 71–75
Sonic Desktop, 296, 429
SonicBlue Rio MP3 player, 81
SonicFire Pro, 429
Sonigistix Monsoon iM700s speakers, 105, 106
Sony
  DVMC-DA2 ADC converter, 241
  i.Link FireWire implementation, 241
  MDR-IF630RK headphones, 106
  Memory Stick, 121, 122
  VCR technology, 238
Sorenson compression, 331
Sound Dogs sound effects, 327
Sound Settings dialog box (iMovie), 440–441
Sound Studio, 470
SoundJam MP3 player, 22
SourceForge MediaPipe, 371
speakers, 26, 104–106
speech balloon, adding to QuickTime movie, 336–339
Speech ⇨Start Speaking (iPhoto), 169
Steadicam camcorder stabilizers, 358
SteadyTracker camcorder stabilizers, 366
stock video footage, 351
storyboarding, 451
streaming QuickTime movie, 346–347
Stripe SubiMovie effect, 285, 286
Subtitle Editor software, 475
SuperDrive, 17, 365, 376, 433–434
SVCD (Super Video Compact Disc)
  described, 17
  DVD player compatibility, 353
  GNU VCDToolsX, creating using, 372
  MPEG file on, 318, 372
  prevalence of, 239
  Toast 5 Titanium, creating using, 369, 372
  United States, availability in, 239
  VCD Builder, creating using, 372
System Preferences (Mac OS X)
  network identity, 204
  sharing, 204
  speech, 169

system requirements
    iDVD, 364, 376, 407, 433–434, 480
    iMovie, 240, 253, 363–365, 479
    iPhoto, 478–479
    iTunes, 24–26, 96–97, 477–478

T

Targa file, importing into iPhoto, 138
`<td>` HTML tag, 203
TDK CD Mark pen, 8
television. *See also* NTSC (National Television System Committee) standard; PAL (phase alternating line) television standard
    aspect ratio, 154, 330
    iDVD conformance to standards, 394, 430–431
    iMovie color considerations when producing for, 301
    iMovie playback through, 256, 300, 302
    interlacing, 431
    VideoCD display area, fitting to, 355
TextEdit utility, 345
theme, iDVD
    application package storage of, 424–425
    background, 382, 393, 424–426
    built-in themes, 388–389
    button, 382–383, 390, 397
    creating, 421, 426
    customizing, 381–383, 392–398, 424–426
    drawer, 381–384, 389, 410
    iDVD Companion, applying from, 417
    motion, 381, 389
    picture with audio, 381, 389
    picture-only, 381, 389
    project, applying to, 399
    saving in Favorites, 398–399
    title, 382
    version 1, using theme from, 426–428
theme, .Mac homepage, 348
3ivx compression, 318, 331
3ivx Decoder compressor, 318
TIFF files
    compression, 194
    iMovie, importing into, 299
    iPhoto, exporting from, 181, 194
    iPhoto, importing into, 138
TIFFany3 software, 204
Tiffen lens filters, 367
timecode, working with in iMovie, 255, 266–267, 279
timeline viewer (iMovie), 244, 251–252, 255, 287–292
Toast Export iPhoto plug-in, 9, 206
Toast 5 Titanium
    audio CD, burning using Jam, 109, 471

audio editing features, 109
cost, 108, 369, 471
encoding, 464
files, temporary, 468
iMovie, using with, 9, 109, 243, 368–369
iPhoto, using with, 226
iTunes, using with, 98, 108–109
Jam version, 108–109, 471
MPEG file, writing to VideoCD, 372
Other button, 462–463
QuickTime, converting to VideoCD using, 109, 462–465
QuickTime plug-in, 9, 109
Save Video CD Stream As dialog box, 464
SVCD, creating, 369, 372
Toast Video CD Options dialog box, 463
utilities included with, 109, 369
VCD operations, 5
VideoCD, burning, 353, 356–357, 372, 445, 468
Toast Video CD Options dialog box (Toast 5 Titanium), 463
`<tr>` HTML tag, 203
transition, iMovie
    applying, 248, 249, 274–275, 276–277, 288
    audio, 269, 288
    choosing, 454–455
    cutting versus, 274–275
    deleting, 278
    direction, specifying, 276
    intercuts, between, 311
    modifying, 278
    one-clip, 277
    plug-in, using, 275, 279, 326–327, 370
    previewing, 276–277
    rendering, 277, 303
    speed, specifying, 276
    still clip, 254, 272, 311–312
    two-clip, 277
    visual effect, combining with, 280–281
tripod, 123, 223, 357, 358
Typewriter iMovie effect, 285

U

Univenture Unikeeps software, 98
USB (universal serial bus)
    card, using third-party, 478, 479
    CD burner, 108
    FireWire compared, 25
    introduced, 17
    microphone, 294
    MP3 player, 80, 107
    speakers, 105

V

VBR (variable bit rate), 18, 41, 42
VCD. *See* VideoCD
VCD Builder, 353, 354–357, 372, 445, 466
VCDHelp.com, 378
VCR (Video Cassette Recorder)
    iMovie, recording from, 256, 302–304
    overview, 237–239
Verse-704 microphone, 294
Version Tracker, 76, 78
VHS (Video Home System), 237–239
video analog-to-digital converter, 240, 241
Video compression, 331
video, editing using Adobe After Effects, 371, 473
video, editing using DVD Studio Pro, 376, 409, 433, 446, 474–475
video, editing using Final Cut Pro, 371, 399, 473–474
video, editing using iMovie
    cutaway, 310
    cut-in, 310
    intercutting, 256, 310–316
    J-cutting, 313–315
    jump cutting, 312
    L-cutting, 313, 315–316
    scoring, 295, 296–298, 327, 370–371
    stock footage, 351
    timecode, working with, 255, 266–267, 279
    title, creating template for, 324
    title, creating using plug-in, 327
    title, creating using timeline viewer, 288
    title, creating using Titles panel, 282–287
    transition, applying, 248, 249, 274–275, 276–277, 288
    transition, audio, 269, 288
    transition between intercuts, 311
    transition, combining with visual effect, 280–281
    transition, cutting versus, 274–275
    transition, deleting, 278
    transition direction, specifying, 276
    transition, modifying, 278
    transition, one-clip, 277
    transition plug-ins, 275, 279, 326–327, 370
    transition, previewing, 276–277
    transition, rendering, 277, 303
    transition speed, specifying, 276
    transition, still clip, 254, 272, 311–312
    transition, two-clip, 277
    visual effect, adding from Effects panel, 278–279
    visual effect, adding from shelf view, 248, 250
    visual effect, adding from timeline viewer, 251, 288
    visual effect, adding using plug-in, 279, 326, 370
    visual effect, built-in, 279–280
    visual effect, Effect In/Effect Out points, 279, 281
    visual effect, transitional, 280–281
video, editing using QuickTime Pro, 242, 334–341
video format overview, 237–239. *See also specific formats*
Video Home System format. *See* VHS
video production. *See also* camcorder, digital
    audio, recording, 251, 294–295, 440
    blackstriping, 267
    budget, 451
    charting, 448–450
    clapboard, 265, 358
    documentation, 448
    electricity supply, 453
    footage, shooting extra, 265, 453
    footage, stock, 351, 453
    lighting, 359–360, 365–366
    microphone, 294–295, 357, 360–362
    planning, 357–358, 447–453
    PMS (Project Management System), using, 449
    project, outlining, 448–450
    redundancy, 440
    schedule, 452–453
    script, 450–451
    shot list, 451
    storyboarding, 451
    takes, shooting multiple, 357
    timecode, working with, 266–267
    tripod, 357, 358
    zooming, 358
VideoCD
    burning using Toast 5 Titanium, 353, 356–357, 372, 445, 468
    chapters, organizing into, 354
    compatibility considerations, 5
    DVD player, playing in, 5, 353
    format written in, 353
    iMovie video, creating from, 353–357
    introduced, 18
    length, 353
    menu-driven, 353–356, 372, 465
    MPEG file, writing to, 372
    naming, 356
    QuickTime, converting to using Toast 5 Titanium, 109, 462–465
    resolution, 354
    sequence, 354–355, 372
    slideshow, burning to, 445, 462–468
    television viewing area, fitting to, 355
    VCD Builder, creating using, 353, 354–357, 372, 445, 466

View Options dialog box (iTunes), 33–34
Virtix iMovie plug-ins, 325, 370
Visual Effects feature (iTunes), 35–36, 85–88, 99, 113–114
Visualizer feature (iTunes), 85–88, 99, 113–114

W

Warp In iMovie effect, 327
Warp Out iMovie effect, 327
Wash In iMovie effect, 327
Wash Out iMovie effect, 327
Water Ripple iMovie effect, 280
WAV files
    introduced, 18
    iTunes Library, adding to, 46
    iTunes, ripping from audio CD using, 41, 42, 57
    PCM, 430
    size, 57
Web, publishing QuickTime movie to, 196, 306, 341–349
Web publishing to .Mac homepage
    album, creating, 183, 185
    cost, 182
    disk space, 341
    FileSharing Web page, 347
    HomePage button, 184
    iDisk, 6, 183, 327, 347–349
    iMovie, using, 347–349
    iPhoto, using, 131, 181–185
    music source, as, 429
    Public folder, 347, 348
    Publish button, 185
    slideshow, 184
    theme, 348
Web publishing using HomePage Web page builder, 6
Web publishing using iDisk, 6, 183
Web publishing using iPhoto
    album, creating, 183, 185
    background color, 200
    background image, 200
    browser considerations, 183
    dialup connection, designing for, 200
    filenames generated, 201
    folders generated, 201
    FTP client, file upload using, 204
    HTML generated, 202–203
    iCard announcement, sending, 185
    Images folder, 201
    index.html file, 183, 201
    IP (Internet Protocol) address settings, 204
    Mac OS X System Preferences, 204
    .Mac/iTools homepage, 131, 181–185
    "Made with Apple iTools" logo, 182
    overview, 6, 124–125
    page title, 199
    password protecting site, 185
    photo caption, 182, 185
    photo size, specifying maximum, 201
    previewing, 201
    QuickTime movie, 196
    scrolling, minimizing, 200
    thumbnail file size considerations, 200
    thumbnail frame style, specifying, 183
    thumbnail size, specifying maximum, 201
    Thumbnails folder, 201
    thumbnails per row/column, specifying, 199–200
    uploading, 183, 204
Web publishing using iTools, 6, 181–185
Web publishing using iTunes, 6–7
Web publishing using iView, 227
Web Sharing feature (Mac OS X), 204
WebDesign software, 202
Web-safe color palette, 301
Window ⇨ Customize Toolbar (iPhoto), 153
WMA (Windows Media Audio) files, 81, 82
WMV files, 318
Word X, using as HTML editor, 202

X

XPod, 76

Z

zoom lens
    camcorder, digital, 358, 360
    camera, digital, 123, 217, 220
    digital zoom versus, 220
Zoomify iTunes plug-in, 113–114

Bonus Chapter

Macworld® Mac® OS X Bible

The following content is an excerpt from the Macworld *Mac OS X Bible*, published by Wiley.

Written by expert authors Dennis Cohen, Lon Poole, and Steve Burnett, the *Macworld Mac OS X Bible* has more than 900 pages of authoritative advice on Apple's revolutionary new operating system.

We hope you enjoy this free bonus chapter.

The *Mac OS X Bible* is available wherever books are sold or at www.wiley.com/compbooks/.

Harnessing Standard Services

In This Chapter

Mail

TextEdit

Grab

Stickies

Summarize

Disk Copy

Other services

I n the old days, users frequently desired to use the spell checker they were accustomed to in one application when using another application, and they were frustrated that they could not do so. Each application provided its own solution for such common tasks as spell checking, sending e-mail, or annotating the open document. Apple attempted to address this need with the technology known as OpenDoc, but it was never really accepted in the marketplace. Apple dropped the technology in 1996-7. Mac OS X provides a more general facility to achieve the goal, and that is the Services submenu of the application menu.

The Services menu allows applications to offer their capabilities to other applications. These *client* applications don't have to know what is being offered ahead of time. The Services menu works quite simply. You select some data in an application, such as the string of text, "We're coming to visit on Sunday." Then you choose a command from an application listed in the Services submenu, such as the Mail command's Mail Text option and the command is executed on the selection, invoking Mail to create a new mail message with "We're coming to visit on Sunday," already placed in the message body. Similarly, in TextEdit you could invoke the Grab service's Selection option to allow you to select a part of the screen to be inserted as an image in your TextEdit document.

Using Services often seems as though you're copying data from one application and pasting it into another, the latter of which modifies the data and copies the result back into the original application. For example, select a folder in the Finder and choose a StuffIt Service that compresses the folder and puts it into an archive. This archive is placed back in the same place as the original folder. However, this action can be one-way as well. For example, select a name in a word processing document and then select a Service that looks up the name by using an LDAP (Lightweight Directory Access Protocol) server, starts your e-mail application, and opens a new message window with the found e-mail address after the To: line.

Several applications included with Mac OS X provide services. This chapter describes the services provided by Mail, TextEdit, Grab, Stickies, Summarize, and Disk Copy.

Mail

The Mail application supplied by Mac OS X provides services to a variety of other applications. A typical use of the Mail service is as follows:

1. **Select a name or e-mail address in the body of your TextEdit document (or other word processor — it has to support Services).**
2. **Select Services ⇨ Mail ⇨ Mail To from the application menu.** The Mac OS X Mail application opens with a new e-mail message addressed as you specified, shown in Figure BC-1.

Figure BC-1: Use the Mail ⇨ Mail To service (top) to create a mail message addressed to the selected name (bottom).

Be aware that the Mail ⇨ Mail To service does not check for a valid e-mail address or name. It merely takes the text you provide and places that text into the To: field of a new mail message. Note that the Mail ⇨ Mail To service breaks the text into strings of less than 256 characters if it is too long.

Similarly, select a block of text, an image, or other material and choose Services ⇨ Mail ⇨ Mail Text from the application menu to create a new e-mail message in Mail with the selected text or image in the body of the e-mail message, as shown in Figure BC-2. Yes, we know that Mail Text is misleading — it specifically mentioned Text, but the Mail ⇨ Mail Text service does allow you to include multi-media in your e-mail.

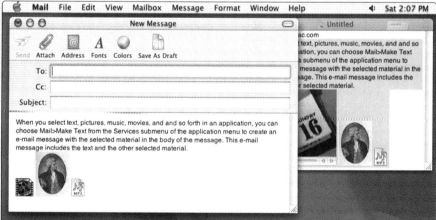

Figure BC-2: Use the Mail ⇨ Mail Text service (top) to make an e-mail message from selected text and other media (bottom).

TextEdit

The TextEdit application, the versatile text editor and word processor included with Mac OS X, provides two services:

✦ Open a file by name

✦ Create a new file containing selected text, pictures, and so forth

To open a file by name, as shown in Figure BC-3, you select text that specifies a full path to the file and then choose Services ⇨ TextEdit ⇨ Open File from the application menu. If the file cannot be found, an error message appears stating that the file could not be opened; however, the error message doesn't tell you why the attempt failed.

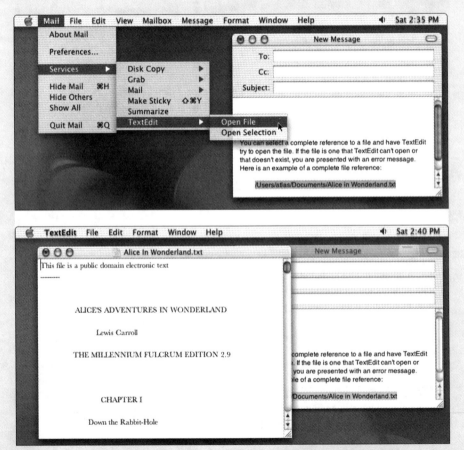

Figure BC-3: Open a file in TextEdit by selecting a full path and using the Services menu.

You can also select a block of text and other media. Then choose Services ⇨ TextEdit ⇨ Open Selection from the application menu to create a new TextEdit document using the selected media, as shown in Figure BC-4. Because both text and other media are combined, you can edit the result. This service is a useful adjunct to clipping files.

Figure BC-4: Use the Services menu (top) to create a TextEdit document from selected text and other media (bottom).

Grab

Apple has long made it easy to take "snapshots" of your Mac screen and parts thereof. Mac OS X provides this capability via the Grab utility. Some of the nicer aspects of the Classic screen capture, such as capturing just a single window, are missing in Mac OS X; however, Grab balances that deficiency by providing Timed Screen captures and providing the dimensions of an image being created from a selection.

Grab lends its services to other applications, allowing you to take a snapshot of the entire screen, a selection, or a timed screen shot. For example, while working in TextEdit you could choose TextEdit ⇨ Services ⇨ Grab ⇨ Screen and a full-screen picture would be inserted in your TextEdit document at the current insertion point.

Screen capture without Grab

Beginning with Mac OS X version 10.1, you can capture the full screen or a selected area without using the Grab utility. The following keystrokes do the trick:

- ⌘-Shift-3 captures the full screen.
- ⌘-Shift-4 provides a cross-hairs pointer to select the area you want captured.

With either keystroke, the screen shot is saved as a TIFF picture file on the Desktop.

Screen capture in the Classic environment

From the very first days of the Mac in 1984, you could take a screen shot by pressing ⌘-Shift-3. In those early days, the image resulted in a MacPaint file reflecting the 512-x-384-pixel screen. Similarly, ⌘-Shift-4 sent that screen image directly to your ImageWriter dot-matrix printer. As display and printer technology advanced, so did these built-in *FKEY* resources (it stood for Function KEY, before there were specific Fn keys on a Mac keyboard).

In the Classic environment, Mac OS 9 provides several ways to capture a screen shot, including the following:

- ⌘-Shift-3 takes a picture of the full Mac screen.
- ⌘-Shift-4 provides a cross-hair cursor to take a picture of a selection.
- ⌘-Shift-CapsLock-4 provides a shutter icon to take a picture of a given window by clicking in it.

Screen captures taken with these keystrokes in the Classic environment are stored at the top level of your Classic startup disk (or folder) by the name Picture *n*, where n increases by one for each one taken. These files are in PICT format and have the Classic application SimpleText set as their creator application.

Clicking in a Mac OS X window or on the Desktop switches you out of the Classic environment without taking the screenshot. Thus, you can't (for example) take a shot of a Mac OS X window by using ⌘-Shift-CapsLock-4 while in a Classic application and clicking in a Mac OS X window — bummer!

One of the more frequent uses of ⌘-Shift-4 under Mac OS 9 was to select an icon-sized image to use as a custom icon or to insert such an image in a document. ⌘-Shift-4, and its Grab equivalent, are unnecessary in Mac OS X. Just drag the icon into a TextEdit document, and you have the icon saved in your text, as seen earlier in Figure BC-2.

Note There is an exception to the above drag-the-icon method. If the file is a graphic file, such as a PICT, JPEG, TIFF, or GIF file, the image in the dragged file is dropped into the document rather than the icon. Go back to the selection method and use Grab if you need the icon of a graphic file.

Stickies

For those fans of Post-It Notes and their electronic counterpart, Stickies, Mac OS X Stickies registers as a service. Any selected text in an application that supports services can be made into a Sticky by choosing Services ⇨ Make Sticky (⌘-Shift-Y) from the application menu. A new sticky appears, launching Stickies if necessary, containing your selected text (up to the maximum size of a Sticky).

Note Although Stickies can contain graphics in Mac OS X, the service ignores any graphics within the selection when it creates the Sticky.

Being a good Mac OS X citizen, Stickies supports services as well. If you have a Sticky open, you can choose from any of the supported services.

Summarize

A service that's available beginning with Mac OS X version 10.1 takes currently selected text and quickly summarizes it by extracting key sentences. This service is unusual because it's provided by an application that you don't use otherwise. The service is called Summarize, and it's provided by the Summary Service application. To use this service, you select some text in a document and choose Services ⇨ Summarize from the application menu. The Summary Service application opens, prepares a summary of the selected text, and displays the summary in a window. Figure BC-5 shows an example of the Summarize service.

Tip If you select some text but the Summarize choice is disabled (dim) in the Services submenu, the Summarize service is not available in the application you're using. You can summarize the selected text by copying it to a document in the TextEdit application. Then select the text in the TextEdit document and choose TextEdit ⇨ Services ⇨ Summarize.

When the summary window appears in the Summary Service application, you can save the summary as a text document by choosing File ⇨ Save As. In addition, you can edit the summary by using the Edit menu and other regular text editing methods. You can even check the spelling in the summary by choosing Edit ⇨ Spelling or Edit ⇨ Check Spelling.

Note You won't find the Summary Service application in your Applications folder. It's buried in the Library folder of the folder named System.

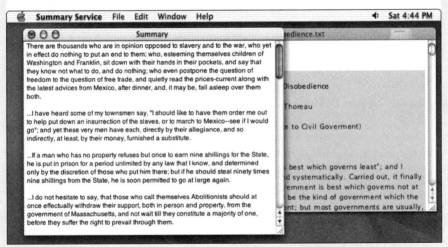

Figure BC-5: Use the Summarize service (top) to prepare a summary of selected text (bottom).

Disk Copy

Probably the least useful service is Disk Copy ⇨ Mount Image. This service makes the Disk Copy's window become visible so that you can drag a disk image file to the window for mounting. Just select some text, and the Mount Image option will be enabled, whether it is a valid pathname to the file or not. If your selected text is not a valid path to a disk image file, you receive an error message to that effect. As we said, this is not a very useful service to the general user.

Other Services

Other applications that you install may provide additional services. For example, the OmniWeb application (www.omnigroup.com) provides a service that tries to open a Web page using selected text as a URL.

Services provided by a newly installed application may not become available until the next time you log in.

Summary

In this chapter, you learned that some Mac OS X applications support a Services submenu in their application menu and some (maybe even the same ones) are available to use as services. You've also seen that some of the applications and utilities shipped with Mac OS X are both service providers and service clients. Check out the full *Mac OS X Bible* for more information on the applications and utilities that come with Mac OS X.

✦ ✦ ✦